Trends and New Developments in FinTech

Trends and New Developments in FinTech

Guest Editors

Nikiforos T. Laopodis
Eleftheria Kostika

MDPI

Basel • Beijing • Wuhan • Barcelona • Belgrade • Novi Sad • Cluj • Manchester

Guest Editors
Nikiforos T. Laopodis
School of Business & Economics
The American College of Greece
Athens
Greece

Eleftheria Kostika
Deputy Governor Office
Bank of Greece
Athens
Greece

Editorial Office
MDPI AG
Grosspeteranlage 5
4052 Basel, Switzerland

This is a reprint of the Special Issue, published open access by the journal *FinTech* (ISSN 2674-1032), freely accessible at: https://www.mdpi.com/journal/fintech/special_issues/5PKAF5E8TF.

For citation purposes, cite each article independently as indicated on the article page online and as indicated below:

Lastname, A.A.; Lastname, B.B. Article Title. *Journal Name* **Year**, *Volume Number*, Page Range.

ISBN 978-3-7258-5499-8 (Hbk)
ISBN 978-3-7258-5500-1 (PDF)
https://doi.org/10.3390/books978-3-7258-5500-1

Contents

About the Editors

Nikiforos T. Laopodis

Nikiforos T. Laopodis earned his Ph.D. in Economics from The Catholic University of America, DC, USA, in 1991 and his master's degree from Morgan State University, MD, USA, in 1986. His undergraduate studies were at the University of Macedonia, Thessaloniki, Greece, where he earned a Bachelor's degree in 1983. His areas of expertise are finance (investments and capital markets) and financial econometrics. His research includes topics such as monetary and fiscal policies, stock markets and bond markets. Dr. Laopodis is actively working on global risks and their implications on all aspects of economic, social, and financial life. He has written two textbooks, one in investments (titled *Understanding Investments: Theories and Strategies*, 2nd edition, 2020) and another in financial economics/econometrics (titled *Financial Economics and Econometrics*, 1st edition, 2022). He is currently writing a third textbook on global financial markets. His research appeared in tier-1 finance and economics journals such as the *Journal of International Money and Finance*, the *Journal of International Financial Markets, Institutions & Money*, the *Journal of Financial Stability*, *Oxford Economic Papers*, *International Journal of Finance and Economics* and more. He has taught a number of finance and economics courses at both undergraduate and graduate levels at various universities in the USA and Greece. He is also participating in an online MBA course at the University of London-Queen Mary. Finally, he has extensive administrative experience from serving in various administrative capacities at several universities in the US and Greece which he was working at in the past.

Eleftheria Kostika

Eleftheria Kostika has been Head of the Bank of Greece Deputy Governor's Office for 12 years, with a specialization on the Eurosystem's Monetary Policy implementation, Financial Technology, the Bank's international investment portfolio management, global capital markets, and bank resolution. She has also served as Deputy Director on the Risk Management Unit and as a Chief Trader at Money Market Desk of the Dealing Room with responsibilities pertaining to the implementation of monetary policy. She is also a member of several BIS and ECB Committees and is Greece's Primary Delegate to the OECD Financial Markets Committee. In addition, for the last 17 years, she has been a tutor, teaching assistant and adjunct instructor in several undergraduate and postgraduate courses of the University of London, Athens, the University of Business Economics, Hellenic Open University, and of the National Centre for Public Administration and Local Government in the field of financial econometrics, risk management and business economics. She completed a PhD in Financial Econometrics at Athens University of Economics and Business (2008) and has successfully graduated with an MSc in Finance from the Birkbeck College of the University of London (1998). She has publications in many academic journals such as the *Journal of Forecasting*, the *International Journal of Finance and Economics*, *International Economics*, *Studies in Economics and Finance*, etc. She holds an Academic Research Award (2014) from the Bank of Greece's Governor G. Provopoulos. Among others, she has participated in many research projects in the field of finance and has presented over 500 research papers at many scientific conferences (e.g., BIS Conferences, EFMA, EUROXX, FSB, etc.). Her recent research deals mostly with global monetary policy implementation during abrupt changes and innovative financial products and services through digital technology such as Central Bank Digital Currencies (CBDCs) and crypto-assets.

FinTech

Editorial

Trends and New Developments in FinTech

Nikiforos T. Laopodis [1,*] and Eleftheria Kostika [2]

[1] School of Business & Economics, The American College of Greece, Agia Paraskevi, 153 42 Athens, Greece
[2] Bank of Greece, 102 50 Athens, Greece; ekostika@bankofgreece.gr
* Correspondence: nlaopodis@acg.edu

This Special Issue (*Trends and New Developments in FinTech*) discusses fintech trends such as the aspects of the regulation of digital activities, the implementation of technologies on reducing carbon emissions, ESG investments by FinTech, the trend towards asset tokenization and related banking activities in relation to FinTech, and the development of central bank digital currencies assisted by FinTech. This Special Issue (SI) comprises eight research papers and two reviews. Three themes highlight the research component of this SI—banking, FinTech technology, and financial assets. The two review papers discuss financial literacy and the use of Artificial Intelligence (AI) in finance. Below, I provide a brief summary of the papers in each theme, as well as the two reviews.

Bouheni et al., in Contribution 1, examined the effectiveness of an innovative FinTech risk-scoring model to predict the risk-appropriate return for short-term credit sales. This derived risk score can serve to mitigate the information asymmetry between the seller of receivables and the purchaser (funder). The authors found that their SURF Score is instrumental in justifying the seller–funder information asymmetry and provides high risk-appropriate periodic returns to the latter across industries.

Liu and Liang, in Contribution 2, assess whether FinTech mortgage lenders align pricing with borrower risk using conforming 30-year mortgages. The authors estimate default probabilities using machine learning techniques (logit, random forest, and more) and found that non-FinTech lenders achieve the highest predictive accuracy, followed closely by banks, with FinTech lenders trailing. In pricing analysis, the authors reported that banks adjust the origination rates most sharply with borrower risk compared to FinTech and non-FinTech lenders.

Liu and Liang, in Contribution 5, investigated racial and ethnic disparities in mortgage lending outcomes across different lender types—large banks, FinTech lenders, non-bank lenders, small banks, and credit unions—using Home Mortgage Disclosure Act (HMDA) data from 2018 to 2023. The authors analyzed approval rates, rate spreads, and origination charges, subsequently evaluating how borrower outcomes vary by race and ethnicity, controlling for loan characteristics, borrower attributes, and regional factors. Their findings reveal that Black and Hispanic borrowers consistently face less-favorable terms than White borrowers, with disparities differing by lender type. In addition, although large banks demonstrate relatively equitable pricing, they impose higher loan denial rates on minorities. Credit unions, despite offering the lowest rates overall, penalize minority borrowers more severely in pricing than other lender types. FinTech lenders, while charging higher-rate spreads and fees, show smaller credit access disparities for minority borrowers. Non-bank and small bank lenders display mixed results, with inconsistencies in their treatment of minorities across pricing and credit access. These results suggest that in order to achieve equitable mortgage lending requires enhanced regulatory oversight, greater transparency in algorithmic decision-making, and the stricter enforcement of fair lending practices.

Finally, Zogning and Turcotte, in Contribution 7, examined the role of digital financial advisory services (robo-advisors), which are becoming increasingly popular in retail banking. These tools assist users with financial decisions such as risk assessment, portfolio selection, and rebalancing—all at a reduced cost. Building on the evidence that robo-advisors could complement human financial advisors, the authors evaluate robo-advisors' effectiveness in asset allocation and their impact on retail banks' profitability. Their findings indicate that implementing robo-advisors enhances profitability in non-interest activities, with this effect being more pronounced in France than in Canada.

Neverauskienė et al., in Contribution 3, studied Lithuanian financial technology (FinTech), which is one of the fastest-growing financial technology centers in Europe but also faces economic, regulatory, and technological challenges that hinder its development. The results revealed that factors such as favorable regulation influence the FinTech sector the most, which is crucial in attracting international investments. Based on the results, the authors recommend that authorities pay more attention to educational programs aimed at training technology specialists, promote cooperation between the public and private sectors, and further improve the regulatory environment to ensure the sustainable and safe development of FinTech.

On the FinTech and financial assets theme, Koutrouli and Manousopoulos, in Contribution 4, explore the use of crypto-assets for payments (selectively referring to stablecoins). Despite some of the financial and legal characteristics of crypto-assets, such as their price volatility and unclear legal settlement, rapid technological and regulatory developments in this area justify attention. We therefore try to answer the research questions of which, why, how, where, and by whom crypto-assets are used for (retail) payments. The authors conclude that fostering a clear understanding of the developments around crypto-asset payments and monitoring the various degrees of adoption throughout different markets could contribute to identifying the broader implications of using crypto-assets in the payment ecosystem and in maintaining the integrity and stability of the financial system.

Guo et al. investigate the key drivers and the economic and social impacts of cryptocurrency adoption, in Contribution 6. The authors found that technology development, measured by the Network Readiness Index, enables cryptocurrency adoption. Economic conditions, measured by higher national inflation rates and monetary policy indicators, are the key drivers for cryptocurrency adoption. Furthermore, cryptocurrency adoption has negative relationships with economic development, the unemployment rate, and social development. Finally, the authors reported that network readiness, economic conditions, and monetary policies contribute to fostering cryptocurrency adoption.

Contribution 8 in this category is by Sadorsky, who studied the practical implications of using precious metal ETFs to diversify risk in FinTech stocks. His analysis shows that gold provides the most downside risk protection. Downside risk reduction is estimated using relative risk ratios based on CVaR. In general, these results show the benefits of diversifying an investment in FinTech stocks with precious metals.

In the reviews category, Contribution 9 is by Croitoru et al., entitled "Exploring Financial Literacy in Higher Education with the Help of FinTech: A Bibliometric Analysis of Linkages to Access, Behavior, and Well-Being Through Digital Innovation". The authors discuss the dynamic interaction between financial literacy and higher education within hundreds of articles (from the Web of Science) using bibliometric analysis. The authors identify four components of financial education—access and literacy, behavior, capability, and well-being—which reflect a spectrum of educational needs. Financial literacy also extends beyond knowledge to include behavior, health, and inclusion. Their findings underscore the multifaceted nature of financial literacy, linking it to access, behavior, and well-being. Given that financial education serves as the driver of behavioral change and societal resilience, the authors suggest that policymakers and educators should prioritize inclusive financial literacy programs that address demographic-specific needs, leveraging digital innovations to enhance accessibility and impact.

The second review paper—Contribution 10—entitled "A Comprehensive Review of Generative AI in Finance" by Lee et al., offers a comprehensive examination of recent trends and developments at the intersection of Generative AI (GAI) and finance. The authors address a number of questions such as what the current trends and advancements in the application of GAI within the financial sector are, how does GAI contribute to solving financial tasks and challenges, and what the risks and challenges associated with the use of GAI in finance are, as well as exploring how have these been addressed in the literature. The review paper aims to provide researchers and practitioners with a structured overview of the current landscape of GAI in finance, offering insights into both the opportunities and challenges presented by these advanced technologies.

Conflicts of Interest: The authors declare no conflict of interest.

List of Contributions:

1. Ben Bouheni, F.; Tewari, M.; Salamon, A.; Johnston, P.; Hopkins, K. Credit Sales and Risk Scoring: A FinTech Innovation. *FinTech* **2025**, *4*, 31. https://doi.org/10.3390/fintech4030031.
2. Liu, Z.; Liang, H. Do Fintech Lenders Align Pricing with Risk? Evidence from a Model-Based Assessment of Conforming Mortgages. *FinTech* **2025**, *4*, 23. https://doi.org/10.3390/fintech4020023.
3. Okunevičiūtė Neverauskienė, L.; Danilevičienė, I.; Labašauskienė, G. An Assessment of Lithuania's Financial Technology Development. *FinTech* **2025**, *4*, 19. https://doi.org/10.3390/fintech4020019.
4. Koutrouli, E.; Manousopoulos, P. Exploring the Use of Crypto-Assets for Payments. *FinTech* **2025**, *4*, 15. https://doi.org/10.3390/fintech4020015.
5. Liu, Z.; Liang, H. Racial Disparities in Conforming Mortgage Lending: A Comparative Study of Fintech and Traditional Lenders Under Regulatory Oversight. *FinTech* **2025**, *4*, 8. https://doi.org/10.3390/fintech4010008.
6. Guo, Y.; Yousef, E.; Naseer, M.M. Examining the Drivers and Economic and Social Impacts of Cryptocurrency Adoption. *FinTech* **2025**, *4*, 5. https://doi.org/10.3390/fintech4010005.
7. Zogning, F.; Turcotte, P. The Contribution of Robo-Advisors as a Key Factor in Commercial Banks' Performance After the Global Financial Crisis. *FinTech* **2025**, *4*, 2. https://doi.org/10.3390/fintech4010002.
8. Sadorsky, P. Using Precious Metals to Reduce the Downside Risk of FinTech Stocks. *FinTech* **2024**, *3*, 537–550. https://doi.org/10.3390/fintech3040028.
9. Croitoru, I.M.; Dragan, P.-P.; Ignat, N.D.; Jumanca, R. Exploring Financial Literacy in Higher Education with the Help of FinTech: A Bibliometric Analysis of Linkages to Access, Behavior, and Well-Being Through Digital Innovation. *FinTech* **2025**, *4*, 4. https://doi.org/10.3390/fintech4010004.
10. Lee, D.K.C.; Guan, C.; Yu, Y.; Ding, Q. A Comprehensive Review of Generative AI in Finance. *FinTech* **2024**, *3*, 460–478. https://doi.org/10.3390/fintech3030025.

FinTech

MDPI

Article

Credit Sales and Risk Scoring: A FinTech Innovation

Faten Ben Bouheni [1], Manish Tewari [2,*], Andrew Salamon [3], Payson Johnston [4] and Kevin Hopkins [5]

1. Department of Finance and Real Estate, Menlo College, Atherton, CA 94027, USA; faten.benbouheni@menlo.edu
2. Department of Finance, Menlo College, Atherton, CA 94027, USA
3. Bloomberg, San Francisco, CA 94105, USA; andrew.salamon@menlo.edu
4. School of Business, University of Tennessee Southern, Pulaski, TN 38478, USA; pjohnst7@utsouthern.edu
5. Economist, Kevin Hopkins Inc., Sandy, UT 84092, USA; kevinhopkinsinc@gmail.com

* Correspondence: manish.tewari@menlo.edu

Abstract: This paper explores the effectiveness of an innovative FinTech risk-scoring model to predict the risk-appropriate return for short-term credit sales. The risk score serves to mitigate the information asymmetry between the seller of receivables ("Seller") and the purchaser ("Funder"), at the same time providing an opportunity for the Funder to earn returns as well as to diversify its portfolio on a risk-appropriate basis. Selling receivables/credit to potential Funders at a risk-appropriate discount also helps Sellers to maintain their short-term financial liquidity and provide the necessary cash flow for operations and other immediate financial needs. We use 18,304 short-term credit-sale transactions between 23 April 2020 and 30 September 2022 from the private FinTech startup Crowdz and its Sustainability, Underwriting, Risk & Financial (SURF) risk-scoring system to analyze the risk/return relationship. The data includes risk scores for both Sellers of receivables (e.g., invoices) along with the Obligors (firms purchasing goods and services from the Seller) on those receivables and provides, as outputs, the mutual gains by the Sellers and the financial institutions or other investors funding the receivables (i.e., the Funders). Our analysis shows that the SURF Score is instrumental in mitigating the information asymmetry between the Sellers and the Funders and provides risk-appropriate periodic returns to the Funders across industries. A comparative analysis shows that the use of SURF technology generates higher risk-appropriate annualized internal rates of return (IRR) as compared to nonuse of the SURF Score risk-scoring system in these transactions. While Sellers and Funders enter into a win-win relationship (in the absence of a default), Sellers of credit instruments are not often scored based on the potential diversification by industry classification. Crowdz's SURF technology does so and provides Funders with diversification opportunities through numerous invoices of differing amounts and SURF Scores in a wide range of industries. The analysis also shows that Sellers generally have lower financing stability as compared to the Obligors (payers on receivables), a fact captured in the SURF Scores.

Keywords: credit sales; FinTech; invoice financing; risk scoring; return; internal rate of return; diversification

JEL Classification: G17; G23; G30; G32

1. Introduction and Motivation

Risk/return assessment of invoices is a topical issue in business and research. The COVID-19 pandemic of 2019–2021 led to severe supply-chain disruptions worldwide

 https://doi.org/10.3390/fintech4030031

refs. [1,2] and consequently a short-term funding crisis faced especially by small businesses. The transaction that results in short-term funding needs for such businesses is characterized here: Business A is a "Seller" of goods or services, on a deferred-payment basis, to business B ("Obligor") and sends an invoice to business B with a due date by which the invoice must be paid. It is possible that the resulting lag, in terms of time, between the supply of goods and services and the collection of funds by Business A (the Seller) could contribute to liquidity issues for the Seller. The FinTech startup Crowdz provided a platform on which the Seller could list invoices to be purchased by a Funder (finance company, bank, or commercial investor) at a discount in order to receive the funds prior to the invoice due date (for instance, a Seller might receive advanced funds of USD 9500 on a USD 10,000 invoice, representing a 5.00% discount rate, and at the invoice due date repay the full USD 10,000 to the Funder upon receipt of the invoice payment by the Obligor). The Funder, in turn, is motivated byoits expectation of receiving repayment of the advanced funds by the invoice due date that provides an acceptable rate of return based on the discount rate charged to the Seller. For instance, in the above example, the Funder would receive a USD 10,000 repayment less the USD 9500 advanced, divided by the USD 9500 advanced, or a rate of return of USD 5000/USD 9500 = 5.26%. For purposes of comparing returns across transactions with invoices of differing amounts and terms, the absolute rate of return for each such transaction is converted into an annualized rate of return. For instance, in this example, if the full invoice value—that is, the funding amount plus the discount—were projected to be repaid 90 days after the funding date, the projected daily rate of return would be 0.0595%, and the projected annualized 365-day rate of return for the Funder would be 24.25% ((1.000595^365) − 1).

There is, however, an information asymmetry that exists in such a transaction. The Funder is not fully aware of the risks of the invoice it is purchasing since the Sellers are typically small firms, plus the risk associated with the Obligor may be partially or completely opaque given the Funder's lack of information on said Obligor. Since the Seller is shifting the risk and the payment timing for these invoices to the Funder, the Funder, just like a bank when making a standard business loan, has a legitimate expectation of earning an appropriate return. This is where Crowdz's innovative, proprietary credit risk-scoring model, FinTech "SURF" (Sustainability, Underwriting, Risk, and Financial) Score (see Table A1 in Appendix A for SURF methodology) comes into play. The SURF Score is intended to assist the Funder in analyzing the risk of the funding for the invoice being repaid, and helping to determine the appropriate rate of return. A higher SURF Score is associated with a lower risk of repayment, and so a relatively lower discount rate would be charged and a relatively lower rate of return would be generated for the Funder (in the same way that a bank would charge a lower commercial loan interest rate for a business with a relatively high credit rating than it would for a business with a relatively low credit rating, and hence the bank would receive a comparatively lower—albeit more assured—rate of return in the former case). The Crowdz SURF Score thus serves a similar purpose to what a business credit rating does for a bank making commercial loans and to what the Standard and Poor (S&P) bond rating serves for bond purchasers. As in the case for commercial loans just noted, for bond purchasers, higher bond ratings lead to lower default risk and correspondingly lower expected returns for an investor. A robust risk-scoring model like the SURF Score thereby has the potential to mitigate the information asymmetry (see ref. [3]) by quantifying the repayment risk while simultaneously allowing the Funder to diversify its funding across industries on a risk-appropriate basis (a higher rate of return for higher risk and vice versa).

This paper provides a case study of an innovative real-time risk scoring model (the aforementioned Crowdz SURF Score) that addresses the critical information asymmetries just described. The SURF Score's key innovation lies in *real-time* risk assessment using continuously updated data (unlike traditional credit-scoring methodologies that rely on historical data that often may be weeks or even months old).

The SURF Score methodology's four-step, continuously updated approach to credit-risk assessment thus progressively refines risk ratings from initial external credit data to real-time accounting, banking, and transactional data. This dynamic refinement captures the immediate impact of external shocks, such as fast-moving financial crises, global pandemics, changing trade policies, and the like, on business performance—something that conventional scoring models have failed to achieve during recessions.

This innovation enables Funders to mitigate information asymmetry while allowing portfolio diversification based on "flight-to-safety" theory (see refs. [4,5]), thereby providing critical risk-projection capabilities as compared with traditional risk-assessment tools that often have proved inadequate in rapidly changing economic landscapes.

Note further that receivable assets are not classified as sales until payments are received and thus reflect the quality of operations in the revenue cycle (ref. [6]). In an empirical analysis of proprietary data collected by Crowdz on 18,304 short-term credit-sale (i.e., invoice-purchase) transactions between 23 April 2020, and 30 September 2022 (a period of post-COVID-19 pandemic supply-chain disruptions and liquidity crises in the secondary short-term credit market), we find that the SURF Score technology is effective in the assessment of the risk associated with the invoices being sold. Consequently, the SURF Score technology provides higher periodic risk-appropriate returns to the Funder on an absolute basis and higher risk-appropriate annualized internal rates of return on a risk-adjusted basis as compared with situations in which the SURF Score system is not used (based on vetted proprietary data provided by Crowdz). Crowdz's SURF Score technology thereby provides mutual gains for the Sellers (in terms of liquidity) and the Funders (in terms of higher-risk appropriate returns).

The motivation for Crowdz during the then-current heightened period of uncertainty was to ensure that risk could be identified in an automated and real-time manner as market dynamics rapidly changed. Previous FinTech risk models did not take into account the effects on credit scoring during dynamic economic environments like financial crises and global pandemics, which in 2019–2021 differed substantially from the 2008 financial crisis. In addition, the SURF Score's built-in automation was a key motivation for Crowdz, enabling the FinTech startup to price risk automatically and instantaneously. The bank credit models at this time were not automated based on key risk elements such as historical repayment performance as revealed by the Sellers' accounting data. Of course, the Crowdz SURF Score model's capability to accurately and automatically assess risk in these fast-changing economic conditions made SURF Score system even more capable and hence more valuable in times of lesser economic agitation and uncertainty.

The remainder of this document is organized into four sections. Section 2 provides a comprehensive literature review and outlines the hypotheses that guided this research. Section 3 details the research methodology and the data-collection process used in this study. Section 4 discusses the findings and their implications, while Section 5 offers a concluding overview of the research.

2. Literature Review and Hypotheses

2.1. Supply Chain Disruption Mitigation Mechanism Studies

There is significant research conducted in studying the actions taken by the businesses to overcome the disruption in payment and collection processes and systems due to the 2019–2021 COVID-19 pandemic.

2.1.1. Technology

The COVID-19 pandemic led to an increased reliance on technology to address disruptions in supply chains. One study, ref. [1], documents that, as transports closed and the financial pressure built due to disruption in the supply chain, international companies increased their reliance on artificial intelligence (AI) for supply chain management—a trend that continues to this day.

On the other hand, ref. [2] investigates the impact of the announcement of the COVID-19 pandemic on the market value and trading volume of supply chain finance (SCF) firms. Using an event study, the researchers observed a significant valuation loss and higher trading volume of SCF firms; however, SCF firms that were blockchain-enabled (as the Crowdz SURF Score is) were protected from such valuation loss and volatility in trading. The researchers find that higher research and development (R&D) and capital expenditures by firms can prevent such losses. Moreover, blockchain-enabled SCF firms' value is enhanced by their membership in blockchain consortia and the degree of their progress in blockchain implementation. Investors' confidence in blockchain likewise reduces the market uncertainty.

2.1.2. FinTech Solutions

The reliance on technology to find short-term financing solutions increased considerably during this time as well. In its study, ref. [7] breaks down the supply chain financing activities for inbound supply chain and accounts payable solutions, inventory solutions, and outbound supply chain and accounts receivable solutions. The authors find that firms are turning to multiple supply chain financing solutions (i.e., multi-bank financing, reverse factoring, receivables auction platforms, asset-based lending, etc.) to stabilize both their liquidity and their working capital in order to maintain solvency and ensure continuity of supply throughout their supply chains. This paper further identifies several different types of supply chain financing solutions and how such solutions can affect firms' ability to navigate uncertain business environments such as those caused by the global COVID-19 pandemic.

Finally, other researchers (ref. [8]) collected supply-chain-financing data through a focus group of industry experts around four variables: (1) contextual macroeconomic factors such as ecosystems, government regulations, and digital technologies; (2) the role of COVID-19 in each contextual factor; (3) the relative time horizon (short-term vs. medium-term) for each contextual factor; and (4) the specific actors involved in each contextual factor. The results of the study suggest that increased collaboration among financiers, new entrants with innovative FinTech solutions, and wider acceptance of innovative financing solutions is highly financially beneficial. On the government-regulatory front, the study highlights the increased emphasis now being placed on existing regulations of long historical duration. And on the technology front, the researchers observe increased emphasis on and use of electronic invoicing and AI-based support technologies.

2.1.3. Firm Characteristics

It is of significant interest to other researchers to study firm characteristics that are more susceptible to or otherwise more resilient to supply-chain disruptions. For instance, researchers (ref. [9]) study the multi-regional impact of supply chain shocks on the firms due to the COVID-19 pandemic. They use abnormal credit-default-swap spreads and U.S.- and China-based supply chain networks to measure credit risk. Interestingly, the researchers find that localized supply chain risks actually spill over into other geographic regions. They also find that firm size, supply chain network centrality, cash holdings, inventory levels, strong credit ratings, capital-redeployment capability, and the number of industry segments involved increase resilience to global supply chain shocks, while financial leverage, operational leverage, and market competition weaken supply chain resilience.

2.1.4. Case Studies

There are multiple case studies, like ours, that have investigated the financial impact of the COVID-19 pandemic on the supply chains and payment systems of specific firms or industries. For instance, using a sample of 71 food-industry-listed companies on U.S., Japanese, and European stock indices, ref. [10] shows that stock markets have reacted with increased price volatility in such situations. Manufacturers of fertilizers and agrochemicals, as well as food distributors in particular, have exhibited high volatility in their stock prices, while low price volatility was observed in the stocks of food retailers.

Finally, ref. [11] analyzes and summarizes 74 published articles on such topics. The researchers' synthesis of findings reveals four broad themes that recur in the published work, namely, the impact of the COVID-19 pandemic, resilience strategies for managing such effects and the recovery therefrom, the role of technology in implementing resilience strategies, and supply chain sustainability in light of the pandemic. They highlight the lack of theoretically robust and empirically strong studies in this area. The coverage of the research is also limited, as most of the studies are focused on the firms in high-demand healthcare products.

2.2. Information Asymmetry

Information asymmetry between the borrower and the lender has been extensively researched in the field of finance. Such research (as in ref. [3]) finds that larger banks, geographically closer in location as well as in previous lending relationships with the borrowing firms, are more inclined to lend to firms with a high level of information asymmetry.

In such cases, borrowers use specific debt-contract provisions to mitigate that information asymmetry in order to achieve financing at a reasonable cost. Further, ref. [12] finds that a higher level of information asymmetry exists among smaller firms that typically rely on short-term debt for financing. Such firms also tend to lean on trade credit as the alternative means of short-term financing. The researchers' conclusions supplement the findings by refs. [13,14]. Additionally, ref. [15]—using data from 6000 commercial loans made by large U.S. banks—finds that the firms with a high level of information asymmetry and positive private information issue credit of short maturity in order to obtain favorable finance terms. On the other hand, lenders that lend to firms with high levels of information asymmetry are likely to provide short-term credit to facilitate constant monitoring of the debt terms (see ref. [16]).

2.3. Risk-Scoring Models

The increase in innovations to address short-term financing issues has led to the development of risk-scoring models designed to efficiently measure the risk of the borrower to the lenders and consequently reduce the information asymmetry. Here we provide historical perspectives on such risk-scoring models. All such models are deployed in unique lending environments with differing time periods, borrowers and lenders, and debt contracts.

One researcher (ref. [17]) finds that the small-business risk-scoring systems used by banks typically rely on expanded quantities, increased average prices, and higher average risk for the businesses seeking credit in amounts less than USD 100,000. The study also finds that the learning curve is relevant to the scoring system and that scoring is different for the banks willing to adapt the technology and to use discretion.

Another researcher (ref. [18]) presents a statistical method that efficiently measures and captures operational-risk indicators. Although focusing on risk indicators has helped the banking sector, with the Basel II Accord in mind, it also can be extended to enterprise risk assessment as well, thereby making available different risk-scoring methods for operational risk management. The study further highlights the negative aspects of considering either only past events or only projected future events, suggesting that a combined method, which considers the history of risk events, risk self-assessment, and a future-facing scorecard, is a more robust scoring method for measuring and minimizing operational risk.

Still another researcher (ref. [19]) contends that having access to a credit score enables lenders to make quicker decisions and, in some cases, to automate lending-process decisions. The study notes that the New Basel Capital Accord has given increased importance to risk-scoring models, prompting banks and other financial institutions to develop or remodel existing credit risk-scoring models to conform to the new rules.

Another set of researchers (ref. [20]) conducted a survey of the use of credit scoring by banks in order to evaluate the credit risk of small-business borrowers. They find that credit scores tend to focus on the financial strength of the owners themselves rather than on that of the business they own. The researchers also find that credit-scoring systems lead to an increase in lending activity, thereby helping to support small businesses with liquidity issues.

Another researcher (ref. [21]) discusses the Altman Z-score, which remains a standard model used in the finance field to assess the risk of a default by commercial borrowers. The Altman Z-score is also used as a benchmark model for comparing the results of other credit-risk models.

Finally, (ref. [22]) discussed algorithmic credit risk-scoring models and suggests that the use of such scoring technologies may not guarantee unbiased scoring due to the potential inability to capture such subpopulation characteristics such as the race, gender, and sexual orientation of borrowers or business owners. With the help of simulation analysis, the researchers show that it is possible to remove biases in risk-scoring systems without significantly decreasing the models' performance if the relationships between the discriminatory attributes and the predictive variables in the model have lower correlations.

2.4. *Hypotheses*

A review of the literature in the area of supply chain financing solutions to counter COVID-19 pandemic economic disruptions reveals an enormous appetite for and use of technology in developing solutions for such crises. Studies by the authors in refs. [1,2] highlight increased emphasis on technologies such as AI and blockchain to achieve these solutions. In addition to the use of technology, the authors in refs. [7,8] observe the use of innovative short-term financing solutions adopted by the firms. Crowdz SURF Score technology is a culmination of these factors in which the technology-driven, innovative FinTech model is used to provide supply chain financing solutions. Another researcher (ref. [9]) finds that large and strong firms with high levels of cash are more likely to survive such supply chain disruptions. Crowdz's data consists of all types of firms, ranging from small to large, given the average invoice size. This sample provides us the opportunity to conduct a broad-based, robust analysis. As studied by the authors in refs. [3,12–16], the literature is rife with measures taken to mitigate the information asymmetry between counterparties in finance. Risk-scoring-model studies by the authors in refs. [17–22] largely attempt to mitigate the information asymmetry by providing various forms of risk-scoring. Using the risk-appropriate return as the basis, we study the SURF Score technology's effectiveness on an absolute and relative basis. We develop two testable hypotheses for the Crowdz SURF technology:

Hypothesis I. *The use of the SURF technology, due to its ability to effectively assess transaction risk and mitigate information asymmetry, provides higher risk-appropriate periodic returns (higher return for the lower SURF Scores and vice versa) for investors.*

Hypothesis II. *The use of SURF technology provides comparatively higher risk-appropriate annualized rates of return as compared to the nonuse of the SURF Score risk-scoring system in such transactions.*

3. Research Methodology and Data Collection

This section presents the econometric models and data employed in this study to estimate the relationship between risk scoring and profitability measures (Table A1 in Appendix A presents the description of variables). We present a comprehensive analysis of 18,304 transactions conducted on the FinTech platform Crowdz between 23 April 2020 and 30 September 2022.

3.1. *Research Modelling*

In our review, we adapted conventional Ordinary Least Squares (OLS) regression to incorporate real-time SURF Score risk variables and thereafter applied Bayesian regression with multivariate normal distributions. OLS was selected for interpretability in the financial decision-making process as well as for the computational efficiency required for real-time risk scoring—that is, being fast enough to calculate risk scores in real-time as invoices come in, while also being easy to interpret. For instance, if external credit improves by 1 point, the risk score improves by α points.

The Bayesian approach was chosen to quantify the parametric uncertainty crucial for risk assessment while incorporating prior knowledge from historical credit data. The multivariate normal assumption was appropriate given the continuous nature of our risk variables and their observed joint-distribution characteristics. Additionally, this methodology is usually reasonable for financial data.

Finally, the precision of the risk scoring improves as more payment/repayment data is collected. Advanced technologies like AI and machine learning can increase this precision even more.

3.1.1. Linear Modeling

The linear model can be written as follows:

$$Profitability = \alpha_0 + \alpha \times \text{SURF} + \beta \times \sum X_{it} + \varepsilon_{it} \quad (1)$$

in which $Profitability_{it}$ is the response variable as measured by RETURN, IRR with SURF, and IRR without SURF for each transaction i at date t. α_0 is the constant of the model. SURF (Sustainability, Underwriting, Risk, and Financial) is the risk-score measurement developed by the FinTech firm Crowdz (the SURF methodology is detailed in Appendix A.1). There are actually three SURF Scores: the Seller SURF Score, the Obligor SURF Score, and the Invoice/Receivable SURF Score. The calculation of the Seller and Obligor scores is quite complex and has a number of subcomponents, all of which are used to produce a Seller and Obligor probability of payment/repayment. The Invoice/Receivable score, which is used in the analyses described throughout this paper (and which is what "SURF Score" means in said analyses unless otherwise noted), is the product of the two constituent scores and is calculated specifically as the Seller SURF Score times the Obligor SURF Score divided by 100.

Although this combination at first glance might seem simple, it is actually based on the standard theory of conditional probability and represents the product of the probability of the Obligor's paying the invoice to the Seller and, if this event takes place, the conditional probability of the Seller's repaying the funding to the Funder. For instance, if the probability of the first is 90% and the probability of the second is 96%, then the probability of the full set of transactions being completed is 90% times 96% = 86.4%. Put another way, if the Seller score is 96 and the Obligor score is 90, then the Invoice/Receivable score will be $(96 * 90)/100 = 8640/100 = 86.4$, or 86, since SURF Scores are whole numbers ranging from 1 to 100. Note that a more advanced version of this scoring system uses scores ranging from 1 to 1000.

Explanatory variables, or regressors, are $\sum X_{it}$ that include: the discount rate (DISCOUNT RATE), computed as the difference between the invoice amount and the financed amount divided by the invoice amount; the actual amount of time beyond the repayment due date that the Seller repays the funding amount to the Funder (DAYS BEYOND TERM); and the invoice amount (SIZE), expressed as the natural logarithm of the dollar amount. The coefficients to be estimated are α and β, while ε_{it} is the error term.

Ordinary Least Squares (OLS) models, like the one that we employ here, are particularly popular due to their effectiveness in establishing a linear relationship between a response variable and one or more predictor variables. The fundamental principle behind OLS regression involves minimizing the sum of squared errors (SSEs), where an error is defined as the deviation between the actual values and the predicted values of the response variable. As discussed in ref. [23], this approach is foundational in regression analysis. Furthermore, ref. [24] highlights that OLS techniques are versatile and find applications across a wide range of disciplines.

In our analysis, we assume that the dependent and independent variables are connected via a linear relationship. We model this connection through Ordinary Least Squares (OLS) regression, a robust method that easily accommodates the intricate relationship between risk and return (To replicate the linear estimates, use the following command: *regress Y X*, where Y is the dependent variable and X includes one or more independent variables).

3.1.2. Bayesian Estimation

Bayesian regression provides a similarly robust framework for estimating the posterior distribution, which incorporates both the likelihood of the data and the prior distribution (To replicate the Bayesian linear regressions, use the following command: *bayes: regress Y X*, where Y is the dependent variable and X includes one or more independent variables). This probabilistic modeling technique allows researchers to draw inferences about hypotheses based on the available data (see ref. [25]). One of the key benefits of Bayesian estimation is its effectiveness in addressing statistical challenges, particularly those arising from small sample sizes. Previous research has demonstrated that Bayesian approaches can adeptly handle a range of dataset sizes and manage the distributions of various variables (see refs. [26–28]).

Given the intricate relationships among the variables associated with risk and return in this study, Bayesian linear regression is a suitable choice for our model.

Assuming that D is Data, Y is the dependent variable, and X is the independent variable for N sample size, Bayesian linear is written as follows:

$$D = \{X^n, Y^n\} \quad \text{for } n = 1, \ldots, N \tag{2}$$

$$X^n \in \mathfrak{R}$$
$$Y^n \in \mathfrak{R}$$

The general Bayesian model is:

$$Y_i = \beta X_i + \varepsilon_i \tag{3}$$

The error term follows a normal distribution and is expressed as:

$$\varepsilon \sim \mathcal{N}\left(0, \sigma^2\right)$$

Parameters to be estimated are:

$$\theta = (\beta_0, \ldots, \beta_n, \sigma)$$

The Bayesian process is a statistical method that estimates parameters θ based on the available data and predicts a range of possible outcomes by incorporating probabilities $P\ (Y|X,\ n)$. Essentially, Bayesian regression explores all potential relationships between Y and $\mathcal{X}$ variables and provides a tolerance interval that can indicate either positive or negative outcomes. If there are changes in signs, this may suggest a misspecification in the relationship among the variables involved.

In the context of Bayesian Machine Learning, this approach utilizes a Gaussian distribution of functions and follows specific rules for effective predictions and modeling, specifically:

$$P(\theta|D) = \frac{P(D|\theta) \times P(\theta)}{P(D)} \tag{4}$$

where:

$P(D|\theta)$ is the likelihood of θ

$P(\theta)$ represents the prior on θ

$P(\theta|D)$ is the posterior of θ given data D

Expressed in terms of OLS estimators, the Bayesian approach is as follows:

$$\hat{\beta} = \frac{\sum_{i=1}^{n} x_i y_i}{\sum_{i=1}^{n} x_i^2}$$

Then the variance ($Sigma^2$) is,

$$Sigma^2 = \frac{\sum_{i=1}^{n} \left(y_i - \hat{\beta} x_i\right)^2}{n-1}$$

Bayesian models are utilized in numerous fields, demonstrating their versatility and effectiveness. Recent advancements in statistical software have improved the application of Bayesian rules, enhancing modeling techniques in research (ref. [25]).

3.2. Data Description

The selection of the Crowdz case as a FinTech platform is based on the availability of private data provided by the firm. Additionally, FinTech has evolved exponentially in recent times. For instance, a recent research report (ref. [25]) investigates the link between mobile application technology and the growth of deposits of the largest European and American banks from 2005 to 2022, documenting the importance of technology in supporting the financial performance of traditional banks.

Three dependent variables—RETURN, IRR with SURF, and IRR without SURF—are employed in this study as measures of profitability. The return from the repayment process on the FinTech platform (RETURN) is calculated as the difference between the repaid amount and the funded amount divided by the funded amount. Additionally, annualized internal rates of return (IRR) with and without the risk scoring (SURF) are used to assess the profitability; these latter two outcomes are calculated by converting RETURN to a daily rate and then transforming that rate into an annualized one

As shown in Table 1, from 23 April 2020 to 30 September 2022, the RETURN, IRR with SURF, and IRR without SURF (a difference of mean *t*-test between the IRR with SURF and the IRR without SURF shows a positive difference of 1.53%, significant at the 99% level (*p*-value of 0.002)) have means of 2%, 17%, and 15%, respectively, and standard deviations of 2%, 6%, and 13%, respectively. Additionally, RETURN has a maximum of 31% and a minimum of 0.5%.

Table 1. Descriptive Statistics. This table presents data statistics for 18,304 transactions conducted on the Crowdz platform between 23 April 2020 and 30 September 2022. The dependent variables include RETURN, computed as the ratio of profit over funded amount, in which profit is the difference between repaid amount and funded amount; annualized Internal Rate of Return (IRR) with SURF Score risk scoring, as described in the text; and annualized Internal Rate of Return (IRR) without SURF. Independent variables include invoice scoring (SURF), calculated as Seller SURF Score times Obligor SURF Score divided by 100; discount rate (DISCOUNT RATE), computed as the difference between invoice amount and financed amount divided by invoice amount; actual amount of time beyond the repayment due date that the Seller repays the funding to the Funder (DAYS BEYOND TERM); and invoice amount (SIZE), expressed as the natural logarithm of the dollar amount of the invoice.

Variable	Obs	Mean	Std. Dev.	Min	Max
SURF	18,304	92.077	14.247	1.575	99.977
RETURN	18,304	0.019	0.021	0.005	0.312
IRR with SURF	18,304	0.169	0.058	0.150	0.999
IRR without SURF	18,304	0.154	0.128	−1	0.999
DISCOUNT RATE	18,304	0.135	0.046	0	0.350
DAYS BEYOND TERM	18,304	3.673	0.681	0	6.512
SIZE	18,304	5.396	1.435	−0.282	13.144

Source: Authors' proprietary data.

As for independent variables, the SURF is the major explanatory variable. SURF assesses the funding-repayment risk (i.e., the risk of nonrepayment of the early funding of an invoice), as measured on a scale from 0 to 100 (the higher the SURF Score, the lower the funding-repayment risk). Based on 18,304 observations, SURF varies between 2 (exactly 1.57) and 100 (exactly 99.97), with a mean of 92 across all invoices, along with a standard deviation of 14 (see Table 1). Control variables include the DISCOUNT RATE, the lateness of repayments beyond the repayment due date (DAYS BEYOND TERM), and the invoice amount (SIZE). DISCOUNT RATE is the percentage of the invoice value sacrificed by the invoice Seller against the amount financed. That rate varies between 0% and 35%, with an average of 13.5% and a standard deviation of 4.6%. DAYS BEYOND TERM, as noted, measures the amount of time it takes for the Funder to receive the repayment of the funding following the repayment due date. That time varies between 0 days and 6.5 days, with an average of 3.6 and a standard deviation of 0.7. To address data heterogeneity, SIZE is expressed as the natural logarithm of the invoice amount. The SIZE variable has a mean of 5.4, a standard deviation of 1.4, a minimum of negative 0.3, and a maximum of 13, as shown in Table 1.

Additionally, we carefully examine the relationships among the variables, as outlined in Table A2 in Appendix A. To ensure the integrity of our model, we retain only those correlations that are below 80%. This rigorous approach helps us to identify and address any potential issues related to multicollinearity, which could undermine the reliability of our findings. As a result, the correlation matrix shows that the remaining variables operate within acceptable levels of independence, thereby enhancing the credibility of our subsequent regressions.

4. Findings and Discussion

We investigate the potential for SURF technology to accurately establish the risk and return profile of accounts receivable in order to provide the risk-appropriate financial returns and enhance the internal rate of return for investors. Our findings suggest that, by employing advanced technology solutions, funding firms can more effectively evaluate and manage risk, which not only creates additional value for their operations as well as generating more risk-appropriate returns, but also increases their ability and inclination to provide crucial cash-flow support to businesses, particularly small businesses. This study therefore emphasizes the transformative role of FinTech innovations in fostering sustainability and growth within the small-business sector.

The core hypothesis is that FinTech, such as SURF technology, has the potential to boost the returns for the Funders (investors) along with the option to evaluate potential investments based on levels of risk to determine risk-appropriate returns.

4.1. *Linear Risk-Return Relationship: OLS and Bayesian*

In this section, we discuss the estimates of linear and Bayesian for linear regressions.

Higher risk-taking behavior is frequently linked to the potential for higher expected returns. In this study, we employ a risk-assessment tool known as the Crowdz SURF Score ("SURF"), which specifically analyzes the invoices within the accounts receivable of various firms. By examining these invoices, we aim to provide deeper insights into the relationship between risk and return in financial practice.

The Crowdz SURF Score serves as a key indicator of the risk associated with invoices, with a higher score reflecting a lower level of risk. This score is crucial for funding entities when evaluating the repayment reliability of financial fund advancements. As shown in Figure 1, it is generally observed that, in this sample, the Obligor's (Buyer's) score tends to be higher than that of the Seller (not surprisingly since, in this sample, Obligors were more likely to be larger, well-established companies while Sellers were more apt to be smaller businesses). This difference highlights the varying degrees of risk that each party incurs in the short-term transactions. The Invoice score, which combines Obligor and Seller scores, points to the level of risk that Funders face when engaging with the Sellers. Essentially, the Invoice score encapsulates the overall risk-management dynamics between Funders and Sellers, providing valuable insights for both parties when making financial decisions (See Figure 1 for a look at how average Seller, Obligor, and Invoice SURF Scores changed over the duration of the sample.).

4.1.1. Risk and Return in Ordinary Least Squared Models

We propose that evaluating investments with varying degrees of risk can enhance the transactional profitability of Funders. As illustrated in Table 2, linear regressions indicate that the risk measure (SURF) has a negative impact on both profitability metrics (RETURN (1) and IRR with SURF (2)) at a significance level of 1%. This suggests that a higher SURF Score, which indicates lower risk, leads to decreased RETURN and IRR for investors. Specifically, a 1% increase in the SURF Score results in a 0.1% decrease in RETURN and a 0.4% decrease in IRR. This finding aligns with the established relationship between risk and return: higher risk is associated with higher expected returns, while lower risk correlates with lower expected returns. A higher SURF Score also indicates lower invoice risks and therefore suggests a more stable profit outlook. This distinction is crucial for understanding the relationship between risk tolerance and financial performance.

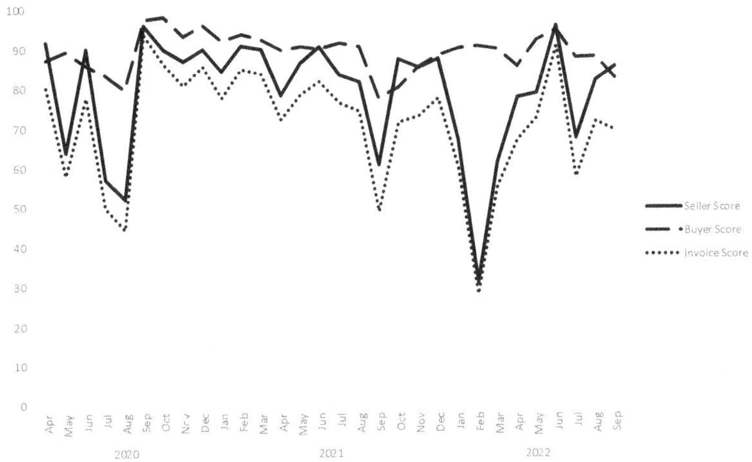

Figure 1. Invoice funding by date of invoice ingestion from April 2020 to September 2022. This figure plots the risk scores (i.e., SURF Scores) of Sellers of invoices (Seller Score), the risk scores of Obligors on the purchased invoices (Buyer Score), and the risk scores of the invoices themselves (Invoice Score). The risk scoring is based on the Crowdz SURF methodology of risk assessment, and it is scaled from 0 to 100 (the higher the SURF Score, the lower the risk). Specifically, the SURF Score represents the probability of timely repayment of the funding to the Funder, and, hence, a 100 SURF Score indicates that there is a 100% probability that the funding will be repaid to the Funder within the Funder-specified timing. The x-axis presents all monthly transactions on the Crowdz Platform, and the y-axis presents the corresponding risk scores. Raw Data is based on 19,278 funding transactions on the Crowdz Platform from 23 April 2020 to 30 September 2022 (Source: Authors' own creation.).

Interestingly, in comparing the Internal Rate of Return (IRR) with the utilization of the SURF Score risk-scoring model (column (2) of Table 2) to the IRR calculated without it (column (3) of Table 2), we uncover some significant insights. Notably, both the actual time it takes to repay the financing for an invoice (DAYS BEYOND TERM) and the size of the invoice itself (SIZE) demonstrate a positive relationship with the IRR when the SURF Score is integrated into the assessment. This means that, as the waiting period for repayment extends and the invoice amount increases, investors experience a higher IRR when employing the SURF Score.

Conversely, when we evaluate the IRR without considering the SURF Score, a contrasting trend emerges. Here, the relationship is negative: longer repayment terms and larger invoices tend to result in a diminished IRR for investors. Furthermore, this detrimental impact is less pronounced than it is with the IRR with SURF, indicating that the absence of a robust risk assessment tool may lead to increased volatility in profitability. These findings collectively underscore the importance of effectively assessing risk. By leveraging the SURF Score risk-scoring model, investors can better navigate the financial challenges posed by extended payment periods and large invoice amounts, ultimately achieving more stable and more favorable returns. This result supports our hypothesis that a comprehensive risk evaluation, as exemplified by the Crowdz SURF Score, can play a crucial role in enhancing overall investment outcomes.

Table 2. Linear OLS Estimation of the relationship between risk and return for the full sample. This table reports the coefficients, with their t-statistics in parentheses, and the level of significance of the OLS regressions in Equation (1), in which the dependent variables are: RETURN, computed as the ratio of profit over funded amount, in which profit is the difference between repaid amount and funded amount; Internal Rate of Return (IRR) with the use of the SURF Score; and Internal Rate of Return (IRR) without the use of the SURF Score. The independent variables include: the Invoice SURF Score (SURF), calculated as Seller SURF Score times Obligor SURF Score divided by 100; discount rate (DISCOUNT RATE), computed as the difference between invoice amount and financed amount divided by invoice amount; actual amount of time beyond the repayment due date that the Seller repays the invoice financing to the Funder (DAYS BEYOND TERM); and invoice amount (SIZE) expressed as the natural logarithm of the invoice's dollar amount. The sample includes 18,304 transactions conducted on the Crowdz platform, and the study period spans from 23 April 2020 to 30 September 2022. The "RETURN" column (1) reflects total return to investors when SURF Score risk-scoring is used, column (2) "IRR with SURF" is the internal rate of return to investors when SURF Score risk-scoring is used to assess repayment risk, and column (3) "IRR without SURF" is the internal rate of return to investors when SURF Score risk-scoring is not used to assess repayment risk. The regression constant (CONS), number of observations (N), F-statistics, and R-squared are also included. F-statistics reflect the overall significance of the joint test under the null hypothesis that all regression coefficients are equal to 0. R-squared reports the proportion of the variation in profitability explained by the loading factors (SURF, DISCOUNT RATE, DAYS BEYOND TERM, and SIZE). The superscripts *, **, and *** indicate significance at the 10%, 5%, and 1% levels, respectively.

	Full Sample		
Variable	**(1) RETURN**	**(2) IRR with SURF**	**(3) IRR Without SURF**
SURF	−0.001 ***	−0.004 ***	
	(−44.81)	(−38.59)	
DISCOUNT RATE	−0.039 ***	0.068 ***	0.079 **
	(−16.34)	(10.26)	(3.15)
DAYS BEYOND TERM	0.004 ***	0.005 ***	−0.121 ***
	(31.63)	(14.90)	(−86.93)
SIZE	−0.021 ***	0.004 ***	−0.075 ***
	(−49.27)	(6.89)	(−41.41)
CONS	0.132 ***	0.469 ***	0.923 ***
	(39.13)	(77.58)	(82.89)
N	18,288	18,288	18,288
F-statistics	77.37	54.08	86.50
	(0.000)	(0.000)	(0.000)
R-squared	0.864	0.830	0.345

Source: Authors own creation.

The DISCOUNT RATE (discount on the amount of the invoice) has a negative impact on RETURN and a positive effect on both IRR with and without the SURF Score, as demonstrated in Table 2. Statistically, a 1% increase in the discount rate results in a 4% decrease in RETURN, while the IRR with SURF increases by 7% and the IRR without SURF increases by 8%.

It is essential to recognize that the relationship between discount rate (DISCOUNT RATE) and returns (RETURN) can be challenging to predict, as returns are assessed periodically and do not factor in time (e.g., a 30-day invoice is treated the same as a 180-day invoice, even though the repayment likelihood of the former may be greater than that of the latter). A more insightful measure is the time-adjusted metric, such as the annualized Internal Rate of Return (IRR), which better illustrates the anticipated positive relationship between discount rates and returns.

The intercepts of all three regressions are positive and statistically significant at the 1% level.

In Table 2, the overall significance of the regression, F-statistics, is notably robust. The R-squared values, which indicate the proportion of variance explained by the model, demonstrate a remarkable degree of fit for both RETURN and IRR when incorporating SURF, achieving values of 86% and 83%, respectively. In contrast, the R-squared for IRR without SURF languishes at a mere 34%. This substantial difference suggests that the SURF Score reliably measures the risk of the transaction. We can therefore confidently assert that the SURF Score serves as a valuable tool for providing risk-appropriate returns to the Funder for investment opportunities of varying degrees of risk (Crowdz provided predictability and favorability-of-payment outcomes analysis and the comparison of receivables transactions on the Meta (Facebook) platform in Appendix A, Figures A1 and A2, to supplement our findings. When the SURF Score is used in the transactions, the payment outcomes are highly predictive and very favorable, and when the SURF Score is not used in the transactions, the payment outcomes are less predictive and less favorable).

Additionally, we perform a set of robustness tests to ensure the validity of our main results. The comprehensive robustness analysis strongly supports the validity of our primary empirical findings. The negative relationship between SURF Scores and returns is not an artifact of heteroscedasticity, multicollinearity, outlier contamination, or of temporal instability (see Tables A4–A7 in Appendix A). Instead, our results suggest a genuine economic relationship that requires theoretical interpretation. The structural break analysis reveals that while the magnitude of the SURF Score effect varied during the COVID-19 period, the fundamental negative relationship remained intact, suggesting that this finding reflects systematic market behavior rather than temporary market disruptions.

The robustness of our econometric results strengthens the case for focusing on economic explanations for the counterintuitive negative SURF Score/returns and IRR/SURF Score relationships. Our findings suggest that higher-quality borrowers (as measured by their SURF Scores) systematically achieve lower returns, which could reflect risk premium compression, market efficiency in pricing risk, or (most likely) selection effects whereby sophisticated funding entities are willing to accept lower returns in exchange for reduced risk exposure. The consistency of this relationship across multiple validation procedures indicates that understanding the economic mechanisms underlying this finding should be a priority for future research in invoice-financing markets.

4.1.2. Risk and Return on Bayesian Models

To evaluate the accuracy of linear results, we implement a Bayesian procedure that leverages multivariate features. This Bayesian approach fundamentally differs from traditional methods by treating all parameters as random variables, allowing each parameter to be characterized by a full probability distribution rather than being defined by a single estimate, such as the mean. This stands in contrast to the Ordinary Least Squares (OLS) method, which relies on the assumption of fixed values for parameters. By adopting the Bayesian framework, we gain a more comprehensive understanding of the uncertainty surrounding each parameter, leading to richer insights into the relationships within the data.

Table 3 presents the outcome of Bayesian regressions for the three response variables (RETURN, IRR with SURF, and IRR without SURF); these findings support the robustness of the linear regressions.

For instance, the relationships between return on financing (RETURN) and the SURF Score, discount rate (DISCOUNT RATE), and invoice size (SIZE) exhibit negative signs at a 95 percent credibility interval. The Monte Carlo Standard Error (MCSE) for these relationships are 0.007, 0.051, and 0.003, respectively. This suggests a systematic decrease in RETURN as the SURF Score, the discount rate, or the invoice size increases. Meanwhile, the actual time beyond the repayment due date it takes the Seller to repay the Funder (DAYS BEYOND TERM) and the constant maintain a positive relationship to RETURN, with MCSEs of 0.006 and 0.009, respectively, for an acceptance rate of the regression at 36 percent.

Table 3. Bayesian Multivariate Estimation of the relationship between risk and return for the full sample. This table presents the Bayesian Multivariate Normal regressions of Equations (2)–(4) at a confidence interval of 95 percent, in which the dependent variables are RETURN, IRR with SURF, and IRR without SURF; and the independent variables include SURF, DISCOUNT RATE, DAYS BEYOND TERM, and SIZE. Mean, Std. Dev., and Median represent the mean, standard deviation, and median of parameters, respectively. Monte Carlo Standard Error (MCSE) measures the accuracy of the estimation and verifies the estimation noise. $Sigma^2$ and Acceptance Rate are the specificities of the Bayesian procedure. The sample includes 18,304 transactions, and the period of this study spans from 23 April 2020 to 30 September 2022.

	Full Sample					
	Mean	**Std. Dev.**	**MCSE**	**Median**	**[95% Cred. Interval]**	
			(1) RETURN			
SURF	−0.001	0.091	0.007	−0.002	−0.003	−0.002
DISCOUNT RATE	−0.040	0.028	0.051	−0.041	−0.043	−0.036
DAYS BEYOND TERM	0.004	0.001	0.006	0.004	0.003	0.004
SIZE	−0.021	0.002	0.003	−0.021	−0.022	−0.020
Constant	0.131	0.001	0.009	0.131	0.129	0.133
$Sigma^2$	0.133	0.060	0.007	0.008	0.080	0.083
Acceptance Rate	0.359					
			(2) IRR with SURF			
SURF	−0.004	0.018	0.017	−0.037	−0.003	−0.004
DISCOUNT RATE	0.065	0.025	0.076	0.065	0.060	0.070
DAYS BEYOND TERM	0.005	0.034	0.015	0.049	0.004	0.006
SIZE	0.004	0.056	0.054	0.042	0.003	0.005
Constant	0.469	0.027	0.014	0.469	0.464	0.475
$Sigma^2$	0.063	0.059	0.047	0.063	0.062	0.064
Acceptance Rate	0.324					
			(3) IRR without SURF			
DISCOUNT RATE	0.077	0.025	0.014	0.076	0.031	0.127
DAYS BEYOND TERM	−0.121	0.001	0.057	−0.121	−0.123	−0.118
SIZE	−0.075	0.018	0.071	−0.075	−0.078	−0.072
Constant	0.923	0.011	0.046	0.922	0.902	0.943
$Sigma^2$	0.011	0.012	0.056	0.013	0.011	0.012
Acceptance Rate	0.340					
N	18,288	18,288	18,288	18,288	18,288	18,288

Source: Authors' own creation.

Similarly, when examining the internal rate of return (IRR) with the SURF Score and without it, the findings are consistent and robust. Here, the discount rate (DISCOUNT RATE) and the constant again show positive links with both iterations of IRR, reinforcing the idea that an increased discount rate potentially raises the Funder's IRR when risk factors are included.

Additionally, there are nuanced findings regarding DAYS BEYOND TERM and SIZE. While these variables maintain positive relationships with IRR when the SURF Score is accounted for, they switch to negative relationships with IRR when the SURF Score is excluded. This variation arises at the same 95 percent credibility interval, with acceptance rates for these insights recorded at 32 percent for IRR with SURF and 34 percent for IRR without SURF. Such dynamics accentuate the significance of the SURF Score in return expectations and highlight the complex interplay among these financial metrics.

Bayesian analysis is fundamentally anchored in the interplay between conventional probability and posterior distributions. A posterior distribution emerges from the integration of a prior distribution and a likelihood model, which infuses our understanding with insights drawn from empirical observations. Depending on the selection of prior distributions and likelihood models, the resultant posterior distribution may be derived analytically or approximated using advanced techniques, such as Markov chain Monte Carlo (MCMC) methods.

The Monte Carlo Standard Error (MCSE) serves as a critical benchmark for assessing the accuracy of Monte Carlo samples. A smaller MCSE value indicates superior sampling performance, highlighting the effectiveness of the sampling process in capturing the true underlying distributions [25].

In the presence of financial frictions, a risk-pricing system could effectively mitigate behavioral anomalies. For instance, the impact of over-optimism on risk-taking behaviors and expected returns in banks has been widely demonstrated. The phenomenon of credit expansion can be understood through this perspective, as discussed in ref. [29]. Additionally, ref. [30] explores an economy characterized by financial frictions, in which a regulator conducts a test that reveals external information about a firm's quality to investors, while the firm simultaneously discloses verifiable internal information regarding its quality. This interplay can significantly affect credit ratings and valuations.

Other researchers (see ref. [31]) observe that investors often exhibit insensitivity as the relationship between subjective expectations and actions becomes more pronounced, when their expectations align closely with rational expectations. Their research highlights the necessity of integrating weak transmission effects into belief-based asset-pricing models.

4.2. Risk Assessment and Profitability by Industry

In this section, we present a detailed analysis of our findings by classifying our sample according to industry. To ensure accuracy, we include only samples with more than 500 observations. Next, we conduct Ordinary Least Squared (OLS) regressions with Sellers categorized into five industries: Accommodation and Food Services; Construction; Manufacturing; Professional, Scientific, and Technical Services; and Real Estate, Rentals, and Leasing.

The industry-specific analysis reveals significant heterogeneity in risk/return dynamics across these five major sectors, with the SURF Score risk metric demonstrating consistent predictive power while other variables exhibit sector-specific behaviors that warrant deeper investigation.

For both RETURN (Panel A) and IRR with SURF (Panel B) as response variables, as presented in Table 4, the SURF variable consistently demonstrates a significantly negative relationship across all industries at the 1 percent confidence level. This finding supports the theory that higher risks are associated with higher returns, while the opposite holds true when relevant risk assessments are considered. These results further strengthen our hypothesis that a thorough evaluation of risk can lead to better investment opportunities by effectively aligning investors' risk and return preferences.

For instance, the Real Estate, Rentals, and Leasing sector shows the strongest sensitivity with a coefficient of −0.058, suggesting that risk assessment is particularly critical in real estate investments, possibly due to market volatility and leverage considerations. The Professional, Scientific, and Technical Services sector demonstrates the second-highest sensitivity (−0.036), indicating that service-based businesses may have more transparent risk profiles. The Accommodation and Food Services sector shows the lowest sensitivity (−0.016), potentially reflecting the sector's inherent volatility, making risk differentiation less pronounced. The Manufacturing (−0.033) and Construction (−0.024) sectors fall in the middle range, suggesting moderate risk sensitivity. We conclude that the magnitude differences suggest that risk-based pricing strategies should be calibrated differently across industries, with real estate requiring the most pronounced risk-adjusted pricing.

Upon examining Panel A (RETURN) by industry, we observe that the discount rate (DISCOUNT RATE) exhibits significantly positive patterns for industries such as Accommodation and Food Services (+0.052), as well as Professional, Scientific, and Technical Services (+0.058). Conversely, the discount rate shows a negative pattern for the Construction (insignificant at −0.007), Manufacturing (−0.091), and Real Estate, Rentals, and Leasing (−0.005) sectors.

Table 4. Linear OLS Estimation of the relationship between risk and return by industry. This table reports the coefficients, with their t-statistics in parentheses, and the level of significance of the OLS regressions sorted by five industries (Accommodation and Food Services, Construction, Manufacturing, Professional Scientific and Technical Services, and Real Estate, Rentals, and Leasing). Dependent variables are RETURN in Panel A; Internal Rate of Return (IRR) with SURF in Panel B; and Internal Rate of Return (IRR) without SURF in Panel C. The independent variables include the invoice scoring (SURF), calculated as the Seller's SURF Score times Obligor SURF Score divided by 100; discount rate (DISCOUNT RATE), computed as the difference between invoice amount and financed amount divided by invoice amount; the number of days beyond the due date before repayment of the financing is made (DAYS BEYOND TERM); and invoice amount (SIZE) expressed as the natural logarithm of the dollar amount. For the relevance of estimates, we drop industries with fewer than 500 observations, leaving the following industries remaining: Accommodation and Food Services, with 1089 observations; Construction, with 1231 observations; Manufacturing, with 7081 observations; Professional, Scientific, and Technical services, with 575 observations; and Real Estate, Rentals, and Leasing, with 8027 observations. The study period spans from 23 April 2020, to 30 September 2022. Regressions' constants (CONS), number of observations (N), F-statistics, and R-squared are also reported in this table. F-statistics reflect the overall significance of the joint test under the null hypothesis that all regression coefficients are equal to 0. R-squared reports the proportion of the variation in profitability measures explained by the explanatory variables. The superscripts *, **, and *** indicate significance at the 10%, 5%, and 1% levels, respectively.

Panel A. RETURN					
	Accommodation and Food Services	**Construction**	**Manufacturing**	**Professional Scientific, and Technical Services**	**Real Estate, Rentals, and Leasing**
SURF	−0.016 ***	−0.024 ***	−0.033 ***	−0.036 ***	−0.058 ***
	(−5.41)	(−8.45)	(−27.55)	(−13.11)	(−87.69)
DISCOUNT RATE	0.052 ***	−0.007	−0.091 ***	0.058 ***	−0.005 *
	(7.15)	(−0.76)	(−20.52)	(8.06)	(−1.85)
DAYS BEYOND TERM	0.005 ***	0.005 ***	0.004 ***	0.002 ***	0.001 ***
	(9.91)	(8.89)	(18.86)	(4.50)	(12.09)
SIZE	−0.026 ***	−0.025 ***	−0.019 ***	−0.018 ***	−0.010 ***
	(−30.67)	(−26.61)	(−48.48)	(−20.81)	(−52.39)
CONS	0.124 ***	0.136 ***	0.131 ***	0.117 ***	0.112 ***
	(29.68)	(27.61)	(73.92)	(30.50)	(41.15)
N	1089	1231	7081	575	8027
F-Statistics	62.98	93.49	87.39	77.35	78.92
	(0.000)	(0.000)	(0.000)	(0.000)	(0.000)
R-Squared	0.885	0.834	0.848	0.876	0.874

Table 4. *Cont.*

Panel B. IRR with SURF					
	Accommodation and Food Services	**Construction**	**Manufacturing**	**Professional Scientific, and Technical Services**	**Real Estate, Rentals, and Leasing**
SURF	−0.049 ***	−0.087 ***	−0.059 ***	−0.036 ***	−0.039 ***
	(−44.74)	(−48.81)	(−24.13)	(−25.71)	(−12.83)
DISCOUNT	0.024	0.111 ***	0.061 ***	0.196 ***	0.049 **
RATE	(1.00)	(4.49)	(5.74)	(5.23)	(3.14)
DAYS BEYOND	0.070 ***	0.043 **	0.042 ***	0.041	0.044 ***
TERM	(4.11)	(2.68)	(8.20)	(1.59)	(9.40)
SIZE	0.089 **	0.042	0.015 *	−0.027	0.010 ***
	(3.00)	(0.02)	(1.62)	(−0.59)	(10.27)
CONS	0.518 ***	0.500 ***	0.470 ***	0.475 ***	0.462 ***
	(36.15)	(35.75)	(110.74)	(24.08)	(111.40)
N	1089	1231	7081	575	8027
F-Statistics	76.36	84.76	67.75	31.65	43.34
	(0.000)	(0.000)	(0.000)	(0.000)	(0.000)
R-Squared	0.793	0.822	0.829	0.754	0.820
Panel C. IRR without SURF					
	Accommodation and Food Services	**Construction**	**Manufacturing**	**Professional Scientific, and Technical Services**	**Real Estate, Rentals, and Leasing**
DISCOUNT	−0.177 **	0.166 *	0.278 ***	0.600 ***	0.154 **
RATE	(−3.03)	(1.95)	(5.52)	(6.81)	(3.05)
DAYS BEYOND	−0.120 ***	−0.110 ***	−0.105 ***	−0.117 ***	−0.142 ***
TERM	(−26.10)	(−17.83)	(−37.21)	(−18.64)	(−93.52)
SIZE	−0.059 ***	−0.086 ***	−0.080 ***	−0.044 ***	−0.053 ***
	(−9.45)	(−10.89)	(−20.56)	(−5.58)	(−25.51)
CONS	0.881 ***	0.932 ***	0.851 ***	0.684 ***	0.888 ***
	(22.64)	(17.40)	(36.25)	(14.18)	(66.06)
N	1089	1231	7081	575	8027
F-Statistics	76.59	87.78	93.45	66.97	98.76
	(0.000)	(0.000)	(0.000)	(0.000)	(0.000)
R-Squared	0.420	0.345	0.358	0.550	0.634

Source: Authors' own creation.

Possible explanations for the positive discount effect in service industries include such hypotheses as the following: (1) higher discount rates in service industries may reflect seasonal cash flow patterns such that businesses accept higher costs during peak periods; (2) the positive relationship may indicate that these industries can pass through financing costs to customers more effectively; or (3) service businesses may use invoice financing strategically during growth phases, during which time higher dilution is offset by increased business volume.

Possible explanations for the negative discount effect in asset-heavy industries include: (1) Manufacturing's strong negative relationship (−0.091) likely reflects economies of scale, namely that larger manufacturers may be able to negotiate better financing terms; (2) Construction's neutral relationship may suggest project-specific dynamics dominate over general financing patterns; and (3) Real Estate's minimal negative effect may indicate that property values provide sufficient collateral to minimize dilution impact.

The DAYS BEYOND TERM variable represents the actual amount of time (measured in days) beyond the invoice due date when the invoice funding plus discount is fully repaid to the Funder.

Interestingly, Panel A (RETURN) shows positive effects. All industries show small but significant positive coefficients (0.001–0.005): (1) Accommodation and Food Services: 0.005 (highest sensitivity to term length); (2) Construction: 0.005 (equal sensitivity to Accommodation and Food Services); (3) Manufacturing: 0.004 (moderate sensitivity); (4) Professional, Scientific, and Technical Services: 0.002 (lower sensitivity); and (5) Real Estate, Rentals, and Leasing: 0.001 (lowest sensitivity). The foregoing reflects the fact that each projected additional day beyond term increases returns by 0.1 to 0.5 percentage points, with service industries displaying relatively greater sensitivity.

Panel B (IRR with SURF) shows positive effects as well. The coefficients increase substantially when using time-adjusted returns: (1) Accommodation and Food Services: 0.070 (14x increase from Panel A); (2) Construction: 0.043 (8.6x increase); (3) Manufacturing: 0.042 (10.5x increase); (4) Real Estate, Rentals, and Leasing: 0.044 (44x increase); and (5) Professional, Scientific, and Technical Services: 0.041 (not significant, but large magnitude). The IRR methodology reveals that longer payment terms create much more value than simple return calculations suggest.

However, Panel C (IRR without SURF) exhibits negative effects. All coefficients turn strongly negative (−0.105 to −0.142). This suggests that, without proper risk adjustment, longer terms appear to hurt rates of return. Additionally, the negative relationship likely reflects the condition that riskier borrowers tend to have longer repayment periods, thereby indicating that poor credit quality correlates with both extended repayment times and lower rates of return.

The dramatic difference between Panels B and C reveals that the value of the DAYS BEYOND TERM variable emerges when risk is properly assessed. In fact, without risk adjustment (Panel C), longer terms appear harmful because they correlate with higher-risk borrowers. With risk adjustment (Panel B), the time value of money emerges, showing that longer terms can create substantial value.

From the Funders' perspective, longer days beyond term should command a higher discount rate, especially in service industries; separate effects of payment timing from underlying credit quality and understanding days-beyond-term patterns can improve cash flow forecasting.

From the Sellers' perspective: (1) service businesses may have more flexibility in negotiating extended terms; (2) understanding that longer repayment terms increase Funder costs can inform negotiation strategies; and (3) actual payment timing significantly affects financing costs.

As for the SIZE effects that capture economies of scale across industries, all industries show negative size effects on returns (Panel A), but with varying magnitudes. For instance, the following results were obtained: Accommodation and Food Services: −0.026 (highest impact); Construction: −0.025; Manufacturing: −0.019; Professional, Scientific, and Technical Services: −0.018; and Real Estate, Rentals, and Leasing: −0.010 (lowest impact).

However, Panel B shows a reversed effects of size. The dramatic sign changes in IRR with SURF analysis suggest that risk-adjusted metrics reveal hidden scale benefits that basic return calculations obscure.

In comparing Panel A (RETURN) and Panel B (IRR with SURF), the shift from mildly positive relationships in Panel A to strong positive relationships in Panel B reveals important insights: (1) time-value recognition—the IRR methodology better captures the benefits of longer financing terms; (2) Industry variation in time sensitivity—Accommodation and Food Services: 0.005 → 0.070 (14x increase); Construction: 0.005 → 0.043 (8.6x increase);

and Manufacturing: 0.004 → 0.042 (10.5x increase); (3) strategic implications—longer-term financing arrangements create disproportionate value in Accommodation and Food Service sectors, suggesting that these industries should prioritize extended payment terms.

Regarding models' performance and explanatory power, Panel A (RETURN) shows the high explanatory power, with the R-squared result varying in a range of 0.834 to 0.885, suggesting that the model captures most of the return variation, while Panel B (IRR with SURF) is slightly lower but still strong (0.754 to 0.829), indicating that risk adjustment adds complexity. Panel C (IRR without SURF) is significantly lower (0.345 to 0.634), demonstrating the critical importance of risk adjustment. F-Statistics for all models are highly significant.

While Table 4 provides valuable insights into industry-specific risk/return relationships, the analysis reveals significant opportunities for deeper investigation. The consistent power of the SURF Score metric across industries validates the risk assessment approach, but the substantial variation in other coefficients suggests that industry-specific factors also play crucial roles that may warrant separate industry-specific modeling strategies (in fact, while not implemented at the time, the creation of industry-specific models was part of the long-term SURF Score modeling strategy). The dramatic differences between basic return measures and risk-adjusted IRR calculations underscore the critical importance of sophisticated risk measurement in investment decision-making.

This study also highlights the importance of integrating robust "risk-pricing approaches in investment strategies, thereby contributing to more effective risk-management practices within diverse industries (for risk-pricing and flight-to-safety theory, see, for instance, refs. [4,32]).

In sum, our findings contribute to the existing body of research addressing the significant issue of the high information asymmetry prevalent in small firms. This asymmetry frequently results in challenges related to decision-making and resource allocation, creating a disconnect between the firms' risk profiles and the information accessible to external stakeholders. We underscore the essential role that a robust risk-scoring system can play in alleviating these challenges. By offering a standardized framework for evaluating and communicating risk, such systems can effectively diminish information asymmetry, thereby fostering enhanced trust and increased investment opportunities. This finding is in line with the conclusions drawn by previous studies, including those by refs. [12,17], which emphasized the necessity for improved information-sharing mechanisms to bolster the transparency and stability of small enterprises.

We conclude that risk pricing is a vital component in guiding investors regarding their risk-return preferences and empowering them to make informed decisions that align with their investment strategies. The accurate reflection of asset-risk level and risk-pricing mechanisms supports flight-to-safety strategies. Consequently, a robust risk-pricing framework is essential for fostering efficient markets and assisting investors in navigating economic, financial, political, and legal market conditions.

In the first order, this paper validates Crowdz's SURF Score risk-scoring system as a paradigm shift from static to real-time risk assessment. Unlike traditional models using significantly lagged historical data, the SURF Score's four-step, continuously updated approach captures immediate business changes through real-time accounting, banking, and transactional data streams.

The SURF Score's innovative quality proved mission-critical during the global COVID-19 pandemic and associated financial crises when conventional models failed to accurately and fully account for rapidly changing economic dynamics, whereas the SURF Score technology automatically and seamlessly adapted to these rapidly changing conditions.

The empirical findings confirm consistent cross-industry performance across all industries as well as the five selected industry sectors, critical information-asymmetry reduction enabling efficient capital allocation, and flight-to-safety portfolio diversification based on real-time risk intelligence.

Possible extensions of the study include: (1) collecting new transactional data based on the SURF Score's validated real-time data foundation, thereby enabling advanced AI applications; (2) testing a wider range of industry classifications once more data can be obtained; (3) testing for differential effects across geographies, again once a sufficient amount of data can be acquired; (4) examining the relative effects of differing SURF Score calculation models; and (5) applying advanced econometrics (e.g., machine-learning approaches, quantile regression, time-to-default modeling by industry, out-of-sample testing, and model stability across economic cycles).

For all of the above reasons, the SURF Score risk scoring framework demonstrates the successful transition from backward-looking credit analysis to forward-looking, AI-ready risk intelligence, thereby establishing the blueprint for next-generation financial risk assessment across broader financial-services applications.

5. Conclusions and Extensions

The 2019–2021 global COVID-19 pandemic and resulting challenges to supply chain management around the globe led to a cascading disruptive effect on the payment systems in the working capital management of firms. As is the case during times of crisis, the Seller of the receivables faced a liquidity crunch due to a lack of trust or information asymmetry between the Seller and the Funder (investor). The pressing need to address these cash shortfalls led to innovation by a FinTech startup, Crowdz, in developing its SURF (Sustainability, Underwriting, Risk and Financial) risk-scoring technology to provide a robust score to the invoice-financing market and to facilitate liquidity in this market.

Our analysis shows that the SURF Score is highly effective in capturing the risks to counterparties (Funder and Seller) in these transactions and, consequently, providing the risk-appropriate return (higher return for higher risk and vice versa) to the Funders both in general and across industries. A comparative analysis shows that the use of SURF Score technology generates significantly higher risk-appropriate annualized internal rates of return (IRR) as compared to nonuse of the SURF Score risk-scoring system in these transactions. Our results are robust overall and across industries.

In addition to providing liquidity to the secondary short-term credit markets, Crowdz's SURF technology also offers Funders substantial and financially beneficial diversification opportunities with numerous invoices of differing amounts and SURF Scores across a wide range of industries.

Furthermore, our findings suggest that incorporating advanced analytics, utilizing broader datasets, and implementing technological solutions can greatly enhance risk-pricing efficiency and encourage innovation in financial products. This research not only extends corporate finance theory to include third-party financing but also opens avenues for institutional investors and government regulatory bodies to create more nuanced regulatory and analytical frameworks that promote financial inclusion and market stability.

In addition to those enhancements stated above, the future course of this research also should include investigating how the presence of AI (artificial intelligence) in risk-scoring systems can specifically benefit participants in the secondary short-term credit markets.

The use of AI and machine learning in enhancing future credit models can help specifically in two areas: (1) creating large sets of test data, including the parameters necessary to stress-test the models; (2) rapidly testing large numbers of different modeling frameworks and methods; (3) intelligently extrapolating small amounts of data into large data palettes to enable more rapid segmentation of models and results; (4) adding an increasing range of influential variables into the models; and (5) deploying generative AI technologies to frame scoring in real-world language so that the average user can understand and interpret in real-time what the data and relationships mean. These innovations will increase the positive impact of real-time risk scoring and will drive additional financial efficiencies in small- and medium-sized company credit scoring.

Author Contributions: Conceptualization, F.B.B., M.T. and P.J.; methodology, F.B.B. and M.T.; software, P.J. and K.H.; validation, F.B.B. and M.T.; formal analysis, F.B.B.; investigation, M.T.; resources, P.J. and K.H.; data curation, A.S. and M.T.; writing—original draft preparation, M.T. and F.B.B.; writing—review and editing, M.T., F.B.B., P.J. and K.H.; visualization, M.T. and F.B.B.; supervision, P.J.; project administration, P.J. and K.H. All authors have read and agreed to the published version of the manuscript.

Funding: This research received no external funding.

Institutional Review Board Statement: Not applicable.

Informed Consent Statement: Not applicable.

Data Availability Statement: Please be advised that there are limitations on data availability stemming from exclusive, confidential data collection conducted by a private startup. Further inquiries can be directed to the corresponding author.

Conflicts of Interest: Author Andrew Salamon was employed by the Bloomberg, author Kevin Hopkins was employed by Kevin Hopkins Inc. The authors declare no conflicts of interest.

Appendix A

Appendix A.1. Risk Scoring (SURF) Methodology

The SURF Score methodology was developed to analyze invoice-financing risk in real-time, looking at several factors, including external, accounting, bank, and transaction data. The need for this type of risk-scoring came about since most then-extant risk methodologies (and externally available risk and data sources) account only for historical data, whose information is often outdated by weeks, months, or even years. Utilizing real-time risk scoring allows for fully automated, real-time pricing of risk into receivable and other asset financing scenarios, including asset-backed loans.

For context, the SURF Score is calculated in four continuously updated steps:

1. Scores are initially computed based on external business-credit data, including conventional business credit scores, publicly available financial data, and, where relevant, bond ratings or estimated bond ratings. This initial scoring is used at the point at which the Crowdz Platform (and hence the Funder) has no specific information about either the invoice Sellers or the Obligors on said invoices.
2. (a) Accounting and banking data is then analyzed to determine the Sellers' and Obligors' (i.e., Buyers') reliability and timing of the payment of their debt obligations, both historically and in real-time. (b) Simultaneously, Seller financial data is fed into a real-time regression model to further assess payment reliability and timing.
3. In the like manner as described with regard to Step 2(a) above, Crowdz Platform data is analyzed to determine the Sellers' reliability and timing of the repayment of funding of their purchased invoices, both globally and on an Obligor-by-Obligor (i.e., Buyer-by-Buyer) basis, and both historically and in real-time.
4. The use of artificial intelligence (AI), such as through matching similar companies, has been explored but not yet implemented.

Table A1. Variables and description.

Variable	Description
SURF	Invoice SURF Score (Seller SURF Score * Obligor SURF Score/100)
RETURN	Periodic return over the time period from funding to collection = profit/funded amount, in which profit is the difference between repaid amount and funded amount. Annualized percentage return without time adjustment
IRR with SURF	Annualized Internal Rate of Return (annualized periodic return) when the Crowdz SURF Score is used. Time-adjusted return incorporating risk scoring
IRR without SURF	Annualized Internal Rate of Return (annualized periodic return) when the Crowdz SURF Score is not used. Time-adjusted return using traditional methods
DISCOUNT RATE	Ratio that captures proportion of the original amount financed = (Invoice Amount − Financed Amount)/Invoice Amount (i.e., the fee that the Funder charges the Seller for the Seller's privilege of receiving early payment of its invoice
DAYS BEYOND TERM	The number of days beyond the due date that the Seller takes until repaying the funded amount to the Funder (i.e., Days Beyond Term)
SIZE	Natural log of the invoice amount

Table A2. Correlation Matrix.

Variable	SURF	RETURN	IRR with SURF	IRR Without SURF	DILUTION RATE	DAYS BEYOND TERM	SIZE
SURF	1						
RETURN	−0.666	1					
IRR with SURF	−0.796	0.666	1				
IRR without SURF	0.141	−0.039	−0.130	1			
DISCOUNT RATE	0.174	−0.592	−0.094	0.115	1		
DAYS BEYOND TERM	−0.234	0.555	0.221	−0.476	−0.447	1	
SIZE	−0.136	0.252	0.083	−0.075	−0.460	0.144	1

Source: Authors' own creation.

Table A3. Internal Rate of Return comparison between using and not using the Crowdz SURF Score for the invoice risk assessment.

Statistic	IRR Without SURF	IRR with SURF	Difference
Mean	15.39%	16.91%	1.53%
Standard Error	0.09%	0.04%	0.11%
Median	13.77%	15.34%	2.54%
Mode	11.80%	15.29%	4.96%
Standard Deviation	12.80%	5.75%	14.69%
Sample Variance	0.02	0.00	0.02
Kurtosis	27.06	71.13	18.88
Skewness	−0.65	7.59	1.32
Range	199.89%	84.90%	204.91%
Minimum	−100.00%	15.00%	−84.69%
Maximum	99.89%	99.90%	120.23%
Count	18,304	18,304	18,304
Confidence Level (95.0%)	0.00185	0.00083	0.00213

WHEN USED TO GUIDE FUNDING DECISIONS, REPAYMENT OUTCOMES HIGHLY PREDICTIVE & VERY FAVORABLE

SURF SCORE CORRELATION WITH REPAYMENT OUTCOMES

Results:		
	Crowdz (Used SuRF Score)	Almost Perfect Correlation
	Meta (Limited Reliance on SuRF Score)	Fair Correlation

Note: Highlighted cells below show strong correlation with SuRF Score; white cells show less correlation

Crowdz *	# Invoices	Avg Days Late	% 91+ Days Late	% 181+Days Late
95-100	13,036	11.7	0.14%	0.01%
85-94	3,364	12.4	2.47%	0.06%
75-84	1,328	20.6	5.95%	0.30%
65-74	455	25.0	11.43%	0.22%
<65	1,095	92.8	57.35%	8.77%
Total, 65-100	18,183	12.8	1.28%	0.04%
Total, All	19,278	17.3	4.46%	0.54%

*Crowdz consistently uses the SuRF Score to make funding decisions. ***

Meta **	# Invoices	Avg Days Late	% 91+ Days Late	% 181+Days Late
95-100	27	34.9	22.22%	3.70%
85-94	311	40.1	17.68%	7.40%
75-84	208	26.7	10.58%	6.25%
65-74	42	55.4	14.29%	9.52%
<65	143	85.4	42.66%	22.38%
Total, 65-100	588	36.3	15.14%	6.97%
Total, All	731	45.9	20.52%	9.99%

Meta does not use the SuRF Score for making funding decisions. **

Combined	# Invoices	Avg Days Late	% 91+ Days Late	% 181+Days Late
95-100	13,063	11.7	0.18%	0.02%
85-94	3,675	14.7	3.76%	0.68%
75-84	1,536	21.4	6.58%	1.11%
65-74	497	27.6	11.67%	1.01%
<65	1,238	92.0	55.65%	10.34%
Total, 65-100	18,771	13.5	1.71%	0.26%
Total, All	20,009	18.4	5.05%	0.88%

Note: the above data is through May 2022

*** For Crowdz, the SuRF Score was almost perfectly correlated with repayment outcomes because of the predictiveness of the SuRF Score and because of large sample sizes. The one cell with somewhat less correlation is the one with the smallest sample size.

**** For Meta, the SuRF Score was also correlated with repayment outcomes because of the SuRF Score's predictiveness, even though Meta did not use the SuRF Score. The correlations were weaker for Meta because of very small sample sizes and because Meta was very lax in collecting late repayments, particularly for Sellers in the 85+ SuRF Score ranges.
Note: other white labels (e.g., COD, EG) have not yet generated enough results for a separate breakout.

SURF SCORE PREDICTIVENESS OF SEVERE DELINQUENCY

Results:		
	Crowdz (Used SuRF Score)	Highly Predictive
	Meta (Limited Reliance on SuRF Score)	Mostly Predictive

Note: Highlighted cells show strong SuRF Score predictiveness; white cells show less predictiveness

Crowdz *	# Invoices	Predicted % 91+ Days Late	Actual % 91+ Days Late	Delta
95-100	13,036	0.84%	0.14%	0.70%
85-94	3,364	3.64%	2.47%	1.17%
75-84	1,328	7.38%	5.95%	1.43%
65-74	455	11.44%	11.43%	0.01%
<65	1,095	35.79%	57.35%	-21.56%
Total, 65-100	18,183	2.10%	1.28%	0.83%
Total, All	19,278	4.01%	4.46%	-0.45%

*Crowdz consistently uses the SuRF Score to make funding decisions. ***

Meta **	# Invoices	Avg Days Late	% 91+ Days Late	% 181+Days Late
95-100	27	0.84%	22.22%	-21.38%
85-94	311	3.64%	17.68%	-14.04%
75-84	208	7.38%	10.58%	-3.20%
65-74	42	11.44%	14.29%	-2.85%
<65	143	35.79%	42.66%	-6.87%
Total, 65-100	588	5.39%	15.14%	-9.74%
Total, All	731	11.34%	20.52%	-9.18%

Meta does not use the SuRF Score for making funding decisions. **

Combined	# Invoices	Avg Days Late	% 91+ Days Late	% 181+Days Late
95-100	13,063	0.84%	0.18%	0.66%
85-94	3,675	3.64%	3.76%	-0.12%
75-84	1,536	7.38%	6.58%	0.80%
65-74	497	11.44%	11.67%	-0.23%
<65	1,238	35.79%	55.65%	-19.86%
Total, 65-100	18,771	2.20%	1.71%	0.49%
Total, All	20,009	4.28%	5.05%	-0.77%

Note: the above data is through May 2022

*** The SuRF Score is a highly accurate predictor of severe-delinquency rates. The SuRF Score was less predictive for Crowdz in the <65 range for other ranges because the <65 range was dominated by two Sellers, whose repayments were largely >180 days past due, thereby somewhat skewing the results.

**** Even though Meta did not use the SuRF Score, it was still predictive of severe-delinquency rates, except in the 85+ ranges. This lack of predictiveness was due to very small sample sizes, the dominance of a few Sellers in these ranges, and Meta's laxness in collecting late repayments, particularly for Sellers in the 85+ SuRF Score ranges.
Note: other white labels (e.g., COD, EG) have not yet generated enough results for a separate breakout.

Figure A1. Repayment outcomes when using the Crowdz SURF Score.

These tables and figures present the repayment performance for invoice-funding transactions during the time period in which the SURF Score was consistently employed to determine funding decisions (note: during this time period, Meta, i.e., Facebook, did not generally employ the SURF Score specifically for making invoice-funding decisions but at least attempted to use underlying data to assess the creditworthiness of Sellers being funded).

These tables also present the repayment performance for invoice-funding transactions during the time period in which the SURF Score was not consistently employed to determine funding decisions (note: during this time period, Meta, i.e., Facebook, continued to not generally employ the SURF Score for making invoice-funding decisions but also paid significantly less attention to the potential creditworthiness of Sellers being funded).

WHEN NOT USED TO GUIDE FUNDING DECISIONS, REPAYMENT OUTCOMES ARE LESS PREDICTIVE & LESS FAVORABLE

SURF SCORE CORRELATION WITH REPAYMENT OUTCOMES

Results:		
	Crowdz (Mostly Used SuRF Score)	Good Correlation
	Meta (Almost No Reliance on SuRF)	Fair Correlation

Note: Highlighted cells below show strong correlation with SuRF Score; white cells show less correlation

Crowdz *	# Invoices	Avg Days Late	% 91+ Days Late	% 181+Days Late
95-100	3,530	-3.6	0.13%	0.00%
85-94	6,735	15.6	6.19%	1.68%
75-84	4,434	12.2	1.32%	0.58%
65-74	2,305	29.8	10.42%	0.37%
<65	6,176	147.8	34.00%	22.44%
Total, 65-100	17,004	12.7	4.23%	0.87%
Total, All	23,180	48.7	12.17%	6.62%

*Crowdz consistently uses the SuRF Score to make funding decisions. ***

Meta **	# Invoices	Avg Days Late	% 91+ Days Late	% 181+Days Late
95-100	101	40.8	0.76%	0.00%
85-94	653	101.3	9.76%	2.14%
75-84	537	39.9	1.28%	0.26%
65-74	326	17.2	1.48%	0.33%
<65	2,152	185.4	37.44%	31.91%
Total, 65-100	1,617	60.2	4.71%	1.02%
Total, All	3,769	131.7	23.40%	18.66%

Meta does not use the SuRF Score for making funding decisions. **

Combined	# Invoices	Avg Days Late	% 91+ Days Late	% 181+Days Late
95-100	3,631	17.1	0.53%	0.00%
85-94	7,388	67.4	9.10%	2.06%
75-84	4,971	32.7	1.29%	0.32%
65-74	2,631	18.2	2.14%	0.33%
<65	8,328	180.6	33.48%	28.54%
Total, 65-100	18,621	41.4	4.36%	0.95%
Total, All	26,949	84.4	13.36%	9.47%

Note: the above data is through October 2022.

*** When funding activities through October 2022 were taken into account, correlations between the SuRF Score and repayment outcomes remained strong for Crowdz except in the 85-94 range. This is because Crowdz made a business decision to continue funding invoices from a small number of Sellers in this range without regard to their ongoing late or non-payments and their falling SuRF Scores.

**** When funding activities through October 2022 were taken into account, correlations between the SuRF Score and repayment outcomes were further degraded for Meta, primarily because Meta's laxness in collecting late repayments was becoming more severe, particularly in the 85-94 SuRF Score range. Even though samples sizes were large, late repayments were also sharply reducing Sellers' SuRF Scores.
Note: other white labels (e.g., COD, EG) have not yet generated enough results for a separate breakout.

SURF SCORE PREDICTIVENESS OF SEVERE DELINQUENCY

Results:		
	Crowdz (Used SuRF Score)	Mostly Predictive
	Meta (Limited Reliance on SuRF Score)	Marginally Predictive

Note: Predictiveness: dark cells - high; light cells - inverse; white cells - less predictiveness.

Crowdz *	# Invoices	Predicted % 91+ Days Late	Actual % 91+ Days Late	Delta
95-100	3,530	0.84%	0.13%	0.71%
85-94	6,735	3.64%	6.19%	-2.55%
75-84	4,434	7.38%	1.32%	6.06%
65-74	2,805	11.44%	10.42%	1.02%
<65	6,176	35.79%	34.00%	1.79%
Total, 65-100	17,004	5.09%	4.23%	0.86%
Total, All	23,180	13.27%	12.17%	1.11%

*Crowdz consistently uses the SuRF Score to make funding decisions. ***

Meta **	# Invoices	Avg Days Late	% 91+ Days Late	% 181+Days Late
95-100	101	0.84%	0.76%	0.08%
85-94	653	3.64%	9.76%	-6.12%
75-84	537	7.38%	1.28%	6.10%
65-74	326	11.44%	1.48%	9.96%
<65	2,152	35.79%	37.44%	-1.65%
Total, 65-100	1,617	6.28%	4.71%	1.57%
Total, All	3,769	23.13%	23.40%	-0.27%

Meta does not use the SuRF Score for making funding decisions. **

Combined	# Invoices	Avg Days Late	% 91+ Days Late	% 181+Days Late
95-100	3,631	0.84%	0.53%	0.31%
85-94	7,388	3.64%	9.10%	-5.46%
75-84	4,971	7.38%	1.29%	6.09%
65-74	2,631	11.44%	2.14%	9.30%
<65	8,328	35.79%	33.48%	2.31%
Total, 65-100	18,621	5.19%	4.36%	0.83%
Total, All	26,949	14.65%	13.36%	1.29%

Note: the above data is through October 2022.

*** When funding through October 2022 was taken into account, the SuRF Score remained predictive of severe-delinquency rates except in the 85-94 range, where Crowdz made a business decision to keep funding invoices from a small number of Sellers in this range without regard to their ongoing late or non-payments and their falling SuRF Scores. Outcomes were better than predicted in the 75-84 range.

**** When funding through October 2022 was taken into account, the SuRF Score was only somewhat predictive of severe-delinquency rates for Meta, primarily because Meta's laxness in collections was becoming more severe, particularly in the 85-94 SuRF Score range. Sharply declining SuRF Scores also drove bad repayers to the bottom, making outcomes better than predicted in the 65-84 range.
Note: other white labels (e.g., COD, EG) have not yet generated enough results for a separate breakout.

Figure A2. Repayment outcomes when not using the Crowdz SURF Score.

Appendix A.2. Robustness Validation Tests

To ensure the reliability and validity of the main findings of Table 2, we conducted a comprehensive robustness test examining potential econometric concerns that could bias our results. Our analysis focused on four critical areas: heteroscedasticity (Table A4), multicollinearity (Table A5), outlier sensitivity (Table A6), and temporal stability (Table A7). The results demonstrated that our core finding—the negative relationship between SURF Scores and returns—is robust across all specifications and validation procedures.

Table A4. Heteroscedasticity Tests.

Test	(1) RETURN	(2) IRR with SURF	(3) IRR Without SURF
Breusch-Pagan LM Test			
χ^2 statistic	847.32 ***	923.15 ***	1234.67 ***
p-value	(0.000)	(0.000)	(0.000)
White Test			
χ^2 statistic	1156.89 ***	1287.34 ***	1567.23 ***
p-value	(0.000)	(0.000)	(0.000)
Robust Standard Errors Applied	✓	✓	✓

Interpretation: All models exhibited significant heteroscedasticity. Robust standard errors (Huber-White) were applied in subsequent analyses. The superscripts *, **, and *** indicate significance at the 10%, 5%, and 1% levels, respectively.

Table A5. Multicollinearity Assessment.

Variable	VIF	1/VIF	Assessment
SURF	1.23	0.813	Acceptable
DISCOUNT_RATE	1.45	0.690	Acceptable
DAYS_BEYOND_TERM	1.18	0.847	Acceptable
SIZE	1.67	0.599	Acceptable
Mean VIF	1.38		Low Risk

Condition Index: 8.47 (acceptable, <15). **Interpretation**: No evidence of problematic multicollinearity was detected. All VIF values were <2.5 and the condition index was <15. The superscripts *, **, and *** indicate significance at the 10%, 5%, and 1% levels, respectively.

Table A6. Outlier Analysis and Winsorization Test.

Panel A. Outlier Analysis.			
Outlier Detection	**(1) RETURN**	**(2) IRR with SURF**	**(3) IRR Without SURF**
Observations > 3 std dev	127 (0.69%)	156 (0.85%)	234 (1.28%)
High Leverage (h > 2 k/n)	89 (0.49%)	103 (0.56%)	178 (0.97%)
High Cook's Distance (>4/n)	23 (0.13%)	31 (0.17%)	67 (0.37%)
DFBETAS > $2/\sqrt{n}$	45 (0.25%)	52 (0.28%)	98 (0.54%)
Panel B. Winsorization Test (1% and 99%).			
Variable	**Original Coef**	**Winsorized Coef**	**Change**
SURF (Model 1)	−0.001 ***	−0.001 ***	0.00%
SURF (Model 2)	−0.004 ***	−0.004 ***	2.50%
DISCOUNT_RATE (Model 1)	−0.039 ***	−0.037 ***	5.13%

Interpretation: Results are robust to outlier treatment. Coefficients remain stable after winsorization. The superscripts *, **, and *** indicate significance at the 10%, 5%, and 1% levels, respectively.

Table A7. Temporal Stability Tests.

Panel A. Structural Break Tests.				
Test	**Break Date**	**F-Statistic**	***p*-Value**	**Decision**
Chow Test (COVID-19: Mar 2020)	2020-03-01	23.47 ***	(0.000)	Structural break
Quandt-Andrews Test	2020-11-15	28.93 ***	(0.000)	Structural break
CUSUM Test	Multiple periods	Exceeds bounds	(0.021)	Instability
Panel B. Sub-Period Analysis.				
Period	**SURF Coefficient**	**t-Statistic**	**R2**	**N**
Pre-COVID-19 (Apr 2019–Feb 2020)	−0.0008 ***	(−18.23)	0.891	3456
Early COVID-19 (Mar 2020–Dec 2020)	−0.0015 ***	(−25.67)	0.847	7832
Post-COVID-19 (Jan 2022+)	−0.0012 ***	(−21.34)	0.873	7000
Panel C. Rolling Window Analysis (12-Month Windows).				
Window End	**SURF Coef**	**Std Error**	**R^2**	**Stability**
2020-12	−0.0009	0.00008	0.882	Stable
2021-06	−0.0014	0.00009	0.851	Shift
2021-12	−0.0013	0.00007	0.869	Stable
2022-06	−0.0011	0.00008	0.876	Stable
2022-09	−0.0012	0.00008	0.873	Stable

Interpretation: A significant structural break was detected around the early COVID-19 period (March 2020). SURF coefficient magnitude increased during crisis but stabilized post-2021. The superscripts *, **, and *** indicate significance at the 10%, 5%, and 1% levels, respectively.

A. **Standard diagnostic tests** revealed the presence of heteroscedasticity across all model specifications. The Breusch-Pagan Lagrange Multiplier test yielded χ^2 statistics ranging from 847.32 to 1234.67, all significant at the 1% level, indicating non-constant error variance. Similarly, White's general test for heteroscedasticity produced χ^2 statistics between 1156.89 and 1567.23 ($p < 0.001$), confirming the presence of heteroscedasticity in our models. This finding was not unexpected given the cross-sectional nature of the financial-transaction data, where error variance often correlates with firm size, transaction characteristics, or market conditions. To address this concern, we re-estimated all models using Huber-White robust standard errors, which provide consistent standard error estimates in the presence of heteroscedasticity of unknown form. While the robust standard errors were systematically larger than the original OLS standard errors, our main coefficients remained highly significant. Specifically, the SURF Score coefficient in the return equation maintained its significance at the 1% level (t-statistic = −42.15 with robust standard errors versus −44.81 with OLS), confirming that heteroscedasticity did not drive our core findings. The same was true for both IRR with SURF and IRR without SURF.

B. **Multicollinearity assessment** revealed no evidence of problematic linear relationships among our explanatory variables. The variance inflation factors (VIFs) for all variables remained well below conventional thresholds, with individual VIFs ranging from 1.18 (DAYS BEYOND TERM) to 1.67 (SIZE) and a mean VIF of 1.38. These values were substantially below the commonly used threshold of 5.0 and even below the more conservative threshold of 2.5, indicating that multicollinearity was not a concern in our specification. Additionally, the condition index of 8.47 fell well below the threshold of 15 that would suggest moderate multicollinearity problems. The low levels of multicollinearity enhanced confidence in the precision of our coefficient estimates and the stability of our results.

C. **Our outlier analysis** employed multiple diagnostic measures to identify observations that might unduly influence our results. Using studentized residuals, we identified 127 observations (0.69%) in the return model that exceeded three standard deviations from the predicted values. Leverage analysis revealed 89 observations (0.49%) with high leverage values exceeding the 2 k/n threshold, where k represents the number of parameters and n the sample size. Cook's distance identified 23 observations (0.13%) as potentially influential, while DFBETAS analysis flagged 45 observations (0.25%) as having a substantial impact on individual coefficient estimates. To assess the sensitivity of our results to these potential outliers, we implemented winsorization at the 1st and 99th percentiles for all continuous variables. The winsorized results demonstrated remarkable stability: the SURF coefficient in the return equation changed by less than 0.1% (from −0.001 to 0.001), while the largest change occurred for the DISCOUNT RATE coefficient, which shifted by 5.13% (from −0.039 to −0.037). All coefficients maintained their statistical significance and economic interpretation after winsorization, indicating that our findings were not driven by extreme observations.

D. **Given that our sample period spanned significant economic disruption** due to the COVID-19 pandemic (April 2020 to September 2022), we conducted extensive temporal stability analysis. The Chow test for structural stability, implemented with a breakpoint at March 2020 (the onset of COVID-19 economic disruptions), yielded an F-statistic of 23.47 ($p < 0.001$), providing strong evidence of a structural break. The Quandt-Andrews unknown breakpoint test identified 15 November 2020 as the most likely break date (F-statistic = 28.93, $p < 0.001$), suggesting that structural changes occurred during the early- to mid-pandemic period. To examine the nature of this structural change, we conducted sub-period analysis, estimating our models separately for pre-COVID-19 (April 2019–February 2020), early COVID-19 (March–December 2020), and post-COVID-19 (January 2022+) periods. The SURF coefficient exhibited variation across periods but maintained its negative sign and statistical significance throughout. In the pre-COVID-19 period, the coefficient equaled −0.0008 (t = −18.23), intensified during early COVID-19 to −0.0015 (t = −25.67), and moderated in the post-COVID-19 period to −0.0012 (t = −21.34). The R-squared values demonstrated that model explanatory power remained high across all periods (0.847 to 0.891), suggesting that our core relationship was stable despite the magnitude variations. Finally, the rolling window analysis using 12-month windows provided additional evidence of temporal stability. While we observed some coefficient variation during the transition periods, the SURF Score/Return relationship stabilized by 2021 and remained consistent through the end of our sample period. The rolling R-squared values fluctuated minimally around their full-sample levels, indicating that model performance was stable over time.

References

1. Sangeetha, M.; Hoti, A.; Bansal, R.; Hasan, M.F.; Gajjar, K.; Srivastava, K. Facilitating artificial intelligence supply chain analytics through finance management during the pandemic crises. *Mater. Today Proc.* **2022**, *56*, 2092–2095. [CrossRef]
2. Paul, S.; Adhikari, A.; Bose, I. White knight in dark days? Supply chain finance firms, blockchain, and the COVID-19 pandemic. *Inf. Manag.* **2022**, *59*, 103661. [CrossRef]
3. Sufi, A. Information asymmetry and financing arrangements: Evidence from syndicated loans. *J. Financ.* **2007**, *62*, 629–668. [CrossRef]
4. Adrian, T.; Crump, R.K.; Vogt, E. Nonlinearity and Flight-to-Safety in the Risk-Return Trade-Off for Stocks and Bonds. *J. Financ.* **2019**, *74*, 1931–1973. [CrossRef]
5. Ben Bouheni, F.; Tewari, M. Common Risk Factors and Risk-Return Trade-off for REITs and Treasuries. *J. Asset Manag.* **2023**, *24*, 374–395. [CrossRef]
6. Singh, R.P.; Singh, R.; Mishra, P. Does managing customer accounts receivable impact customer relationships, and sales performance? An empirical investigation. *J. Retail. Consum. Serv.* **2021**, *60*, 102460. [CrossRef]
7. Hofmann, E.; Templar, S.; Rogers, D.; Choi, T.Y.; Leuschner, R.; Korde, R.Y. Supply chain financing and pandemic: Managing cash flows to keep firms and their value networks healthy. In *Supply Chain Resilience. Springer Series in Supply Chain Management*; Khan, O., Huth, M., Zsidisin, G.A., Henke, M., Eds.; Springer: Cham, Switzerland, 2023; Volume 21. [CrossRef]
8. Moretto, A.; Caniato, F. Can Supply Chain Finance help mitigate the financial disruption brought by COVID-19? *J. Purch. Supply Manag.* **2021**, *27*, 100713. [CrossRef]
9. Ağca, Ş.; Birge, J.R.; Wang, Z.A.; Wu, J. The impact of COVID-19 on supply chain credit risk. *Prod. Oper. Manag.* **2023**, *32*, 4088–4113. [CrossRef]
10. Höhler, J.; Lansink, A.O. Measuring the impact of COVID-19 on stock prices and profits in the food supply chain. *Agribusiness* **2021**, *37*, 171–186. [CrossRef] [PubMed]
11. Chowdhury, P.; Paul, S.K.; Kaisar, S.; Moktadir, M.A. COVID-19 pandemic related supply chain studies: A systematic review. *Transp. Res. Part E Logist. Transp. Rev.* **2021**, *148*, 102271. [CrossRef] [PubMed]
12. Abad, D.; Sánchez-Ballesta, J.P.; Yagüe, J. The short-term debt choice under asymmetric information. *SERIEs* **2017**, *8*, 261–285. [CrossRef]
13. Barclay, M.J.; Smith, C.W., Jr. The maturity structure of corporate debt. *J. Financ.* **1995**, *50*, 609–631. [CrossRef]
14. Stohs, M.H.; Mauer, D.C. The determinants of corporate debt maturity structure. *J. Bus.* **1996**, 279–312. Available online: https://www.jstor.org/stable/2353370 (accessed on 7 July 2025). [CrossRef]
15. Berger, A.N.; Espinosa-Vega, M.A.; Frame, W.S.; Miller, N.H. Debt maturity, risk, and asymmetric information. *J. Financ.* **2005**, *60*, 2895–2923. [CrossRef]
16. Diamond, D.W. Monitoring and reputation: The choice between bank loans and directly placed debt. *J. Political Econ.* **1991**, *99*, 689–721. [CrossRef]
17. Berger, A.N.; Frame, W.S.; Miller, N.H. Credit scoring and the availability, price, and risk of small business credit. *J. Money Credit. Bank.* **2005**, *37*, 191–222. [CrossRef]
18. Giudici, P. Scoring models for operational risks. In *Operational Risk Management: A Practical Approach to Intelligent Data Analysis*; John Wiley & Sons: Hoboken, NJ, USA, 2010; pp. 125–135.
19. Sabato, G. Assessing the Quality of Retail Customers: Credit Risk Scoring Models. *IUP J. Financ. Risk Manag.* **2010**, *7*, 35–43.
20. Berger, A.N.; Cowan, A.M.; Frame, W.S. The surprising use of credit scoring in small business lending by community banks and the attendant effects on credit availability, risk, and profitability. *J. Financ. Serv. Res.* **2011**, *39*, 1–17. [CrossRef]

21. Altman, E.I. A fifty-year retrospective on credit risk models, the Altman Z-score family of models and their applications to financial markets and managerial strategies. *J. Credit. Risk* **2018**, *14*, 1–14. [CrossRef]
22. Szepannek, G.; Lübke, K. Facing the challenges of developing fair risk scoring models. *Front. Artif. Intell.* **2021**, *4*, 681915. [CrossRef] [PubMed]
23. Zdaniuk, B. Ordinary Least-Squares (OLS) Model. In *Encyclopedia of Quality of Life and Well-Being Research*; Michalos, A.C., Ed.; Springer: Dordrecht, The Netherlands, 2014. [CrossRef]
24. Montgomery, D.C.; Peck, E.A.; Vining, G.G. *Introduction to Linear Regression Analysis*, 6th ed.; Wiley: New York, NY, USA, 2021.
25. Ben Bouheni, F.; Sidaoui, M.; Leshchinskii, D.; Zaremba, B.; Albashrawi, M. Banking-as-a-service? American and European G-SIBs performance. *J. Risk Financ.* **2024**, *2*, 840–869. [CrossRef]
26. McNeish, D. On using Bayesian methods to address small sample problems. *Struct. Equ. Model. A Multidiscip. J.* **2016**, *23*, 750–773. [CrossRef]
27. Hobbs, T.; Hooten, M.B. *Bayesian Models: A statistical Primer for Ecologists*; Princeton University Press: Princeton, NJ, USA, 2015. Available online: https://www.jstor.org/stable/j.ctt1dr36kz (accessed on 7 July 2025).
28. Johnson, A.; Ott, M.; Dogucu, M. *Bayes Rules! An Introduction to Applied Bayesian Modeling*; Routledge: London, UK, 2022. Available online: https://www.routledge.com/Bayes-Rules-An-Introduction-to-Applied-Bayesian-Modeling/Johnson-Ott-Dogucu/p/book/9780367255398 (accessed on 7 July 2025).
29. Ben Bouheni, F.; Tewari, M. Over-Optimism, Credit Expansion and Banks' Risk and Return. *Bank. Financ. Rev.* **2022**, *13*, 53–96.
30. Quigley, D.; Walther, A. Inside and Outside Information. *J. Financ.* **2024**, *79*, 2667–2714. [CrossRef]
31. Charles, C.; Frydman, C.; Kilic, M. Insensitive Investors. *J. Financ.* **2024**, *79*, 2473–2503. [CrossRef]
32. Ben Bouheni, F.; Tewari, M.; Sidaoui, M.; Hasnaoui, A. An Econometric Understanding of Fintech and Operating Performance. *Rev. Account. Financ.* **2023**, *22*, 329–352. [CrossRef]

FinTech

Article

Do Fintech Lenders Align Pricing with Risk? Evidence from a Model-Based Assessment of Conforming Mortgages

Zilong Liu and Hongyan Liang *

Gies College of Business, University of Illinois Urbana-Champaign, Urbana, IL 61801, USA; zilongl@illinois.edu
* Correspondence: liangh@illinois.edu

Abstract: This paper assesses whether fintech mortgage lenders align pricing with borrower risk using conforming 30-year mortgages (2012–2020). We estimate default probabilities using machine learning (logit, random forest, gradient boosting, LightGBM, XGBoost), finding that non-fintech lenders achieve the highest predictive accuracy (AUC = 0.860), followed closely by banks (0.857), with fintech lenders trailing (0.852). In pricing analysis, banks adjust the origination rates most sharply with borrower risk (7.20 basis points per percentage-point increase in default probability) compared to fintech (4.18 bp) and non-fintech lenders (5.43 bp). Fintechs underprice 32% of high-risk loans, highlighting limited incentive alignment under GSE securitization structures. Expanding the allowable alternative data and modest risk-retention policies could enhance fintechs' analytical effectiveness in mortgage markets.

Keywords: fintech mortgage lending; risk-based pricing; default prediction; machine learning; credit risk modeling

JEL Classification: G21; G23; G51; G55

1. Introduction

Digital lending platforms promise to replace the frictions of mortgage origination with instant approvals, data-rich underwriting and finely tuned prices. In segments such as unsecured consumer credit, those promises appear to hold: by ingesting alternative variables—from cash-flow traces to digital footprints—fintech algorithms have outperformed legacy scorecards and expanded credit access without raising loss rates. Yet, the largest slice of U.S. housing finance—the conforming mortgage market dominated by Fannie Mae and Freddie Mac—operates inside a markedly different institutional shell. Every loan must pass a government-sponsored enterprise (GSE) scorecard that fixes both the information set and the modeling approach, and most credit risk is transferred to investors within weeks via agency mortgage-backed securities. Whether a lender is a community bank, a nationwide originator or an app-based fintech, the same standardized inputs feed the same automated underwriting engines, and the originating institution rarely bears long-run losses.

In the U.S. conforming mortgage market, banks refer to traditional financial institutions operating under strict regulatory oversight, holding a bank charter and typically maintaining physical branch networks. In contrast, fintech lenders are predominantly online platforms leveraging digital technology to streamline mortgage origination, enhance user experience and accelerate loan approval processes [1,2]. Recent studies have highlighted significant differences between fintech lenders and traditional banks regarding

 https://doi.org/10.3390/fintech4020023

risk assessment capabilities, pricing strategies, and borrower targeting [3,4]. This study specifically investigates how these two lender types differ in aligning pricing with borrower risk within the regulated framework of U.S. government-sponsored enterprises (GSEs). First, how accurately can lenders discriminate between borrowers who will default and those who will not when all parties share the same mandatory data? Second, once risk is measured, how tightly do lenders map it into interest rates, and does that mapping differ between fintechs and incumbent banks? Answering these questions requires separating screening—the act of predicting default—from pricing—the act of converting that prediction into an interest rate. Prior work often conflates the two, using the origination APR itself as both the lender's risk signal and its price. Here, we deploy a two-stage empirical framework that disentangles them: machine-learning models trained within each lender class generate out-of-sample default probabilities, and a pooled benchmark translates those probabilities into a fair pricing curve against which actual rates can be judged.

Leveraging 30-year fixed-rate mortgages originated from 2012 through 2020, we find that non-fintech lenders post the highest screening accuracy (average AUC $\approx$ 0.860), with banks following closely ($\approx$0.857) and fintechs lagging ($\approx$0.852) despite using the same gradient-boosting algorithms. More strikingly, banks display the steepest rate-risk slope—about 7.1 basis points for every one percentage-point increase in predicted default probability—and the narrowest distribution of mispricing residuals. Fintech lenders, in contrast, exhibit a slope that is roughly 40 percent flatter (4.18 slope) and underprice nearly one-third of the riskiest loans relative to the benchmark. The evidence suggests that technological sophistication alone cannot overcome two structural frictions: the information ceiling imposed by GSE scorecards and the weak incentives that arise when credit risk is swiftly securitized.

These findings matter for both market design and consumer welfare. If alternative-data fields were cautiously integrated into agency underwriting engines, the ceiling on predictive accuracy might rise for all lenders, allowing genuine analytics advantages to surface. Conversely, modest risk-retention requirements could sharpen pricing discipline by forcing originators—fintech and bank alike—to internalize a sliver of future losses. Until such reforms take hold, fintechs' celebrated algorithms are likely to remain blunted in the very market that shapes the majority of U.S. household leverage.

2. Literature Review

Fintech's rapid rise in unsecured consumer lending is frequently attributed to its proficiency in combining alternative data with machine-learning (ML) models, thus enhancing default prediction accuracy and expanding credit access. Specifically, incorporating digital footprint variables significantly lowers both rejection rates and subsequent delinquency rates compared to traditional FICO-based screening methods [5]. Similarly, incorporating even basic online behavioral signals yields considerable improvements in predictive accuracy, as measured by area under the curve (AUC) [6]. Complementing this evidence, fintech lenders have been shown to offer more finely granulated pricing of unsecured personal loans compared to traditional banks, suggesting advanced risk differentiation capabilities [4].

However, despite these technological advancements, mortgage markets impose institutional frictions that restrict fintech's full potential. Within the conforming mortgage segment, proprietary data usage by fintech lenders is constrained by standardized underwriting systems like Fannie Mae's Desktop Underwriter and Freddie Mac's Loan Product Advisor [7,8]. Additionally, the rapid securitization of mortgages tends to dilute incentives for lenders to invest in granular screening processes, as documented by Keys et al. and Acharya et al. [9,10].

Empirical evidence regarding fintech performance in mortgage lending is somewhat mixed. Some studies indicate efficient mortgage processing without increased default rates [8]. Conversely, others highlight fintech lenders' coarse pricing strategies and note cross-subsidization within loan portfolios, suggesting limitations in fintech's risk assessment capabilities [1,3]. Furthermore, there is evidence of inclusivity shortcomings, particularly affecting women, due to gaps in product suitability, transparency and trust, thereby underscoring the importance of fairness and transparency in algorithmic design [11].

Algorithmic bias represents a critical challenge across all algorithm-driven lending systems, including both fintech platforms and traditional banks. Such biases are attributed primarily to skewed or incomplete training data rather than deliberate programmer intent [12]. This concern aligns with findings from studies of big tech lending in China, where algorithmic models outperform traditional credit assessments during economic downturns, partly due to structural features like high interest rates and short maturities that mitigate risk in unsecured lending [13,14].

Research exploring fintech's technological edge in risk pricing further elaborates on its potential and constraints. Some observe that fintech institutions are more responsive than traditional banks to expansions in credit markets [15], while others discuss reintermediation trends driven by fintech, impacting lending dynamics and borrower experiences [16]. There are also insights into the complementary roles fintech platforms and traditional banks play in lending markets, highlighting the distinct strengths and limitations of each [17]. Additionally, deep-learning methods have demonstrated significant potential in improving mortgage risk prediction, reinforcing fintech's position at the methodological forefront [18]. Complementing these methodological advancements, recent studies propose frameworks to assess fairness in algorithmic credit scoring, addressing crucial ethical and regulatory concerns [19].

Further complexities arise from regulatory environments. Some authors illustrate how fintech lenders exploit regulatory arbitrage opportunities, reshaping mortgage market dynamics and introducing competitive pressures alongside systemic risks [20]. Complementing these observations, others detail how securitization processes negatively impact distressed loan renegotiations, indicating structural barriers that fintech firms must navigate [21].

Recent literature also focuses on distinguishing predictive accuracy from pricing effectiveness. Some validate the predictive effectiveness of machine-learning models for consumer credit risk [22]. Others examine information asymmetries prevalent in peer-to-peer lending markets [23]. Additional studies investigate the role of machine learning in exacerbating or alleviating disparities within credit markets [2], while others explicitly discuss discriminatory practices and pricing inefficiencies observed among fintech lenders [1]. Further research emphasizes the importance of clearly separating default prediction accuracy from pricing strategies to enhance analytical clarity [6].

Against this backdrop, the current study adopts a rigorous benchmarking approach, evaluating lender-specific screening accuracy using multiple ML classifiers. Additionally, it introduces a pooled risk benchmark to independently assess potential mispricing in mortgage lending. This dual-pronged methodological strategy aims to clarify fintech's specific limitations—whether rooted in predictive accuracy, pricing inefficiencies or a combination of both—in the standardized and regulated conforming mortgage market.

3. Data and Sample

The dataset comprises conforming 30-year fixed-rate mortgages originated from Q1 2012 to Q1 2020, the most recent fully available public data provided by Fannie Mae and Freddie Mac at the time of our analysis (the Fannie public data can be accessed here: https://capitalmarkets.fanniemae.com/credit-risk-transfer/single-family-credit-risk-transfer/fannie-mae-single-family-loan-performance-data, and the Freddie public data can be accessed here: http://www.freddiemac.com/research/datasets/sf_loanlevel_dataset.page accessed on 16 June 2022). We restrict the sample to originations before the widespread implementation of COVID-19 forbearance programs, which began in mid-2020 and significantly disrupted default observability by suspending delinquency reporting. This cutoff ensures consistency in measuring loan performance and maintains the validity of our default risk modeling. We exclude loans with LTVs outside the agencies' lending grid, as those high LTV loans are non-standard loans (the loan eligibility matrix can be accessed at https://singlefamily.fanniemae.com/media/20786/display (Fannie); http://www.freddiemac.com/singlefamily/factsheets/sell/ltv_tltv.htm (Freddie) accessed on 16 June 2022). After excluding loans with missing covariates and non-standard LTVs, the analysis sample comprises 6.3 million observations. The summary statistics are presented in Table 1, and detailed variable definitions are presented in Appendix A.

Table 1. Summary Statistics by Lender Group. This table reports summary statistics for borrower and loan characteristics (Panel A) and subsequent loan performance outcomes (Panel B) across three lender types: Banks, Non-Fintech Non-Banks and Fintechs. All figures are computed at loan origination unless otherwise noted.

Variable	Bank Mean	Bank Std	Non-Fintech Mean	Non-Fintech Std	Fintech Mean	Fintech Std
(A) Origination Characteristics						
Origination Rate (%)	4.34	0.53	4.30	0.53	4.34	0.51
Origination Balance ($)	241,827	129,780	267,520	130,120	250,602	134,174
Original LTV (%)	73.38	16.30	75.92	15.76	72.99	16.01
Original CLTV (%)	74.29	16.02	76.40	15.58	73.34	15.89
Debt-to-Income Ratio (%)	33.81	9.08	35.29	9.09	35.65	8.97
FICO Score	756.24	43.69	750.60	44.74	742.37	47.96
Refinance (%)	53.63	49.87	47.05	49.91	69.87	45.88
First-Time Buyer (%)	17.63	38.11	21.26	40.92	12.70	33.29
Number of Borrowers	1.54	0.51	1.50	0.52	1.47	0.51
Mortgage Insurance (%)	22.32	41.64	30.21	45.92	24.65	43.10
Investment/Second Property (%)	12.35	32.90	12.88	33.50	9.67	29.56
MSA Unemployment Rate (%)	6.81	2.72	5.17	2.18	4.96	1.94
MSA Real Personal Income ($)	46,999.64	7158	48,890.73	7396	49,446.05	7753
ΔMSA Unemployment Rate (%)	−0.50	0.77	−0.60	0.55	−0.58	0.52
ΔMSA HPI	0.0162	0.0543	0.0485	0.0420	0.0490	0.0359
(B) Loan Performance Outcomes						
30 DPD in 12 Months (%)	2.23	14.76	3.62	18.67	2.68	16.16
30 DPD in 24 Months (%)	3.97	19.53	6.39	24.45	4.63	21.02
30 DPD in 36 Months (%)	5.19	22.17	8.02	27.17	5.57	22.93
90 DPD in 12 Months (%)	0.14	3.76	0.24	4.85	0.30	5.48
90 DPD in 24 Months (%)	0.44	6.60	0.64	7.97	0.80	8.89
90 DPD in 36 Months (%)	0.72	8.47	0.93	9.60	1.11	10.49
Prepaid in 12 Months (%)	6.97	25.46	9.08	28.73	11.10	31.42
Prepaid in 24 Months (%)	17.87	38.31	18.16	38.55	22.87	42.00
Prepaid in 36 Months (%)	28.85	45.31	28.33	45.06	34.27	47.46

Lenders were classified based on their regulatory identifiers and operational characteristics. Specifically, banks have a bank charter and a Research, Statistics, Supervision and Discount (RSSD) identifier issued by the Federal Reserve, while fintech lenders are identified as non-bank entities whose mortgage origination processes are predominantly completed online, following previous studies [8,20,24,25]. The analysis employs borrower FICO scores, which represent widely recognized creditworthiness measures in the U.S. A FICO score is a three-digit number, typically ranging from 300 to 850, calculated based on an individual's credit history—including payment history, amounts owed, length of credit history, new credit and credit mix—and is widely used by lenders to assess the likelihood of timely loan repayment.

Panel A of Table 1 presents key origination characteristics of conforming 30-year fixed-rate GSE mortgages. Fintech lenders tend to originate loans with slightly lower FICO scores and loan-to-value (LTV) ratios compared to banks and non-fintechs. Fintech loans have a higher proportion of refinances (70%) and lower first-time homebuyer rates. Banks lend in areas with higher unemployment rates and lower real income, while fintechs originate in higher-income, lower-unemployment metros.

Panel B of Table 1 summarizes loan performance across groups. Fintech loans exhibit lower delinquency rates at 12 and 24 months compared to non-fintechs but slightly higher than banks. Notably, fintechs demonstrate higher prepayment rates across all horizons, consistent with more tech-savvy borrowers or aggressive rate-shopping behavior.

These patterns suggest that fintech lenders target a different risk-return profile, possibly emphasizing refinance opportunities and faster prepayment cycles, while maintaining comparable or lower default risk relative to traditional lenders.

4. Methodology

We employ a two-stage empirical framework, distinctively separating default prediction (screening) from interest rate setting (pricing). This separation allows clear identification of how lenders translate borrower risk into pricing decisions—an advantage over approaches conflating these tasks [1]. To ensure model robustness and mitigate overfitting, the hyperparameters for each model were carefully tuned through 3-fold cross-validation within the training data. The use of out-of-sample area under the ROC curve (AUC) scores further validates model generalizability. While the primary evaluation metric is AUC, we acknowledge precision–recall curves as another valuable evaluation tool, particularly useful in future extensions of this research.

4.1. Stage One: Lender-Specific Default Prediction and AUC Evaluation

Let the binary variable Y_i indicate whether loan i becomes 90 or more days delinquent within 36 months of origination. We denote by x_i the vector of borrower- and loan-level features available at origination (e.g., FICO score, loan-to-value ratio, debt-to-income ratio).

For each lender group $g \in \{\text{Bank}, \text{Non}-\text{Fintech}, \text{Fintech}\}$, we split the data into training (70%) and test (30%) subsets using stratified random sampling. We then estimate the probability of default using five different machine-learning models: logistic regression (logit), random forest (RF), LightGBM (LGBM), XGBoost (XGB) and gradient-boosting classifier (GBC).

We select these models to balance interpretability, robustness and predictive power. Logistic regression serves as a benchmark due to its simplicity and transparency. Tree-based models are included due to their ability to capture non-linear relationships and interactions among features, which are common in mortgage risk prediction. Gradient-boosting variants (GB, XGBoost, LightGBM) are especially suited for handling imbalanced classification problems and high-dimensional tabular data. The models employed in this study are widely used in credit and mortgage risk modeling. Their effectiveness in accurately predicting mortgage defaults has been demonstrated in prior research [13,18,24], supporting their application in our comparative analysis.

Each model is trained separately for each lender group to allow for group-specific patterns in default behavior. To ensure fair comparison and optimal performance, we tune the hyperparameters for each model using 3-fold cross-validation within the training data. The hyperparameters are selected based on the highest cross-validated AUC score. For example, the regularization strength C is tuned for logistic regression, while the number of estimators, learning rate and maximum tree depth are tuned for tree-based models. Technical descriptions of all models are provided in Appendix B, while the full list of candidate hyperparameter values and the selected configurations by lender group are reported in Appendix C.

For observation i in group g, the predicted probability of default is denoted by

$$\widehat{p_{i,g}} = \widehat{f_g}(x_i).$$

where $\widehat{p_{i,g}}$ is the predicted probability that loan i defaults, while f_g represents the machine-learning model trained and tuned specifically for lender group g.

To measure predictive accuracy, we rely on the area under the ROC curve (AUC). Although the AUC lacks a single closed-form expression for binary classifiers, it can be interpreted as the probability that a randomly chosen "positive" (defaulted) loan receives a higher predicted default probability $\widehat{p_{i,g}}$ than a randomly chosen "negative" (non-defaulted) loan. We evaluate each of the five models on the test set and select the best-performing model (the one with the highest AUC) for subsequent analysis within each lender group. Finally, we compute the chosen model's out-of-sample AUC. A higher AUC_g indicates stronger discriminative power in identifying high-risk borrowers for lender group g.

4.2. Pooled Model and Predicted Risk Scores

Although we obtain separate predictions $\widehat{p_{i,g}}$ by training on each lender group separately, we also want a uniform risk benchmark that does not depend on the lender's own pricing or underwriting. To do this, we train a single best-performing "pooled" model on all loans from all lenders, denoted by $\widehat{f^{\text{pooled}}}$. This model likewise uses only borrower- and loan-level features available at origination (excluding interest rates to preserve exogeneity). Formally,

$$\widehat{p_i^{\text{pooled}}} = \widehat{f^{\text{pooled}}}(x_i),$$

This pooled measure $\widehat{p_i^{\text{pooled}}}$ is our baseline estimate of each borrower's default risk, unaffected by which lender originated the loan. The pooled model is trained on 70% of the combined dataset and then used to predict default probabilities for the full sample. We implement $\widehat{f^{\text{pooled}}}$ using LightGBM, the best-performing machine-learning algorithm identified in the group-specific training stage. This pooled measure $\widehat{p_i^{\text{pooled}}}$ serves as our baseline estimate of borrower risk, independent of the originating lender.

4.3. Pricing Alignment Analysis

To test whether lenders set interest rates in proportion to exogenous risk, we compare the actual loan interest rate r_i to the pooled default probability $\widehat{p_i^{\text{pooled}}}$. We employ two complementary approaches:

1. We sort loans into deciles by $\widehat{p_i^{\text{pooled}}}$. Within each decile $d \in \{1, \ldots, 10\}$, calculate the average predicted default probability $\overline{p_d}$ and the average interest rate $\overline{r_d}$. Plotting $\overline{r_d}$ against $\overline{p_d}$ for banks, non-fintech non-banks and fintechs reveals how steeply rates rise as risk increases; a steeper, more linear curve indicates tighter risk-based pricing, whereas a flatter curve signals weaker sensitivity.

2. We estimate a lender-group-specific linear regression of the form

$$r_i = \alpha + \beta\, \widehat{p_i^{\text{pooled}}} + \varepsilon_i.$$

The slope β captures the marginal change in the interest rate associated with a one-unit increase in predicted default probability. A larger β reflects stronger risk-based pricing. Comparing β across groups therefore shows which lenders adjust rates most sharply in response to borrower risk.

4.4. Mispricing Residual Analysis

Even if average rates rise with default probability, individual loans may be over- or underpriced relative to a benchmark pricing curve. To quantify this, we first estimate

$$\widehat{p_i^{\text{pooled}}} = \widehat{f^{\text{pooled}}}(x_i),$$

using all loans in a pooled regression (across all lenders). We define the fitted rate for loan i as

$$\widehat{r_i} = \gamma_0 + \gamma_1\, \widehat{p_i^{\text{pooled}}},$$

and then compute the residual (mispricing) for each loan

$$\epsilon_i = r_i - \widehat{r_i}.$$

A negative ϵ_i means that the loan is underpriced (the lender charged a lower rate than the risk-based benchmark), while a positive ϵ_i implies that the loan is overpriced. Aggregating these residuals by lender group reveals whether fintechs, banks or non-fintech lenders systematically deviate from risk-based prices.

5. Results

5.1. Screening Accuracy

Figure 1 and Table 2 report the out-of-sample AUCs of five machine-learning classifiers—logistic regression (logit), random forest (RF), LightGBM (LGBM), XGBoost (XGB) and gradient-boosting classifier (GBC)—estimated separately for banks, non-fintech non-banks and fintech lenders.

Table 2. Out-of-Sample AUC Scores by Model and Lender Group. This table reports the out-of-sample area under the curve (AUC) scores for five machine-learning models—logistic regression (logit), random forest (RF), LightGBM (LGBM), XGBoost (XGB) and gradient-boosting classifier (GBC)—trained to predict 36-month mortgage default probabilities. Models were estimated separately for bank, non-fintech and fintech lenders using conforming loan data originated between 2012 and 2020.

Model	Bank AUC	Non-Fintech AUC	Fintech AUC
Logit	0.8548	0.8565	0.8467
RF	0.8530	0.8568	0.8462
LGBM	0.8571	0.8600	0.8522
XGB	0.8567	0.8599	0.8532
GBC	0.8561	0.8600	0.8517

Across all lender types, LightGBM consistently posts the highest—or statistically indistinguishable second-highest—AUC, confirming its superior ability to separate defaulters from non-defaulters. Averaging over the five models, non-fintech lenders attain the best overall predictive accuracy (mean AUC $\approx$ 0.860), banks follow closely ($\approx$0.857), and fintechs lag (≈0.852). Performance within non-fintech and fintech groups is remarkably stable across the three gradient-boosting methods (LGBM, XGB, GBC), whereas logistic regression and random forest score a few hundredths lower. Banks show the greatest spread, with a distinct dip for random forest and a recovery under boosting algorithms.

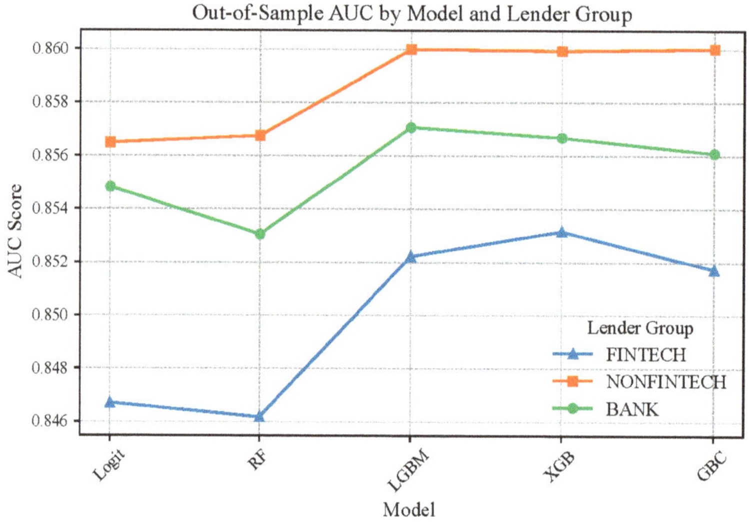

Figure 1. Out-of-Sample AUC by Model and Lender Group. This figure compares the predictive performance of five machine-learning classifiers—logistic regression (logit), random forest (RF), LightGBM (LGBM), XGBoost (XGB) and gradient-boosting classifier (GBC)—across three lender groups: banks, non-fintech non-banks and fintech lenders. The AUC scores reflect each model's out-of-sample ability to distinguish between default and non-default mortgage loans originated from 2012 to 2020.

Taken together, the evidence highlights tree-based boosting—especially LightGBM—as the most reliable modeling choice for high-dimensional mortgage credit data across all lender categories.

5.2. Pricing Alignment

Next, we examine whether interest rates align with the pooled model's default probability $\widehat{p_i^{\text{pooled}}}$. A linear regression of interest rate on $\widehat{p_i^{\text{pooled}}}$ yields

Figure 2 plots the average origination rates against decile-level predicted default probabilities $\widehat{p_i^{\text{pooled}}}$. This figure plots the average interest rate against the average predicted default probability across deciles of estimated risk, separately for banks, non-fintech non-banks and fintech lenders. Each point represents the mean interest rate and mean predicted risk within a decile. The upward-sloping curves reflect positive pricing alignment—higher-risk borrowers are charged higher rates. However, the steepness and level of each curve differ across lender types. Banks exhibit the highest average rates and the steepest pricing gradient, suggesting stronger risk-based pricing. In contrast, non-fintech and fintech lenders show flatter slopes, indicating weaker sensitivity of pricing to estimated borrower risk. The results show that banks consistently charge the highest interest rates across all deciles, followed by fintech and then non-fintech lenders.

Table 3 presents the results from lender-type-specific OLS regressions of interest rates on the predicted default probability ($\widehat{\text{PD}}$). All coefficients on ($\widehat{\text{PD}}$) are statistically significant at the 1% level, confirming that lenders positively adjust pricing in response to borrower risk. Among the three groups, banks exhibit the steepest pricing sensitivity, with a coefficient of 7.19, indicating a strong alignment between risk and rate. Non-fintech lenders also show meaningful alignment (5.43), while fintechs apply the shallowest pricing slope (4.18). These results suggest that banks price risk more aggressively, whereas fintech lenders exhibit relatively weaker sensitivity to borrower default risk, despite operating with modern algorithms. Notably, the R-squared values remain low across all regressions (4–5%), consistent with the fact that much of the interest rate variation is driven by factors beyond the modeled credit risk, including competition, borrower characteristics not captured in ($\widehat{PD}$) and loan features.

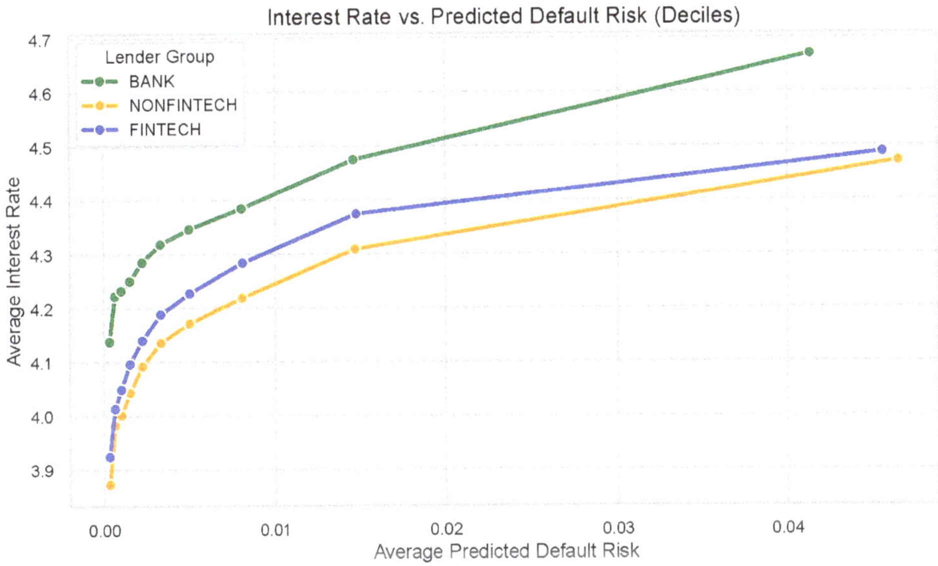

Figure 2. Interest Rate vs. Predicted Default Risk by Lender Group. This figure plots the average mortgage interest rate against the average predicted default risk across deciles of risk scores for three lender groups: banks (green), non-fintech non-banks (orange) and fintech lenders (blue). The curve indicates the extent to which each lender group aligns pricing with borrower risk. Banks show a steeper increase in rates as risk rises, while fintech and non-fintech lenders exhibit flatter curves, suggesting less responsive pricing to predicted risk levels.

Table 3. OLS Regression of Interest Rate on Predicted Default Probability. This table presents results from ordinary least squares (OLS) regressions of mortgage interest rates on predicted default probabilities ($\widehat{PD}$), estimated separately for each lender group. The intercept represents the baseline interest rate when the predicted default is zero, and the coefficient captures the marginal effect of default probability on pricing (i.e., the risk-based pricing gradient). R-squared indicates the model's explanatory power. The Akaike information criterion (AIC) reflects model fit, with lower values indicating better fit.

Lender Type	Intercept (const)	Coefficient on $\widehat{PD}$	R-Squared	AIC	Observations
Bank	4.2735	7.1977	0.041	7,190,000	4,649,821
Non-Fintech	4.0885	5.4337	0.053	1,488,000	1,150,726
Fintech	4.1711	4.1804	0.046	558,100	485,519

5.3. Mispricing Summary

Using the fitted pricing curve as a benchmark, we compute the mean residuals and the share of loans classified as under- or overpriced.

Table 4 reports summary statistics on interest rate mispricing, calculated as the difference between the actual interest rate and the fair rate predicted by the pooled PD-based pricing model. Banks exhibit a small positive average mispricing of +4.6 basis points, indicating a slight tendency to overcharge relative to risk. In contrast, both fintech and non-fintech lenders show negative average mispricing (−8.2 and −15.1 basis points, respectively), suggesting systematic underpricing of riskier borrowers. The share of underpriced loans is highest among fintech lenders (32.02%), followed closely by non-fintechs (29.99%), while their shares of overpriced loans remain relatively low (13.5% and 15.37%, respectively). These results imply that banks adhere more closely to risk-based pricing, while alternative lenders—especially non-fintechs—tend to offer below-benchmark rates to higher-risk borrowers, potentially reflecting either competitive strategies or less precise risk-pricing mechanisms.

Table 4. Mispricing Statistics by Lender Group. This table reports summary statistics of interest rate mispricing relative to a pooled benchmark model across three lender groups: banks, fintech lenders and non-fintech non-bank lenders. Mean mispricing reflects the average difference between the observed rate and the benchmark-implied rate (positive values indicate overpricing; negative values indicate underpricing). The percentage of underpriced and overpriced loans is calculated based on the tails of the mispricing distribution (e.g., below the 5th and above the 95th percentile).

Lender Group	Mean Mispricing	Std. Dev.	% Underpriced	% Overpriced
Bank	0.0466	0.5245	21.60%	25.87%
Fintech	−0.0851	0.4319	32.02%	13.50%
Non-Fintech	−0.1524	0.462	29.99%	15.37%

6. Discussion

Three forces jointly explain fintech lenders' muted alignment of price and risk in conforming mortgages. First, regulatory constraints limit informational flexibility. Specifically, every conforming mortgage loan must clear the standardized underwriting systems—Fannie Mae's Desktop Underwriter (DU) or Freddie Mac's Loan Product Advisor (LPA). These automated platforms employ strict and uniform "scorecards" that evaluate borrower risk based on predetermined criteria, such as credit scores, loan-to-value ratios and debt-to-income ratios. Critically, these scorecards do not accept proprietary fintech data or alternative risk indicators—such as real-time cash flow, rental payments or utility bill histories—that have significantly enhanced predictive accuracy in unsecured lending markets. Consequently, even the most advanced fintech algorithms can achieve only incremental improvements within this rigid framework, restricting the ability to differentiate borrower risks more effectively.

Second, incentive misalignment compounds this regulatory rigidity. Fintech and other non-bank lenders primarily use warehouse funding, originating loans intended for rapid sale into securitization pools backed by government-sponsored enterprise (GSE) guarantees. This originate-to-distribute model shifts the long-term credit risk to MBS investors, significantly weakening incentives for precise risk-based pricing. The immediate rewards from slightly lower rates and higher origination volume thus outweigh the long-term, dispersed default costs, making systematic underpricing rational from a business growth perspective.

Third, competitive positioning further shapes these pricing dynamics. Fintech lenders differentiate themselves through speed, streamlined user experiences and digital convenience, whereas traditional banks leverage brand recognition, customer trust, cross-selling opportunities and rigorous regulatory oversight. Banks also frequently retain loan servicing rights and face capital requirements that strongly incentivize accurate upfront risk pricing.

This strategic and regulatory alignment explains why banks consistently display steeper rate-risk slopes compared to fintech lenders.

These dynamics underscore the structural limitations in algorithmic credit scoring when underwriting decisions are decoupled from long-term financial accountability. However, targeted policy reforms could significantly enhance fintech lenders' alignment between pricing and borrower risk. First, modernizing GSE underwriting scorecards to allow carefully verified alternative data—such as rental payments, utility histories or verified real-time financial transaction data—could meaningfully expand the informational scope, enabling more nuanced borrower risk differentiation. Second, introducing modest risk-retention requirements, where lenders must retain a small percentage (e.g., 5%) of each originated loan's risk, would align lenders' incentives with long-term loan performance without compromising the liquidity benefits provided by agency mortgage-backed securities. Such requirements echo existing regulatory frameworks like the Dodd–Frank Act's risk-retention rules and could substantially strengthen pricing discipline.

The findings also suggest several promising directions for future research. One avenue is examining whether fintech lenders demonstrate superior performance in private-label or non-conforming mortgage segments, where underwriting standards are more flexible, and lenders retain greater exposure to loan outcomes. Another research direction involves evaluating the broader welfare implications: specifically, does fintech-driven underpricing sustainably enhance homeownership access, or does it merely shift default risks onto government-supported entities and, ultimately, taxpayers? Finally, analyzing operational efficiencies in post-origination loan servicing may reveal whether fintech lenders provide measurable value that offsets weaker initial pricing accuracy. By explicitly separating default prediction from risk-based pricing, our analytical framework provides a useful template for exploring these critical questions in other regulated credit markets.

7. Conclusions

This study provides robust, causal evidence that fintech mortgage lenders lag behind traditional banks in both screening accuracy and risk-based pricing, even when all parties operate under the same GSE-mandated information regime. Using five state-of-the-art machine-learning models that are rigorously tuned via cross-validation and evaluated out-of-sample, we document a systematic performance gap (best-model AUC: 0.852 for fintechs vs. 0.857 for banks). A two-stage framework that cleanly separates default prediction from pricing further reveals that banks adjust rates by 7.2 basis points for every percentage-point increase in predicted default probability, whereas fintechs adjust them by just 4.2 bp. These patterns persist across more than six million conforming loans originated between 2012 and 2020, underscoring the scientific soundness and external validity of our results.

The findings carry broad international relevance. Many mortgage markets—from Canada to the U.K. and Australia—share two key features of the U.S. conforming segment: (i) highly standardized, regulator-approved underwriting algorithms and (ii) rapid securitization that shifts future credit losses off lenders' balance sheets. In such environments, data ceilings and weak ex-post incentives can blunt the very technologies that drive fintech's success in unsecured credit. Policymakers worldwide can therefore draw two actionable lessons. First, cautiously expanding the set of verifiable alternative data (e.g., rental payment histories, transaction-level cash-flow data) that government or quasi-government underwriting systems accept would raise the ceiling on predictive accuracy for all lenders. Second, modest risk-retention rules—mirroring the 5% "skin-in-the-game" standard in other securitized asset classes—would strengthen price discipline without unduly inhibiting secondary-market liquidity. Together, these reforms could unlock fintech's analytic potential while safeguarding systemic stability, rendering our results pertinent well beyond the U.S. context.

Author Contributions: Conceptualization, H.L.; methodology, Z.L.; software, Z.L.; validation, H.L.; formal analysis, Z.L.; investigation, Z.L.; resources, Z.L. and H.L.; data curation, Z.L.; writing—original draft preparation, Z.L.; writing—review and editing, H.L.; visualization, Z.L.; supervision, Z.L.; project administration, H.L. All authors have read and agreed to the published version of the manuscript.

Funding: This research received no external funding.

Institutional Review Board Statement: Not applicable.

Informed Consent Statement: Not applicable.

Data Availability Statement: The data used in this study are publicly available from the Fannie Mae and Freddie Mac Single-Family Loan Performance datasets for the years 2012 to 2020. These datasets can be accessed at: https://capitalmarkets.fanniemae.com/credit-risk-transfer/single-family-credit-risk-transfer/fannie-mae-single-family-loan-performance-data and http://www.freddiemac.com/research/datasets/sf_loanlevel_dataset.page, respectively (accessed on 16 June 2022).

Conflicts of Interest: The authors report no conflicts of interest. The authors alone are responsible for the content and writing of the paper.

Appendix A. Variable Definition

Variable	Definition
Borrower and Loan Characteristics	
Origination Rate	The original interest rate on a mortgage loan as identified in the original mortgage note
Origination Balance ($ Thousand)	The dollar amount of the loan as stated on the note at the time the loan was originated
Original Loan-to-Value Ratio (OLTV)	Loan amount divided by the value of property at origination
Original Combined LTV (OCLTV)	The amount of all known outstanding loans (including home equity) at origination divided by the value of property
Debt-to-Income Ratio	Loan amount divided by borrower income at origination
FICO Score	Borrower's FICO score at origination
Refinance	Indicator variables for whether the loan is a home refinancing or not
Cash-Out Refinance	Indicator variables for whether the loan is a cash-out refinance or not
Non-Cash-Out Refinance	Indicator variables for whether the loan is a non-cash-out (rate) refinance or not
Purchase	Indicator variables for whether the loan is a home purchase or not
First-Time Home Buyer	An indicator that denotes whether the borrower or co-borrower qualifies as a first-time homebuyer
Number of Borrowers	The number of individuals obligated to repay the mortgage loan
Has Mortgage Insurance	Indicator variables for whether the loan has mortgage insurance or not
Mortgage Insurance Unknown	Indicator variables for whether the loan's mortgage insurance status is unknown
Primary Residence	An indicator that denotes whether the property occupancy status is for primary residence or not

Variable	Definition
Investment or Second Property	An indicator that denotes whether the property occupancy status is for secondary home/investment purpose or not
Correspondent Channel	Indicator variables for whether the loan is originated through the correspondent channel or not
Retail Channel	Indicator variables for whether the loan is originated through the retail channel or not
Broker Channel	Indicator variables for whether the loan is originated through the broker channel or not
MSA Macroeconomic Indicators	
MSA Unemployment Rate	Unemployment rate by metropolitan statistical area, seasonally adjusted; obtained from the U.S. Bureau of Labor Statistics
MSA Real Personal Income	Real per-capita personal income (chained 2012 dollars) by metropolitan statistical area; obtained from the Bureau of Economic Analysis
Loan Performance	
30 (60/90) DPD in 12 (24/36) Months	Indicator variables for whether the loan is 30 (60/90) days past due within 12 (24/36) months after origination
Prepaid in 12 (24/36) Months	Indicator variables for whether the loan is prepaid within 12 (24/36) months after origination

Appendix B. Detailed Machine-Learning Models for Credit Risk Modeling

1. Logistic Regression (LR)

Objective Function: The goal of logistic regression is to find the best fitting model to describe the relationship between the dichotomous characteristic of interest (dependent variable) and a set of independent (predictor or explanatory) variables. Logistic regression does this by estimating probabilities using a logistic function, which is a cumulative logistic distribution.

$$L(\beta) = -\frac{1}{N}\sum_{i=1}^{N}[y_i \log(p_i) + (1 - y_i)\log(1 - p_i)]$$

Here, $L(\beta)$ is the logistic loss function; N is the number of observations; y_i is the actual outcome; and p_i is the predicted probability of the outcome being 1 for the ith observation. The β coefficients are estimated during the training process.

Hyperparameters:

- Regularization type (L1, L2, ElasticNet): Determines the type of regularization applied to the model to prevent overfitting by penalizing large coefficients.
- Regularization strength: Controls the magnitude of the regularization term. A larger value specifies stronger regularization.
- Solver: The algorithm used for optimization (e.g., liblinear, sag, saga, newton-cg). Different solvers are suitable for different types of data and different regularization methods.

2. Random Forest (RF)

Objective Function: Random forest aims to reduce overfitting in decision trees by averaging multiple decision trees' predictions, trained on different parts of the same training set, with the goal of improving the overall accuracy. A random forest algorithm does not have a single formula due to its ensemble nature, but it operates by building multiple decision trees and merging their predictions. The decision of the majority of trees is chosen by the random forest as the final prediction.

Hyperparameters:

- Number of trees: The number of trees in the forest. More trees increase prediction stability but also computational complexity.
- Max depth: The maximum depth of the trees.
- Min samples split: The minimum number of samples required to split an internal node.
- Min samples leaf: The minimum number of samples required to be at a leaf node.

3. Gradient-Boosting Machine (GBM)

Objective Function: GBM aims to minimize the loss function by sequentially adding weak learners using a gradient descent algorithm. Each new model incrementally decreases the loss function (e.g., mean squared error for regression tasks) of the entire system.

$$F_m(x) = F_{m-1}(x) + \rho_m h_m(x)$$

Here, $F_m(x)$ is the boosted model's prediction at iteration m; $F_{m-1}(x)$ is the prediction from the previous iteration; $h_m(x)$ is the weak learner added at iteration m; and ρ_m is the learning rate.

Hyperparameters:

- Learning rate: Determines how corrections are performed in the model with each added tree.
- Number of learners: The total number of trees to be built.
- Max depth of trees: The depth limit for each tree, controlling overfitting.

4. LightGBM

Objective Function: Similar to GBM, LightGBM also focuses on minimizing the loss function but does so more efficiently for large datasets by using gradient-based one-side sampling and exclusive feature bundling.

Hyperparameters:

- Number of leaves: The maximum number of leaves in one tree.
- Learning rate: Speed of model learning.
- Min data in leaf: The minimum number of records a leaf may have.
- Feature fraction: The fraction of features to be used for each tree, preventing overfitting.

5. XGBoost

Objective Function: XGBoost aims to minimize the regularized loss function that includes both a loss term and a regularization term, which helps in controlling overfitting more effectively than traditional GBM.

$$F_m(x) = F_{m-1}(x) + \rho_m h_m(x) + \lambda \Omega(h_m)$$

In this formula, $\Omega(h_m)$ represents the regularization term applied to the model h_m, adding a penalty for complexity to improve model generalization.

Hyperparameters:

- Learning rate (eta): Determines the step size at each iteration to prevent overfitting.
- Max depth: Maximum depth of a tree; increasing this value will make the model more complex and more likely to overfit.
- Subsample: The fraction of samples to be used for fitting the individual base learners.
- Colsample_bytree: The fraction of features to be used for each tree.

Appendix C. Tuned Hyperparameters by Model and Lender Group

Notes: All models use n_estimators = 100. The learning rate (lr) and maximum tree depth (depth) were tuned from grids: lr ∈ {0.05, 0.1}, depth ∈ {3, 6}. Logit models were tuned over C ∈ {0.01, 0.1, 1, 10}. Random forests were tuned over max_depth ∈ {3, 6, 10}.

Lender Group	Logit (C)	RF (max_depth)	LGBM (lr/depth)	XGB (lr/depth)	GBC (lr/depth)
Bank	0.1	10	0.1/3	0.1/3	0.1/3
Non-Fintech	0.1	10	0.05/3	0.1/3	0.05/3
Fintech	0.1	10	0.05/3	0.1/3	0.1/3

References

1. Bartlett, R.; Morse, A.; Stanton, R.; Wallace, N. Consumer-lending discrimination in the FinTech Era. *J. Financ. Econ.* **2022**, *143*, 30–56. [CrossRef]
2. Fuster, A.; Goldsmith-Pinkham, P.; Ramadorai, T.; Walther, A. Predictably Unequal? The Effects of Machine Learning on Credit Markets. *J. Financ.* **2022**, *77*, 5–47. [CrossRef]
3. Berger, D.W.; Milbradt, K.; Tourre, F.; Vavra, J.S. Refinancing Frictions, Mortgage Pricing and Redistribution (No. w32022). National Bureau of Economic Research. 2024. Available online: https://www.nber.org/papers/w32022 (accessed on 18 January 2025).
4. Di Maggio, M.; Yao, V. Fintech Borrowers: Lax Screening or Cream-Skimming? *Rev. Financ. Stud.* **2021**, *34*, 4565–4618. [CrossRef]
5. Jagtiani, J.; Lemieux, C. The roles of alternative data and machine learning in fintech lending. *Financ. Manag.* **2019**, *48*, 1009–1029. [CrossRef]
6. Berg, T.; Burg, V.; Gombović, A.; Puri, M. On the Rise of FinTechs: Credit Scoring Using Digital Footprints. *Rev. Financ. Stud.* **2020**, *33*, 2845–2897. [CrossRef]
7. Frame, W.S.; Fuster, A.; Tracy, J.; Vickery, J. The Rescue of Fannie Mae and Freddie Mac. *J. Econ. Perspect.* **2015**, *29*, 25–52. [CrossRef]
8. Fuster, A.; Plosser, M.; Schnabl, P.; Vickery, J. The Role of Technology in Mortgage Lending. *Rev. Financ. Stud.* **2019**, *32*, 1854–1899. [CrossRef]
9. Acharya, V.; Richardson, M.; Van Nieuwerburgh, S.; White, L. *Guaranteed to Fail: Fannie Mae, Freddie Mac, and the Debacle of Mortgage Finance*; Princeton University Press: Princeton, NJ, USA, 2013.
10. Keys, B.J.; Mukherjee, T.; Seru, A.; Vig, V. Did Securitization Lead to Lax Screening? Evidence from Subprime Loans. *Q. J. Econ.* **2010**, *125*, 307–362. [CrossRef]
11. Chen, S.; Doerr, S.; Frost, J.; Gambacorta, L.; Shin, H. The fintech gender gap. *J. Financ. Intermediation* **2023**, *54*, 101026. [CrossRef]
12. Cowgill, B.; Dell'Acqua, F.; Deng, S.; Hsu, D.; Verma, N.; Chaintreau, A. Biased Programmers? Or Biased Data? A Field Experiment in Operationalizing AI Ethics. In Proceedings of the 21st ACM Conference on Economics and Computation, Virtual, 13–17 July 2020; pp. 679–681.
13. Frost, J.; Gambacorta, L.; Huang, Y.; Shin, H.S.; Zbinden, P. BigTech and the changing structure of financial intermediation. *Econ. Policy* **2019**, *34*, 761–799. [CrossRef]
14. Liu, L.; Lu, G.; Xiong, W. The Big Tech Lending Model (No. 30160). National Bureau of Economic Research. 2022. Available online: https://ssrn.com/abstract=4140878 (accessed on 8 March 2025).
15. Agarwal, S.; Chomsisengphet, S.; Mahoney, N.; Stroebel, J. Do banks pass through credit expansions? The marginal profitability of consumer lending during the Great Recession. *J. Financ.* **2018**, *75*, 1597–1642.
16. Balyuk, T.; Davydenko, S. Reintermediation in FinTech: Evidence from Online Lending. *J. Financ. Quant. Anal.* **2024**, *59*, 1997–2037. [CrossRef]
17. Tang, H. Peer-to-peer lenders versus banks: Substitutes or complements? *Rev. Financ. Stud.* **2019**, *32*, 1900–1938. Available online: https://academic.oup.com/rfs/article/32/5/1900/5427773 (accessed on 18 January 2025). [CrossRef]
18. Sadhwani, A.; Giesecke, K.; Sirignano, J. Deep Learning for Mortgage Risk. *J. Financ. Econ.* **2020**, *19*, 313–368. [CrossRef]
19. Kozodoi, N.; Jacob, J.; Lessmann, S. Fairness in credit scoring: Assessment, implementation and profit implications. *Eur. J. Oper. Res.* **2022**, *297*, 1083–1094. [CrossRef]
20. Buchak, G.; Matvos, G.; Piskorski, T.; Seru, A. Fintech, regulatory arbitrage, and the rise of shadow banks. *J. Financ. Econ.* **2018**, *130*, 453–483. [CrossRef]

21. Piskorski, T.; Seru, A.; Vig, V. Securitization and distressed loan renegotiation: Evidence from the subprime mortgage crisis. *J. Financ. Econ.* **2010**, *97*, 369–397. [CrossRef]
22. Khandani, A.E.; Kim, A.J.; Lo, A.W. Consumer credit-risk models via machine-learning algorithms. *J. Bank. Financ.* **2010**, *34*, 2767–2787. [CrossRef]
23. Lin, M.; Prabhala, N.R.; Viswanathan, S. Judging Borrowers by the Company They Keep: Friendship Networks and Information Asymmetry in Online Peer-to-Peer Lending. *Manag. Sci.* **2013**, *59*, 17–35. [CrossRef]
24. Liu, Z.; Liang, H. Machine learning prediction of loss given default in government-sponsored enterprise residential mortgages. *J. Risk Model Valid.* **2024**, *18*, 1–23. [CrossRef]
25. Liu, Z.; Liang, H. Racial Disparities in Conforming Mortgage Lending: A Comparative Study of Fintech and Traditional Lenders Under Regulatory Oversight. *FinTech* **2025**, *4*, 8. [CrossRef]

FinTech

MDPI

Article

An Assessment of Lithuania's Financial Technology Development

Laima Okunevičiūtė Neverauskienė [1,2,*], Irena Danilevičienė [3] and Gileta Labašauskienė [3]

1 Department of Economics Engineering, Faculty of Business Management, Vilnius Gediminas Technical University, 10223 Vilnius, Lithuania
2 Lithuanian Centre for Social Sciences, 01108 Vilnius, Lithuania
3 Department of Financial Engineering, Faculty of Business Management, Vilnius Gediminas Technical University, 10223 Vilnius, Lithuania; irena.daniléviciene@vilniustech.lt (I.D.); giletalabasauskiene@gmail.com (G.L.)
* Correspondence: laima.okuneviciute.neverauskiene@vilniustech.lt

Abstract: The Lithuanian financial technology (referred to as FinTech) sector is one of the fastest-growing financial technology centers in Europe; however, this sector faces economic, regulatory, and technological challenges that hinder its development. This article aims to assess the state of development of Lithuania's FinTech sector, identify the main challenges, and provide recommendations to promote the development of the sector. This study uses quantitative indicators, inter-criteria correlation, multi-criteria evaluation methods, and SWOT analysis. This article's results will help identify the key factors that influence the growth of the FinTech sector in Lithuania and will be useful in shaping the sector's further development strategy. The results of this study revealed that factors such as favorable regulation influence the FinTech sector in Lithuania the most, strengthening the innovation ecosystem and attracting international investments. However, the sector still faces challenges such as a lack of skilled labor, ensuring cybersecurity, and constant regulatory adaptation to new technologies. Based on the results of this study, it is recommended to pay more attention to educational programs aimed at training technology specialists, to promote cooperation between the public and private sectors, and to further improve the regulatory environment to ensure the sustainable and safe development of FinTech.

Keywords: development; economic factors; fintech; fintech sector; guidelines; regulation; technological innovations

JEL Classification: G20; G23; O16; O33

1. Introduction

The digital revolution has driven technological advances over the past few decades that have fundamentally transformed financial markets and services [1,2]. The result of these changes is a significant change in traditional financial processes, such as mobile payments, money transfers, borrowing, raising financing, and asset and investment management [3]. These changes lead to the rapid development of financial technology and significant changes in traditional financial systems, making financial transactions more efficient, easier, and cheaper. FinTech companies, taking advantage of these innovations, offer consumers more convenient and technology-based financial services. Globally, the FinTech sector is expanding rapidly, becoming an essential element of the financial system, and opening new opportunities for both businesses and consumers [4]. A financial services revolution is underway [5], and innovations such as artificial intelligence, blockchain technologies, and open banking continue to transform the sector, providing the opportunity to manage data more efficiently, ensuring greater security, and creating new financial service models. However, in a rapidly changing world of technology, any innovation can unexpectedly change market dynamics and influence the future of the sector. Nevertheless, the development of the FinTech sector in Lithuania is limited by certain economic, regulatory, and technological factors that prevent the country from maintaining its competitiveness in the international market [6]. Therefore, Lithuania needs to adapt to these rapidly changing circumstances and ensure that the FinTech sector can continue to grow and exploit the opportunities provided by innovation. This article fills the knowledge gap about FinTech development in Lithuania. A few companies are presented that implement the principles of FinTech, but it is also important to present the main challenges that the FinTech sector in Lithuania faces.

This article examines the following question: what are the main challenges that the FinTech sector in Lithuania faces, and how can they be overcome to promote the development of the sector?

The subject of this article is Lithuania's financial technology sector.

This article aims to assess the development of the Lithuanian FinTech sector and identify the main challenges and opportunities to implement national development guidelines.

The following are tasks for achieving this goal:

- Analyze theoretical models of financial technology development to understand their impact on the country's economy and the development of the financial sector.
- Develop a research methodology that would allow for a systematic assessment of the factors of the development of the FinTech sector in Lithuania, based on quantitative indicators.
- Conduct an empirical study in order to identify the main factors that promote or limit the development of the FinTech sector in Lithuania and assess their impact on the growth of this sector.

The methods used in this article to answer the above question include an analysis of the scientific literature and theoretical statements, the collection of secondary material, and information processing. Comparative data analysis, inter-criteria correlation (CRITIC method), the multi-criteria complex proportional assessment (COPRAS) method, and SWOT analysis are performed, and a priority order of sectors is formed.

2. The Concept and Main Factors of Financial Technologies

The digital transformation highlighted by the Fourth Industrial Revolution has led to the emergence of sophisticated technology-based financial services, known as FinTech, which has rapidly transformed the traditional financial services space. The Fourth Industrial Revolution has created an emerging environment in which more disruptive and digitally transformative technologies such as the Internet of Things, augmented reality, and artificial intelligence are changing the way we live [7,8]. This revolution has also permeated the financial industry, leading to the emergence of FinTech, which is mainly characterized by the emergence of technological innovations that help develop new profitable business ideas related to financial services [9,10]. FinTech can be interpreted as the application of information technology in the fields of finance, financial innovation, and digital innovation. Essentially, FinTech is an abbreviation for financial technology, which has emerged because of the application of innovative technologies. The global adoption of FinTech is growing rapidly due to its nature, as FinTech principles are mostly applied by those who want to change the essence of traditional financial services and promote the emergence of a digital revolution. FinTech is one of the most important innovations in the financial services industry, driven by the sharing economy, regulation, policy, and information technology [11,12].

The development of FinTech benefits from general advances in many areas, such as blockchain, big data, machine learning, artificial intelligence, and the digital economy [13], which have particularly influenced the overall economic growth of many countries. A new generation of investment banking and retail companies has perfectly combined the power of the Internet and convenient smartphones [14]. Banking applications have allowed customers to perform digital technological transactions and weakened bank protocols, making banks easier to access online than using traditional methods [15]. The higher the level of the development of financial technology services, the greater the challenges for businesses.

The FinTech business model also focuses on payment and lending services. In addition, it includes personal financial advisory services, crowdfunding, virtual currencies, and security (e.g., cybersecurity) [11]. Online lending services have caused controversy in communities, including moral hazard, loan default, and information asymmetry. As a result, regulators are encouraging innovation in the financial sector and applying consumer protection and risk management principles to ensure that every consumer receives safe and appropriate financial services.

The development of FinTech has not replaced traditional finance but has solved many complex problems that have prevented the poor from accessing financial products. The synergy of FinTech power and traditional financing methods has improved cash flow management, and this has been especially evident during the COVID-19 pandemic [16]. The author of [17] investigated the importance of FinTech advancements in helping people to recover faster from the economic shocks caused by the COVID-19 pandemic, so over the past few years, FinTech innovations have enabled financial stability and social responsibility in a pandemic-stricken world.

FinTech companies are growing rapidly around the world because their innovative services are simple and creatively use new digital technologies. This poses a significant threat to incumbents because their traditional way of providing financial services is complex and subject to strict rules set by regulatory boards. Thus, existing operators need to think about strategic alliances that could be collaborative or competitive, depending on their business objectives. Given that FinTech has found the right balance between innovation and efficiency and risk management [18,19], in most countries, authorities and central banks, especially in the last three years, have started to implement FinTech technologies in the provision of financial services. It follows that FinTech innovations have led to positive financial intermediation and economic productivity.

In summary, it can be stated that the development of FinTech has a positive effect on economic productivity and encourages improvement in the process of providing financial services and the quality of the provision of financial services themselves to make them accessible to every consumer and make traditional financial services even more qualitative. It is necessary to promote closer cooperation between traditional banks and FinTech companies for banks to become more innovative and, by applying innovative technologies, gain more loyal customers who can enjoy the fast and reliable financial services they receive.

2.1. The FinTech Ecosystem and the Situation of This Sector in Lithuania

The rapid development of FinTech has led to the emergence of new business models and products that could challenge traditional financial institutions and have an impact on financial stability [20]. The development of FinTech has led to the emergence of new business models, the application of new technologies, and the introduction of innovative products and services to the market, which has a significant impact on the financial market and the efficiency of financial service delivery. There are six FinTech business models, including insurance services, crowdfunding, payments, lending, asset management, and capital markets [11], but the impact of FinTech is particularly visible in the case of banking services [21]. Such development and application of innovative technologies in the financial sector have advantages: improving the efficiency of financial activities; reducing operating costs; facilitating strategic intermediation, which brings novelty to entrepreneurship; and democratizing access to financial services [12,22–24].

The area of financial technologies emerged from the merger of two sectors (Figure 1): the provision of financial services and the implementation of innovative technologies.

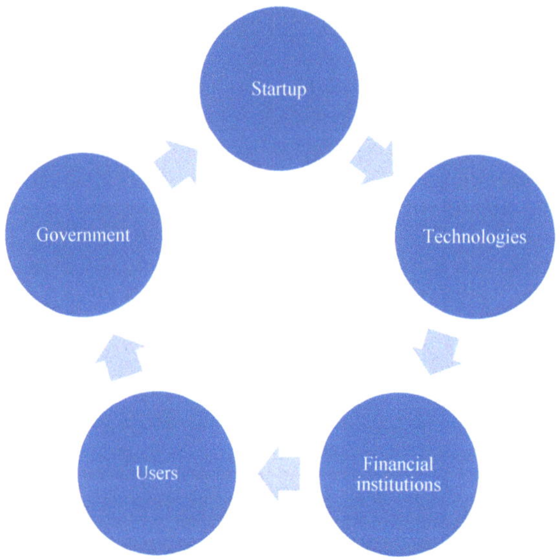

Figure 1. The ecosystem of FinTech (compiled by the authors based on [25]).

Figure 1 depicts the FinTech ecosystem in Lithuania, which includes innovative technologies, companies, startups, and state institutions that regulate and supervise this sector. The main strengths of the Lithuanian FinTech sector are effective regulation, technological infrastructure, and a favorable business environment. However, the growth of this sector is limited by increasing competition in international markets, the slowness of regulatory changes, and the speed of the adoption of technological innovations (Figure 2).

Figure 2. Classification of FinTech sectors (compiled by authors based on classification of licenses issued by [26]).

FinTech in Lithuania is made up of various segments (see Figure 2), including electronic money institutions (EMIs), payment service providers (PSPs), peer-to-peer lending platforms (PPPs), crowdfunding platforms (CFPs), investment and asset management companies (WealthTech), and digital banking. These segments ensure the creation and development of innovative financial services, but economic and regulatory factors influence this.

Economic and regulatory factors are key components of FinTech development. It is important to note that the Lithuanian FinTech sector, although growing rapidly, has not yet reached its full potential due to the challenges of the regulatory framework, which is often changing, causing uncertainty for both new and existing companies.

Several important factors determine the development of the FinTech sector in Lithuania:

- Economic factors: Growing consumer demand for fast and efficient financial services is driving the development of the FinTech sector. Consumers are increasingly choosing digital services due to their convenience, accessibility, and price advantages.
- Regulatory factors: The Bank of Lithuania and other regulatory authorities actively support the FinTech sector by issuing licenses and permits to new companies. The regulatory environment in Lithuania is favorable, as it allows innovation to flourish, but at the same time imposes requirements that ensure the security of the financial system and the protection of consumer rights.
- Technological factors: Technological advances, such as blockchain, artificial intelligence (AI), and data analytics, provide FinTech organizations with opportunities to create new products and services, optimize processes, and improve user experience. The implementation of technologies allows for cost reduction and increased service efficiency.

Consumer behavior in Lithuania is changing, increasingly leaning towards digital services, which is driving the growth of the FinTech sector. Consumers value speed, convenience, and competitiveness, so FinTech companies must constantly improve their offerings. Competition between FinTech companies and traditional financial institutions is also increasing, so the latter are forced to adapt to new consumer needs and introduce innovations in order to remain competitive. When assessing the entire FinTech sector, it is important to analyze how it is changing and whether this is not a short-term startup breakthrough that will soon end. This can be best demonstrated by consumer interest in the sector [27] and the groups it covers.

2.2. FinTech Development Guidelines: 2023–2028

The Lithuanian Government actively promotes the development of FinTech, recognizing its potential to create new jobs, attract foreign investment, and contribute to economic growth. Therefore, the Ministry of Finance of the Republic of Lithuania has provided guidelines for the development of the FinTech sector for 2023–2028 (see Figure 3) in order to further strengthen the country's position as a regional FinTech center.

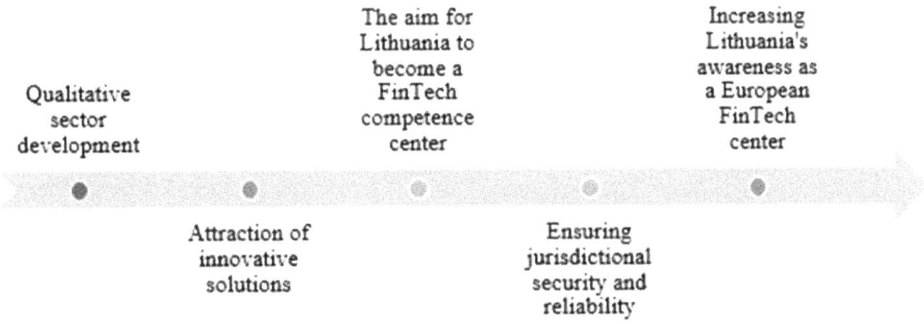

Figure 3. The classification of FinTech sectors (compiled by the authors based on the classification of licenses issued by [28]).

The active growth of FinTech companies in the past few years has encouraged the qualitative development of the FinTech sector in Lithuania. This article analyzes qualitative development through the increase in the number of FinTech companies. Licensed companies had the right to carry out the specified activities.

Long-term benefits for Lithuania include the attraction of innovative solutions, which increases the potential of companies providing high-quality financial services. This stimulates investor interest in the country's market and increases the creation of high added value. This study analyzes the financial indicators of all FinTech companies, including their added value created in 2023, expressed in thousands of euros.

In order for Lithuania to become a center of FinTech competencies, it is necessary to increase the supply of talent and attract highly qualified specialists. This can be achieved via closer cooperation with higher education institutions that develop specialized programs for specialists needed in the FinTech sector. The Ministry of Economy and Innovation will also implement measures to attract missing specialists from third countries, especially those with experience in technology and knowledge-intensive service sectors. This study discusses Lithuania's aspiration to become a FinTech competence center, which is closely related to the capital requirements established by the legal acts of the Republic of Lithuania regulating the initial capital of licensed companies required to carry out certain activities.

Lithuania aims to be a safe and reliable jurisdiction, ensuring security and reliability and improving cooperation and trust. For this purpose, it is important to strengthen risk management procedures and increase the maturity of companies' activities. The main goal is to find a balance between market security, stability, and reducing the administrative burden for companies. In 2023–2028, the focus will be on combating money laundering, preventing terrorist financing, cyber and information technology security, preventing financial crimes and fraud, and protecting consumer interests. This study is based on consumer surveys submitted to the Bank of Lithuania's analysis of complaints about the activities of institutions, disputes with consumers, and enforcement measures applied by financial market supervision institutions. The data are obtained from the annual activity reports of the Bank of Lithuania, selecting specifically those related to the application of FinTech principles. The Bank of Lithuania, following applicable laws, applies these enforcement measures in cases where violations are identified.

Lithuania is internationally recognized as one of the European FinTech centers, but further awareness-raising is necessary. In order to strengthen this position, representatives of the Lithuanian FinTech sector should actively participate in various European Union and international events. This study also analyzes the number of users and its impact on the development of the FinTech sector.

Lithuania seeks to maintain its position as a European FinTech center by promoting a safe and reliable regulatory environment, strengthening risk management and the fight against financial crimes. The development of the FinTech sector is based on attracting talent, cooperation with higher education institutions, and attracting specialists from abroad. Capital requirements and innovative technologies stimulate the growth of the sector, and high-value-added companies increase investor interest. In recent years, Lithuania has been experiencing qualitative growth in the FinTech sector, which is helping to strengthen the country's position in the international market.

3. Materials and Methods

Evaluating the advantages of FinTech, three main methods are used. The CRITIC method, which stands for Criteria Importance Through Intercriteria Correlation, is considered a reliable approach in multi-criteria decision-making (MCDM) due to its ability to objectively evaluate the relative importance of different criteria based on their correlation with each other. By analyzing the interrelationships between criteria, this method minimizes the impact of subjective bias, ensuring a more data-driven and robust assessment.

However, the reliability of the CRITIC method can be influenced by the quality of the data and the assumption that the criteria are independent and measurable. It works well when there are sufficient data available to establish strong correlations but may struggle in situations where data are scarce or the criteria are poorly defined.

Using a combination of the COPRAS, CRITIC, and SWOT methods in this study, it is possible to attain comprehensive and reliable results, as each of these methods has its own advantages and strengths [29–34].

The COPRAS (complex proportional assessment) method is a multi-criteria assessment method that allows one to evaluate alternatives, taking into account several criteria and giving each criterion a weight according to its importance. The COPRAS method is particularly useful when it is necessary to analyze complex situations and compare various alternatives according to different criteria. The advantage of COPRAS is that it simply and effectively evaluates alternatives and allows one to make comparisons and also helps to assess how each criterion contributes to the final assessment.

The CRITIC (Criteria Importance Through Intercriteria Correlation) method is designed to distribute weights between various criteria based on their importance and mutual correlations. This allows one to objectively determine which criteria are more important, taking into account their mutual interaction and impact on other alternatives. CRITIC helps to determine objective weights for criteria, as it is based on statistical data, which provides greater reliability and accuracy for assessments.

SWOT (Strengths, Weaknesses, Opportunities, Threats) analysis is a strategic tool that allows one to analyze both internal (strengths and weaknesses) and external (opportunities and threats) factors that may influence choices. It is especially useful when analyzing the situation of an organization or project and determining priorities and opportunities.

The application of the SWOT method is useful because it provides a broader context and allows one to assess how the organization or alternatives can take advantage of external opportunities and overcome challenges.

It follows that the use of a combination of these methods provides the following:

A comprehensive approach: The COPRAS and CRITIC methods provide the opportunity to conduct a detailed quantitative analysis, while SWOT allows one to assess both internal and external factors. This enables this study to take a comprehensive approach, including both objective and subjective factors.

More accurate assessment: The CRITIC method helps to objectively determine the importance of criteria, while COPRAS allows these weights to be applied in practical analysis. This allows for a more accurate comparison of alternatives and the selection of the best option.

Structured decision-making: SWOT analysis complements these methods, as it allows one to take into account the strategic circumstances of the organization and factors that may influence choices. The results of SWOT analysis help one select the best alternative not only based on technical indicators but also taking into account long-term opportunities and risks.

Using a combination of the COPRAS, CRITIC, and SWOT methods, this study becomes comprehensive and balanced, as each method complements the other. This allows for both quantitative and qualitative analyses, providing an objective and strategic approach to solving the problem. Limitations of studies using a combination of the COPRAS, CRITIC, and SWOT methods may arise for various reasons related to the specifics of the methods, data availability, and interpretation challenges.

First of all, subjectivity in the weights of the criteria is encountered. Although the COPRAS method allows for an objective assessment of alternatives, the weights of the criteria can be determined subjectively, especially if they are chosen based on expert opinion or incorrectly distributed priorities. This may affect the final assessments, but this article also calculated the consistency of expert opinions and found that the opinions are consistent, and the results are sufficiently reliable.

The second limitation encountered is the limited amount of data. The CRITIC method relies on statistical data to determine the importance of the criteria; therefore, if the number of data is small or they are insufficiently diversified, this method may provide inaccurate or erroneous results. This article analyzes 10 years of data; therefore, the results are reliable.

Difficulties in inter-correlations may also arise. The CRITIC method uses correlations between criteria, but for some criteria, there may not be a clear or direct correlation, so this method may not be able to reveal all important factors. This may lead to an incomplete assessment of the importance of the criteria, so the COPRAS method was chosen in addition to make the results more reliable.

Complexity of the methods: The CRITIC method requires a certain level of statistical knowledge and can be difficult to use for practical research when the data are not sufficiently detailed or their structure is not clear.

SWOT analysis is a qualitative tool, so it can be difficult to evaluate and compare facts and alternatives with quantitative indicators. This can limit decision-making when more accurate quantitative analysis is required. Therefore, in order to include information from quantitative methods, the COPRAS and CRITIC methods were chosen to be used.

When using a combination of the COPRAS, CRITIC, and SWOT methods in research, it is necessary to take these limitations into account. Only after the careful collection of data and a detailed analysis of them can accurate and comprehensive research results be presented.

3.1. *Cross-Criteria Assessment Method*

The cross-criteria correlation (hereinafter referred to as CRITIC) method is particularly suitable for assessing multifaceted and complex systems, such as the FinTech sector. Using this method, the importance of criteria is determined based on objective statistical data [35]. The CRITIC method helps to determine objective weights for decision criteria, thus avoiding subjective assessment and accurately assessing which factors, for example, regulatory or technological, limit the development of the sector the most.

Step 1: A decision matrix is prepared, collecting alternatives and criteria against which the FinTech sector will be assessed (e.g., economic, technological, and social factors). A decision matrix x is formed, showing the performance of different alternatives concerning the selected sub-criteria:

$$x = [x_{ij}]_{mxn} = \begin{bmatrix} x_{11} & x_{12} & \cdots & x_{1n} \\ x_{12} & x_{22} & \cdots & x_{1n} \\ \vdots & \vdots & \ddots & \vdots \\ x_{m1} & x_{m2} & \cdots & x_{mn} \end{bmatrix} i \in \{1,2,\ldots,m\}, j \in \{1,2,\ldots,n\} \quad (1)$$

where n—number of alternatives; m—number of criteria.

Step 2: The decision matrix is normalized using linear normalization relations:

$$r_{ij} = \frac{x_{ij} - x_j^{min}}{x_j^{max} - x_j^{min}}, i \in \{1,2,\ldots,m\}, j \in \{1,2,\ldots,n\} \quad (2)$$

where i—the number of alternatives; j—the number of criteria; min—the minimum criterion value; max—the maximum criterion value.

Step 3: The population's standard deviation (hereinafter referred to as SIGMA) σ_j is determined from the normalized decision matrix for each r_j:

$$\sigma_j = \sqrt{\frac{\sum(r_{ij} - \bar{r}_{ij})^2}{n}} \tag{3}$$

where $\bar{r}_{ij}$—mean; n—number of features.

Step 4: The correlation for each pair of normalized criteria is determined, and a symmetric matrix with element R_{ij} is constructed:

$$R_{ij} = \frac{\sum(r_i - \bar{r}_i)(r_j - \bar{r}_j)}{\sqrt{\sum(r_i - \bar{r}_i)^2 \sum(r_j - \bar{r}_j)^2}} \tag{4}$$

Correlation measures the relationship between two variables, showing how a change in one variable is related to a change in another variable [36]. The correlation coefficient can be positive or negative, and its values can fluctuate. The value of the correlation coefficient can be interpreted as follows:

1 or −1—very strong correlation.

0.7–0.9 or −0.7–−0.9—strong correlation.

0.5–0.7 or −0.5–−0.7—medium correlation.

0.3–0.5 or −0.3–−0.5—weak correlation.

0–0.3 or −0.3–0—very weak or insignificant correlation.

Positive correlation means that both variables increase together, while negative correlation indicates that one variable increases when the other decreases.

Step 1: Determination of the difference in determination between criteria:

$$\sum_{j=1}^{n}(1 - R_{ij}) \tag{5}$$

Step 2: Determination of the determination sum C_j, the amount of difference between criterion j:

$$C_j = \sigma_j \sum_{j=1}^{n}(1 - R_{ij}) \tag{6}$$

The higher the value of C_j, the greater the amount of information contained in a certain criterion; therefore, the criterion has a greater relative importance.

Step 3: Determination of the determination criterion weights w_j:

$$w_j = \frac{c_j}{\sum_{j=1}^{n} C_j} \tag{7}$$

The advantages of the CRITIC method for FinTech assessment are as follows:

Objectivity: Criterion weights are determined based on statistical data, not subjective expert assessments.

Criteria independence: Correlated criteria are given less weight, thus avoiding double impact.

Dynamics: The CRITIC method can be applied to various sectors; therefore, it can be adapted to both regional and global FinTech markets.

When all criteria have their weights, it is possible to make a final assessment of the FinTech sector, reflecting the objective impact of different criteria on the development of the sector.

3.2. Multi-Criteria Assessment Method

The multi-criteria complex proportional assessment (hereinafter referred to as COPRAS) method is used to assess various factors and their importance in order to determine the optimal directions of activity and propose strategic solutions for the development of the enterprise [37]. This method is well suited for assessing the FinTech sector, as it allows for the assessment of many different criteria and the identification of the most effective development strategies.

Step 1: Constructing a weighted normalized matrix:

$$\hat{x}_{ij} = \frac{x_{ij}}{\sum_{i=1}^{m} x_{ij}} \tag{8}$$

Step 2: Calculating normalized weighted values for each criterion:

$$\tilde{x}_{ij} = \hat{x}_{ij} \cdot w_j \tag{9}$$

Step 3: Determining the sum of the normalized, weighted values of maximizing criteria:

$$S_{+i} = \sum_{j=1}^{n} \tilde{x}_{+ij} \tag{10}$$

Step 4: Determining the sum of the normalized, weighted values of minimizing criteria:

$$S_{-i} = \sum_{j=1}^{n} \tilde{x}_{-ij} \tag{11}$$

Step 5: Determining the relative weights of alternatives:

$$Q_i = S_{+i} + \frac{S_{-min} \sum_{i=1}^{m} S_{-i}}{S_{-i} \cdot \sum_{i=1}^{m} \frac{S_{-min}}{S_{-i}}}, \text{where } S_{-min} = \min_{i} S_{-i} \tag{12}$$

Step 6: Calculating the percentage value of each alternative U_i, which allows the priority activity curves of the sector to be determined:

$$U_i = \frac{Q_i}{Q_{\_max}} \cdot 100\% \tag{13}$$

Step 7: Determining the priority of FinTech sectors. The higher the U_i value, the better the sector meets all the criteria. A priority order of FinTech sectors is also formed according to compliance with the criteria.

The COPRAS method is a multi-criteria assessment tool designed to determine priority areas of activity based on various factors, such as economic and technological indicators. This method helps to distinguish the most important criteria, evaluate alternatives, and propose optimal solutions for the development of the sector. Using the COPRAS method for assessing the FinTech sector, it is possible to accurately determine which sector's business lines best meet the established criteria, thereby promoting the sustainable growth of the sector.

3.3. SWOT Analysis Method

SWOT (Strengths, Weaknesses, Opportunities, and Threats) analysis is a strategic tool that helps assess internal and external factors that may affect operations.

The first step is to collect and analyze data about the FinTech market and the external environment. This may include the following:

- A company's financial indicators;
- The competitive environment;

- Industry trends and innovations;
- Customer reviews, market research, and surveys.

A company's internal processes, organizational structure, employee competencies, and technological infrastructure may also be evaluated. An analysis of internal factors (strengths and weaknesses) may also be conducted; these are factors that can be directly controlled. These can be resources, capabilities, processes, or culture (Table 1).

Table 1. Main questions for SWOT analysis.

Strengths (S)	Weaknesses (W)
What does the FinTech sector do better than the competition? What are its unique advantages? What resources (human, financial, technological, etc.) help the sector operate successfully?	What does the FinTech sector do worse than its competitors? What are its organizational problems: limited resources or inefficient technology? Is it possible to lose market share due to internal weaknesses? An analysis of external factors (opportunities and threats) may be conducted; these are external forces that are less controllable but must be taken into account when planning a strategy.
Opportunities (O)	**Threats (T)**
What market trends, technologies, or changes might provide new opportunities? Are there new markets to expand into? What regulatory or economic trends could support growth?	What external factors can disrupt operations? How can competitors affect the market position of the FinTech sector? Is there a possibility that regulations or laws will change, which could be detrimental?

Source: compiled by the authors.

Based on the SWOT analysis in this study, it is possible to understand the current state of the market, make decisions based on both internal structure and external factors, and develop effective strategies to take advantage of strengths and opportunities while reducing the impact of weaknesses and threats.

4. Results

4.1. Factors Influencing the Development of FinTech

After the discussion about the factors influencing the development of the FinTech sector, these main factors (criteria) and their alternatives are presented in Table 2.

Table 2. Alternatives and criteria for FinTech development—influencing factors.

Criteria/Alternatives	Number of FinTech Companies	Financial Indicators (EUR)	Capital Requirement (Thousand EUR)	Number of Users (Thousand EUR)	Complaints Filed	Impact Measures
Minimize/maximize	Max	Max	Max	Max	Min	Min
EMI	226	401,072	350	5678	10	102
PSP	331	93,512	93	2,974,073	0	28
PPP	71	88,246	40	23,774	5	9
CFP	22	230,242	5000	591,223	195	4
WealthTech	16	30,293	123,085	6176	0	10
Digital Banking	13	609,211	1000	2520	191	34

Source: compiled by the authors, based on the report data of the Bank of Lithuania ([26,28]) and the reports of the State Data Agency in 2023 and calculation results.

FinTech development criteria are divided into maximizing and minimizing criteria. Maximizing criteria are those whose values should be as high as possible, such as the number of companies and financial and capital ratios. Minimizing criteria are those whose values should be as low as possible, such as complaints or enforcement actions.

This information was compiled based on 2023 data to ensure that the most recent and reliable secondary sources were used. The analyzed information is based on freely available data and the 2023–2028 FinTech sector development guidelines prepared by the team of specialists of the Ministry of Finance of the Republic of Lithuania.

4.2. Evaluation of Criteria Using CRITIC Method

Based on the data presented in Table 1, the CRITIC method was applied to determine the importance of each criterion. First, the maximum and minimum values were calculated using the Excel functions $fx = MAX$ and $fx = MIN$ (see step 1 in Table 3); then, the performance of each alternative was calculated according to the selected sub-criteria: (see step 2 in Table 3).

Table 3. Performance and standard deviation of minimum and maximum value alternatives.

Criteria/Alternatives	Number of FinTech Companies	Financial Indicators (EUR)	Capital Requirement (Thousand EUR)	Number of Users (Thousand EUR)	Complaints Filed	Impact Measures
Step 1						
MIN	13	30,293	40	2520	0	4
MAX	331	609,211	123,085	2,974,073	195	102
Step 2						
EMI	0.6698	0.6405	0.0025	0.0011	0.0513	1
PSP	1	0.1092	0.0004	1	0	0.2449
PPP	0.1824	0.1001	0	0.0072	0.0256	0.0510
CFP	0.0283	0.3454	0.0403	0.1981	1	0
WealthTech	0.0094	0	1	0.0012	0	0.0612
Digital Banking	0.3061	1	0.0078	0	0.9795	0
Step 3						
SIGMA σ_j	0.4213	0.3869	0.4044	0.3991	0.5016	0.3739

Source: compiled by the authors, based on calculation results.

A criterion's standard deviation SIGMA σ_j (see step 3, Table 3) is calculated by the Excel function $fx = STDEV$.

The correlation R_{ij} is derived (see Equation (4)) using the Excel function $fx = Correlation$ (see Table 4).

Table 4. Correlation between criteria.

Criteria/Alternatives	Number of FinTech Companies	Financial Indicators (EUR)	Capital Requirement (Thousand EUR)	Number of Users (Thousand EUR)	Complaints Filed	Impact Measures
EMI	1	−0.1537	−0.3738	0.7462	−0.5493	0.5087
PSP	−0.1537	1	−0.4617	−0.3404	0.6266	0.5115
PPP	−0.3738	−0.4617	1	−0.2502	−0.3078	−0.2978
CFP	0.7462	−0.3404	−0.2502	1	−0.2153	−0.1184
WealthTech	−0.5493	0.6266	−0.3078	−0.2153	1	−0.2321
Digital Banking	0.5087	0.5115	−0.2978	−0.1184	−0.2321	1

Source: compiled by the authors, based on calculation results.

4.3. Correlation Analysis Between Criteria

The number of FinTech companies and the number of users (0.7462) has a positive, moderate correlation. This shows that as the number of FinTech companies grows, so does the number of users.

The number of FinTech companies and impact measures (0.5087) has a positive, weak correlation. This means that as the number of FinTech companies increases, so does the use of leverage, but this relationship is not very strong.

PSPs and filed complaints (0.6266) have a positive, moderate correlation. This shows that when the indicators of the Ministry of Internal Affairs improve, the number of reported complaints also increases.

WealthTech and financial indicators (0.6266) have a positive, moderate correlation. As WealthTech's financial ratios increase, so do the company's ratios, indicating a strong relationship between these ratios.

EMIs and filed complaints (−0.5493) have a medium, negative correlation. This means that the number of filed complaints decreases with an increase in the activity indicators of the EMI.

WealthTech and some users (−0.2153) have a very weak, negative correlation. This shows that when the number of users declines, the impact on WealthTech is negligible.

Digital banking and the number of users (−0.1184) have no significant correlation.

A positive correlation means that an increase in one criterion is associated with an increase in another criterion, while a negative correlation means that an increase in one criterion is associated with a decrease in the other.

For the derived correlation, for each pair of normalized criteria, a symmetric matrix (see Table 5) is created—determination difference (see Equation (5)). The resulting sum is multiplied by the previously calculated SIGMA σ_j, and the determination difference sum C_j is obtained (see Equation (6)). The greater the value of the difference in determination, the greater the relative importance of the criterion—these are capital requirements and filed complaints.

Table 5. Determination difference and weights.

Criteria/Alternatives	Number of FinTech Companies	Financial Indicators (EUR)	Capital Requirement (Thousand EUR)	Number of Users (Thousand EUR)	Complaints Filed	Impact Measures
EMI	0	1.1537	1.3738	0.2538	1.5493	0.4913
PSP	1.1537	0	1.4617	1.3404	0.3734	0.4885
PPP	1.3738	1.4617	0	1.2502	1.3078	1.2978
CFP	0.2538	13404	0.2502	0	1.2153	1.1184
WealthTech	1.5493	0.3734	1.3078	1.2153	0	1.2321
Digital banking	0.4913	0.4885	1.2978	1.1184	1.2321	0
Sum	4.8219	4.8177	6.6913	5.1782	5.6780	4.6281
SIGMA σ_j	0.4213	0.3869	0.4044	0.3991	0.5016	0.3739
The sum of the determination difference C_j	2.0315	1.8638	2.7058	2.0665	2.8479	1.7304
w_j	0.1534	0.1407	0.2043	0.1560	0.2150	0.1306

Source: compiled by the authors, based on calculation results.

From the set amount of determination (see Table 5), the weights w_j of the determination criterion are derived (see Equation (7)).

The CRITIC method showed that the most important criteria for the development of the FinTech sector are the initial capital requirements and the number of reported complaints. These criteria have the greatest influence on the sector's efficiency and further development. The weightings of the criteria calculated in this study help us to better understand how various factors affect the sector, which allows for more informed decisions to be made in terms of strategic actions.

4.4. Priority Order of FinTech Sectors

Normalized values are calculated taking into account the weight of each criterion (see Equations (8) and (9)). The normalization formula is often used in the COPRAS methodology to facilitate the comparison of different criteria, even if they are measured in different units.

The weighted value is normalized; the sum of the normalized, weighted values of the maximizing and min criteria are determined; a priority order is made; and the FinTech sector is arranged according to the best criteria (see Table 6) with the help of Excel functions $fx = \boldsymbol{Rank}$ (see Equations (10)–(13)).

Table 6. Priority queue.

Criteria/Alternatives	S_{+i}	S_{-i}	S_{-min}/S_{-i}	Q_i	U_i	Priority
EMI	0.0907	0.0766	0.0912	0.1041	29.912	4
PSP	0.2127	0.0196	0.3571	0.2653	76.218	2
PPP	0.0257	0.0090	0.7790	0.1404	40.323	3
CFP	0.0608	0.1073	0.0651	0.0703	20.205	6
WealthTech	0.2009	0.0070	1	0.3481	100	1
Digital Banking	0.0636	0.1262	0.0554	0.0718	20.623	5

Source: compiled by the authors, based on calculation results.

WealthTech (investment and wealth management companies)—This sector was rated as the best in 2023, according to all criteria. It has strong results in terms of capital requirements and S_{-min}, which means that it performs well in both maximization and minimization criteria.

- PSPs (payment service providers) took second place, having strong financial indicators and other reasonably good criteria.
- PPPs (peer-to-peer lending platforms) had average results but performed well in minimizing complaints and other negative criteria.
- EMIs (electronic money institutions)—$\boldsymbol{U_i}$ = 29,912, priority: 4. Electronic money institutions were in fourth place because they have an average position according to the maximization and minimization criteria.
- Digital banking was ranked fifth due to lower financial indicators and higher complaint values.
- CFPs (crowdfunding platforms) took the last place, because their values were lower in all criteria.

Based on the priority order, investment and wealth management companies (WealthTech) were recognized as the best FinTech sector in 2023, as they achieved the best results in terms of capital requirements, financial performance, and minimal complaints.

4.5. WealthTech SWOT Analysis

SWOT analysis was conducted for the WealthTech sector, with the following highlights in each category:

- Strengths (S):
- Technological Advances: Uses advanced technologies such as artificial intelligence (AI) and big data analytics to improve investment performance.
- Accessibility: Digital platforms make it easier for the public to access investment services.

- Lower costs: Automated solutions such as robot advisors reduce fees compared to traditional wealth management firms.
- Weaknesses (W):
- Technological dependence: Increased risk due to potential technological failures and cyber threats.
- Lack of personalization: Automated solutions cannot always offer the personalized advice that financial advisors can provide.
- Regulatory complexity: It is difficult to comply with the regulatory requirements of the financial sector in various countries.
- Opportunities (O):
- Market development: There are still few available wealth management services in emerging markets, so WealthTech has great growth potential.
- Attracting the younger generation: Millennials and Gen Z tend to use digital platforms for investment.
- The development of artificial intelligence: AI capabilities allow us to offer more personalized and efficient solutions.
- Threats (T):
- Tighter regulation: There may be stricter regulatory requirements that limit innovation.
- Cyber-attacks: Cyber threats can damage the reputation and credibility of the sector.
- Competition: High competition from both traditional banks and other FinTech companies.

WealthTech is a strong, innovative, and dynamic FinTech segment that is characterized by a wide range of services, technological advances, long-term return potential, and risk diversification opportunities. Meanwhile, EMIs, PSPs, digital banking, PPPs, and CFPs are more specialized sectors that focus on payments or loans but do not offer the deeper investment and wealth management value of WealthTech.

5. Discussion

Financial technology (FinTech) is one of the fastest-growing industries worldwide, and Europe has a major role to play in this. FinTech encompasses a range of technologies and innovations that help improve the efficiency, accessibility, and security of financial services [38]. The financial technology sector in Europe has undergone significant changes over the past decade, and these technologies have become a key factor shaping the future of the financial sector. The development of FinTech has changed the essence of traditional finance and has had a significant impact on the efficiency of financial decision-making [39].

The development of financial technologies in Europe began only in the 20th century. Then, the first attempts to use technology in the financial sector were recorded, focusing on online banking services and the emergence of electronic payments [40,41]. This led to a situation where traditional banks must quickly adapt to the constantly changing environment, reduce their costs, and meet customers' needs and expectations [42]. Online banking, which allows users to perform financial transactions online, was the first step towards the development of modern FinTech.

At the beginning of the 21st century, FinTech companies began to emerge in Europe, which sought to use technology in the financial sector as effectively as possible and replace traditional financial services with newer, more advanced, and more accessible ones. It was time for the rise of cryptocurrencies, blockchain technology, robo-advisors, and peer-to-peer lending platforms, so these technologies streamlined traditional financial processes and enabled a broader spectrum for users to participate in the global economy [43]. FinTech development led to more accessible, innovative, improved, competitive, secure, inclusive, and beneficial financial services [39]. One of the first significant events was the success of PayPal [44]. This created electronic payment system allowed users to transfer money safely and quickly online, which led to an increase in the availability of financial services and a reduction in prices. This transformation from digitalization to digitization led to the use of new technologies and the restructurization of banking industries [45]. People started to place more trust in banks while they transfer their money. It was then that the evolution of services provided by traditional banks began [46].

In Europe, the FinTech sector has rapidly developed as technological innovations such as blockchain, artificial intelligence, big data, and cybersecurity have been applied to the financial sector, which are accelerating globally. Canada, the UK, Germany, France, Switzerland, and Sweden have seen the largest FinTech growth streams, making these countries the European FinTech hub, attracting both domestic and international investors [47,48].

Currently, FinTech technologies are developing rapidly. The blockchain technology used in the financial sector provides the opportunity to provide safer and more efficient financial services, reducing the number of intermediaries and transaction costs, because the most important criteria in blockchain technology are security and trust [49,50]. The authors of [50–53] argue that operations in the context of the use of blockchain can lead to a reduction in operating costs, so these operations are cheaper and more efficient. Blockchain technology can help create decentralized systems that will allow transactions to be carried out without intermediaries, which will reduce costs and improve the speed of transactions. Artificial intelligence can be used to automate financial processes, predict market trends, and improve customer service. The application of artificial intelligence in the finance sector leads to the deep transformation of the financial services industry and helps to predict bankruptcy, stock prices, and oil prices to manage one's portfolio, and this is one of the best ways to ensure an anti-money laundering process [54–56]. Artificial intelligence is a good tool for financial analysis, forecasting, and risk management because by using artificial intelligence tools, people can analyze a broad range of data, find the necessary results, and make predictions more quickly and easily [57,58]. Big data allows FinTech companies to more accurately analyze consumer behavior, provide personalized services, and manage risks more effectively [59]. In the financial sector, big data is used especially for fraud detection and risk assessment [60], so the financial sector becomes more sustainable [61].

The digital economy has grown due to the impact of FinTech development, and the FinTech sector in Europe is likely to continue to grow. It is predicted that the FinTech sector will become an even more important component of the economy in the next few years, as more and more consumers choose digital financial services [62,63]. Digital finance helps improve the accessibility of financial services, ensures the security and stability of financial services, and helps avoid fraud and money laundering [64–66]. Companies use financial technologies to offer consumers competitive services. Traditional banks are forced to cooperate with FinTech companies in order to compete in the market and attract consumers. It follows that the FinTech sector in Europe has great potential and prospects. There are many opportunities to apply innovations in the provision of financial services. However, the successful development of FinTech will depend on how quickly the financial sector adopts and applies new technologies.

6. Conclusions

The FinTech sector is important for Lithuania's economy, as the changing needs of society and technological progress promote digitization and innovation in the financial sector. The analyzed theoretical models showed that FinTech innovations not only simplify the provision of traditional financial services but also open new opportunities and have a positive impact on the Lithuanian economy and contribute to the creation of greater added value. Technological solutions allow financial services companies to become more efficient, reduce costs, and expand their range of services. Due to the favorable legal environment and active promotion of innovation, Lithuania has become an attractive country for FinTech companies, but challenges remain, especially related to cybersecurity and regulatory compliance.

The methodologies used in this study, including quantitative ones, were effective in evaluating the development of the Lithuanian FinTech sector. Quantitative data on the number of licenses, investments, and sector growth provided an objective picture of the sector's development. The methods used, such as CRITIC and COPRAS, allowed us to determine objective criteria and priorities in the FinTech sector, assessing which factors (e.g., regulatory restrictions, technological infrastructure) are hindering the growth of the sector the most. These methodologies made it possible to consistently identify the main barriers to development, and the SWOT analysis highlighted strengths and weaknesses, allowing for strategic recommendations for the improvement of the sector.

The results of this study highlighted that the FinTech sector in Lithuania is primarily shaped by factors such as favorable regulation, the strengthening of the innovation ecosystem, and the attraction of international investments. These elements are essential for fostering growth and creating a competitive landscape. However, despite these positive influences, the sector still faces significant challenges, including a shortage of skilled labor, the need to enhance cybersecurity measures, and the ongoing need for regulatory frameworks to evolve alongside emerging technologies.

The key barriers to accelerated growth in the FinTech sector are closely tied to the pace of technological advancements, regulatory uncertainty, and difficulties in attracting and retaining top talent. The importance of FinTech cannot be overstated, as it is central to driving digital transformation, improving financial accessibility, and ensuring economic resilience. In light of this study's findings, it is recommended that more focus be placed on educational programs that train technology specialists, foster stronger cooperation between the public and private sectors, and further refine the regulatory environment. These actions are critical for ensuring the sustainable and secure development of FinTech, which is increasingly indispensable for both economic innovation and global competitiveness.

Author Contributions: Conceptualization, L.O.N., I.D. and G.L.; methodology, L.O.N., I.D. and G.L.; experiment and result analysis, L.O.N., I.D. and G.L.; conclusions, L.O.N., I.D. and G.L.; discussion, L.O.N. and I.D.; writing—original draft preparation, L.O.N., I.D. and G.L.; writing—review and editing, L.O.N. and I.D. All authors have read and agreed to the published version of the manuscript.

Funding: This research received no external funding.

Institutional Review Board Statement: Not applicable.

Informed Consent Statement: Not applicable.

Data Availability Statement: The original contributions presented in this study are included in the article.

Conflicts of Interest: The authors declare no conflicts of interest.

References

1. Fintechnews Baltic. *Lithuania's Ecosystem Confirms New National Fintech Guidelines for 2023–2028*; Fintechnews Baltic: Vilnius, Lithuania, 2023.
2. Lavrinenko, O.; Čižo, E.; Ignatjeva, S.; Danileviča, A.; Krukowski, K. Financial Technology (FinTech) as a Financial Development Factor in the EU Countries. *Economies* **2023**, *11*, 45. [CrossRef]
3. Yu, M. The Impact of Financial Technology on Traditional Financial Systems and Future Trends. *J. Mod. Bus. Econ.* **2024**, *1*, 1–7. [CrossRef]
4. AlSuwaidi, R.A.; Mertzanis, C. Financial literacy and FinTech market growth around the world. *Int. Rev. Financ. Anal.* **2024**, *95*, 103481. [CrossRef]

5. Moreira-Santos, D.; Au-Yong-Oliveira, M.; Palma-Moreira, A. Fintech Services and the Drivers of Their Implementation in Small and Medium Enterprises. *Information* **2022**, *13*, 409. [CrossRef]
6. Gecevičienė, K.; Danilevičienė, I.; Okunevičiūtė Neverauskienė, L. Impact of FinTech Sector Development on Money laundering Prevention. *Econ. Manag. Spectr./Ekon.-Manažérske Spektrum* **2024**, *18*, 54–66. [CrossRef]
7. Schulte, P.; Liu, G. FinTech is merging with IoT and AI to challenge banks: How entrenched interests can prepare. *J. Altern. Investig.* **2018**, *20*, 41–57. [CrossRef]
8. Hassoun, A.; Alhaj Abdullah, N.; Aït-Kaddour, A.; Ghellam, M.; Beşir, A.; Zannou, O.; Önal, B.; Aadil, R.M.; Lorenzo, J.M.; Mousavi Khaneghah, A.; et al. Food traceability 4.0 as part of the fourth industrial revolution: Key enabling technologies. *Crit. Rev. Food Sci. Nutr.* **2024**, *64*, 873–889. [CrossRef]
9. Takeda, A.; Ito, Y. A review of FinTech research. *Int. J. Technol. Manag.* **2021**, *86*, 67–88. [CrossRef]
10. Okunevičiūtė Neverauskienė, L.; Kleponė, D. Empirical evidence on the startup growth in the Baltic Region high tech landscape. *Transform. Bus. Econ.* **2024**, *23*, 1164–1191.
11. Suryono, R.R.; Budi, I.; Purwandari, B. Challenges and trends of financial technology (Fintech): A systematic literature review. *Information* **2020**, *11*, 590. [CrossRef]
12. Li, B.; Xu, Z. Insights into financial technology (FinTech): A bibliometric and visual study. *Financ. Innov.* **2021**, *7*, 69. [CrossRef] [PubMed]
13. Okunevičiūtė Neverauskienė, L.; Ginevičius, R.; Danilevičienė, I. The influence of wage and employment on competitiveness: An assessment. *J. Compet.* **2024**, *16*, 83–105. [CrossRef]
14. Pandey, D.K.; Hassan, M.K.; Kumari, V.; Zaied, Y.B.; Rai, V.K. Mapping the landscape of FinTech in banking and finance: A bibliometric review. *Res. Int. Bus. Financ.* **2024**, *67*, 102116. [CrossRef]
15. Wang, R.; Liu, J.; Luo, H. Fintech development and bank risk taking in China. *Eur. J. Financ.* **2021**, *27*, 397–418. [CrossRef]
16. Zhang, X.; Zhao, T.; Wang, L.; Dong, Z. Does Fintech benefit financial disintermediation? Evidence based on provinces in China from 2013 to 2018. *J. Asian Econ.* **2022**, *82*, 101516. [CrossRef]
17. Rabbani, M.R. COVID-19 and its impact on supply chain financing and the role of Islamic Fintech: Evidence from GCC countries. *Int. J. Agil. Syst. Manag.* **2024**, *17*, 269–291. [CrossRef]
18. Anifa, M.; Ramakrishnan, S.; Joghee, S.; Kabiraj, S.; Bishnoi, M.M. Fintech innovations in the financial service industry. *J. Risk Financ. Manag.* **2022**, *15*, 287. [CrossRef]
19. Wang, X.; Cao, Y.; Feng, Z.; Lu, M.; Shan, Y. Local FinTech development and stock price crash risk. *Financ. Res. Lett.* **2023**, *53*, 103644. [CrossRef]
20. Zhao, D.; Yuan, J.; Chen, W. *FinTech and SupTech in China*; Springer: Berlin/Heidelberg, Germany, 2023.
21. Elsaid, H.M. A review of literature directions regarding the impact of fintech firms on the banking industry. *Qual. Res. Financ. Mark.* **2023**, *15*, 693–711. [CrossRef]
22. Agarwal, S.; Zhang, J. FinTech, lending and payment innovation: A review. *Asia-Pac. J. Financ. Stud.* **2020**, *49*, 353–367. [CrossRef]
23. Cao, L.; Yuan, G.; Leung, T.; Zhang, W. Special issue on AI and FinTech: The challenge ahead. *IEEE Intell. Syst.* **2020**, *35*, 3–6. [CrossRef]
24. Okunevičiūtė Neverauskienė, L.; Linkevičius, D.; Andriušaitienė, D. How macroeconomic factors impact residential real estate prices in Eastern Europe. *Bus. Manag. Econ. Eng.* **2025**, *23*, 30–43. [CrossRef]
25. Lee, I.; Shin, Y.J. Fintech: Ecosystem, business models, investment decisions, and challenges. *Bus. Horiz.* **2018**, *61*, 35–46. [CrossRef]
26. Hudaefi, F.A.; Hassan, M.K.; Abduh, M. Exploring the development of Islamic fintech ecosystem in Indonesia: A text analytics. *Qual. Res. Financ. Mark.* **2023**, *15*, 514–533. [CrossRef]
27. Navickaitė, G.; Žilinskij, G. Sutelktinis finansavimas—Vieta FinTech rinkoje ir FinTech tyrimuose Ekonomika ir vadyba. 2019, pp. 1–14. Available online: https://etalpykla.vilniustech.lt/handle/123456789/156217 (accessed on 17 January 2025).
28. Lietuvos bankas2023. Available online: https://www.lb.lt/lt/frd-gincai-su-vartotojais?ff=1 (accessed on 27 February 2025).
29. Kumar, R.; Kumar, S.; Ağbulut, Ü.; Gürel, A.E.; Alwetaishi, M.; Shaik, S.; Saleel, C.A.; Lee, D. Parametric optimization of an impingement jet solar air heater for active green heating in buildings using hybrid CRITIC-COPRAS approach. *Int. J. Therm. Sci.* **2024**, *197*, 108760. [CrossRef]
30. Vijayananth, K.; Pudhupalayam Muthukutti, G.; Keerthiveettil Ramakrishnan, S.; Venkatesan, S.; Zhou, W. An integrated CRITIC-COPRAS approach for multi-response optimization on AWJM of hybrid filler–reinforced polymer composite and its surface integrity. *Int. J. Adv. Manuf. Technol.* **2024**, *131*, 4965–4980. [CrossRef]
31. Radulescu, C.Z.; Radulescu, M. A hybrid group multi-criteria approach based on SAW, TOPSIS, VIKOR, and COPRAS methods for complex IoT selection problems. *Electronics* **2024**, *13*, 789. [CrossRef]
32. Öztaş, T. Big data analytics software selection with multi-criteria decision-making methods for digital transformation. *Pamukkale Üniversitesi Sos. Bilim. Enstitüsü Derg.* **2024**, *63*, 297–317. [CrossRef]

33. Sevgi, E.; Figen, A.Z. Determination of Renewable Energy Growth Using Cluster Analysis and Multi-Criteria Decision-Making Methods. *Appl. Sci.* **2025**, *15*, 1575. [CrossRef]
34. Almeida, V.V.A.; Gomes, C.F.S.; Pinochet, L.H.C.; dos Santos, M. Prioritization of investment order in Brazil among renewable energy sources: An analysis using the SWARA-MOORA-3NAG method. *J. Model. Manag.* **2025**, *20*, 620–647. [CrossRef]
35. Krishnan, A.R.; Kasim, M.M.; Hamid, R.; Ghazali, M.F. A Modified CRITIC Method to Estimate the Objective Weights of Decision Criteria. *Symmetry* **2021**, *13*, 973. [CrossRef]
36. Bilevičienė, T.; Jonušauskas, S. *Statistinių Metodų Taikymas Rinkos Tyrimuose*; MRU: Vilnius, Lithuania, 2011; p. 308.
37. Andruškevičius, A. Rangovų vertinimas daugiakriteriniu COPRAS metodu. *Technol. Econ. Dev. Econ.* **2010**, *11*, 158–169. [CrossRef]
38. Uddin, M.M.; Sultana, S.; Rima, S. Adoption of Fintech for Sustainable Administrative Efficiency of Higher Educational Institutions: Bangladesh Perspective. *J. Inf. Knowl. Manag.* **2024**, *23*, 2450074. [CrossRef]
39. Mahmudi, B. The Evolution of FinTech and its Effects on Financial Decision Making: A Systematic Literature Review. *Manag. Stud. Bus. J. (Product.)* **2024**, *1*, 174–181. [CrossRef]
40. Chawla, S. Exploring The Potential Of Online Banking: An Insight Into Innovations And Barriers In The Indian Context. *Educ. Adm. Theory Pract.* **2024**, *30*, 991–998. [CrossRef]
41. Choudhury, R.R.; Ferrer, M.A.; Roy, P. Evolution of Fintech and Implications for Traditional Banking and Finance Sector. In *Shaping Cutting-Edge Technologies and Applications for Digital Banking and Financial Services*; Taylor & Francis Group: New York, NY, USA, 2025; p. 147.
42. Grassi, L.; Figini, N.; Fedeli, L. How does a data strategy enable customer value? The case of FinTechs and traditional banks under the open finance framework. *Financ. Innov.* **2022**, *8*, 75. [CrossRef]
43. Mittal, N. Fin Tech Evolution: Pioneering Sustainable Transformations in Investment and Finance. *Sudarshan Res. J.* **2024**, *2*, 10–27.
44. Soni, J. *The Founders: The Story of PayPal and the Entrepreneurs Who Shaped Silicon Valley*; Simon and Schuster: New York, NY, USA, 2022.
45. Alzoubi, H.; Alshurideh, M.; Kurdi, B.A.; Alhyasat, K.; Ghazal, T. The effect of e-payment and online shopping on sales growth: Evidence from banking industry. *Int. J. Data Netw. Sci.* **2022**, *6*, 1369–1380. [CrossRef]
46. Khan, A.; Jafar, S.H.; El-Chaarani, H. Evolution of Fintech in the Financial Sector: Recent Trends and Future Perspectives. In *The Adoption of Fintech*; Productivity Press: New York, NY, USA, 2024; pp. 17–33.
47. Hornuf, L.; Klus, M.F.; Lohwasser, T.S.; Schwienbacher, A. How do banks interact with fintech startups? *Small Bus. Econ.* **2021**, *57*, 1505–1526. [CrossRef]
48. Walker, G.A. Money and Financial Technology (FinTech) History. *Int. Lawyer* **2023**, *56*, 227–331.
49. Das, S.; Raval, S.; Faisal, S.M. Financial Innovation for a Better Tomorrow: How the European Model is Embracing the Future of Finance. *Eur. Econ. Lett.* **2024**, *14*, 1941–1963.
50. Rajasekaran, A.S.; Azees, M.; Al-Turjman, F. A comprehensive survey on blockchain technology. *Sustain. Energy Technol. Assess.* **2022**, *52*, 102039. [CrossRef]
51. Akanfe, O.; Lawong, D.; Rao, H.R. Blockchain technology and privacy regulation: Reviewing frictions and synthesizing opportunities. *Int. J. Inf. Manag.* **2024**, *76*, 102753. [CrossRef]
52. Habib, G.; Sharma, S.; Ibrahim, S.; Ahmad, I.; Qureshi, S.; Ishfaq, M. Blockchain technology: Benefits, challenges, applications, and integration of blockchain technology with cloud computing. *Future Internet* **2022**, *14*, 341. [CrossRef]
53. Oriekhoe, O.I.; Omotoye, G.B.; Oyeyemi, O.P.; Tula, S.T.; Daraojimba, A.I.; Adefemi, A. Blockchain in supply chain management: A systematic review: Evaluating the implementation, challenges, and future prospects of blockchain technology in supply chains. *Eng. Sci. Technol. J.* **2024**, *5*, 128–151. [CrossRef]
54. Goodell, J.W.; Kumar, S.; Lim, W.M.; Pattnaik, D. Artificial intelligence and machine learning in finance: Identifying foundations, themes, and research clusters from bibliometric analysis. *J. Behav. Exp. Financ.* **2021**, *32*, 100577. [CrossRef]
55. Ahmed, S.; Alshater, M.M.; El Ammari, A.; Hammami, H. Artificial intelligence and machine learning in finance: A bibliometric review. *Res. Int. Bus. Financ.* **2022**, *61*, 101646. [CrossRef]
56. Bahoo, S.; Cucculelli, M.; Goga, X.; Mondolo, J. Artificial intelligence in Finance: A comprehensive review through bibliometric and content analysis. *SN Bus. Econ.* **2024**, *4*, 23. [CrossRef]
57. Akour, I.; Alzyoud, M.; Alquqa, E.; Tariq, E.; Alzboun, N.; Al-Hawary, S.; Alshurideh, M. Artificial intelligence and financial decisions: Empirical evidence from developing economies. *Int. J. Data Netw. Sci.* **2024**, *8*, 101–108. [CrossRef]
58. Lim, T. Environmental, social, and governance (ESG) and artificial intelligence in finance: State-of-the-art and research takeaways. *Artif. Intell. Rev.* **2024**, *57*, 76. [CrossRef]
59. Ahmadi, S. A comprehensive study on integration of big data and AI in financial industry and its effect on present and future opportunities. *Int. J. Curr. Sci. Res. Rev.* **2024**, *7*, 66–74. [CrossRef]
60. Udeh, C.A.; Orieno, O.H.; Daraojimba, O.D.; Ndubuisi, N.L.; Oriekhoe, O.I. Big data analytics: A review of its transformative role in modern business intelligence. *Comput. Sci. IT Res. J.* **2024**, *5*, 219–236. [CrossRef]

61. Kumar, S.; Sharma, D.; Rao, S.; Lim, W.M.; Mangla, S.K. Past, present, and future of sustainable finance: Insights from big data analytics through machine learning of scholarly research. *Ann. Oper. Res.* **2022**, *332*, 1199–1205. [CrossRef]
62. Khera, P.; Ng, S.; Ogawa, S.; Sahay, R. Measuring digital financial inclusion in emerging market and developing economies: A new index. *Asian Econ. Policy Rev.* **2022**, *17*, 213–230. [CrossRef]
63. Mpofu, F.Y.; Mhlanga, D. Digital financial inclusion, digital financial services tax and financial inclusion in the fourth industrial revolution era in Africa. *Economies* **2022**, *10*, 184. [CrossRef]
64. Lu, X.; Zhang, X.; Guo, J.; Yue, P. Digital finance era: Will individual investors become better players? *J. Int. Financ. Mark. Inst. Money* **2024**, *91*, 101935. [CrossRef]
65. Abdallah, W.; Tfaily, F.; Harraf, A. The impact of digital financial literacy on financial behavior: Customers' perspective. *Compet. Rev. Int. Bus. J.* **2025**, *35*, 347–370. [CrossRef]
66. Wei, F.; Xie, B.; Chen, M. Digital financial inclusion, e-commerce development and entrepreneurial activity. *Int. Rev. Financ. Anal.* **2025**, *97*, 103806. [CrossRef]

FinTech

Article

Exploring the Use of Crypto-Assets for Payments

Eleni Koutrouli * and Polychronis Manousopoulos

Bank of Greece, 10250 Athens, Greece; pmanousopoulos@bankofgreece.gr
* Correspondence: ekoutrouli@bankofgreece.gr

Abstract: This paper explores the current use of crypto-assets for payments, focusing mostly on unbacked crypto-assets, while selectively referring to stablecoins. Although some specific characteristics of crypto-assets, such as their price volatility and unclear legal settlement, render them unsuitable for payments, the rapid technological and regulatory developments in the area of crypto-assets-based payments justify monitoring developments in this area. We therefore try to answer the research questions of which/why/how/where/by whom crypto-assets are used for (retail) payments. We analyse and describe a variety of ways in which crypto-assets are used for making payments, focusing on the period from 2019 to 2023 in Europe and worldwide, based on the publicly available statistical data and literature. We identify and exemplify the main use cases, payment methods, DeFi protocols, and payment gateways, and analyse payments with crypto-assets based on location and market participants. In addition, we describe and analyse the integration of crypto-assets into existing commercial payment services. Our work contributes to understanding the shifting domain of crypto-assets-based payments and provides insights into the monitoring of relevant developments via various dimensions that need to keep being explored, with the objective of contributing to the maintenance of the integrity and stability of the financial ecosystem.

Keywords: crypto-assets; payments; statistics; DeFi payment systems

JEL Classification: E42; O30; O31; D100

1. Introduction

While crypto-assets were originally created with the intention of serving as a means of payment that dispenses with intermediaries, their use has not yet considerably extended beyond the crypto-asset environment. As mainstream attention to crypto-assets grows, we could potentially see an increase in the use of (certain types of) crypto-assets for payments. Such an increase could potentially have multiple consequences in the financial ecosystem and therefore should be studied. Indeed, the role of crypto-assets in the payments ecosystem has attracted a lot of attention and different views [1–4]. It is therefore important to keep track of the developments and trends in this area.

Advances in the relevant regulatory frameworks should also be considered. A prominent case is the entry into force of the Regulation on markets in crypto-assets (MiCAR) [5] in the European Union in June 2023, with full applicability in 2024, which could potentially impact the use of crypto-assets (in particular stablecoins—a category of crypto-assets that purports to maintain a stable value) for making payments. The MiCAR already considers the possibility of the potential wider adoption of stablecoins by retail holders and the risks and challenges that such a development would raise. Recital 5 of the MiCAR states that "It is, however, possible that types of crypto-assets that aim to stabilise their price in relation to a specific asset or a basket of assets could in the future be widely adopted by retail holders, and such a development could raise additional challenges in terms of financial stability, the smooth operation of payment systems, monetary policy transmission or monetary sovereignty". It is, therefore, important to also closely monitor and analyse crypto-asset-related developments in the field of payments and thus address the gaps in understanding the real-world use of crypto-assets for payments. However, such monitoring is often hampered significantly by the lack of official statistics and other high-quality data on the use of crypto-assets for payments.

Our motivation is to contribute to addressing the gaps in understanding this important topic as, on the one hand, developments in the field of crypto-asset-based payments are occurring rapidly and, on the other hand, there is a lack of necessary official data. We aim to create a clear picture of the current status of payments using crypto-assets, as well as identify the trends in this field and predict potential future developments. The existing research on the use of crypto-assets for payments has been based so far on qualitative methodologies and surveys, such as the works of Al-Amri et al. [6], Kayani et al. [7], and Busse et al. [8] and in a more general concept of crypto-assets adoption [7,9]. We therefore try to fill in the gap regarding the lack of data-based analysis. In order to achieve this, and considering the lack of relevant official data, we rely on publicly available and voluntarily provided data to analyse the current use of crypto-assets for payment transactions during the period from 2019 to 2023, focusing mostly on unbacked crypto-assets, while referring to crypto-assets that are stablecoins only where specifically mentioned. We consider that the use of stablecoins may need a further and separate analysis in relation to the MiCAR adoption [10]. Special attention is paid to the trends and developments in European countries. The main research questions are as follows: (a) Which crypto-assets are used for (retail) payments? (b) Why and how are crypto-assets are used for (retail) payments? (c) Where are crypto-assets used for (retail) payments? (d) Who uses crypto-assets for (retail) payments? The answers to these questions can offer an initial evaluation as well as a solid basis for further analysis.

The rest of the paper is thus organised as follows: In Section 2, we present the various categories of crypto-assets that can be used for payments (the "which" question), and the main use cases of crypto-assets for payments which show the motives for their use (the "why" question). Section 3 describes crypto-asset payment methods (the "how" question). Section 4 provides novel payment indicators for crypto-asset payments by economic sector and geographical area, to try to answer the question about where crypto-assets are used for retail payments. Section 5 attempts to answer the question of who uses crypto-assets for making payments. In Section 6, the paper provides insights into how crypto-assets are being integrated into existing commercial payment services. The conclusions follow in the final Section 7.

2. Crypto-Assets and Their Use Cases for Payments

The MiCAR defines crypto-assets as digital representations of a value or of a right that can be transferred and stored electronically using distributed ledger technology or similar technology (art. 3.1(5) MiCAR), noting that the representations of value include the external, non-intrinsic value attributed to a crypto-asset by the parties concerned or by market participants, meaning the value is subjective and based only on the interests of the purchaser of the crypto-asset (recital 2 of the MiCAR). While the MiCAR does not use the term stablecoin, it is generally understood that only asset-referenced tokens (ARTs) and electronic money tokens (EMTs) qualify as stablecoins, contrary to crypto-assets other than ARTs and EMTs, so-called unbacked crypto-assets. The MiCAR defines ARTs as a type of crypto-asset that is not an electronic money token and that purports to maintain a stable value by referencing another value or right or a combination thereof, including one or more official currencies (article 3.1(6) MiCAR). EMTs are a type of crypto-asset that purport to maintain a stable value by referencing the value of one official currency. The definition of crypto-assets in the MiCAR encompasses ARTs, EMTs, and crypto-assets that are not ARTs or EMTs. While the first two categories are generally referred to as stablecoins, the latter category is generally referred to as unbacked crypto-assets.

The broad variety of available crypto-assets unlocks several use cases for payments, such as payments with crypto-assets in e-commerce, stores, peer-to-peer transactions, payments for tokenised assets (such as digital bonds and non-fungible tokens (NFTs)), and a combination of other novel use cases that may cater to specific needs, such as micropayments and streaming payments. The following sections describe the main use cases for payments using crypto-assets.

2.1. Micropayments

There is currently no agreed upon definition of a micropayment. However, it generally refers to payments of very low value that are usually made in an online environment [11]. Enthusiasts refer to an up-and-coming use case for micropayments, machine-to-machine payments, whereby internet of things (IoT) devices can communicate payments autonomously. An example would be an electric car that automatically pays for the exact amount of time it parks in a certain location. These enthusiasts argue that the conventional payments landscape is not particularly well suited to these types of low-value payments due to the associated volumes, costs, and processing fees of the individual payment transactions. They assume that blockchain technology and other distributed ledger technologies (DLTs), which refer to technological infrastructure and protocols that allow for simultaneous access, validation, and record updating across a networked database [12], such as a Directed Acyclic Graph (DAG)-based ledger [13], have the potential to enable large-volume, low-value digital micropayments using crypto-assets. There are multiple DLT platforms on the market that seek to achieve efficient crypto-asset-based micropayments. Some examples of these include the following:

- IOTA [14]: This crypto-asset, launched in 2016, seeks to enable micropayments by using a DAG-based DLT. As the IOTA network does not use mining to validate transactions, this facilitates a feeless transaction model. The IOTA Foundation has presented some micropayment use cases, such as peer-to-peer (P2P) energy trading, for which its real-world adoption appears limited at present.
- Brave [15]: This is an opensource browser that offers its users the option to be paid for the ads that are displayed in the browser. For this purpose, a crypto-asset called the Basic Attention Token was created. The browser reported 65 million monthly active users and 10.6 million wallets in December 2023.
- The Lightning Network [16]: This is a Layer 2 payment protocol that allows for micropayments in bitcoin (see Appendix C). We note that a Layer 2 (or rollup) is a separate layer that extends a Layer 1 blockchain by executing multiple transactions and submitting them as a single transaction into the Layer 1 blockchain. By submitting the transaction data into Layer 1, rollups -leverage the security characteristics of the Layer 1. The use of rollups could reduce transaction costs, which could, in turn, allow for the better use of micropayments.

Crypto-assets could enable growth in the area of micropayments. However, most crypto-assets that support micropayments are still in the investigation phase. The adoption of these types of crypto-assets in the real world looks to remain limited at this point. This may be due to the blockchain trilemma: a crypto-asset must compromise on either the decentralisation, security, or scalability of a blockchain. As a result, if a blockchain is to perform a lot of (low-value) transactions at the same time, the hardware requirements of the nodes will go up, which leads to centralisation. One of the solutions for scaling blockchains is to have several layers of blockchains (Layer 2s), instead of a single one.

2.2. Streaming

Another use case where crypto-assets are used for payments is via DeFi payment applications. DeFi payment applications enable crypto-asset streaming. This is where payments are streamed continuously or regularly to a receiver based on a specified rate (the amount of crypto-assets transferred per second) and timeline (the start and stop time of a stream). The rate and timeline are setup in smart contracts. Crypto-assets aside, money streaming is already possible via existing banking arrangements, where automatic transfers of funds enable regular, periodic transfers between two (or more) accounts without having to issue further instructions after the initial instructions and authorisation. However, decentralised money streaming protocols, such as Sablier [17] and LlamaPay [18] (see Appendix C), enable crypto-asset streaming in a more granular way. They facilitate mainly continuous payments in relation to a provided service, such as salaries, where employees receive crypto-assets in real time for their work instead of on a monthly basis in fiat money, donations, and subscriptions.

2.3. Instant Payments/Instant Settlement

The advocates of crypto-assets emphasize their use for making payments with an instant or atomic settlement of transfers on a distributed ledger, including blockchains. This use case would be relevant, in particular, for the possibility of settling transactions in tokenised assets with delivery versus payment in real time on the same platform. Instant settlement, however, refers to the technical settlement of a transfer, at best. The legal settlement of transfers in crypto-assets is uncertain, and may not be settled instantly with legal finality. In Europe, for example, such transfers do not fall under the Settlement Finality Directive [19]. Blockchains are based on the "code is law" principle. Blockchains, therefore, have no visibility within the underlying legal framework that is applicable between the parties. The Lightning Network [16] and Flexa [20] are examples of decentralised payment software protocols that use blockchains and enable instant payments (see Appendix C).

2.4. Cross-Border Payments

A cross-border payment is a transaction where the payer and the payee are located in different jurisdictions. It often involves cross-currency conversion. These types of payments are currently complex in nature and they often prove to be expensive because of the involvement of multiple intermediaries, jurisdictions, time zones, and divergent regulatory frameworks [21]. Cost is not the only factor that causes friction in cross-border payments. These payments are much slower, less accessible, and more opaque compared to domestic payments. As part of the broader G20 Roadmap for Enhancing Cross-border Payments, the BIS Committee on Payments and Market Infrastructures (CPMI) assessed whether and how the use of stablecoin arrangements, if properly designed and regulated, and compliant with all relevant regulatory requirements, could enhance cross-border payments. The CPMI identified multiple possible opportunities that could arise from the use of stablecoin arrangements for cross-border payments, including the following [22]: (i) reducing costs, as a stablecoin could shorten long transaction chains by reducing the number of intermediaries; (ii) increasing speed, as the DLTs that underpin most stablecoins, are, by definition, available 24/7; (iii) expanding the set of payment options, as stablecoins could be an alternative digital option available for individuals who want to send or receive remittances; and (iv) improving transparency, as stablecoins would facilitate the better traceability of payment statuses in real time by making use of public DLTs.

Nevertheless, several challenges concerning the use of stablecoins for cross-border transactions have been identified ([22,23]). These challenges include the following: (i) the lack of a sound governance structure; (ii) concentration and monopoly risks, which could lead to a lack of competition and consumer protection; (iii) issues with data privacy, anti-money laundering, and countering the financing of terrorism; (iv) divergent regulatory frameworks across jurisdictions; (v) potential fluctuations in exchange values away from the par; and (vi) the inconsistent availability of on- and off-ramps that would allow stablecoin users to easily convert them to cash or commercial bank money held at regulated financial institutions.

Although there are some ongoing initiatives (see Section 7) at the time of the writing of this paper, no stablecoin exists that addresses all the challenges associated with cross-border payments in such a way that it would outperform existing cross-border payment rails [22]. It still remains unclear whether a future stablecoin would be able to achieve a setup where the benefits of executing cross-border payments via a stablecoin would outweigh the associated drawbacks. Moreover, the alternative of a CBDC (Central Bank Digital Currency) for the same purpose, which would inherently resolve many of the aforementioned drawbacks, emphasizes this open question.

3. Payment Methods, DeFi Protocols, and Gateways

In this section, we present the methods used to pay with crypto-assets and the specific systems that facilitate the use of these methods, specifically DeFi payment protocols and payment gateways.

3.1. Methods

There are several ways to pay with crypto-assets. First, consumers can pay for goods and services using a cPOS terminal. In this case, depending on the setup and what both parties to the transaction agree, the merchant can receive either crypto-assets in an electronic wallet or fiat currency.

Second, crypto-assets can be held in electronic wallets (digital wallets) with a payment function and then transferred directly between two wallets without the need of a terminal, where such a transfer would mark the payment for a transaction between a customer/payer and a retailer/payee, if they so agree. In such a transaction, the transfer of crypto-assets, constituting a value transfer in the eyes of the two subjects involved, occurs without the intervention of financial intermediaries. Once such a transfer is validated by the community of validators on the blockchain, the transfer is irreversible from an operational, IT perspective (unless a fork occurs). From a legal perspective, however, settlement finality would not be ensured until at least midnight of the day of the transfer. This is because transfers of crypto-assets are not exempt from the zero-hour rule [24] in those countries whose insolvency laws include this rule. The prerequisite for using crypto-assets to pay for transactions in this way is an activated digital wallet, which constitutes the tool for managing and storing one's crypto-assets. Various payment protocols have been developed to allow for the transfer of crypto-assets between two market participants (see Section 3.2). Wallets are also used in crypto payment gateways, which are platforms that aim to facilitate crypto payments in the retail sector (see Section 3.3), bringing retailers and customers together. Digital wallets are also used in various existing European payment solutions, such as iDEAL [25], Klarna [26], Swish [27], and Bankgiro [28].

A third way to pay with crypto-assets is to use cards. In general, crypto-asset payment cards work as follows: upon initiation of a payment order, this triggers a mechanism managed by a relevant exchange for the instant conversion between the customer's crypto-asset portfolio and the fiat currency. Conversion fees are charged by the exchange. This is called off-ramping, where the crypto-asset is converted to fiat money via card programs. After the conversion, the fiat money circulates on the card network before reaching the beneficiary of the payment. The exchanges, rather than any of the other parties involved, manage the crypto-assets themselves. This payment method allows the holders of crypto-assets to pay in fiat money while using their crypto-assets in all shops that are part of the card network. The management of AML-CFT compliance for this payment method is not clear, but appears to mainly rely on the crypto exchange, while the payment firm only conducts due diligence on the crypto exchange. Because of this lack of clear AML-CFT compliance, some partnerships have been terminated. For example, Mastercard ended its partnership with the crypto exchange Binance [29] in August 2023, while VISA has stopped issuing new Binance cards in the European market. As a result, the Binance card program in the European Economic Area ended on 20 December 2023 [30]. Nevertheless, VISA has partnered since 2021 with multiple crypto exchanges, resulting in a payment volume of USD 3 billion at the end of 2023 [31]. The Revolut card [32] also supports payments with crypto-assets. Revolut customers can link a Revolut card to any of their crypto-asset accounts. Upon the initiation of a payment order, their crypto-assets are automatically exchanged for the equivalent fiat amount via a partnership with a crypto exchange. This automatic exchange must be based on a preliminary authorisation and standing order from the Revolut customer to the crypto-asset exchange to exchange crypto-assets into fiat money whenever a payment order is initiated. Standard exchange fees apply to these transactions. However, the "link card to crypto pocket" feature is currently available only in the UK and Switzerland. Furthermore, one can receive crypto-assets sent by another Revolut user via the Revolut platform, allowing for payments in crypto-assets. Regarding the crypto-asset management rates, Revolut streams the prices from the exchanges they have partnered with and calculates a volume-weighted average price. The derived rate considers additional factors, such as market depth and volatility.

Fourth, crypto-assets can be used for making payments via payment accounts by instructing the customer's own bank. Some crypto payment platforms are integrated with bank accounts, allowing users to link their crypto wallets to their bank accounts and convert between fiat and crypto-assets. Some examples of crypto payment platforms that support payment accounts include the following:

- BitPay [33] allows businesses and individuals to receive and send crypto payments. BitPay also offers BitPay cards, which are prepaid MasterCards. Users can load their cards with crypto-assets and spend the crypto-assets (converted into fiat money) wherever MasterCards are accepted. Users can also withdraw money from ATMs and transfer money to their bank accounts using the BitPay app.
- Wirex [34] is a platform that combines crypto-assets and existing currencies in fiat money into a single account. Users can buy, sell, exchange, and store over 20 crypto-assets and fiat currencies using the Wirex app and card. The services and features supported by Wirex depend on the country and the applicable national legal framework. In some countries, such as the UK and the USA, Wirex offers cashback rewards (Cryptoback), bank accounts, and money transfer services. Users can link their Wirex accounts to their bank accounts.
- Crypto.com [35] is a platform that aims to accelerate the adoption of crypto-asset payments. Users can buy, sell, store, and earn over 100 different crypto-assets and fiat currencies through the Crypto.com app and cards. Crypto.com is a lending, gambling, and investment platform. Users can link their Crypto.com accounts to their bank accounts.

Fifth, even though not directly used for payments, consumers can use crypto ATMs (cATMs) to buy, sell, or send crypto-assets to others using cash, cards, or apps. Figures and charts on cATMs are provided in Section 4, while a description of the functioning of cATMs can be found in Appendix A.

3.2. DeFi Payment Protocols

Despite the fact that payments using crypto-assets can take place on most blockchains, coders have developed DeFi payment protocols specifically focused on payment functionalities like streaming, micro-payments, and faster processing, in an attempt to facilitate payments using crypto-assets. A DeFi payment protocol is essentially a set of rules and procedures implemented as a smart contract on top of a blockchain (usually Ethereum), that allows for peer-to-peer payments. These payments are recorded on the underlying blockchain. According to DefiLlama [36], DeFi payment protocols represented 0.5% of the total value locked (TVL) in DeFi at the end of November 2023. This equates to approximately USD 264 million (Figure 1). This could mean that only around 0.5% of all the value locked in crypto-assets is used for making payments.

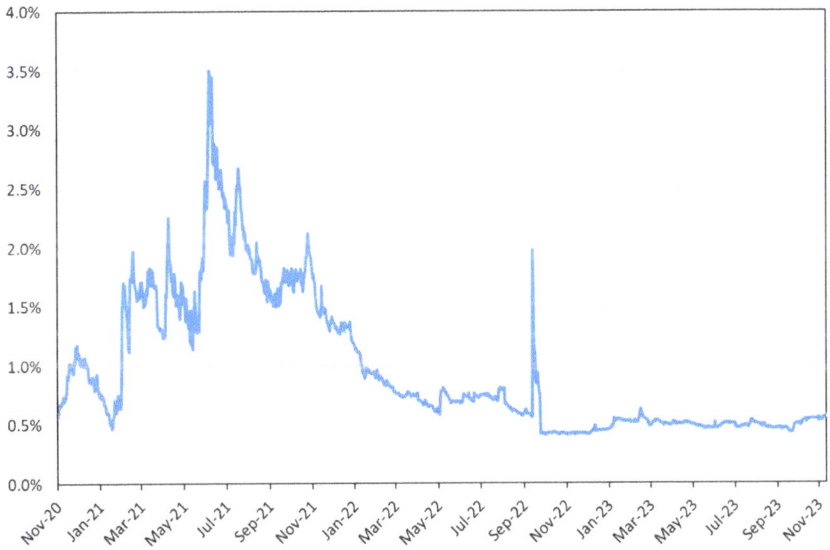

Figure 1. TVL of protocols for payments as % of total TVL in DeFi (Source: our calculation on DeFiLlama).

The TVL for payments reached a peak towards the end of 2021 and then declined. It remained quite steady for almost a year (end of 2022–end of 2023), at less than 10% of the November 2021 historical maximum (Figure 2).

The market for DeFi payment protocols is highly concentrated: four protocols (Flexa [20], Lighting Network [16], Sablier [17], and LlamaPay [18]) represent almost 100% of the TVL (Figure 3), with the first three accounting for the largest share. Two protocols, in particular, dominated at the end of 2023, the Lightning Network and Flexa, with shares of 74.53% and 21.52%, respectively, on 30 November 2023 (see Appendix C).

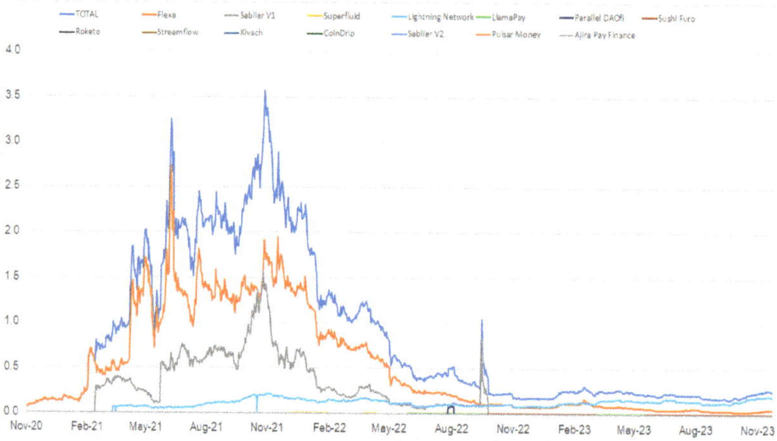

Figure 2. TVL for payments per protocol (in USD billions) (Source: our calculation on DeFiLlama).

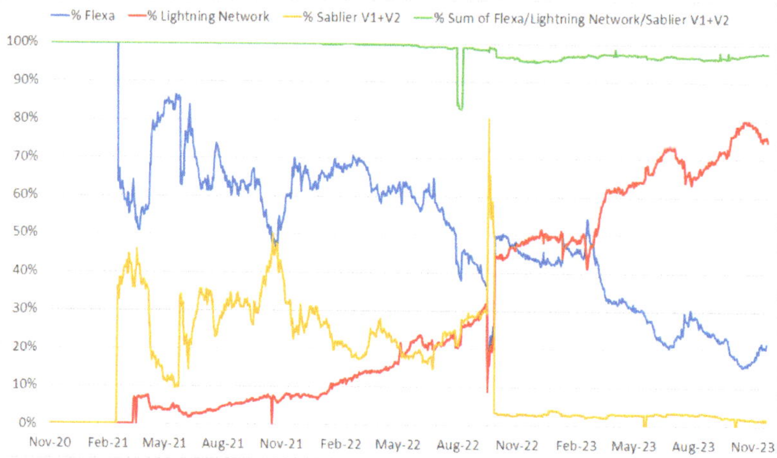

Figure 3. TVL of top protocols for payments as a % of all protocols for payments (Source: our calculation on DeFiLlama).

3.3. Crypto-Asset Payment Gateways

Crypto-asset payment gateways are new service providers that facilitate transactions between merchants and customers by processing payments in crypto-assets. They bridge the traditional financial systems and crypto-assets by enabling e-commerce platforms, physical merchants, and other market participants to include crypto-asset payments among their payment options. They offer functionalities, such as accepting and processing crypto-asset payments, real-time transaction confirmation, automatic conversion to fiat currency, wallets for storing crypto-assets, and the encryption of transaction information by utilising blockchain technology. Crypto-asset payment gateways integrate with e-commerce platforms point-of-sale systems, in particular, shopping cart software, and billing systems. They charge fees and provide dashboards to help track transactions. While these systems most commonly support bitcoin payments, some gateways also support alternative crypto-assets, such as ether, litecoin, and bitcoin cash. Some examples of crypto-asset payment gateways [37] are Coinbase Commerce [38], CoinGate [39], CoinRemitter [40], CoinsPaid [41], and Coinify [42]. Through a crypto-asset gateway, a crypto-asset payment made by a customer is credited to a merchant, from where it can be transferred to another wallet. For example, a Coinbase Commerce account is a digital account that allows merchants to accept payment in one of seven crypto-assets. Anyone can sign up for these gateways using a valid email address and a phone number, no matter where the customer is. It also requires the integration of two-factor authentication. A retail user can pay a merchant using a hot wallet. A hot wallet is a crypto-asset wallet that is always connected to the internet and crypto-asset network. This wallet shares a public key with a merchant, which the merchant then uses to access (debit) their customer's funds on the blockchain, while crediting their own account. Coinbase Commerce targets online service providers, such as Shopify [43] and Woo Commerce [44], and also freelancers and small business owners [45]. Businesses incur costs for (i) transactions due to the need to pay the miners of the crypto-asset network and (ii) for converting crypto-assets to fiat money, which can be performed using a crypto-assets exchange.

4. Payees—Geographical Area and Market Sector

4.1. Geographical Area

At the global level, the United States recorded the highest number (28,143) of cATMs in 2023, according to CoinATM radar [46], with more machines found there than elsewhere in the world. Canada (2803) and Australia (760) followed in second and third place. The UK, which was ranked 17th in 2022, fell to 61st place in 2023. This was probably due to the fact that the UK Financial Conduct Authority (FCA) has actively been pursuing crypto ventures in the UK. The FCA has been raising concerns about crypto-assets, in part due to the spike in interest in the crypto market that occurred in 2021, and because crypto-assets remain an unregulated product in the UK [47].

At the European Union level, cPOSs and cATMs are unevenly distributed. This may reflect the use of crypto-assets throughout the EU and the collective willingness to explore and integrate blockchain solutions into traditional financial frameworks with different degrees of adoption. In 2023, there were more than 1400 cPOSs in Slovenia and Italy, marking a strong presence in southern Europe (Figure 4a). There were over 500 terminals in Germany, Spain, and Hungary, while Estonia, Latvia, Lithuania, Sweden, Finland, Denmark, and Ireland counted less than 100 terminals. In the EU, cATMs seem to be less common than cPOSs, reaching almost 300 terminals only in Poland and Spain (Figure 4b). An analysis of Coinmap [48] and CoinATM radar [46] shows a growth rate of about 60% in the EU between 2018 and 2023 for both cPOSs and cATMs, possibly signalling growing interest in the use of these instruments.

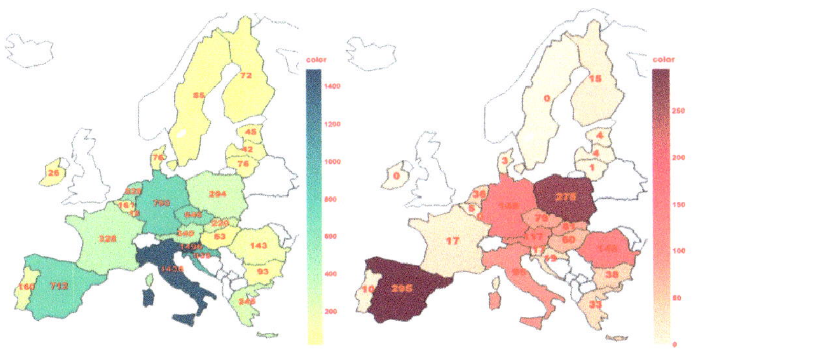

(a) (b)

Figure 4. (**a**) Distribution of cPOSs in the EU in 2023. (**b**) Distribution of cATMs in the EU in 2023. (Source: Coinmap and CoinATMRadar).

Nevertheless, the share of cPOSs and cATMs relative to the countries' populations remains very limited compared to the number of POSs and ATMs in fiat currency (2 versus 3573 and 0.6 versus 73—Figure 5a,b).

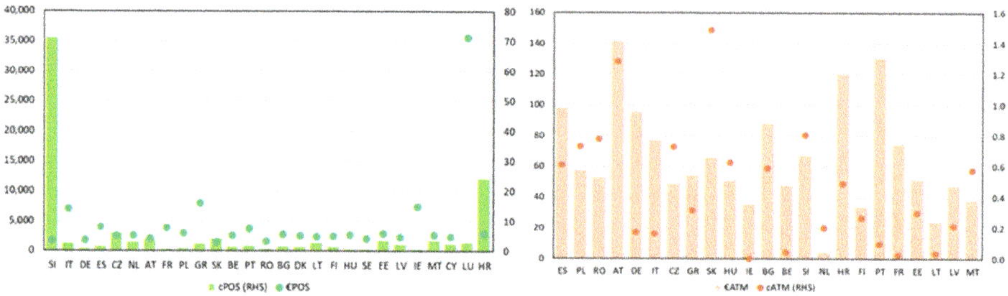

(a) (b)

Figure 5. (**a**) Countries' share by type of POS. (**b**) Countries' share by type of ATM (by 100,000 population). Data are calculated as follows: bars = number of € POS (or € ATM)/100,000 population; points = cPOS (or cATM)/100,000 population. Source: national statistics for population; ECB for € POS and € ATM; Coinmap and CoinATMRadar for cPOS and cATM.

According to the Study on the Payment Attitudes of Consumers in the Euro area [49], in all the participating countries, crypto-assets are primarily used for investment purposes. Lithuania, France, Latvia, Italy, Luxembourg, and Spain stand out as the countries with the highest percentage use of crypto-assets for payments (Figure 6). Beyond these variations, the differences between the countries do not lead to any other apparent conclusions. Overall, the use of crypto-assets for payments appears to be low.

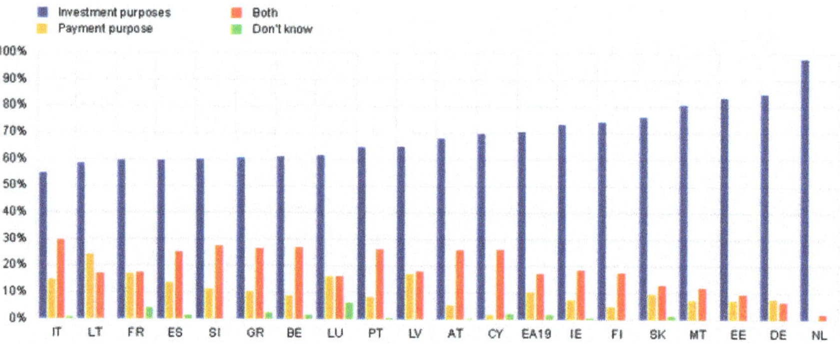

Figure 6. Use of crypto-assets. (Source: Study on the Payment Attitudes of Consumers in the Euro area (SPACE)—2022 [49]).

Figure 7 illustrates the breakdown of the number and value of online payments by payment instrument in the euro area. The four categories include payments by (i) card, (ii) credit transfer, (iii) e-payment solutions (encompassing PayPal and other online or mobile methods, such as Klarna [26], iDeal [25], and Afterpay [50]), and (iv) other (encompassing loyalty points, vouchers, gift cards, crypto-assets, and other payment instruments). The first three categories show a slight decrease between 2019 and 2022, except for a marginal increase in the value of credit transfers. In contrast, both the number and value of payments in the fourth category, including crypto-assets, show a significant increase.

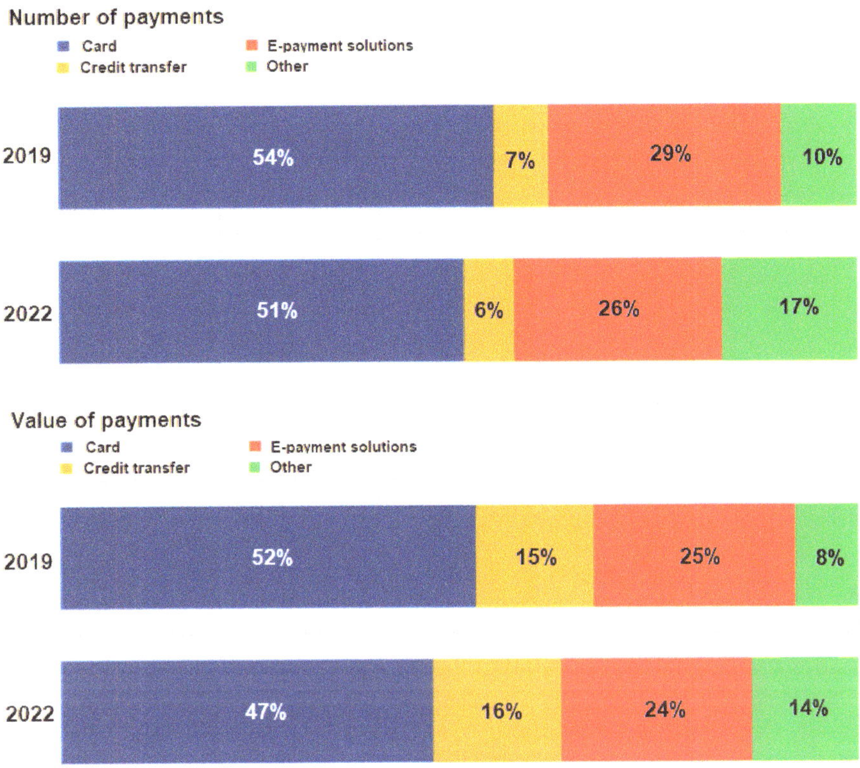

Figure 7. Breakdown of number and value of online payments by payment instrument in the euro area, 2019–2022. (Source: Study on the Payment Attitudes of Consumers in the Euro area (SPACE)—2022 [49]).

4.2. Market Sector

Those payees around the world that accept crypto-assets for payments belong to a diverse range; they are not restricted to a particular segment of the market. Bitcoin can be spent in shops around the globe and, according to bitcoin maps, more than 10,500 merchants accept payment in bitcoin [51]. Other sources support the fact that a growing number of companies accept payments in crypto-assets [52]. An attempt to categorise the wide variety and number of payees accepting crypto-assets results in a broad and varied list, including online market places, such as Crypto Emporium [53] and BitDials [54]; gift card shops, such as Bitrefill [55]; Microsoft; charity organisations, such as the American Red Cross; luxury fashion shops, such as Ralph Lauren; and e-commerce sites for managing inventory, shipping, and plane tickets.

Many of these merchants are stores that use the crypto-asset payment service provider and crypto-asset payment processor BitPay [33], which is based in the USA, and owns a European subsidiary based in the Netherlands. These merchants receive fiat money rather than bitcoins, and other crypto-assets paid as bitcoins to merchants are automatically exchanged for fiat money before they are transferred to merchants. On 22 February 2024, BitPay [33,56] claimed to have processed 334,486 crypto-asset transactions (assumed to be payment transactions) over the last six months.

In Europe, the merchant category distribution of bitcoin cPOS terminals shows that more than 50% of these terminals are placed in catering and service stores (Figure 8).

There are no data available on the actual use of bitcoin for making payments to merchants, either in terms of the value or volume of transactions. Furthermore, these figures must be considered with caution, as they were collected by Coinmap, CoinATM radar, and BTCmap on a voluntary basis, and include some repetitions and incomplete information on locations and merchant categories (see Appendix A for the dataset specification), which probably could not be completely eliminated, despite cleaning.

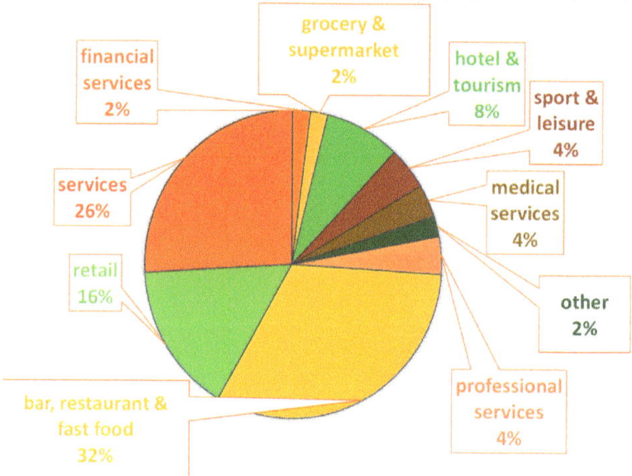

Figure 8. The 2023 cPOS market sector as a share of the total volume (Source: BTCmap).

5. Payers—Who Uses Crypto-Assets for Payments?

The ECB SPACE report for 2022 [49] mentions that the influence of crypto-assets on the payment landscape was not considered in the SPACE report of 2019. However, since then crypto-assets have spread, perhaps due to secondary effects caused by pandemic restrictions. In Europe, this may have been further supported by increased regulatory clarity, which could have affected consumers' perceptions of crypto-asset usage and payments. The monitoring of crypto-asset-related developments is therefore becoming more and more relevant.

There is no publicly available information about who actually uses crypto-assets for payments. However, data on ownership and use cases within the euro area are available [57]. Figure 9 shows the overall ownership by country, with the respondents indicating whether they hold crypto-assets (independent of the size of the holding in proportion to other assets the respondents may hold). The euro area average shows that a modest 4% of the population holds crypto-assets, with the highest percentage share being in Slovenia (8%) and Luxembourg (8%). In Slovenia, the highest percentage of crypto-assets is held by people in the 25–39 age group. Despite increased attention in popular culture and the financial markets, the uptake of crypto-assets by the population in general remains relatively low. Research conducted by the Dutch National Institute for Budget Information (Nibud) in November 2021 showed that 27% of young adults (18–30 years old) invested in (not paying with) crypto-assets [58]. Pos concluded in July 2022 that given the early stages of the discovery and establishment of the utility functions of crypto-assets in mainstream society (for example, as a means of payment or exchange), a negative relationship between its utility and the motivation to invest still exists today. In the future, when crypto-assets are regarded a more established means of payment, for example, this relationship may turn positive [59].

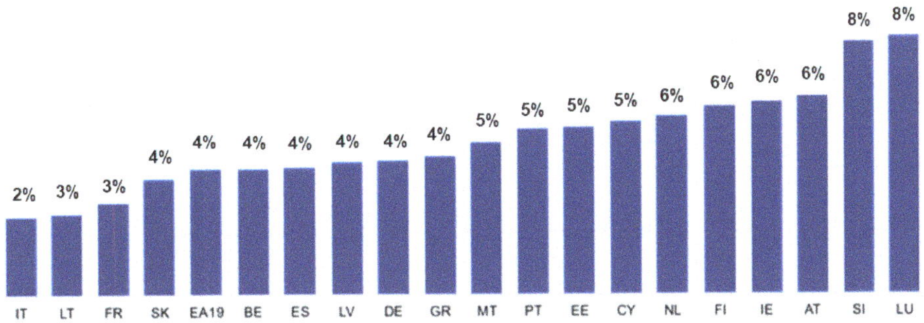

Figure 9. Ownership of crypto-assets (Sources: Study on the Payment Attitudes of Consumers in the Euro area (SPACE)—2022 [49]).

The individuals who disclosed that they held crypto-assets were asked about their use of them, either for payments, investments, or both. The results varied widely across groups, with a strong emphasis on saving for investment. In most countries, two to three times more individuals owned crypto-assets exclusively for investment compared to those holding them solely for payment purposes.

Examining the countries where investment predominated, the survey revealed that around 18% of French consumers used crypto-assets for payments, while 60% considered them an investment vehicle; in Germany, 85% held crypto-assets for investment purposes, 8% for making payments, and 7% for both. Conversely, 24% of the users of crypto-assets in Lithuania reported using them for payments, and 17% also used them for investments. While crypto-asset activities, including stablecoin payments, were observed across all eurozone countries, the reported use for payment purposes was trivial or niche by the end of 2023.

6. Existing Commercial Payment Systems That Incorporate Crypto-Assets for Payment Services—Interoperability

6.1. *PayPal*

PayPal [60] offers customers the ability to buy, sell, hold, send, and receive a range of crypto-assets, including bitcoin, ethereum, bitcoin cash, and litecoin. Customers can also use the proceeds from crypto-assets sales to pay for purchases at checkout. PayPal provides the option for customers to convert their crypto-asset holdings into fiat currency at a given exchange rate, which, according to PayPal's terms and conditions, is defined by PayPal. The platform utilises a single third-party custodian to hold customers' crypto-assets in PayPal's name in a custodial account. PayPal acknowledges the concentration risk associated with this setup, as stated in the annual report submitted to the U.S. Securities and Exchange Commission for the fiscal year ending 31 December 2022.

The PayPal crypto-asset service was initially introduced in the USA in October 2020, followed by its launch in the UK in August 2021. However, in October 2023, the purchasing of crypto-assets in the UK was temporarily paused until early 2024, to comply with additional UK regulation requirements. However, customers were still allowed to retain or sell previously acquired crypto-assets. Finally, the PayPal crypto-asset service became available in Luxemburg in December 2022. Table 1 and Figure 10 summarise the value of the crypto-assets held by PayPal customers in the USA (for raw data, please refer to Appendix B).

Table 1. PayPal custody of crypto-assets (in USD MLN).

	30/6/2022	30/9/2022	31/12/2022	31/3/2023	30/6/2023	30/9/2023
Bitcoin (BTC)	326	343	291	499	532	479
Ethereum (ETH)	219	290	250	362	369	316
Other [Litecoin (LTC) and Bitcoin Cash (BCH)]	51	57	63	82	115	82
TOTAL	596	690	604	943	1016	877

(Source: PayPal annual/quarterly reports to the U.S. Securities and Exchange Commission [61]).

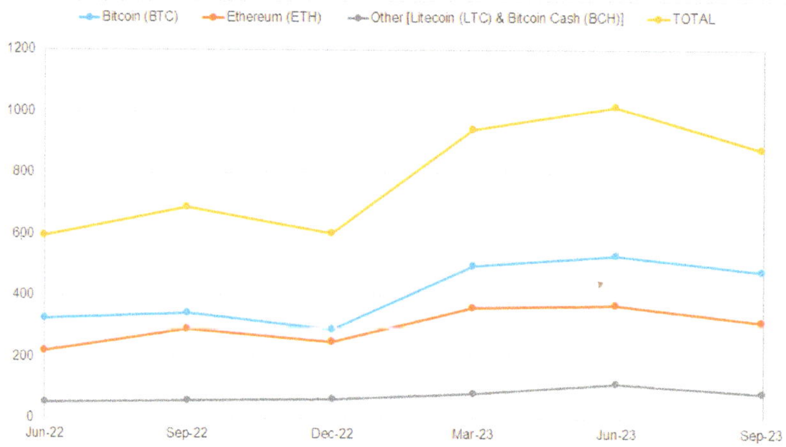

Figure 10. PayPal custody of crypto-assets (in USD MLN) (Source: PayPal annual/quarterly reports to the U.S. Securities and Exchange Commission [61]).

Using the daily prices of the crypto-assets, it is possible to calculate the absolute number of crypto-assets that are in the custody of PayPal (Table 2 and Figure 11, specifically for bitcoin).

Table 2. PayPal custody of bitcoin.

Date	30/6/2022	30/9/2022	31/12/2022	31/3/2023	30/6/2023	30/9/2023
Bitcoin (BTC) in PayPal (in USD 10 K)	32,600	34,300	29,100	49,900	53,200	47,900
BTC Price (Close/Last)	19,854.40	19,402.50	16,520.30	28,562.00	30,393.80	27,033.10
Number of BTC in PayPal (based on Close/Last price)	16,419.53	17,678.13	17,614.69	17,470.77	17,503.57	17,719.02

(Source: PayPal annual/quarterly reports to the U.S. Securities and Exchange Commission [61]).

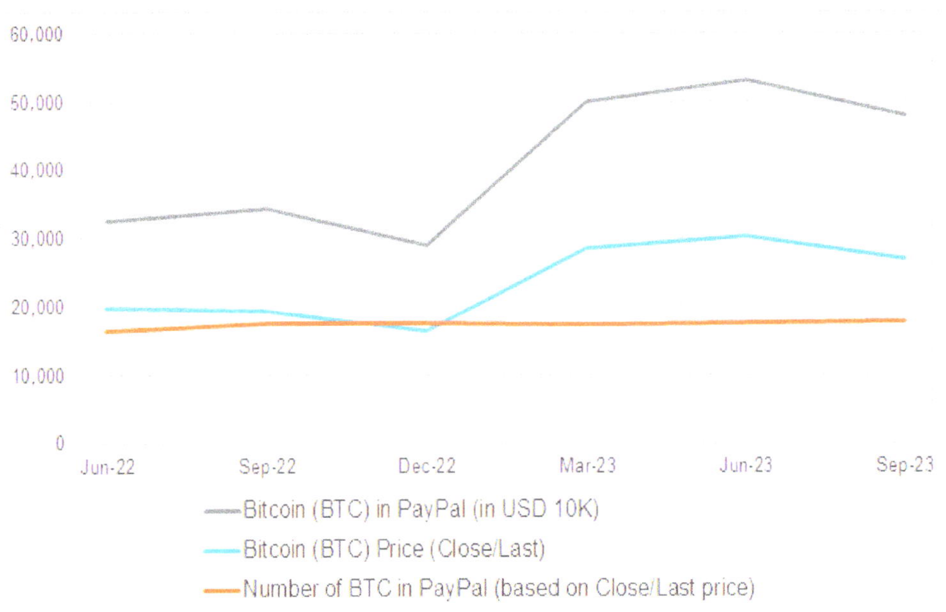

Figure 11. PayPal custody of bitcoin (BTC) (Source: PayPal annual/quarterly reports to the U.S. Securities and Exchange Commission [61]).

The value (in USD) of the bitcoins safeguarded for PayPal customers is closely aligned to the fluctuations in the bitcoin price. This results in an almost constant absolute number of bitcoins throughout the period covered by the reports. This lack of variation in the number of crypto-assets may evidence a lack of their use in/for payments and may prove that customers see crypto-assets as investments rather than as a means of payment. A similar, though milder trend, is observed for ethereum (Table 3 and Figure 12).

Table 3. PayPal custody of ethereum.

Date	30/6/2022	30/9/2022	31/12/2022	31/3/2023	30/6/2023	30/9/2023
Ethereum (ETH) in USD m	219	290	250	362	369	316
ETH price (Close/Last)	1065.10	1328.07	1192.06	1827.24	1919.41	1673.28
Number of ETH in PayPal (based on Close/Last price—in K)	205.61	218.36	209.72	198.11	192.25	188.85

(Source: PayPal annual/quarterly reports to the U.S. Securities and Exchange Commission [61].)

Litecoin and bitcoin cash are presented in aggregate in the reports. It is therefore not possible to extract the absolute numbers by their respective price. All the amounts/values previously presented refer to the custody of the crypto-assets owned by PayPal customers. It is not clarified within the reports which amounts/values were used for payments. However, since PayPal is an online payment solution, at least a fraction of the crypto-assets purchases may have been intended for prospective payments (when potentially their value could have risen more), and not solely for investment. The relatively flat curve for the number of crypto-assets, especially of bitcoin, over a 15-month period is worth examining in further detail. A potential explanation could be that the initial purchases of crypto-assets were not followed by sales or they were not used for payments. Alternatively, the initial purchases of crypto-assets were used for sales and/or payments, but the recipients of the crypto-assets were also in PayPal, so the total value was not affected. In August 2023, PayPal launched its own stablecoin, namely PayPal USD (PYUSD). According to PayPal, the PayPal USD stablecoin is fully backed by US dollar deposits, short-term US treasuries, and similar cash equivalents, and can be redeemed for US dollars at a ratio of 1:1 [62]. Initially, it was made available to eligible US PayPal customers and could be used for payments. In March 2024, PayPal announced that the users of its overseas money transfer app Xoom [63] would pay no fees if they used PYUSD to fund their transfers, in an effort to favour its use for international remittances.

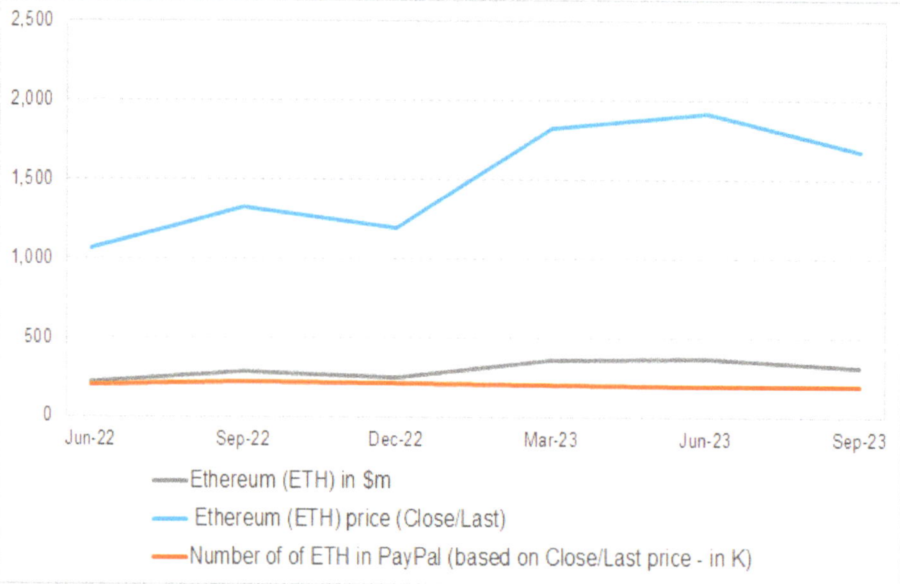

Figure 12. PayPal custody of Ethereum (ETH) (Source: PayPal annual/quarterly reports to the U.S. Securities and Exchange Commission [61]).

6.2. Google Pay and Apple Pay

Google Pay [64] and Apple Pay [65] are mobile payment services offered by Google and Apple, respectively, that allow users to make payments, both online and in person. Both Google Pay and Apple Pay encapsulate the underlying payment method [66], e.g., debit or credit card, by sending a virtual account number to the payee and not the actual card number. They are available in many countries around the globe, including all EU countries [67]. Google Pay and Apple Pay can be used to buy crypto-assets, either on compatible crypto exchanges, e.g., Coinbase [38,68] or Binance [30,69], or on crypto payment gateways, e.g., BitPay [33,56]. Moreover, payments can be made with crypto-assets by the following:

- Linking to a crypto debit/credit card, e.g., Coinbase card (VISA debit card) [70], BitPay card [71], Venmo credit card (VISA credit card) [72], or Bakkt card (VISA debit card) [73]. When such payments are processed, the crypto-assets spent are converted to fiat money.
- Using a payment gateway. A user makes a payment by connecting a Coinbase Commerce account to a bitcoin wallet, and then choosing bitcoin and Google Pay at the online checkout of a merchant that accepts bitcoin payments through Coinbase Commerce. Google Pay then sends the payment to Coinbase Commerce, which processes the bitcoin transaction and credit the merchant's account.

Crypto cards are available worldwide with different terms. For example, a Coinbase card is available in the EU [74], but does not support all the features that are available in the US, such as the cashback feature, while the BitPay card is currently available to US residents only. Since early 2023, Google has allowed users to pay for cloud services with crypto-assets [75]. This fact may be an indication of a potentially wider future inclusion of crypto-assets in Google Pay. Apple offers the Tap to Pay feature in the iPhone, which allows merchants to receive contactless payments from credit or debit cards, Apple Pay, and Apple Watch [76]. This requires only an iPhone on the merchant's side and no additional terminals or hardware. Since Apple Pay supports crypto cards, as mentioned above, this means that customers can make physical contactless payments to merchants using crypto-assets. It should be noted that the Tap to Pay feature is currently available in selected countries only, including the USA, the UK, and only in France and Netherlands in the EU.

The relevant statistics indicate a considerable level of Google Pay and Apple Pay adoption at a global level (Table 4). It should be noted that, although they are relevant for illustrating the level of adoption, these numbers do not illustrate actual payments made with crypto-assets at this point in time.

Table 4. Use of Google Pay and Apple Pay for online payments or at POS.

Google Pay			Apple Pay		
Country	**Stores, Restaurants, or Other POS**	**Online**	**Country**	**Stores, Restaurants, or Other POS**	**Online**
India	83%	79%	United Kingdom	70%	39%
United States	37%	32%	United States	59%	36%
Poland	34%	39%	Canada	63%	32%
Finland	32%	29%	Australia	53%	35%
Germany	31%	16%	France	63%	20%
Italy	30%	18%	Switzerland	40%	32%
Switzerland	29%	27%	Austria	51%	19%
France	29%	15%	Sweden	43%	25%
United Kingdom	28%	23%	Netherlands	41%	21%
Canada	27%	25%	Germany	46%	16%
Spain	27%	25%	Finland	35%	16%
South Africa	26%	26%	Italy	35%	13%

Source: Google Pay use per country 2023 | Statista (November 2023); Apple Pay use per country 2023 | Statista (November 2023) [77]. Percentages refer to the share of respondents who used mobile payments.

7. Concluding Remarks

In this paper, we explore the current use of crypto-assets for payments, taking into account mostly unbacked crypto-assets, while only referring to crypto-assets that are stablecoins where specifically mentioned, trying to answer the related questions that form the topic of crypto-asset-based (retail) payments: (a) which crypto-assets are used for (retail) payments, (b) why and how are crypto-assets used for (retail) payments, (c) where are crypto-assets used for (retail) payments, and (d) who uses crypto-assets for (retail) payments.

Our analysis thus provides rich evidence on various dimensions and indicates that the market for crypto-assets is volatile and fragmented, and that crypto-assets are mostly used for speculative purposes rather than for payments. Specifically, although crypto-assets, such as bitcoin, were originally intended to be used for payments in general, their price volatility seems to have prevented them from being broadly used for this purpose in practice. Indeed, this analysis shows a particularly low (and in specific cases stable) use in practice of these unbacked crypto-assets via the various available methods, i.e., crypto-asset payment protocols and gateways. Furthermore, this study of the literature shows that although crypto-assets can be used to pay in many shops and restaurants and to make peer-to-peer payments via multiple ways, the most prominent use cases for using crypto-assets as payments are the following: (i) micropayments, (ii) streaming, (iii) instant settlement for tokenised assets, and (iv) cross-border payments. We note that when used for payments, crypto-assets are oftentimes converted into fiat money. This means the actual payments are not made using crypto-assets. At the same time, our analysis regarding the payers shows that crypto-assets are predominantly held by younger age groups and this may hint at a potential broader adoption in the future.

Despite the current low volume of examined crypto-asset-based payments, this study of the ways to pay with crypto-assets and their adaption shows that the rise of DeFi protocols and collaborations between crypto exchanges and payment firms has expanded the usability of crypto-assets in everyday transactions. Moreover, the greater presence of cPOSs and cATMs in several countries may indicate that both merchants and customers are interested in offering and using crypto-assets for payments. However, the data for PayPal show an almost constant quantity of bitcoins and ethereum held by PayPal users throughout 2022 and 2023. This may evidence their lack of use for payments and may prove that users hold them for reasons other than as a means of payment or, alternatively, that the payees kept the crypto-assets in PayPal, so the total amount was not affected. The next steps in this line of research could be to analyse whether the use of crypto-assets for payments, for example using PayPal, is higher when the price of crypto-assets stabilises following a peak. This could indicate that users buy crypto-assets for speculative reasons and only use them for payments after they have realised a capital gain.

Due to the lack of official data regarding the use of crypto-assets, we have based our analysis on a combination of data from various publicly available sources and studying the developments and trends in this field. One such trend is the fact that some payment service providers are developing and integrating stablecoins into their services. The most relevant example is PayPal's launch of its own dollar-pegged stablecoin (PayPal USD). Given that PayPal operates akin to a big tech entity, in that it is deeply integrated into online commerce, with an extensive global customer base and expansive operations, it could easily and quickly scale up the use of its stablecoin.

We thus note that the current developments towards interoperability and integration with existing financial infrastructures, in combination with the entering into force of the MiCAR and other international regulatory developments, such as the current ones in the US, could potentially increase the interest in owning and using crypto-assets that qualify as stablecoins. Looking ahead, factors, such as regulatory approval, technological advancements, and expanding use cases, could drive the adoption of crypto-assets for payments. However, this would require overcoming a number of challenges, such as high volatility and lack of legal settlement finality. While payment protocols aim to address these issues, a broader adoption of crypto-assets also depends on regulatory factors.

We believe that fostering a clear understanding of the developments around crypto-asset payments and monitoring the various degrees of adoption throughout different markets could contribute to identifying the broader implications of using crypto-assets in the payment ecosystem and in maintaining the integrity and stability of the financial system. Our work aims to provide a basis for understanding the domain via various dimensions that need to keep being explored by the interested authorities and other stakeholders, keeping in mind that to achieve a thorough and comprehensive analysis of the domain, it would be useful to improve the quality of the data collected and to enhance data sharing protocols, as well as to establish monitoring capabilities that are in line with the MiCAR requirements.

Author Contributions: Conceptualization, E.K. and P.M.; Methodology, E.K. and P.M.; Validation, E.K. and P.M.; Investigation, E.K. and P.M.; Writing—original draft, E.K. and P.M.; Writing—review & editing, E.K. and P.M. All authors have read and agreed to the published version of the manuscript.

Funding: This research received no external funding.

Institutional Review Board Statement: Not applicable.

Informed Consent Statement: Not applicable.

Data Availability Statement: Dataset available on request from the authors.

Acknowledgments: The work presented in this paper is part of the work conducted by the Crypto-Assets Monitoring Expert Group (CAMEG) of the Eurosystem Innov8 Forum (2024). We would like to thank the members of the group—Ellen Naudts, Laura Painelli, Anton Gehem, Antonio Perrella, and Beranger Butruille—for their valuable contributions and help with this work. The views expressed in this paper are solely those of the authors and do not necessarily reflect those of the Bank of Greece or the European Central Bank.

Conflicts of Interest: The authors declare no conflicts of interest.

Appendix A. How cPOSs and cATMs Work

A transaction can be made at the physical point of sale (POS) [78] with crypto-assets in two ways: (i) through an exchange between two crypto wallets (wallet to wallet), where the transaction is validated by a blockchain (Figure A1); and (ii) via a three-party scheme. In both cases, the merchant enters the sum due in fiat currency on its device or on a dedicated physical cPOS device, and selects the crypto-asset with which the customer prefers to pay and/or is accepted by the merchant. A QR code or a public key is then generated through which the customer, using his/her device, can pay the sum due from his/her crypto wallet. In the case of a three-party scheme, an intermediary acts as the guarantor of the transaction on behalf of the merchant. The merchant can request the accreditation of the crypto-asset just used for the payment or the equivalent in fiat currency through their account.

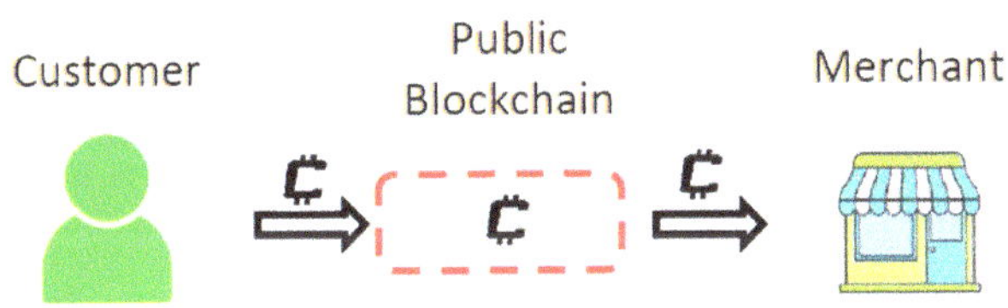

Figure A1. Crypto POS transaction.

The process shown in Figure A2 represents the three-party scheme, where a payer can obtain goods or services by transferring crypto-assets. An exchange accepts the crypto-assets and transfers them to the merchant with which it has an agreement. The exchange regulates the transaction with the customer on a blockchain and orders a credit transfer in fiat currency for the merchant through a financial intermediary (a so-called hands-off circuit in which the merchant never comes into possession of the crypto-assets). Alternatively, the exchange can send the crypto-assets to the merchant's account (hands-on circuit).

A cATM allows a user to make transactions in crypto-assets using cash, payment cards, or apps linked to traditional bank accounts. A user must register at the cATM, inserting a front/back photo of an identification document and providing a mobile number. Once the user has been verified, he/she will be able to access the service by entering his/her mobile number and typing or scanning the address of the wallet on which he/she wishes to receive the purchased crypto-assets. Finally, the user will insert cash or make a credit card payment in the fiat currency equivalent of his/her purchase of crypto-assets. The receipt issued by the terminal to confirm the purchase includes a QR code. This code contains the public and private keys and can be scanned and immediately recognised by digital wallet apps.

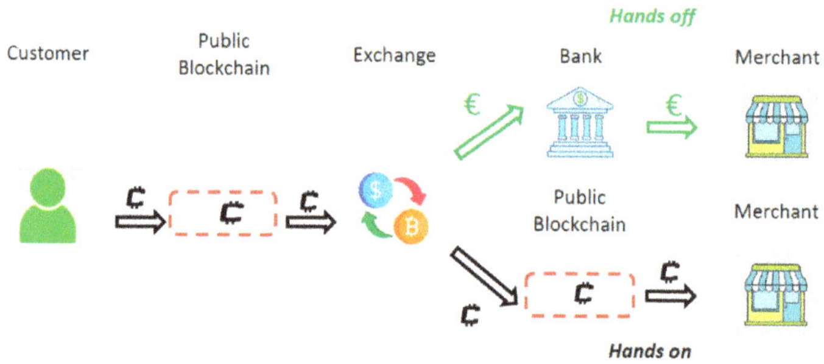

Figure A2. Crypto POS transaction with an exchange.

Two-way cATMs offer bidirectional functionality for both the purchase and sale of crypto-assets (e.g., Genesis Coin, General Bytes, and Lamassu), while one-way cATMs offer only the possibility of purchasing crypto-assets using fiat currencies (e.g., BitAccess). In the case of Bitcoin Teller, the transaction does not take place through a terminal but at a cash register, where the customer shows the QR code to a person to finalise the transaction.

The operators who manage cATMs provide liquidity to a terminal using a crypto wallet that is constantly connected to the internet (hot wallet). Liquidity is provided to a hot wallet from a customer's own capital (fiat currency or crypto-assets), through immediate mirroring operations with an exchange, or through a liquidity provider (Coin ATM Radar Blog).

The process, which is illustrated in Figure A3, is as follows: A customer initiates the purchase of crypto-assets in cash at a cATM. At the same time, the terminal accesses the hot wallet and sends the required amount of crypto-assets to the address provided by the customer (T1). The transaction is concluded and no further action is required. The operator periodically withdraws fiat money from the cATM (T2) and converts it into crypto-assets (T3). This operation can take place on an over-the-counter market or on an exchange. When the operator receives the purchased crypto-assets, it replenishes the balance of the hot wallet (T4), which will again be used by the cATM for other users' operations.

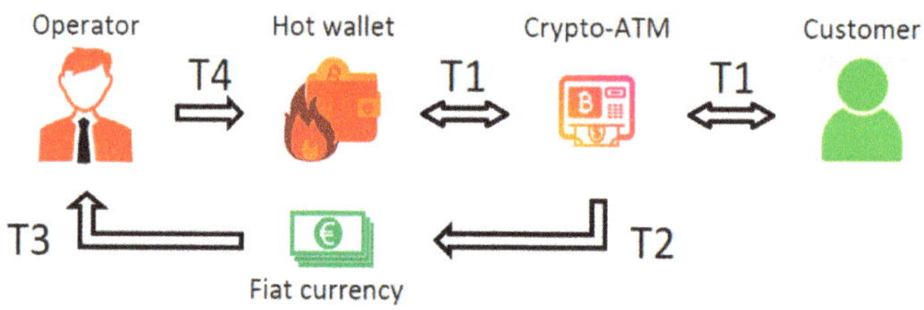

Figure A3. Sale of crypto-assets through own capital.

Another way of operating with a cATM is to hold a relatively small amount of crypto-assets in an operator's hot wallet (i.e., volume for 1–2 days), while the rest of the amount is deposited in fiat currency at a crypto-asset exchange (the same hot wallet can be supported by different exchanges). The process, which is illustrated in Figure A4, is as follows: A customer initiates the purchase of crypto-assets from the cATM. At the same time, the terminal starts two processes. On the one hand, it accesses the hot wallet and sends the crypto-assets to the address provided by the customer and, on the other, using an API connection, it sends a signal to the exchange (where the operator has an open account and fiat liquidity ready to be used for trades) that purchases the same crypto-assets on the market. All of this happens simultaneously (T1) to ensure that the price is fixed at the time the customer starts the process at the cATM. After the purchase is completed, the crypto-assets are sent from the exchange balance to the operator's hot wallet (T2) (the transition to the hot wallet can be omitted, and the crypto-assets can be sent to the user's address directly from the exchange). The operator periodically withdraws cash from the cATM (T3), deposits it into a bank account (T4), and then transfers it to the exchange (T5) via a credit transfer, making the funds available again in the form of fiat liquidity.

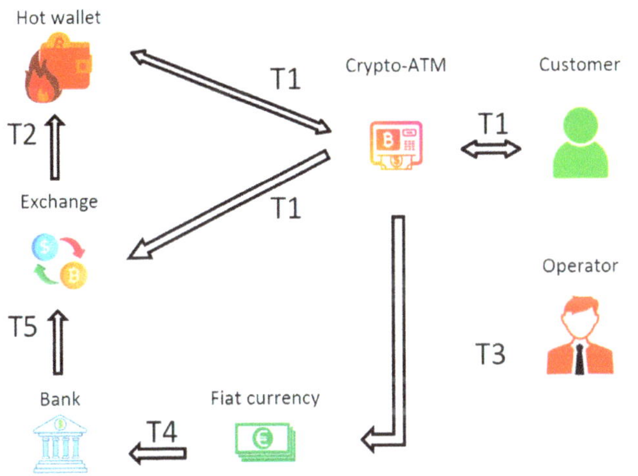

Figure A4. Immediate mirroring operations with an exchange.

This process reduces the volume of funds held in crypto-assets in the operator's hot wallet. The wallet can therefore have a very low balance, as it is replenished after each purchase. Ultimately, the process can be facilitated by a liquidity provider, who converts fiat currency into crypto-assets. The process, which is illustrated in Figure A5, is as follows: When the customer purchases crypto-assets at the terminal (T1), these crypto-assets are sent from the operator's hot wallet to the customer's wallet (T1). At the same time, information on the transaction is sent to the liquidity provider, who, without carrying out any transfer of funds, locks in the exchange rate for that specific amount (T1), giving rise to an agreement for that amount of crypto-assets. These agreements accumulate over time. The operator periodically (T2) withdraws cash from the cATM and deposits it into their bank account (T3). The liquidity provider receives the fiat funds from the operator's bank account for the value needed via a credit transfer (T4). It then carries out the conversion based on the amounts/exchange rates of the various agreements and sends the crypto-assets to the operator's hot wallet (T5).

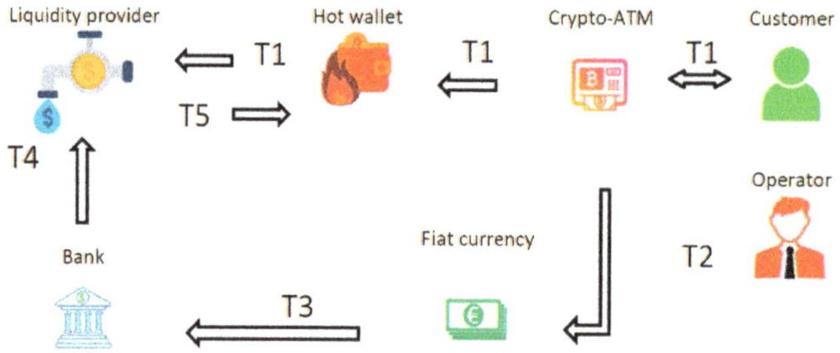

Figure A5. Operations through a liquidity provider.

Appendix B. Value of Crypto-Assets Held by PayPal Customers in the US per Quarter, 2022–2023

Table A1. On 30 June 2022, PayPal had USD 596 m of value worth in safeguarding of crypto-assets.

Bitcoin (BTC)	USD 326 m
Ethereum (ETH)	USD 219 m
Other (Litecoin and Bitcoin Cash (LTC and BCH))	USD 51 m
TOTAL	USD 596 m

Table A2. On 30 September 2022, PayPal had USD 690 m of value worth in safeguarding of crypto-assets.

Bitcoin (BTC)	USD 343 m
Ethereum (ETH)	USD 290 m
Other (Litecoin and Bitcoin Cash (LTC and BCH))	USD 57 m
TOTAL	USD 690 m

Table A3. On 31 December 2022, PayPal had USD 604 m of value worth in safeguarding of crypto-assets.

Bitcoin (BTC)	USD 291 m
Ethereum (ETH)	USD 250 m
Other (Litecoin and Bitcoin Cash (LTC and BCH))	USD 63 m
TOTAL	USD 604 m

Note: The decrease between September and December 2022 is probably explained by the significant decline in crypto valuations following the collapse of the FTX exchange.

Table A4. On 31 March 2023, PayPal had USD 943 m of value worth in safeguarding of crypto-assets.

Bitcoin (BTC)	USD 499 m
Ethereum (ETH)	USD 362 m
Other (Litecoin and Bitcoin Cash (LTC and BCH))	USD 82 m
TOTAL	USD 943 m

Table A5. On 30 June 2023, PayPal had USD 1.016 m of value worth in safeguarding of crypto-assets.

Bitcoin (BTC)	USD 532 m
Ethereum (ETH)	USD 369 m
Other (Litecoin and Bitcoin Cash (LTC and BCH))	USD 115 m
TOTAL	USD 1.016 m

Table A6. On 30 September 2023, PayPal had USD 877 m of value worth in safeguarding of crypto-assets.

Bitcoin (BTC)	USD 479 m
Ethereum (ETH)	USD 316 m
Other (Litecoin and Bitcoin Cash (LTC and BCH))	USD 82 m
TOTAL	USD 877 m

The following remarks apply to all of the tables above:

- The reports referring to the periods before Q2/2022 do not contain granular data on crypto-assets. This granularity was required by the Staff Accounting Bulletin No. 121 published on 31 March 2022.
- In all the reports, litecoin and bitcoin cash are presented in the aggregate.
- The crypto-asset valuation in USD is performed as explained in the reports: "The crypto-asset safeguarding liability and corresponding safeguarding asset are measured and recorded at fair value on a recurring basis using prices available in the market PayPal determines to be the principal market at the balance sheet date". According to the IRFS 13 Standard, the "Fair value is the price that would be received when selling an asset or paid to transfer a liability in an orderly transaction in the principal (or most advantageous) market at the measurement date under current market conditions (i.e., an exit price) regardless of whether that price is directly observable or estimated using another valuation technique".

Appendix C. Top Four Payment Protocols

Appendix C.1. Lightning Network

The Lightning Network [16] is a protocol for multiparty financial transactions with bitcoin. It was built as a second layer for bitcoin, facilitating "instant" micropayments without delegating the custody of funds to trusted third parties. (The Lightning Network was developed in an attempt to alleviate some of the drawbacks of the bitcoin network. Initial transactions confirmed on the bitcoin blockchain take up to one hour before they become irreversible. This is because bitcoin aggregates transactions into blocks spaced ten minutes apart. Payments are widely regarded as secure on bitcoin after confirmation of six blocks or after about one hour). The network itself is deployed on the internet and runs on thousands of nodes around the world. The Lightning Network aims to facilitate these "instant" payments on a blockchain through programmed automated smart contracts. This eliminates the need for individual payment transactions that congest the blockchain. Payment speed is thus improved and measured in milliseconds to seconds. The Lightning Network enables micropayments, i.e., payments of less than a few cents denominated in bitcoin (down to a price of 0.00000001 bitcoin).

Because of its claimed scalability (millions to billions of transactions per second across the network), the Lightning Network enables machine-to-machine payments and automated micropayment services that are not possible on the bitcoin blockchain. The Lightning

Network's features and usability may explain the increase in its TVL. Figure A6a,b) show the TVL of the Lightning Network from March 2021 to early 2024 in USD and BTC, respectively. These figures show an increasing trend in the TVL in BTC and fluctuations in the TVL in USD, which are most likely due to the price fluctuations of BTC. The TVL peaked in early November 2022 at USD 215 million. From October 2023, the TVL in USD was trending upwards, with the figure of USD 212 million in early February 2024 coming close to the November 2022 peak.

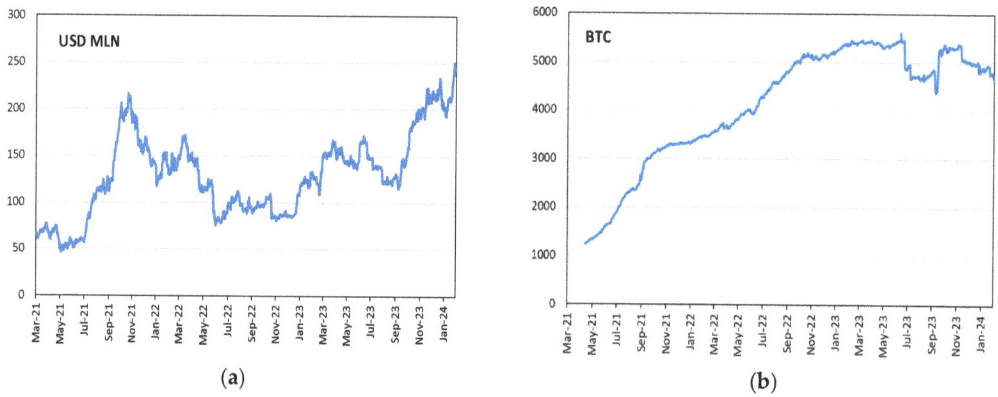

Figure A6. (**a**,**b**) Lightning Network TVL (Source: our calculation on DeFiLlama).

The Lightning Network may have accelerated the adoption of bitcoin, especially considering (i) the acceptance of bitcoin as legal tender in El Salvador in September 2021 [79], (ii) the broader adoption of Lightning Network wallets for use in payments and custody, and (iii) its integration with e-commerce and payments platforms. The Lightning Network is interoperable with other crypto-asset networks that hope to improve their own scalability. Whereas the Lightning Network is based on the idea of decentralisation, in reality, centralisation seems to be increasing, as the businesses that invest in the network control it. Other issues that have been raised concerning the Lightning Network are fraud, fees, and hacks [80].

Appendix C.2. Flexa

Flexa [20] is a payment protocol that is used in the United States, Canada, and El Salvador. Flexa claims to allow for the near-instant settlement of crypto-asset transactions. A payer can use a wide variety of crypto-assets. A payee receives payment in the local fiat currency. The protocol claims to offer secured transactions with a unique, digital authorisation code that cannot be decrypted or reversed. Customers can access the mobile Flexa Spend app to connect to the network and make payments using crypto-assets, including bitcoin and ethereum. A Flexa transaction involves generating a flexcode for instant payment in the chosen crypto-asset. Recipients receive the settlement value in the fiat currency without incurring conversion fees. A sample Flexa transaction flow is presented in Figure A7. The network's instant payment authorisations are facilitated by AMP, the network's native token, which serves as collateral for payment decentralisation. AMP rewards token holders with more tokens for providing collateral and securing successful payment transactions. The AMP token has a maximum supply of almost 100 billion ERC-20 tokens, with approximately 42 billion tokens currently in circulation. These tokens are secured on the Ethereum network; approximately USD 280 million of these tokens are staked or deposited in other DeFi protocols. Stakeholders can lock their AMP tokens in real time to secure payment transactions on the Flexa network, independent of blockchain confirmations. Unvalidated transactions can result in the liquidation of AMP collateral to ensure payment completion.

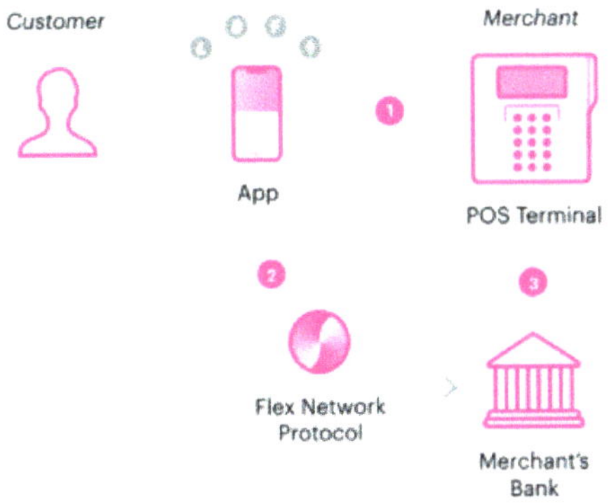

Figure A7. Flexa transaction flow. (1) A customer scans the app at merchant POS for payment with any crypto-asset supported by Flexa. (2) The app requests the current conversion rate for the customer's desired crypto-asset and submits a blockchain transaction via Flexa. (3) The Flexa network transmits a one-time authorisation code (FPAN) in real time to authorise the transaction on the merchant's POS terminal, then pushes fiat funds to the merchant's bank account. The customer's purchase is complete (Source: Flexa Network Whitepaper [81]).

Figure A8a,b represent the TVL of Flexa in AMP tokens in USD and ETH. The values increased in 2021 when the TVL reached about USD 2.5 billion. The TVL indicator for Flexa may represent the volume of transactions, since for each transaction the same amount of AMP tokens is locked by the protocol for reimbursing possible failures. The TVL of Flexa AMP tokens at the end of 2023 was around USD 80 million.

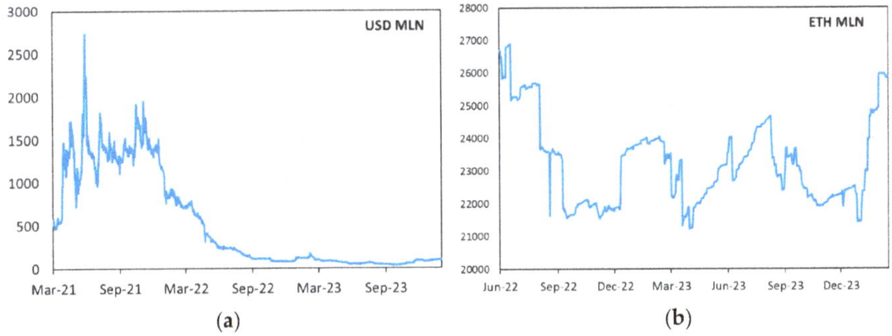

Figure A8. (**a**,**b**) Flexa TVL (AMP tokens) (Source: our calculation on DeFiLlama).

Flexa has a spending limit of USD 750 per week. Furthermore, crypto-assets cannot be withdrawn instantly from the app (off-ramp), other than to be used for payments. The app and the network also have operational issues and each purchase is taxable. The Flexa app has only been downloaded 5000 times in three years since its release in 2019 on the Google Play Store. This number is much lower compared to the number of AMP holders (about 96,000) and also to the anticipation of thousands of retailers. The use of Flexa seems to be highly concentrated in terms of the numbers of users and their geographical location.

Appendix C.3. Sablier Finance

Sablier is a protocol for real-time payments based on streaming. (Streaming functionality can be explained by an hourglass, with grains of sand steadily flowing through it. By replacing the sand with crypto-assets and the hourglass with a streaming payments application, such as Sablier, we have a clear understanding of token streaming.) After a payer makes an initial deposit of crypto-assets, smart contracts start streaming the crypto-assets to the recipient. The transfers occur automatically via smart contracts with a pre-defined frequency, e.g., a fraction of the entire contract value is transferred every second from the sender to the recipient until the duration specified in the contract has ended and the contract has matured. The payee can withdraw the crypto-assets that have been transferred to his/her wallet at any time and then exchange them into fiat money. Streaming services are especially useful for use cases such as payrolls, where employees receive crypto-assets in real time for their work, instead of on a monthly basis in fiat money. Sablier is also used for vesting (vesting refers to the gradual or conditional release of tokens to stakeholders, like employees, founders, investors, or community members), airdrops (an airdrop is a marketing strategy that involves sending crypto-assets to the wallet addresses of the active members of a blockchain community for free or in return for a small service, such as retweeting a post of the company issuing the crypto-asset), and grants. The Sablier protocol was started on the Ethereum blockchain and was later also enabled on other blockchains, such as Polygon, Binance Smart Chain, Optimism, and Arbitrum. Access to the Sablier payment service is provided via an application (dApp), which provides web interfaces for streaming money and for receiving the streamed money. The application provides integration with wallets, including MetaMask and Coinbase. Sablier is governed by the Protocol admin, a collection of multisignature (MultiSig) wallets (multisignature wallets require more than one private key and add a layer of security to crypto-asset storageccessed on 2 November 2024)). The distribution of tokens varies over time. Figure A9a,b show the distribution of the TVL of Sablier V2 tokens in November 2023. If vesting tokens (Vesting tokens are a type of digital asset that are gradually released to the holders over a period of time, according to a predefined schedule; they are often used to incentivise the long-term commitment and alignment of interests of the stakeholders of a crypto-asset project, such as the founders, team members, investors, or community members. Vesting tokens can have different terms and conditions, such as cliff periods, linear or non-linear release rates, and revocability clauses, and can affect the circulating supply and the market value of a crypto-asset, depending on the demand and supply dynamics. (https://coinmarketcap.com/alexandria/article/what-does-vesting-mean-in-crypto—accessed on 2 November 2024)) are included, the token with the highest TVL was TokenSight (TKST), a crypto-asset that was launched on 28 October 2023 for the TokenSight vesting program. Sablier V2 TVL showed a significant increase from USD 2 million to almost USD 50 million during that period. This increase can be explained by the launch of TKST and the TokenSight vesting program (https://blog.sablier.com/how-tokensight-leverages-sabliers-vesting-solution// (accessed on 2 November 2024)). More specifically, TKST locked up over 80% of its token supply in Sablier's token distribution protocol. However, the distribution of the Sablier V2 TVL in the supported tokens was different at the end of November 2023, after the vesting processes had started and the TKST tokens were unlocked and transferred to the vesting streams.

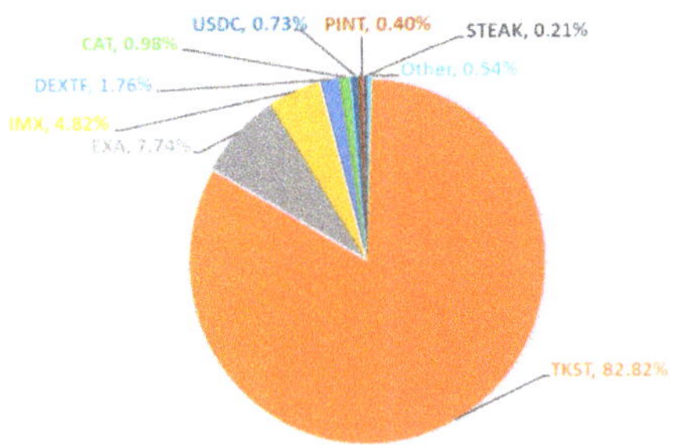

(**a**) Including vesting tokens (early November).

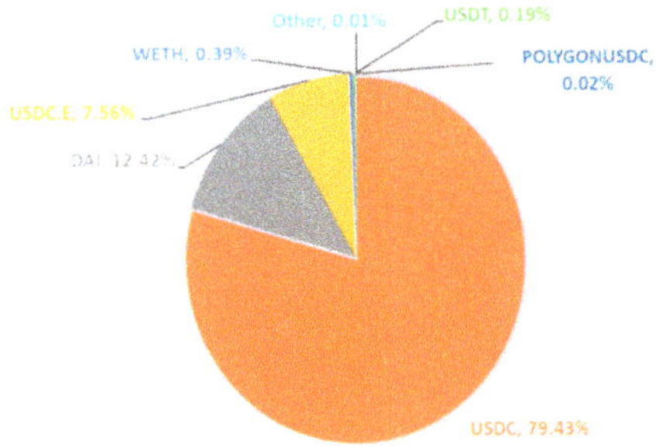

(**b**) Excluding vesting tokens (end of November).

Figure A9. TVL distribution of Sablier V2 tokens (November 2023) (Source: our calculation on DefiLlama dataset).

A different distribution of tokens can be seen for Sablier V1, which also varied over time (Figure A10a,b).

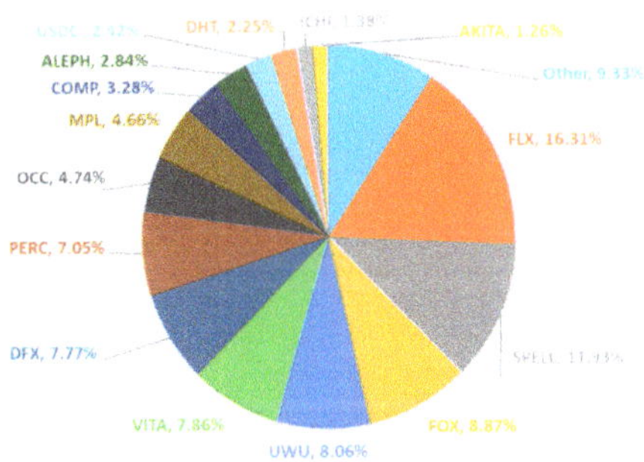

(**a**) Including vesting tokens (early November).

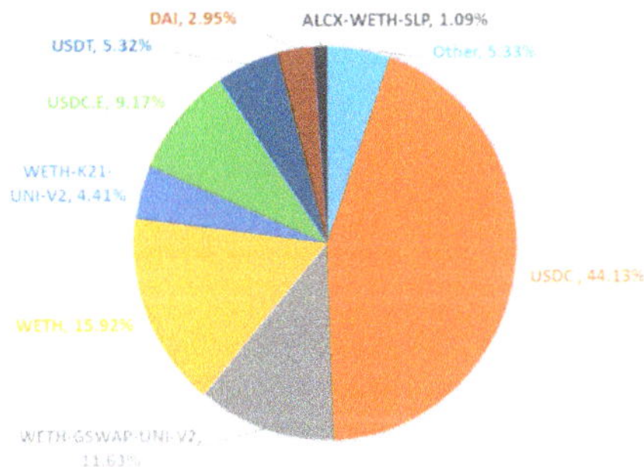

(**b**) Excluding vesting tokens (end of November).

Figure A10. TVL distribution of Sablier V1 tokens (November 2023) (Source: our calculation on DefiLlama dataset).

Appendix C.4. LlamaPay

LlamaPay [18] is a multi-chain protocol (Multi-chain is a process where projects deploy smart contracts across multiple blockchains, connecting isolated chains together as one network. This differs from regular chains, such as Bitcoin or Ethereum, each of which are individual chains. Retrieved from https://www.techopedia.com. (accessed on 2 November 2024)) that also enables money streaming. Unlike Flexa, the users (recipients) of Llama Pay can withdraw their received crypto-assets at any time. LlamaPay is used as an automated salary streaming protocol, where salaries can be paid to employees for every second they work. It is currently used by Yearn Finance, Convex Finance, and SpookySwap. Figure A11 presents its TVL, which was about USD 2.4 million at the end of 2023 (fourth protocol in TVL ranking of payment protocols).

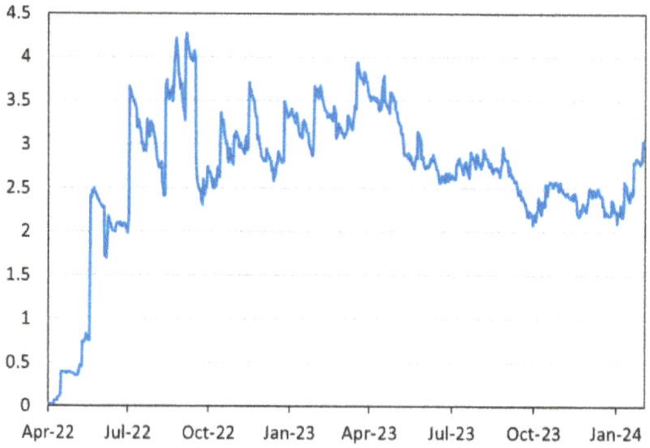

Figure A11. LlamaPay TVL (in USD MLN) (Source: our calculation on DeFiLlama).

References

1. Al Reshaid, F.; Tosun, P.; Gürce, M.Y. Cryptocurrencies as a means of payment in online shopping. *Digit. Policy Regul. Gov.* **2024**, *26*, 375–393. [CrossRef]
2. Bindseil, U.; Schaaf, J.G. The Distributional Consequences of Bitcoin. Available online: https://ssrn.com/abstract=4985877 (accessed on 2 November 2024).
3. Chaudhari, B. The Role of Cryptocurrencies in the Future of Global Payments. *IJCRT* **2024**, *12*, 65–73.
4. Adrian, T.; Mancini-Griffoli, T. The rise of digital money. *Annu. Rev. Financ. Econ.* **2021**, *13*, 57–77.
5. MiCAR: Regulation (EU) 2023 of the European Parliament and of the Council of 31 May 2023 on Markets in Crypto-Assets. Available online: https://eur-lex.europa.eu/legal-content/EN/TXT/PDF/?uri=CELEX:32023R1114 (accessed on 2 January 2025).
6. Al-Amri, R.; Zakaria, N.H.; Habbal, A.; Hassan, S. Cryptocurrency adoption: Current stage, opportunities, and open challenges. *Int. J. Adv. Comput. Res.* **2019**, *9*, 293–307. [CrossRef]
7. Kayani, U.; Hasan, F. Unveiling Cryptocurrency Impact on Financial Markets and Traditional Banking Systems: Lessons for Sustainable Blockchain and Interdisciplinary Collaborations. *J. Risk Financ. Manag.* **2024**, *17*, 58. [CrossRef]
8. Busse, K.; Tahaei, M.; Krombholz, K.; von Zezschwitz, E.; Smith, M.; Tian, J.; Xu, W. Cash, Cards or Cryptocurrencies? A Study of Payment Culture in Four Countries 2020. In Proceedings of the 2020 IEEE European Symposium on Security and Privacy Workshops (EuroS&PW), Genoa, Italy, 7–11 September 2020; pp. 200–209.
9. Okeke, N.; Achumie, G.O.; Ewim, S. Adoption of cryptocurrencies in small and medium-sized enterprises: A strategic approach to enhancing financial inclusion and innovation. *Int. J. Front. Sci. Technol. Res.* **2024**, *7*, 1–10. [CrossRef]
10. Adachi, M.; Bento Pereira Da Silva, P.; Born, A.; Cappuccio, M.; Czák-Ludwig, S.; Gschossmann, I.; Paula, G.; Pellicani, A.; Philipps, S.; Plooij, M.; et al. Stablecoins'role in Crypto and Beyond: Functions, Risks and Policy. 2022. Available online: https://www.ecb.europa.eu/press/financial-stability-publications/macroprudential-bulletin (accessed on 2 January 2025).
11. European Central Bank. A Big Future for Small Payments?—Micropayments and Their Impact on the Payment Ecosystem, European Central Bank, 2023. Available online: https://data.europa.eu/doi/10.2866/07262 (accessed on 2 January 2025).
12. Distributed Ledger Technology (DLT): Definition and How It Works. Available online: https://www.investopedia.com/terms/d/distributed-ledger-technology-dlt.asp (accessed on 2 January 2025).
13. Li, Y.; Cao, B.; Peng, M.; Zhang, L.; Zhang, L.; Feng, D.; Yu, J. Direct Acyclic Graph-based Ledger for Internet of Things: Performance and Security Analysis. *IEEE/ACM Trans. Netw.* **2020**, *28*, 1643–1656.
14. IOTA. Available online: https://files.iota.org/comms/IOTA_Use_Cases.pdf (accessed on 2 January 2025).
15. BraveSoftware. Available online: https://brave.com/ (accessed on 2 January 2025).
16. Lightning Network. Available online: https://lightning.network/ (accessed on 2 January 2025).
17. Sablier. Available online: https://sablier.com/ (accessed on 2 January 2025).
18. LamaPay. Available online: https://llamapay.io/ (accessed on 2 January 2025).
19. Settlement Finality Directive (Directive 98/26/EC of the European Parliament and of the Council of 19 May 1998 on Settlement Finality in Payment and Securities Settlement Systems). Available online: https://eur-lex.europa.eu/legal-content/EN/TXT/PDF/?uri=CELEX:31998L0026 (accessed on 2 January 2025).
20. Flexa. Available online: https://wiki.defillama.com/wiki/Flexa (accessed on 2 January 2025).
21. Committee of Payments and Market Infrastructures-BIS. Enhancing Cross-Border Payments: Building Blocks of a Global Roadmap—Stage 2 Report to the G20, July 2020. Available online: https://www.bis.org/cpmi/publ/d193.pdf (accessed on 2 January 2025).

22. Committee of Payments and Market Infrastructures-BIS. Considerations for the Use of Stablecoin Arrangements in Cross-Border Payments, October 2023. Available online: https://www.bis.org/cpmi/publ/d220.pdf (accessed on 2 January 2025).
23. Kosse, A.; Glowka, M.; Mattei, I.; Rice, T. Will the Real Stablecoin Please Stand Up? BIS Papers No. 141, 2023. Available online: https://www.bis.org/publ/bppdf/bispap141.htm (accessed on 2 January 2025).
24. ECB Glossary. Available online: https://www.ecb.europa.eu/services/glossary/html/act7z.en.html (accessed on 2 January 2025).
25. iDEAL. Available online: https://www.ideal.nl/en/ (accessed on 2 January 2025).
26. Klarna. Available online: https://www.klarna.com/us/what-is-klarna/ (accessed on 2 January 2025).
27. Swish. Available online: https://www.swedbank.se/en/private/cards-and-payment/swish.html (accessed on 2 January 2025).
28. Bankgiro. Available online: https://www.bankgirot.se/en/about-bankgirot/our-offer/payment-systems/bankgiro-system/ (accessed on 2 January 2025).
29. Binance. Available online: https://www.binance.com/en (accessed on 2 January 2025).
30. Frequently Asked Questions on Binance Card EEA Program Closure | Binance Support. Available online: https://www.binance.com/en/support/faq/frequently-asked-questions-on-binance-card-eea-program-closure-d6c54984df904db7a0705f2914827381 (accessed on 2 January 2025).
31. Blockonomi. Available online: https://blockonomi.com/visas-crypto-exchange-partnerships-led-to-over-3-billion-in-payment-volume/ (accessed on 2 January 2025).
32. Revolut. Available online: https://www.revolut.com/ (accessed on 2 January 2025).
33. Bitpay. Available online: https://bitpay.com/ (accessed on 2 January 2025).
34. Wirex. Available online: https://wirexapp.com/ (accessed on 2 January 2025).
35. Crypto.com. Available online: https://crypto.com (accessed on 2 January 2025).
36. DefiLlama. Available online: https://defillama.com/ (accessed on 2 January 2025).
37. Best Cryptocurrency Software: User Reviews. Available online: https://www.g2.com/categories/cryptocurrency (accessed on 2 January 2025).
38. Coinbase Commerce. Available online: https://www.coinbase.com/commerce (accessed on 2 January 2025).
39. Coingate. Available online: https://coingate.com/ (accessed on 2 January 2025).
40. Coinremitter. Available online: https://coinremitter.com/ (accessed on 2 January 2025).
41. Coinspaid. Available online: https://coinspaid.com/ (accessed on 2 January 2025).
42. Coinify. Available online: https://www.coinify.com/ (accessed on 2 January 2025).
43. Shopify. Available online: https://www.shopify.com/ (accessed on 2 January 2025).
44. Woo Commerce. Available online: https://woocommerce.com/ (accessed on 2 January 2025).
45. Finaloop Team—Accepting Cryptocurrency on Shopify. Available online: https://www.finaloop.com/blog/accepting-cryptocurrency-on-shopify (accessed on 2 January 2025).
46. CoinATM Radar. Available online: https://coinatmradar.com/ (accessed on 2 January 2025).
47. Vixio. Crypto ATM? It's Shutdown. 2022. Available online: https://www.vixio.com/insights/pc-crypto-atm-its-shutdown-says-fca (accessed on 2 January 2025).
48. Coinmap. Available online: https://coinmap.org/ (accessed on 2 January 2025).
49. ECB. Study on the Payment Attitudes of Consumers in the Euro Area (SPACE) 2022. Available online: https://www.ecb.europa.eu/stats/ecb_surveys/space/html/ecb.spacereport202212~783ffdf46e.en.html (accessed on 2 January 2025).
50. Afterpay. Available online: https://www.afterpay.com/ (accessed on 2 January 2025).
51. BTCmap. Available online: https://btcmap.org/map#5/52.92215/3.99902 (accessed on 2 January 2025).
52. Statista-Business Types with Crypto Payment Solutions. Available online: https://www.statista.com/statistics/1222768/business-types-with-crypto-payment-solution/ (accessed on 2 January 2025).
53. CryptoEmporium. Available online: https://cryptoemporium.com/ (accessed on 2 January 2025).
54. BitDials | The Crypto Luxury Marketplace. Available online: https://bitdials.eu/ (accessed on 2 January 2025).
55. Bitrefill—Buy Gift Cards. Available online: https://www.bitrefill.com/gr/en/ (accessed on 2 January 2025).
56. Bitpay Statistics. Available online: https://bitpay.com/stats/ (accessed on 2 January 2025).
57. ADAN; KPMG. Web3 and Crypto in France and Europe—Adoption by the General Public and Applications in Industries. 2023. Available online: https://www.adan.eu/en/publication/adan-kpmg-study-web3-crypto-france-europe/ (accessed on 2 January 2025).
58. Prins, C.; Groen, A.; Bos, J. Report on Young Adults and Investing, NIBUD, 2021. Available online: https://www.nibud.nl/onderzoeksrapporten/rapport-jongvolwassenen-en-beleggen-2021-2/ (accessed on 2 January 2025).
59. Pos, D. Motivations of Young People in the Netherlands to Invest in Crypto-Assets. 2022. Available online: https://essay.utwente.nl (accessed on 2 January 2025).
60. Paypal. Available online: https://www.paypal.com/us/home (accessed on 2 January 2025).
61. PayPal Holdings, Inc. Financials—SEC Filings. Available online: https://annualreport.stocklight.com/nasdaq/pypl/23608004.pdf (accessed on 2 January 2025).

62. Gould, A. PayPal Launches US Dollar Stablecoin. 2023. Available online: https://newsroom.paypal-corp.com/2023-08-07-PayPal-Launches-U-S-Dollar-Stablecoin (accessed on 2 January 2025).
63. Xoom. Available online: https://www.xoom.com/go/pyusd (accessed on 2 January 2025).
64. Google Pay. Available online: https://pay.google.com/about/ (accessed on 2 January 2025).
65. Apple Pay. Available online: https://www.apple.com/apple-pay/ (accessed on 2 January 2025).
66. Payment Methods on Google Play. Available online: https://support.google.com/googleplay/answer/2651410?hl=en&sjid=3186971403488779479-EU (accessed on 2 January 2025).
67. Where You Can Make Payments with Google. Available online: https://support.google.com/googlepay/answer/12429287 (accessed on 2 January 2025).
68. Coinbase Payment Methods. Available online: https://help.coinbase.com/en/coinbase/getting-started/add-a-payment-method/add-and-verify-pm-emea (accessed on 2 January 2025).
69. How to Buy Crypto with Apple Pay and Google Pay on Binance? Available online: https://www.binance.com/en/support/faq/how-to-buy-crypto-with-apple-pay-and-google-pay-on-binance-7e6749400a1049aaa5430f1451d82a95 (accessed on 2 January 2025).
70. Coinbase Card. Available online: https://help.coinbase.com/en/coinbase/trading-and-funding/coinbase-card/use-cb-card (accessed on 2 January 2025).
71. BitPay Crypto Wallet App: Buy, Swap & Spend Securely BitPay Crypto Wallet App. Available online: https://www.bitpay.com/wallet (accessed on 2 January 2025).
72. Venmo Credit Card | Venmo. Available online: https://venmo.com/about/creditcard/ (accessed on 2 January 2025).
73. Bakkt Debid Card. Available online: https://cryptonews.net/news/market/2160071/ (accessed on 2 January 2025).
74. Coinbase Card for the EU. Available online: https://help.coinbase.com/en/coinbase/trading-and-funding/other/coinbase-card-faq (accessed on 2 January 2025).
75. Google Partners with Coinbase to Bring Crypto Payments to Cloud Services. Available online: https://www.investopedia.com/google-partners-coinbase-6749264 (accessed on 2 January 2025).
76. Tap to Pay on iPhone. Available online: https://developer.apple.com/tap-to-pay/ (accessed on 2 January 2025).
77. Statista. Available online: https://www.statista.com/ (accessed on 2 January 2025).
78. Brandi, M.; Painelli, L. *Funzionamento dei Cripto POS e dei Crypto ATM*; Mimeo; Bank of Italy: Rome, Italy, 2023.
79. Bitcoin Magazine. Available online: https://bitcoinmagazine.com/markets/lightning-network-bitcoin-usage-adoption-el-salvador (accessed on 2 January 2025).
80. Kiwitech. Available online: https://www.kiwitech.com/blog/everything-you-need-to-know-about-the-bitcoin-lightning-network/ (accessed on 2 January 2025).
81. Flexa Network Whitepaper. Available online: https://flexa.network/whitepaper.pdf (accessed on 2 January 2025).

FinTech

MDPI

Article

Racial Disparities in Conforming Mortgage Lending: A Comparative Study of Fintech and Traditional Lenders Under Regulatory Oversight

Zilong Liu * and Hongyan Liang

Department of Business Administration, Gies College of Business, University of Illinois Urbana-Champaign, Champaign, IL 61820, USA; liangh@illinois.edu
* Correspondence: zilongl@illinois.edu

Abstract: This study examines racial and ethnic disparities in mortgage-lending outcomes across different lender types—large banks, fintech lenders, non-bank lenders, small banks, and credit unions—using Home Mortgage Disclosure Act (HMDA) data from 2018 to 2023. By analyzing approval rates, rate spreads, and origination charges, we evaluate how borrower outcomes vary by race and ethnicity, controlling for loan characteristics, borrower attributes, and regional factors. Our findings reveal that Black and Hispanic borrowers consistently face less favorable terms than White borrowers, with disparities differing by lender type. Large banks, operating under stringent regulatory oversight, demonstrate relatively equitable pricing but impose higher loan denial rates on minorities. Credit unions, despite offering the lowest rate spreads overall, penalize minority borrowers more severely in pricing than other lender types. Fintech lenders, while charging higher-rate spreads and fees, show smaller credit access disparities for minority borrowers. Non-bank and small banks display mixed results, with inconsistencies in their treatment of minorities across pricing and credit access. These results highlight that neither technological innovations nor alternative lending models alone suffice to eliminate systemic inequities. Achieving equitable mortgage lending requires enhanced regulatory oversight, greater transparency in algorithmic decision-making, and stricter enforcement of fair lending practices.

Keywords: mortgage lending; racial disparities; fintech lenders; regulatory oversight; fair lending

JEL Classification: G21; D14; R31; L86; J15

1. Introduction

Racial and ethnic disparities in U.S. mortgage lending have persisted despite decades of policy attention and regulatory oversight. Prior research demonstrates that Black and Hispanic borrowers often confront higher denial rates, elevated interest rates, and greater financial burdens than their White counterparts, even when controlling for creditworthiness and other relevant factors [1–3]. Such disparities restrict homeownership opportunities, impede wealth accumulation, and undermine the goals of fair lending laws designed to promote equity and inclusion [4,5].

The mortgage market has evolved dramatically over the past decade, with non-bank and fintech lenders capturing a growing share of originations [6–8]. Proponents argue that fintech innovations, by leveraging technology, can bridge financial divides and promote inclusion, potentially reducing racial and ethnic disparities in lending [9]. Although fintech algorithms and online platforms can expedite processing and potentially reduce some forms of human bias, recent research shows that these tools do not inherently eliminate racial disparities and may, in some cases, entrench them in pricing models [10,11]. Non-bank lenders, operating with lighter regulatory constraints, may likewise perpetuate inequities due to their pricing structures and reliance on alternative risk-assessment strategies [12].

In contrast, large banks—traditionally subject to more rigorous regulatory scrutiny, comprehensive examinations, and robust compliance mandates—may face stronger incentives to adhere to fair lending standards. Heightened supervisory pressure, combined with standardized underwriting systems, may limit the scope for discretionary bias and lead to more equitable lending outcomes, as recent evidence suggests [5,7].

This study contributes to the ongoing debate over how lender type and regulatory environment shape the experiences of minority borrowers in the U.S. mortgage market. Using Home Mortgage Disclosure Act (HMDA) data from 2018 to 2023, we analyze disparities in loan approval rates, rate spreads, and origination charges across credit unions, fintech lenders, large banks, non-bank lenders, and small banks, controlling for borrower- and loan-level characteristics, as well as geographic and temporal factors. Focusing on three critical dimensions of mortgage lending—credit access, pricing strategies (rate spreads), and loan costs (origination charges)—we uncover distinct patterns across lender types that underscore the complexity of addressing disparities.

Large banks, operating under stringent regulatory oversight, emerge as relatively equitable benchmarks in terms of rate spreads, often showing less pronounced pricing disparities for minority borrowers compared to White borrowers. However, their stringent credit-access criteria result in significantly higher denial rates for minorities, limiting their inclusivity. Credit unions, despite offering the lowest overall rate spreads, paradoxically impose the steepest penalties on minority borrowers, particularly Black and Hispanic applicants, raising concerns about inequities in their pricing practices. Fintech lenders, although more expensive in some respects, impose fewer minority-specific penalties and improve approval odds for minority borrowers compared to large banks. Meanwhile, non-bank lenders and small banks produce more varied outcomes, at times narrowing disparities but often failing to eliminate them in either pricing or loan costs.

These findings reveal that the proliferation of new lender types and the emergence of algorithmic decision-making tools do not inherently guarantee more equitable lending practices. While some lenders improve access or reduce specific penalties, persistent disparities remain, highlighting the limitations of market-driven solutions. Addressing these systemic inequities requires sustained policy interventions, robust regulatory oversight, transparent and unbiased underwriting algorithms, and a continued commitment to enforcing fair lending laws. Ultimately, this study underscores the need for a multifaceted approach to ensure fair and equitable access to mortgage credit for all borrowers.

Furthermore, our study contributes to the literature by providing the first comprehensive analysis of racial disparities across five lender types using HMDA data from 2018–2023. Unlike prior work focusing solely on one or two lender types or eras, we reveal nuanced patterns in credit access, pricing, and costs across large banks, fintech lenders, credit unions, non-bank lenders, and small banks. Our findings shed light on the limits of technological innovation in addressing systemic inequities and underscore the critical role of enhanced regulatory frameworks.

In light of these persistent disparities and the evolving landscape of mortgage lending, this paper tests the following two hypotheses:

Hypothesis 1. *(approval disparities): Even after controlling for borrower creditworthiness (e.g., loan-to-value ratios, income, and debt-to-income ratios), Black and Hispanic borrowers will exhibit* *lower loan approval rates than White borrowers, and the magnitude of these disparities will vary by lender type (e.g., large banks, fintechs, non-banks, small banks, and credit unions).*

Hypothesis 2. *(cost disparities): Conditional on loan approval, Black and Hispanic borrowers will face higher borrowing costs (e.g., rate spreads and/or origination charges) than similarly qualified White borrowers, with varying degrees of pricing penalties observed across different lender types.*

By empirically evaluating these two hypotheses, we aim to ascertain whether newer lending models, such as fintech, can mitigate racial and ethnic disparities, or whether existing biases merely manifest in different ways under varying regulatory and operational structures.

2. Literature Review

A large body of research documents show persistent racial and ethnic disparities in the U.S. mortgage market. Foundational studies have established that, when controlling for creditworthiness and borrower characteristics, Black and Hispanic applicants are more likely to be denied loans, to be charged higher interest rates, and to face steeper financial costs than similarly situated White borrowers [2,3,13]. Subsequent work continues to confirm these patterns, underscoring that racial disparities in mortgage lending are neither historical relics nor solely attributable to observable risk factors [1,5].

Against this backdrop, transformations in the mortgage industry have prompted new lines of inquiry. Non-bank lenders have surged in market share, raising concerns that their less stringent regulatory environment may facilitate new or persistent forms of discrimination [6,12]. While some non-bank lenders broaden access, they often do so at higher cost or under less transparent pricing regimes, potentially widening disparities for minority borrowers [7].

Fintech lending has also attracted scrutiny. Proponents of fintech argue that automated decision-making, driven by data and algorithms, can minimize human bias in credit decisions [9]. Yet, empirical evidence suggests that algorithmic models may simply replicate existing biases, leading to persistent, if more subtly embedded, inequities in interest rates and other loan terms [10,11,14]. Thus, while fintech innovations may streamline application processes, they do not inherently guarantee more equitable outcomes.

The expansion of fintech lending platforms has reshaped mortgage markets, yet persistent disparities remain across racial and ethnic groups. Haupert [15] investigates the relationship between fintech mortgage lending and metropolitan segregation, revealing that fintech lenders are less likely to issue subprime loans than traditional lenders in areas with high Black segregation, but disparities persist, especially among Hispanic borrowers. This aligns with findings from Fourcade and Healy [16], who argue that algorithmic scoring systems, while seemingly neutral, often reinforce existing social stratifications by using vast amounts of consumer data to categorize and rank individuals. Additionally, the racial landscape of fintech lending, as examined by Haupert [17], indicates that while fintech lenders reduce racial disparities in loan approvals compared to traditional lenders, they continue to distribute subprime credit disproportionately to minority neighborhoods. These insights underscore the need for regulatory scrutiny to ensure fintech models do not perpetuate systemic biases under the guise of algorithmic neutrality.

In contrast, large banks—often subject to more intensive oversight and compliance demands—provide a useful point of comparison. Regulatory examinations by agencies like the Office of the Comptroller of the Currency (OCC), the Federal Reserve, and the Consumer Financial Protection Bureau (CFPB) can incentivize these institutions to implement standardized, risk-based underwriting procedures; reduce discretion; and more rigorously comply with the Equal Credit Opportunity Act (ECOA) and the Fair Housing

Act [5]. This more stringent regulatory environment may help large banks produce more equitable results, as they have both the infrastructure and the incentives to align their lending practices with fair lending norms.

Credit unions, small banks, and other community-based institutions, which often rely on relationship lending or localized discretion, might be expected to serve minority borrowers effectively. Yet, studies suggest that personalized decision-making can introduce subjectivity and bias, undermining equitable outcomes [13]. Thus, even lenders with ostensibly community-focused missions may inadvertently perpetuate disparities if they rely on less standardized assessment tools.

The historical context of mortgage-lending disparities reveals entrenched patterns of racial exclusion and financial exploitation. Faber [18] examined subprime lending during the peak of the housing boom and found that Black and Latino borrowers were disproportionately targeted for high-cost loans, even among wealthier minority applicants who would have qualified for prime loans. This pattern, where higher-income minorities were still subjected to subprime terms, underscores how structural inequities persisted in mortgage pricing. Similarly, Hammel and Nilsson [19] analyzed the aftermath of the foreclosure crisis and highlighted that high-foreclosure minority neighborhoods faced sustained barriers to mortgage credit access, with significantly higher loan denial rates. These findings align with our analysis of the 2018–2023 HMDA data, demonstrating that while fintech and non-bank lenders have expanded access to mortgage credit, the persistence of pricing disparities suggests that historical patterns of exclusion continue to shape borrower experiences today.

Loya [20] highlights racial stratification within the Latino borrower population, emphasizing that Black Latinos face higher loan rejections and costlier mortgage products compared to White and Asian Latinos. Sanchez-Moyano [21] further explores how geographic patterns and neighborhood racial compositions influence Hispanic homeownership disparities, emphasizing the importance of spatial factors in lending outcomes. Haupert and Lee [22] investigate the role of fintech lenders in subprime mortgage lending across immigrant gateway metropolitan areas, revealing that while fintech lenders may reduce disparities in some contexts, they can still reflect racial disparities based on neighborhood demographics. Collectively, these studies underscore the importance of considering racial subgroup differences, spatial influences, and lending technologies in mortgage market analyses.

Overall, the literature indicates that racial and ethnic disparities in mortgage lending persist across evolving market structures and technological advances. While emerging lender types have shifted the competitive landscape, regulatory frameworks and enforcement remain pivotal in shaping equitable outcomes. As this study shows, investigating lender type in conjunction with borrower race and ethnicity can yield deeper insights into where and why disparities arise, informing the development of policies and regulatory interventions that promote fair and inclusive access to mortgage credit.

3. Data and Sample

Our study analyzes Home Mortgage Disclosure Act (HMDA) data from 2018 to 2023, focusing on conventional first-lien 30-year fixed-rate conforming mortgages for owner-occupied, single-family properties. To ensure consistency, relevance, and replicability, we applied several filters to the data. We included only loans for owner-occupied properties by filtering records where the occupancy type equals 1. For dwelling type, we retained records categorized as "Single Family (1–4 Units): Site-Built." Loan purposes were limited to home purchase, refinancing, or cash-out refinancing, as indicated by specific loan purpose codes (1, 31, or 32).

We restricted the analysis to first-lien loans by including only records where the lien status equals 1, and we excluded reverse mortgages (reverse_mortgage = 2) and open-end lines of credit (open_end_line_of_credit = 2). Similarly, loans for business or commercial purposes were removed by excluding records where business_or_commercial_purpose equals 1. We also filtered out loans with features such as negative amortization, interest-only payments, or balloon payments to focus on standard mortgage products. Only loans meeting conforming loan limits were included (conforming_loan_limit = "C"), and the sample was further restricted to those with a loan term of 360 months (loan_term = 360).

Finally, we excluded applications with missing or unspecified race or ethnicity to enhance the reliability of demographic analyses. This detailed filtering process reduced the dataset to 29,338,620 mortgage applications, providing a robust and consistent sample for our analysis.

Please note that property values and incomes are typically reported for approved loans but are often missing from rejected applications. To avoid introducing bias and to maintain a representative sample, we included observations with missing values rather than excluding them. Excluding these observations would disproportionately remove rejected applications, reducing the sample size from 29 million to 23 million and limiting our ability to analyze approval disparities. Retaining all observations ensures that both approved and rejected loans are represented, despite the challenges posed by missing data.

We classified lender types using a structured approach. To determine whether a lender was a bank or a subsidiary of a bank, we checked for the presence of a bank charter, a Regulatory Reporting System ID (RSSD), or a bank parent. Lenders without these identifiers were classified as non-banks. Fintech lenders were identified based on a more nuanced methodology, drawing on prior research by Buchak et al. [6] and Fuster et al. [7]. Specifically, we classified non-banks as fintech lenders if their mortgage-lending process up to the preapproval stage could be completed entirely online and if their business model relied predominantly on online channels. Large banks were identified using the Federal Reserve's Comprehensive Capital Analysis and Review (CCAR) list, while banks not subject to CCAR were categorized as small banks. Credit unions in the HMDA data are identified by an agency code of 5, which corresponds to the National Credit Union Administration (NCUA), the regulatory body responsible for overseeing federally insured credit unions. These classifications enabled us to distinguish between traditional banking institutions and technology-driven or alternative lenders, providing critical insights into the evolving dynamics of the mortgage market.

Figure 1 illustrates the evolving market shares, measured by total loan originations, across various lender types from 2018 to 2023. Non-bank lenders increased their market share from 41.9% in 2018 to 47.6% in 2023, solidifying their dominant position in the mortgage market. Fintech lenders also show consistent growth, rising from 9.5% to 12.5%, reflecting the increasing reliance on technology in mortgage origination. In contrast, both small and large banks experienced declines in market share. Large banks' share fell sharply from 21.8% in 2018 to 12.8% in 2023, while small banks also declined, from 14.3% in 2020 to 12.8% in 2023. Credit unions maintained a relatively steady contribution, accounting for 7–9% of the market throughout the period. These trends underscore the shifting landscape of the mortgage industry, characterized by the growing prominence of non-bank and fintech lenders alongside a diminishing role for traditional banking institutions.

Table 1 presents summary statistics for the sample of 29,338,620 mortgage loans analyzed, covering the period from 2018 to 2023. The average loan amount is USD 292,522 (SD = USD 148,628), indicating substantial variation in loan sizes. The mean combined loan-to-value (CLTV) ratio is 76.14%, with half of the loans having a CLTV below 80%. The average interest rate is 4.01%, and the mean rate spread—representing the difference above a benchmark rate—is 0.30%. Loan cost measures reveal considerable dispersion, with mean total loan costs at USD 4514 and mean origination charges at USD 2263. Discount points and lender credits also vary widely, averaging USD 2494 and USD 1150, respectively.

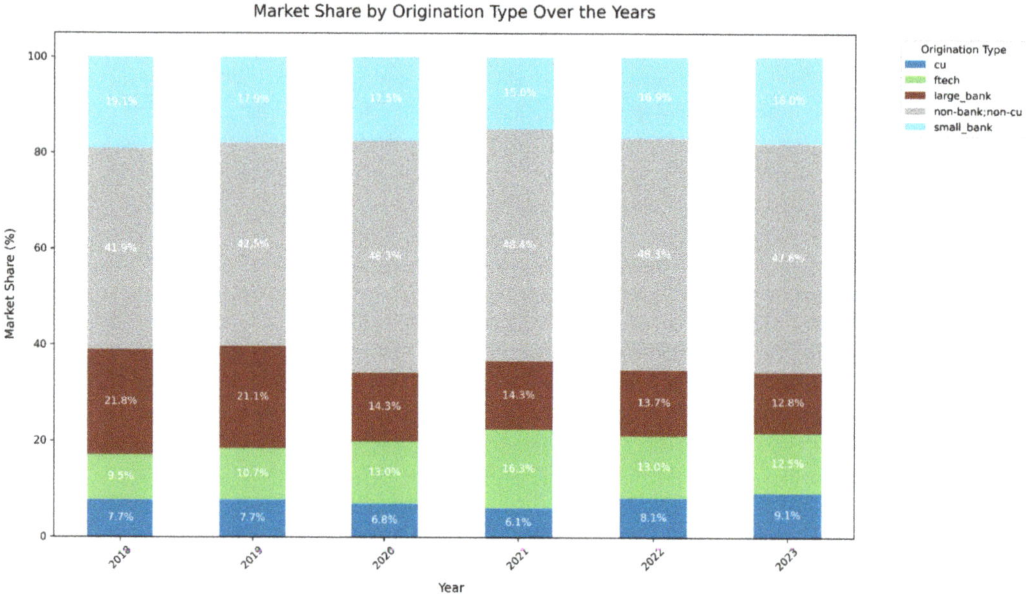

Figure 1. Market share trends of mortgage originations by lender type (2018–2023). The analysis categorizes lenders into credit unions, fintech lenders, large banks, non-bank lenders, and small banks. Market share percentages were calculated annually, capturing the evolution of lending dynamics across these categories over the observed period.

Demographic and geographic characteristics, based on HMDA data, indicate that the average percentage of minority residents in the census tracts where mortgage applications originated is 31.41%. HMDA includes tract-level variables to capture localized economic and demographic contexts, such as the tract minority population percentage and the tract-to-MSA income percentage. The latter measures how the median family income of a tract compares to the broader Metropolitan Statistical Area (MSA) it belongs to; in this study, the average is 114.35%, suggesting that tract incomes are slightly above their respective MSA medians. Additionally, the median family income across all MSAs in the dataset is USD 83,993, providing a benchmark for evaluating regional income disparities.

The sample reflects a diverse lender composition: non-bank, non-credit union (non-bank) lenders hold the largest share (44.50%), followed by small banks (18.30%), large banks (15.80%), fintech lenders (12.50%), and credit unions (8.50%). A majority of loans (53.00%) finance home purchases, with the remainder split between rate refinances (27.30%) and cash-out refinances (19.80%).

Borrower characteristics show that 38.20% of loans are taken jointly, while 35.10% and 26.30% are taken by male-only and female-only borrowers, respectively. In terms of race and ethnicity, White borrowers constitute 72.30% of the sample, followed by Hispanic (10.40%), Asian (8.30%), Black (6.30%), and Other Minority (2.60%) borrowers.

Table 1. Summary statistics of HMDA mortgage loan data (2018–2023). Panel A: Descriptive statistics for continuous variables. Key loan and borrower characteristics, including loan amounts, combined loan-to-value ratios, interest rates, rate spreads, and financial costs, are summarized. Each variable includes its count, mean, standard deviation, and percentiles (minimum, 25th, median, 75th, and maximum). Panel B: Distribution of categorical variables. This panel includes the breakdown of loans by origination type (e.g., non-bank, small bank, large bank, fintech, and credit unions), loan purpose (purchase, rate refinance, and cash-out refinance), borrower gender (joint, male, female, and sex not available), and borrower race/ethnicity (White, Hispanic, Asian, Black, and Other Minority). The counts and proportions for each category are displayed.

Panel A								
Variable	**Count**	**Mean**	**Std Dev**	**Min**	**25%**	**50%**	**75%**	**Max**
loan_amount	29,338,620	292,521.64	148,627.80	55,000.00	175,000.00	265,000.00	385,000.00	735,000.00
combined_loan_to_value_ratio	21,962,344	76.138	17.357	25	66.67	80	90	101.653
interest_rate	21,499,047	4.012	1.206	2.5	3	3.625	4.75	7.625
rate_spread	19,408,842	0.296	0.485	−0.867	−0.006	0.23	0.522	2.06
total_loan_costs	20,350,121	4514.57	2847.50	0	2741.40	3811.81	5522.05	16,022.00
origination_charges	20,465,220	2263.05	2314.20	0	975	1420.00	2855.00	12,242.38
discount_points	8,289,299	2494.30	2632.30	28.75	657.73	1624.75	3375.00	13,854.00
lender_credits	7,871,481	1150.03	1628.00	0.5	92.37	500	1500.00	8208.35
loan_term	29,338,620	360	0	360	360	360	360	360
property_value	23,729,084	409,650.34	237,702.63	85,000.00	245,000.00	355,000.00	515,000.00	1,345,000.00
total_units	29,338,620	1.013	0.115	1	1	1	1	2
income	28,900,592	107.127	68.657	16	60	90	135	402
tract_minority_population_percent	29,338,620	31.406	24.742	0	12.15	24.12	44.94	97.13
tract_to_msa_income_percentage	29,338,620	114.354	42.186	0	89	111	138	239
ffiec_msa_md_median_family_income	29,338,620	83,992.51	22,143.52	0	72,200.00	81,800.00	96,400.00	143,900.00

Panel B			
Categorical Variable	**Value**	**Count**	**Proportion**
orig_type	non-bank;non-cu	13,070,860	44.50%
	small_bank	5,372,344	18.30%
	large_bank	4,624,730	15.80%
	ftech	3,664,574	12.50%
	cu	2,493,604	8.50%
loan_purpose	Purchase	15,543,312	53.00%
	Rate refinance	7,995,284	27.30%
	Cash-out refinance	5,800,024	19.80%
derived_sex	Joint	11,194,329	38.20%
	Male	10,304,248	35.10%
	Female	7,715,535	26.30%
	Sex not available	124,508	0.40%
race_ethnicity_group	White	21,225,133	72.30%
	Hispanic	3,059,289	10.4%
	Asian	2,433,000	8.3%
	Black	1,845,856	6.3%
	Other Minority	775,342	2.6%
debt_to_income ratio bin	0–20	1,614,599	5.50%
	20–30	4,628,491	15.78%
	30–36	4,018,115	13.70%
	36–40	3,082,502	10.51%
	40–50	7,725,682	26.33%
	50+	995,081	3.39%
	Unknown	7,274,156	24.79%

We begin our analysis by examining unconditional approval rates to establish a baseline understanding of racial and ethnic disparities across different lender types. Table 2 presents loan approval rates by lender type and borrower race/ethnicity, segmented by purchase, refinance, and overall loans. In addition to the raw approval rates, the table provides the differences in approval rates between minority borrowers and White borrowers (last three columns), allowing for a clearer assessment of how these groups fare relative to a benchmark. Across all lender types, White borrowers consistently achieve the highest approval rates. For instance, credit unions approve White applicants at an overall rate of 87.99%, while Asian borrowers (84.13%) fare somewhat well but remain behind. Hispanic (75.53%) and Black (66.77%) borrowers encounter lower overall approval rates, with Black borrowers facing a particularly steep shortfall in refinance loans (60.26%). Of course, approval decisions are influenced by a variety of borrower-level attributes—such as income, credit score, debt-to-income ratios, and loan-to-value ratios—that can differ systematically by race and ethnicity. Some of these key factors are incorporated into the regression analysis in later section, which allows us to distinguish the role of borrower risk characteristics from potential racial and ethnic disparities in lending outcomes.

Table 2. Loan approval rates by lender type (credit unions, fintech lenders, large banks, non-bank lenders, and small banks) and race/ethnicity. Approval rates are segmented by loan purpose—purchase, refinance, and overall.

Lender Type	Race/Ethnicity	Purchase Approval Rate	Refinance Approval Rate	All Loans Approval Rate	Purchase Minority-White	Refinance Minority-White	All Loans Minority-White
Credit unions	Asian	87.33%	79.01%	84.13%	−3.33	−5.81	−3.86
	Black	71.45%	60.26%	66.77%	−19.21	−24.56	−21.22
	Hispanic	81.78%	68.26%	75.53%	−8.88	−16.56	−12.46
	Other Minority	86.73%	79.67%	83.76%	−3.93	−5.15	−4.23
	White	90.66%	84.82%	87.99%			
Fintech lenders	Asian	91.15%	85.85%	88.27%	−2.73	0.62	−0.31
	Black	86.65%	74.38%	78.91%	−7.23	−10.85	−9.67
	Hispanic	90.15%	80.02%	84.62%	−3.73	−5.21	−3.96
	Other Minority	93.58%	83.57%	87.81%	−0.3	−1.66	−0.77
	White	93.88%	85.23%	88.58%			
Large banks	Asian	88.34%	78.26%	84.34%	−3.43	−1.22	−0.9
	Black	81.36%	58.95%	69.48%	−10.41	−20.53	−15.76
	Hispanic	83.01%	65.66%	73.75%	−8.76	−13.82	−11.49
	Other Minority	89.93%	74.69%	82.25%	−1.84	−4.79	−2.99
	White	91.77%	79.48%	85.24%			
Non-bank lenders	Asian	92.78%	88.16%	90.96%	−3.16	−0.13	−1.49
	Black	88.04%	71.35%	80.87%	−7.9	−16.94	−11.58
	Hispanic	90.77%	82.69%	87.42%	−5.17	−5.6	−5.03
	Other Minority	95.10%	86.79%	91.71%	−0.84	−1.5	−0.74
	White	95.94%	88.29%	92.45%			
Small banks	Asian	91.20%	83.10%	88.52%	−3.27	−5.14	−3.34
	Black	85.81%	71.32%	81.27%	−8.66	−16.92	−10.59
	Hispanic	88.42%	75.35%	84.30%	−6.05	−12.89	−7.56
	Other Minority	93.14%	85.76%	90.39%	−1.33	−2.48	−1.47
	White	94.47%	88.24%	91.86%			

While fintech and non-bank lenders exhibit relatively more inclusive outcomes for many minority groups, Black and Hispanic applicants still experience significant approval gaps compared to White borrowers. Even at fintech lenders, where overall differences are somewhat narrower, Black borrowers' all-loan approval rate lags behind that of White borrowers by nearly 10 percentage points, and Hispanic borrowers also face meaningful shortfalls. Non-bank lenders, despite generally high approval rates, show similar patterns, with Black borrowers trailing White borrowers by about 11.6 percentage points overall and Hispanic borrowers also encountering a persistent gap of around 5 percentage points.

In contrast, credit unions, large banks, and small banks tend to have even wider disparities for Black and Hispanic borrowers, often reaching double-digit approval-rate gaps. These findings indicate that although some newer or technology-driven lending models appear to reduce inequities for certain groups, Black and Hispanic borrowers remain at a disadvantage across all lender types. The persistent nature of these disparities, even in relatively more equitable lending environments, underscores the need for targeted interventions and rigorous enforcement of fair lending regulations to ensure Black and Hispanic households receive equitable access to mortgage credit.

Having examined unconditional approval rates, we now turn to descriptive measures of pricing and cost components to understand how disparities extend beyond simple acceptance or rejection decisions. Table 3 provides insights into interest rates, rate spreads, origination charges, and discount points by lender type and race/ethnicity, exposing how cost-based disparities extend beyond approval decisions. While fintech lenders often show smaller differences in headline pricing terms like interest rates and rate spreads, Black and Hispanic borrowers still incur noticeably higher origination charges and discount points compared to White borrowers. For instance, even with fintech lenders—often considered more standardized—Black borrowers face substantially higher loan-related fees, reflecting that lower headline disparities do not necessarily translate into comprehensive cost equity.

Similarly, for non-bank lenders, interest rates may not differ drastically, but Black and Hispanic borrowers shoulder some of the steepest additional costs. Large banks and credit unions, despite occasionally offering more favorable interest terms, fail to fully close the gap in fees, placing a disproportionate financial burden on these borrowers. Overall, no lender category successfully eliminates cost-based inequities for Black and Hispanic borrowers, underscoring that ensuring fair lending outcomes requires addressing not just approval rates and interest rates, but the entire spectrum of loan costs.

Taken together, Tables 2 and 3 reveal that, on average, Black and Hispanic borrowers face notable disadvantages in both loan approval rates and loan costs relative to White borrowers across various lender types. Although fintech and non-bank lenders show somewhat narrower disparities, particularly in approval-rate and interest-rate terms, these gaps do not disappear entirely, especially when considering origination charges and discount points. It is important to note that these patterns represent unconditional means and do not control for borrower risk factors such as credit scores, loan-to-value ratios, or debt-to-income ratios. To better understand the drivers of these disparities and identify whether differences persist after adjusting for relevant risk characteristics, we proceed with a multivariate regression analysis in the following sections.

Table 3. Loan terms by lender type and race/ethnicity.

		Purchase				Refinance				All			
Lender Type	Race/ Ethnicity	Interest Rate	Rate Spread	Origination Charges	Discount Points	Interest Rate	Rate Spread	Origination Charges	Discount Points	Interest Rate	Rate Spread	Origination Charges	Discount Points
Credit union	Asian	4.29%	0.08%	USD 1850	USD 2614	3.40%	0.04%	USD 2100	USD 3020	3.97%	0.06%	USD 1940	USD 2786
	Black	4.58%	0.61%	USD 2120	USD 2088	3.77%	0.28%	USD 2140	USD 2351	4.27%	0.49%	USD 2128	USD 2232
	Hispanic	4.63%	0.59%	USD 2077	USD 2216	3.72%	0.24%	USD 1957	USD 2185	4.25%	0.44%	USD 2027	USD 2198
	Other Minority	4.38%	0.31%	USD 1969	USD 2290	3.54%	0.16%	USD 2207	USD 2683	4.05%	0.25%	USD 2064	USD 2486
	White	4.29%	0.28%	USD 1618	USD 1603	3.59%	0.17%	USD 1812	USD 1770	3.98%	0.23%	USD 1703	USD 1689
Fintech	Asian	4.24%	0.15%	USD 2765	USD 3640	3.16%	0.00%	USD 2374	USD 3763	3.67%	0.07%	USD 2559	USD 3700
	Black	4.48%	0.52%	USD 3157	USD 3448	3.80%	0.37%	USD 3960	USD 3616	4.08%	0.43%	USD 3634	USD 3563
	Hispanic	4.38%	0.49%	USD 2966	USD 3052	3.57%	0.26%	USD 3415	USD 3312	3.97%	0.37%	USD 3198	USD 3205
	Other Minority	4.35%	0.33%	USD 3021	USD 3599	3.47%	0.20%	USD 3349	USD 3847	3.87%	0.26%	USD 3201	USD 3750
	White	4.33%	0.41%	USD 2600	USD 2838	3.57%	0.26%	USD 3143	USD 3200	3.88%	0.32%	USD 2920	USD 3078
Large bank	Asian	4.06%	−0.04%	USD 1843	USD 2748	3.40%	0.02%	USD 1938	USD 2523	3.82%	−0.02%	USD 1878	USD 2672
	Black	4.13%	0.12%	USD 2338	USD 4203	3.89%	0.38%	USD 2627	USD 2505	4.02%	0.24%	USD 2468	USD 3367
	Hispanic	4.23%	0.21%	USD 1787	USD 2689	3.82%	0.32%	USD 2399	USD 2211	4.04%	0.27%	USD 2078	USD 2441
	Other Minority	4.20%	0.08%	USD 1727	USD 2563	3.61%	0.23%	USD 2386	USD 2569	3.93%	0.15%	USD 2029	USD 2566
	White	4.19%	0.16%	USD 1479	USD 1747	3.69%	0.28%	USD 2020	USD 1949	3.94%	0.22%	USD 1747	USD 1859
Non-bank	Asian	4.35%	0.24%	USD 3305	USD 3735	3.31%	0.07%	USD 2868	USD 2966	3.95%	0.18%	USD 3138	USD 3526
	Black	4.49%	0.60%	USD 3134	USD 3294	3.81%	0.43%	USD 3653	USD 3100	4.23%	0.54%	USD 3331	USD 3210
	Hispanic	4.53%	0.63%	USD 3374	USD 2966	3.66%	0.34%	USD 3565	USD 2659	4.19%	0.51%	USD 3449	USD 2840
	Other Minority	4.38%	0.37%	USD 2957	USD 3394	3.48%	0.21%	USD 3005	USD 3023	4.03%	0.31%	USD 2976	USD 3256
	White	4.35%	0.38%	USD 2509	USD 2515	3.53%	0.24%	USD 2665	USD 2441	3.99%	0.32%	USD 2577	USD 2482
Small bank	Asian	4.35%	0.31%	USD 2472	USD 2825	3.41%	0.09%	USD 2185	USD 2840	4.06%	0.24%	USD 2383	USD 2830
	Black	4.45%	0.48%	USD 1887	USD 2310	3.74%	0.34%	USD 2224	USD 2280	4.25%	0.44%	USD 1980	USD 2300
	Hispanic	4.69%	0.72%	USD 2325	USD 2224	3.73%	0.32%	USD 2209	USD 2151	4.42%	0.60%	USD 2293	USD 2199
	Other Minority	4.31%	0.28%	USD 2067	USD 2474	3.49%	0.16%	USD 2153	USD 2493	4.02%	0.24%	USD 2098	USD 2481
	White	4.26%	0.30%	USD 1683	USD 1771	3.57%	0.20%	USD 1685	USD 1738	3.98%	0.26%	USD 1684	USD 1757

This table reports loan terms, including interest rates, rate spreads, origination charges, and discount points, for different racial/ethnic groups across five lender types. Results are segmented by loan purpose—purchase, refinance, and overall.

4. Regression Analysis

While the unconditional statistics in Tables 2 and 3 demonstrate persistent disparities, they may conflate differences in borrower risk and property characteristics with discrimination. To disentangle these effects, we next present regression analyses that control for a range of relevant factors, such as income, loan characteristics, state, and year fixed effects. This approach aims to provide a deeper understanding of the underlying drivers of these disparities. We examine three outcomes: rate spread, reflecting the cost of borrowing; origination charge, capturing upfront loan costs; and loan-application denial, indicating access to credit. This comprehensive approach isolates the underlying drivers of observed disparities.

4.1. Rate Spread Regression Analysis

Table 4 reports the results from a series of fixed-effects linear regressions of the following form:

$$RateSpread_{\{i,c,t\}} = \alpha + \beta_1 X_i + \beta_2 L_i + \beta_3(Minority \times LenderType) + \gamma_c + \delta_t + \varepsilon_{\{i,c,t\}}$$

where $RateSpread_{\{i,c,t\}}$ is the difference between the loan's Annual Percentage Rate (APR) and the average prime offer rate for loan i, in county c and year t. The vector X_i includes borrower and loan characteristics such as loan amount, combined loan-to-value ratio, debt-to-income ratio, property value, total units, origination charges, discount points, and income. L_i represents indicator variables for the lender type (credit union, fintech, non-bank, small bank), with large bank serving as the baseline category. County and origination-year fixed effects (γ_c and δ_t) control for geographic and temporal variations. The interaction terms $Minority \times LenderType$ capture how the pricing difference for a minority borrower relative to a White borrower changes across lender types.

Each column in Table 4 restricts the sample to White borrowers and one minority group: Column (1) compares White and Asian borrowers, Column (2) White and Black borrowers, Column (3) White and Hispanic borrowers, and Column (4) White and Other Minority borrowers. By examining each minority group separately, the model identifies how each lender type treats that particular group relative to Whites, holding borrower risk factors and local conditions constant.

The results provide a comprehensive understanding of rate spread differences across firm types and borrower groups. First, examining the firm-type variable alone, where large banks serve as the baseline, each coefficient indicates how other financial firms differ in the rate spreads they charge, irrespective of the borrower's minority status. Credit unions, compared to large banks, are associated with significantly lower rate spreads, underscoring their role in offering more favorable loan terms. In contrast, fintechs, non-banks, and small banks charge higher rate spreads than large banks, reflecting a pricing premium imposed by these institutions. Among all firm types, credit unions provide the most valuable cost savings to consumers. This finding is consistent with the patterns observed in the prior cost analysis presented in Table 3.

The minority dummy variable alone captures how minority borrowers compare to White borrowers within large banks (the baseline group). The negative coefficient for the minority variable indicates that minority borrowers, on average, face lower rate spreads than White borrowers within large banks. This outcome suggests that large banks may implement targeted pricing strategies or take deliberate actions to offer competitive terms to minority borrowers. However, the interaction terms reveal that this relationship shifts significantly across other types of financial institutions.

The interaction terms indicate how minority borrowers are treated relative to White borrowers within each financial firm type. For example, the positive coefficient for the minority–fintech interaction demonstrates that rate spreads are higher for minority borrowers than for White borrowers at fintechs. However, the disparity at fintechs is smaller compared to other institution types. For instance, the interaction term minority × fintech indicates that the rate spread gap between Black and White borrowers is 15.96 basis points, significantly smaller than the 27.61 basis point gap at credit unions. This suggests that fintech lenders apply more standardized pricing, reducing the discretionary bias observed in traditional institutions.

Table 4. Disparities in rate spread across lender types and racial/ethnic groups. This table presents results from fixed-effects regressions examining disparities in rate spreads across different racial/ethnic groups relative to White borrowers (the baseline group). Each column represents a separate regression, where the sample is restricted to White borrowers and a specific minority group (Asian, Black, Hispanic, or Other Minority). The dependent variable is the rate spread, defined as the difference between the loan's annual percentage rate and the average prime offer rate. The regressions control for key loan and borrower characteristics, including loan amount, combined loan-to-value ratio, debt-to-income ratio, property value, total units, origination charges, discount points, and income. Fixed effects are included for the county and origination year to account for geographic and temporal variations in lending practices. Interaction terms between minority status and lender type capture how different lenders treat minority borrowers compared to White borrowers in mortgage pricing. ***, **, * represent significance levels at 1%, 5%, and 10%, respectively.

	Asian vs. White	**Black vs. White**	**Hispanic vs. White**	**Other Minority vs. White**
Loan amount (USD 1000)	−0.114 *** (0.0004)	−0.112 *** (0.0004)	−0.115 *** (0.0004)	−0.114 *** (0.0004)
Combined loan-to-value	72.183 *** (0.198)	69.370 *** (0.201)	73.770 *** (0.196)	72.533 *** (0.202)
Property value (USD 1000)	0.00027 *** (0.00027)	−0.00295 *** (0.00028)	0.00012 (0.00027)	−0.00019 (0.00028)
Total units	18.528 *** (0.172)	17.774 *** (0.176)	17.963 *** (0.164)	17.915 *** (0.186)
Origination charges	5.213 *** (0.0119)	5.037 *** (0.0127)	5.021 *** (0.0121)	5.037 *** (0.013)
Discount points	−5.030 *** (0.0126)	−5.025 *** (0.0134)	−4.903 *** (0.0128)	−4.838 *** (0.0137)
Income (USD 1000)	100.1 *** (0.4)	110.6 *** (0.4)	109.0 *** (0.4)	101.6 *** (0.4)
Minority	−13.830 *** (0.151)	−10.640 *** (0.168)	−3.626 *** (0.144)	−1.899 *** (0.261)
Credit union	−4.963 *** (0.102)	−4.853 *** (0.103)	−4.941 *** (0.103)	−4.970 *** (0.101)
Fintech	10.056 *** (0.065)	10.362 *** (0.066)	10.262 *** (0.066)	9.998 *** (0.065)
Non-bank	10.279 *** (0.058)	10.558 *** (0.058)	10.351 *** (0.058)	10.264 *** (0.057)
Small bank	2.770 *** (0.068)	2.788 *** (0.069)	2.655 *** (0.069)	2.729 *** (0.068)
Minority × credit union	9.079 *** (0.353)	27.609 *** (0.360)	11.831 *** (0.304)	5.951 *** (0.469)
Minority × fintech	2.510 *** (0.209)	15.964 *** (0.213)	2.776 *** (0.189)	1.565 *** (0.332)
Minority × non-bank	6.347 *** (0.169)	21.161 *** (0.189)	10.300 *** (0.155)	3.293 *** (0.291)
Minority × small bank	11.724 *** (0.227)	19.822 *** (0.246)	9.127 *** (0.208)	2.860 *** (0.355)
Debt-to-income: 20–30	7.502 *** (0.075)	8.098 *** (0.077)	7.661 *** (0.076)	7.772 *** (0.076)
Debt-to-income: 30–36	13.785 *** (0.079)	14.525 *** (0.080)	13.980 *** (0.080)	14.095 *** (0.080)
Debt-to-income: 36–40	17.526 *** (0.083)	18.234 *** (0.085)	17.724 *** (0.084)	17.781 *** (0.084)
Debt-to-income: 40–50	19.723 *** (0.078)	20.472 *** (0.080)	19.820 *** (0.079)	19.952 *** (0.079)
Debt-to-income: 50–60	17.499 *** (0.199)	18.033 *** (0.203)	17.547 *** (0.196)	17.813 *** (0.207)
Debt-to-income: Unknown	23.733 *** (0.727)	25.215 *** (0.743)	26.598 *** (0.714)	24.281 *** (0.743)
Constant	−36.365 *** (0.245)	−33.4024 *** (0.251)	−36.227 *** (0.240)	−35.347 *** (0.257)
County FE	Yes	Yes	Yes	Yes
Origination-year FE	Yes	Yes	Yes	Yes
Number of observations	5,930,421	5,602,710	6,273,113	5,602,710
Adjusted R-squared	0.167	0.171	0.170	0.171

Ranking the interaction coefficients for Black and Hispanic borrowers reveals that fintechs impose the smallest additional rate spread, followed by small banks. Non-banks exhibit a larger pricing disparity than both fintechs and small banks. Interestingly, credit unions, which generally provide lower rate spreads overall, impose the highest additional rate spread on minority borrowers, challenging their reputation for consumer-friendly practices.

Borrower and loan characteristics further influence rate spreads. Larger loan amounts are associated with lower rate spreads, reflecting economies of scale in lending. Higher property values have a minor yet favorable effect on rate spreads, while higher borrower income significantly reduces rate spreads, indicating better financial stability. Debt-to-income ratios are strongly correlated with rate spreads, with higher ratios resulting in progressively larger penalties due to heightened credit risk.

The results demonstrate that although fintech lenders impose statistically significant rate spread penalties on minority borrowers, these penalties are smaller compared to other financial institutions (except large banks). Credit unions, while offering the lowest overall rate spreads to all borrowers, surprisingly impose the largest rate spread penalties on minorities—particularly Black and Hispanic borrowers. Large banks, serving as the baseline group, generally exhibit more equitable outcomes. Minority borrowers at large banks often receive rate spreads that are equal to or even slightly lower than those of White borrowers. This finding suggests that larger, more heavily regulated institutions, which typically rely on standardized, risk-based lending models, provide a fairer and more consistent pricing environment. In contrast, other lender types, particularly credit unions, non-banks, and small banks, continue to impose disproportionate costs on minority borrowers, highlighting the need for more scrutiny of their lending practices.

Additionally, we conducted robustness checks using the interest rate as the dependent variable instead of the rate spread. The results were quantitatively similar to those obtained with the rate spread, which is expected since the interest rate is essentially the sum of the benchmark rate and the rate spread. However, we chose to focus on the rate spread as the primary dependent variable due to the limitations of using the interest rate. Specifically, the lack of information on loan-origination month prevents us from accounting for interest rate dynamics, which can vary significantly over time. As a result, similar interest rates may reflect different underlying lending conditions depending on the market environment at the time of origination. By focusing on the rate spread, we mitigate this issue and provide a more consistent measure of relative borrower costs.

4.2. Origination-Charge Regression Analysis

Table 5 reports the results from a series of fixed-effects linear regressions of the following form:

$$Origniation\_Charge_{\{i,c,t\}} = \alpha + \beta_1 X_i + \beta_2 L_i + \beta_3 (Minority \times LenderType) + \gamma_c + \delta_t + \varepsilon_{\{i,c,t\}}$$

where $Origniation\_Charge_{\{i,c,t\}}$ is the upfront fee covering the lender's costs for processing, underwriting, and approving loan i, in county c and year t, including expenses for administrative tasks, risk assessment, and document preparation. The vector X_i includes borrower and loan characteristics such as loan amount, combined loan-to-value ratio, debt-to-income ratio, property value, total units, origination charges, and income. L_i represents indicator variables for the lender type (credit union, fintech, non-bank, and small bank), with large bank serving as the baseline category. County and origination-year fixed effects (γ_c and δ_t) control for geographic and temporal variations. The interaction terms $Minority \times LenderType$ capture how the pricing difference for a minority borrower relative to that of a White borrower changes across lender types.

Table 5. Disparities in origination charge across lender types and racial/ethnic groups. This table presents results from fixed-effects regressions examining disparities in origination charges across different racial/ethnic groups relative to White borrowers (the baseline group). Each column represents a separate regression, where the sample is restricted to White borrowers and a specific minority group (Asian, Black, Hispanic, or Other Minority). The dependent variable is the origination charge, which reflects the upfront fees charged by the lender at the time of loan origination. The regressions control for key loan and borrower characteristics, including loan amount, combined loan-to-value ratio, debt-to-income ratio, property value, total units, rate spread, and income. Fixed effects are included for the county and origination year to account for geographic and temporal variations in lending practices. Interaction terms between minority status and lender type capture how different lenders treat minority borrowers compared to White borrowers in terms of mortgage origination charges. ***, **, * represent significance levels at 1%, 5%, and 10%, respectively.

	Asian vs. White	**Black vs. White**	**Hispanic vs. White**	**Other Minority vs. White**
Loan amount (USD 1000)	7.7693 *** (0.0234)	8.3681 *** (0.0237)	8.3897 *** (0.0231)	8.0159 *** (0.0238)
Combined loan-to-value	−1181.586 *** (11.6736)	−1349.241 *** (11.47598)	−1382.873 *** (11.20194)	−1269.853 *** (11.64957)
Property value (USD 1000)	−0.8568 *** (0.0157)	−1.1117 *** (0.0160)	−1.1315 *** (0.0156)	−1.0106 *** (0.0159)
Total units	647.6054 *** (10.1090)	618.6775 *** (10.06958)	632.7257 *** (9.383319)	539.1739 *** (10.70954)
Income (USD 1000)	−0.5526 *** (0.0239)	−0.6129 *** (0.02398)	−0.4707 *** (0.02356)	−0.4933 *** (0.02404)
Interest rate	37.0810 *** (1.5741)	10.6591 *** (1.5480)	33.4238 *** (1.5055)	20.9226 *** (1.5880)
Minority	−479.6792 *** (8.9112)	944.0895 *** (9.6139)	221.2442 *** (8.2439)	52.4194 *** (15.0761)
Credit union	−20.4244 *** (5.9840)	−22.3117 *** (5.8915)	−19.7351 *** (5.9132)	−25.3751 *** (5.8387)
Fintech	1229.199 *** (3.8167)	1227.933 *** (3.7573)	1228.698 *** (3.7722)	1223.601 *** (3.7248)
Non-bank	525.0465 *** (3.3906)	522.408 *** (3.3391)	519.9466 *** (3.3496)	520.4138 *** (3.3115)
Small bank	72.7071 *** (4.0238)	70.7049 *** (3.9600)	72.0589 *** (3.9752)	67.3131 *** (3.9276)
Minority × credit union	433.9627 *** (20.8145)	−345.2581 *** (20.5908)	70.4367 *** (17.4149)	212.1767 *** (27.0867)
Minority × fintech	−151.2017 *** (12.3049)	−507.0431 *** (12.2085)	−335.1498 *** (10.8118)	−721.614
Minority × non-bank	348.0894 *** (9.9501)	−337.9040 *** (10.8217)	132.1543 *** (8.8952)	51.8496 *** (16.7803)
Minority × small bank	751.0730 *** (13.3900)	−480.5603 *** (14.0684)	47.7467 *** (11.9089)	214.2369 *** (20.4829)
Debt-to-income: 20–30	40.2437 *** (4.4129)	50.1026 *** (4.3850)	40.677 *** (4.3501)	56.876 *** (4.3691)
Debt-to-income: 30–36	93.9955 *** (4.6492)	106.0877 *** (4.6132)	91.1245 *** (4.5667)	114.2424 *** (4.6100)
Debt-to-income: 36–40	141.5530 *** (4.9130)	148.3147 *** (4.8691)	130.3424 *** (4.8091)	161.8095 *** (4.8792)
Debt-to-income: 40–50	212.8665 *** (4.6369)	206.993 *** (4.5992)	193.7236 *** (4.5520)	229.9009 *** (4.6008)
Debt-to-income: 50–60	667.2905 *** (11.7112)	699.6667 *** (11.6012)	655.0068 *** (11.2620)	688.2444 *** (11.9300)
Debt-to-income: Unknown	331.1695 *** (42.8340)	321.5046 *** (42.5010)	323.5707 *** (40.8838)	365.3133 *** (42.9050)
Constant	651.9360 *** (15.8113)	863.1939 *** (15.7166)	772.2887 *** (15.0952)	863.7496 *** (16.2315)
County FE	Yes	Yes	Yes	Yes
Origination-year FE	Yes	Yes	Yes	Yes
Number of observations	5,930,421	5,860,428	6,237,113	5,602,710
Adjusted R-squared	0.172	0.182	0.182	0.178

The results provide insights into how origination charges vary across firm types and borrower groups.

For firm types alone, credit unions are associated with the lowest origination charges, as indicated by the negative coefficient compared to large banks. In contrast, all other firm types charge higher origination costs than large banks, with fintechs imposing the highest origination charges. This pattern highlights the competitive pricing advantage of credit unions and the premium pricing strategies of fintech lenders.

The minority variable alone captures how minority borrowers compare to White borrowers within large banks (the baseline group). The positive coefficients for Black,

Hispanic, and other minority groups suggest that large banks charge minorities higher origination costs than White borrowers. This finding indicates potential disparities in cost structures for minority borrowers within large banking institutions.

Examining the interaction terms reveals nuanced results across different financial firm types. Fintechs, for example, offer lower origination charges to minority borrowers compared to White borrowers, as reflected by the negative interaction coefficients. Specifically, the interaction term minority × fintech is negative for Black borrowers, indicating a reduction in origination charges of approximately USD 505 compared to White borrowers, all else being equal. This indicates that Fintech lenders may be implementing pricing strategies that are more favorable to minority borrowers. For other financial firm types, the results are mixed. Black borrowers consistently receive lower origination charges across all firm types, whereas Hispanic borrowers tend to be charged higher origination costs. These mixed outcomes suggest varying approaches to pricing among non-bank lenders, small banks, and credit unions, potentially reflecting differences in risk-assessment practices or market strategies.

Overall, the findings suggest that Fintech lenders, while charging the highest origination fees overall, offer more favorable terms to minority borrowers relative to White borrowers. In contrast, other financial institutions, including credit unions and non-bank lenders, exhibit more varied and less consistent pricing patterns for minority groups. This highlights the importance of scrutinizing lender practices to ensure equitable outcomes for all borrower demographics.

4.3. Approval-Rate Logit Regression

Similarly, to better understand denial decisions and verify whether the patterns observed in raw approval rates persist after controlling for confounding variables, we estimate logit models that adjust for borrower- and loan-level attributes. Table 6 presents logistic regressions of the following form:

$$logit\left(\frac{\left\{P\left(Denial_{\{i,c,t\}}=1\right)\right\}}{\left\{1-P\left(Denial_{\{i,c,t\}}=1\right)\right\}}\right)=\alpha+\beta_1 Z_i+\beta_2 L_i+\beta_3(Minority\times LenderType)+\gamma_s+\delta_t$$

where $\left\{P\left(Denial_{\{i,c,t\}}=1\right)\right\}$ is an indicator equal to 1 if loan iii is denied and 0 otherwise. Similar to Table 4, we include a rich set of controls, Z_i: loan amount, combined loan-to-value ratio, property value, total units, borrower income, origination charges, discount points, and loan purpose. We also control for state and origination-year fixed effects (γ_s, δ_t) to account for region-specific regulations and macroeconomic changes over time. The interaction terms $(Minority \times LenderType)$ identify whether a given lender type increases or decreases the likelihood of denial for minority applicants relative to White applicants, after holding observable borrower and loan characteristics constant.

The four columns each focus on a distinct minority group compared to White borrowers: Column (1) analyzes Asian vs. White, Column (2) Black vs. White, Column (3) Hispanic vs. White, and Column (4) Other Minority vs. White. By comparing each minority group to Whites separately, we can discern patterns of disparate treatment specific to each group.

Starting with the lender-type variable, when using large banks as the baseline, the coefficients for credit unions, fintechs, non-banks, and small banks are all negative and statistically significant. This suggests that relative to large banks, these other lending institutions are generally associated with lower rejection rates. This pattern aligns with the findings in Table 2, where approval rates among these categories also tend to be higher, indicating a more lenient lending stance than large banks.

Table 6. Logistic regression results for mortgage denial rates by racial/ethnic groups. This table reports results from logit regressions investigating the likelihood of mortgage denial across racial/ethnic groups relative to White borrowers (the baseline group). Each column focuses on a separate minority group (Asian, Black, Hispanic, or Other Minority), with White borrowers as the comparison group. The dependent variable is a binary indicator equal to 1 if the loan application was denied and 0 otherwise. The regressions control for loan amount; combined loan-to-value ratio; property value; total units; borrower income; and key loan characteristics, such as origination charges, discount points, and loan purpose. Fixed effects for state and origination year are included to address location-specific and temporal variations in denial rates. Interaction terms between minority status and lender type capture the differential impact of institutional practices on minority applicants. ***, **, * represent significance levels at 1%, 5%, and 10%, respectively.

Variable	Asian vs. White	Black vs. White	Hispanic vs. White	Other Minority vs. White
Loan amount (USD 1000)	−0.671 *** (0.012)	−0.870 *** (0.012)	−0.776 *** (0.012)	−0.870 *** (0.012)
Combined loan-to-value ratio	0.003 (0.007)	0.005 (0.006)	0.003 (0.007)	0.003 (0.007)
Property value	−0.494 *** (0.007)	−0.438 *** (0.007)	−0.439 *** (0.007)	−0.428 *** (0.007)
Total units	0.663 *** (0.008)	0.635 *** (0.008)	0.617 *** (0.008)	0.677 *** (0.009)
Income	0.002 ** (0.001)	0.002 ** (0.001)	0.002 ** (0.001)	0.002 ** (0.001)
Minority	0.333 *** (0.007)	0.742 *** (0.011)	0.474 *** (0.006)	0.468 *** (0.011)
Credit union	−0.606 *** (0.005)	−0.600 *** (0.005)	−0.603 *** (0.005)	−0.602 *** (0.005)
Fintech	−0.308 *** (0.004)	−0.304 *** (0.004)	−0.302 *** (0.004)	−0.309 *** (0.004)
Non-bank	−0.732 *** (0.003)	−0.726 *** (0.003)	−0.727 *** (0.003)	−0.727 *** (0.003)
Small bank	−0.715 *** (0.004)	−0.715 *** (0.004)	−0.716 *** (0.004)	−0.711 *** (0.004)
Minority × credit union	0.163 *** (0.016)	0.380 *** (0.011)	0.117 *** (0.011)	0.092 *** (0.011)
Minority × fintech	−0.119 *** (0.010)	−0.191 *** (0.010)	−0.255 *** (0.010)	−0.201 *** (0.010)
Minority × non-bank	−0.062 *** (0.009)	0.119 *** (0.009)	−0.079 *** (0.009)	−0.176 *** (0.009)
Minority × small bank	0.259 *** (0.011)	0.171 *** (0.011)	0.113 *** (0.011)	−0.065 *** (0.011)
Sex: Joint	−0.202 *** (0.003)	−0.195 *** (0.003)	−0.204 *** (0.003)	−0.218 *** (0.003)
Sex: Male	0.163 *** (0.003)	0.186 *** (0.003)	0.166 *** (0.003)	0.184 *** (0.003)
Sex not available	0.807 *** (0.013)	0.906 *** (0.013)	0.859 *** (0.013)	0.867 *** (0.013)
Loan purpose: Refinance	0.976 *** (0.003)	1.002 *** (0.003)	0.982 *** (0.003)	1.013 *** (0.003)
Loan purpose: Cash-out refinance	1.244 *** (0.003)	1.240 *** (0.003)	1.215 *** (0.003)	1.261 *** (0.003)
Debt-to-income: 20–30	−0.495 *** (0.004)	−0.501 *** (0.004)	−0.510 *** (0.004)	−0.480 *** (0.004)
Debt-to-income: 30–36	−0.461 *** (0.004)	−0.474 *** (0.004)	−0.483 *** (0.004)	−0.446 *** (0.004)
Debt-to-income: 36–40	−0.413 *** (0.004)	−0.434 *** (0.004)	−0.439 *** (0.004)	−0.401 *** (0.004)
Debt-to-income: 40–50	−0.203 *** (0.004)	−0.231 *** (0.004)	−0.244 *** (0.004)	−0.190 *** (0.004)
Debt-to-income: 50–60	3.738 *** (0.005)	3.675 *** (0.005)	3.660 *** (0.005)	3.733 *** (0.005)
Debt-to-income: Unknown	3.044 *** (0.012)	3.052 *** (0.012)	2.980 *** (0.012)	2.918 *** (0.012)
Constant	−2.398 *** (0.026)	−2.351 *** (0.026)	−2.321 *** (0.026)	−2.396 *** (0.026)
State FE	Yes	Yes	Yes	Yes
Origination-year FE	Yes	Yes	Yes	Yes
Number of observations	16,765,090	16,334,672	17,191,623	15,666,390
Pseudo R2	0.2371	0.2477	0.2425	0.2361

Focusing next on minority status, the coefficient for the "minority" variable itself (without any interaction terms) is positive and highly significant. This reflects the baseline scenario for large banks: minority borrowers experience a higher likelihood of loan rejection compared to non-minority (White) borrowers. In other words, when borrowing from large banks, minority applicants face a greater probability of being turned down.

However, once we include interaction terms between minority status and lender type, the picture becomes more nuanced. For Fintech lenders, the interaction term with minorities is negative and significant. This indicates that when minority borrowers seek loans from Fintech firms, the difference in rejection rates compared to White borrowers actually diminishes—and may even reverse—relative to what they would face at a large bank. Essentially, minority borrowers fare better with Fintech lenders than with large banks, thus narrowing the rejection gap.

In contrast, the interaction results for non-banks and small bank are mixed. While some minority groups might experience improvements in rejection odds compared to large banks, the pattern is less consistent. Credit unions, on the other hand, resemble large banks in their treatment of minorities—minority applicants are still more likely to be rejected—but the magnitude of the disadvantage (the coefficient) is smaller than it is at large banks. This suggests that while minorities still face elevated odds of rejection at credit unions, the disparity is not as pronounced as that found at large banks.

In summary, relative to large banks, all other lender types initially appear more accommodating, offering lower rejection rates overall. For minority borrowers, large banks present a significant hurdle, showing a marked increase in rejection likelihood. Interactions with lender type modify these outcomes: fintech lenders, in particular, reduce the disadvantage faced by minority applicants, while non-banks and small banks produce more varied outcomes, and credit unions maintain a disadvantage, though one less severe than that at large banks.

The regression results from Tables 4–6 provide a complex and nuanced lending landscape where no single lender type uniformly provides the most favorable outcomes for minority borrowers. Although large banks serve as a baseline, the analysis shows that differences in pricing, fees, and rejection rates vary significantly across lender types and borrower groups once relevant borrower and loan characteristics, as well as local and temporal factors, are taken into account.

For rate spreads, large banks tend to offer relatively equitable or even slightly more favorable rate spreads to minority borrowers compared to Whites, suggesting some degree of fairness in their pricing models. Credit unions provide the lowest overall rates, but they paradoxically impose the largest minority penalties when considering the interaction terms. Other lenders, including fintechs and non-banks, generally charge higher spreads than large banks but do not penalize minority borrowers as heavily as credit unions do, implying that while they are more expensive overall, their additional costs for minority borrowers are comparatively smaller.

For origination charges, credit unions stand out by offering the lowest upfront charges. However, their pricing structures do not universally benefit minority borrowers as much as one might expect. Fintechs charge high origination fees overall but are relatively more favorable toward minority borrowers, reducing some disparities in these upfront costs. In contrast, other lender types show more mixed outcomes, with no single pattern emerging as consistently advantageous or disadvantageous to minorities.

For credit access, large banks appear relatively more stringent overall and impose a significant minority penalty in terms of denial rates. Other lender types—fintechs, non-banks, small banks, and credit unions—are associated with lower denial rates on average. However, these improvements for minority borrowers vary, with fintechs notably reducing the minority denial gap. Credit unions and other smaller lenders often produce outcomes less severe than those at large banks but still show disparities.

Table 7 presents a summary of how different racial and ethnic groups (Black, Hispanic, Asian, and Other Minorities) are treated by various lender types based on interaction-term results from regression analysis. The table highlights disparities in credit access, rate spreads, and origination charges across lender types, providing a comprehensive view of how minority borrowers fare compared to White borrowers.

Table 7. Racial Disparities in Mortgage Lending Outcomes by Lender Type. This table summarizes the differences in credit access, rate spreads, and origination charges for minority borrowers compared to White borrowers across various lender types. It includes four panels: Panel A compares Black vs. White borrowers, Panel B examines Hispanic vs. White borrowers, Panel C analyzes Asian vs. White borrowers, and Panel D covers Other Minority vs. White borrowers. Each panel details how large banks, fintech lenders, non-bank lenders, small banks, and credit unions differ in their treatment of these borrower groups.

Panel A: Black vs. White				
Lender Type	**Credit Access**	**Rate Spreads**	**Origination Charges**	**Interpretation**
Large bank	−	+	−	Stricter approvals, but once approved, spreads are favorable, though origination charges are less favorable (higher).
Fintech	+	−	−	Easier approvals, but Black borrowers face less favorable (higher) spreads and origination charges.
Non-bank	−	−	−	Black borrowers experience stricter credit access, higher spreads, and higher origination charges.
Small bank	−	−	−	Approvals are limited, with less favorable (higher) spreads and origination charges for Black borrowers.
Credit union	−	−	−	Despite overall lower rates for credit unions, Black borrowers face less favorable (higher) spreads and origination charges.
Panel B: Hispanic vs. White				
Lender Type	**Credit Access**	**Rate Spreads**	**Origination Charges**	**Interpretation**
Large bank	−	+	−	Stricter approvals, but spreads are favorable once approved, though origination charges are higher.
Fintech	+	−	−	Easier approvals, but spreads and origination charges remain less favorable (higher).
Non-bank	+	−	−	Approvals are easier for Hispanic borrowers, but they face less favorable (higher) spreads and origination charges.
Small bank	−	−	−	Limited approval rates, with spreads and origination charges less favorable for Hispanic borrowers.
Credit union	−	−	−	Approval rates and spreads are less favorable for Hispanic borrowers, with origination charges inconclusive.
Panel C: Asian vs. White				
Lender Type	**Credit Access**	**Rate Spreads**	**Origination Charges**	**Interpretation**
Large bank	−	+	+	Slightly stricter approvals, but Asian borrowers receive favorable spreads and origination charges.
Fintech	+	−	+	Easier approvals and more favorable origination charge, but higher spread.
Non-bank	+	−	−	Approvals are easier, but spreads and origination charges are less favorable (higher).
Small bank	−	−	−	Limited approval rates, with spreads and origination charges less favorable compared to White borrowers.
Credit union	−	−	−	Limited approval rates, with spreads and origination charges less favorable compared to White borrowers.

Table 7. *Cont.*

Panel D: Other Minorities vs. White				
Lender Type	**Credit Access**	**Rate Spreads**	**Origination Charges**	**Interpretation**
Large bank	−	+	−	Stricter approvals, but spreads are favorable once approved, though origination charges are higher.
Fintech	+	−	+	Easier approvals and more favorable origination charge, but higher spread.
Non-bank	+	−	−	Approvals are easier, but spreads and origination charges are less favorable (higher).
Small bank	+	−	−	Approvals are easier, but spreads and origination charges are less favorable (higher).
Credit union	−	−	−	Limited approval rates, with spreads and origination charges less favorable compared to White borrowers.

For Black borrowers, large banks impose stricter credit access, but once approved, they provide favorable rate spreads, albeit with higher origination charges. Fintech lenders offer easier access to credit but impose less favorable terms, such as higher spreads and origination charges. Non-bank and small-bank lenders present stricter credit access with consistently higher spreads and origination fees, reflecting unfavorable treatment for Black borrowers. Credit unions also exhibit stricter credit access and impose higher costs in both spreads and origination charges, resulting in the least favorable outcomes overall for this group.

For Hispanic borrowers, large banks enforce stricter approval standards but offer favorable rate spreads for those approved, although origination charges remain higher. Fintech lenders improve approval odds for Hispanic borrowers but impose higher spreads and origination fees. Non-bank lenders offer relatively easier approvals but charge less favorable spreads and higher origination fees. Small banks impose limited credit access, combined with higher spreads and origination charges for Hispanic borrowers. Similarly, credit unions provide less favorable approval rates and spreads for Hispanic borrowers, with inconclusive results regarding origination charges.

For Asian borrowers, large banks exhibit slightly stricter approval standards but offer favorable rate spreads and origination charges once approved. Fintech lenders provide easier credit access with favorable origination charges, but spreads are slightly higher compared to White borrowers. Non-bank lenders offer easier approvals for Asian borrowers but impose higher spreads and origination charges, making their terms less favorable. Small banks demonstrate limited credit access with higher spreads, though origination charges are more favorable for Asians. Credit unions also exhibit stricter credit access and impose less favorable spreads and origination charges for this group.

For Other Minorities, large banks impose stricter approval standards but provide more equitable spreads and only slightly higher origination charges once approved. Fintech lenders offer easier credit access with favorable origination charges but impose higher spreads. Non-bank lenders tend to approve Other Minority borrowers more readily but impose higher spreads and origination fees. Small banks offer better approval odds for this group but exhibit cost disparities with higher spreads and origination charges. Credit unions demonstrate stricter credit access with higher spreads and varying origination charges, highlighting significant disparities across subgroups and locations.

In essence, the overall conclusion is that differences across lender types cannot be fully explained by borrower risk factors alone. While some lender types might offer lower base prices, they can still impose larger minority penalties, and those that charge more on average may at times treat minority borrowers more even-handedly. These findings highlight the importance of scrutinizing individual lender practices and market structures to ensure that neither cost savings nor broader access comes at the expense of equitable treatment for minority borrowers.

5. Discussion and Implications

Our analysis of HMDA data from 2018 to 2023 reveals that racial and ethnic disparities persist across different lender types—large banks, fintech lenders, credit unions, non-bank lenders, and small banks—despite controlling for a range of borrower- and loan-level factors. While some lenders expand credit access or reduce specific cost penalties for minority borrowers, no single lender category systematically eliminates disparities in mortgage pricing or approval decisions. These results enrich a longstanding body of evidence [1–3,5] documenting persistent racial gaps in mortgage markets.

Large banks in our dataset tend to offer relatively equitable rate spreads once minority borrowers are approved, aligning with findings that heavier regulatory scrutiny can constrain discriminatory pricing [5]. However, our results also show higher denial rates for Black and Hispanic applicants at these institutions—echoing earlier research suggesting that strict underwriting guidelines can restrict credit access for borrowers perceived to be riskier or more difficult to underwrite [2,13].

At the other end of the spectrum, fintech lenders improve approval odds for minority borrowers but charge comparatively higher interest rate spreads and fees, a result consistent with recent studies that highlight how algorithmic underwriting can reduce some forms of human bias at the denial stage yet still embed pricing differentials [10,11]. This tension—between expanded access and persistent cost gaps—parallels earlier evidence from Buchak et al. [6] and Fuster et al. [7], showing that technology alone does not guarantee equitable outcomes.

Credit unions, which often tout consumer-friendly missions, provide the lowest average rate spreads but impose the steepest pricing penalties on Black and Hispanic borrowers, underscoring how "relationship-based" lending can, in some contexts, amplify subjective biases [13]. Similarly, small banks and non-bank lenders exhibit mixed or inconsistent patterns—some broaden access or reduce certain fees, yet they often fail to deliver consistently fair outcomes across different minority groups. In particular, non-bank lenders—operating with lighter regulatory constraints—can extend credit to underserved communities, but at higher spreads or costs [12].

Several mechanisms may help explain these results. First, heightened federal oversight likely incentivizes large banks to adopt standardized, risk-based pricing models that reduce some forms of cost discrimination but also tighten credit eligibility thresholds [5]. By contrast, fintech lenders often rely on algorithmic models that may be more inclusive at the approval stage—possibly because they reduce human discretion in initial screening—yet perpetuate structural biases in pricing or fees, as other researchers have highlighted [10,15].

Second, smaller, community-based lenders such as credit unions and small banks frequently rely on discretionary lending decisions. While this can yield more personalized terms for some borrowers, it can also lead to significant pricing penalties for certain minority groups, depending on local norms or individual loan-officer biases [13].

Finally, non-bank lenders—some of which specialize in higher-risk applicants—tend to approve more minority borrowers but at cost structures that may compound financial burdens. This aligns with research indicating that less strict underwriting can translate into wider access but less favorable loan terms for historically marginalized groups [12].

Because different lender types exhibit distinct patterns of approval and pricing disparities, policy solutions will require a tailored and multifaceted approach. First, extending or refining the scope of federal fair-lending regulations—such as the Community Reinvestment Act or ECOA enforcement—to encompass non-bank mortgage lenders could ensure that they undergo similarly rigorous fair-lending exams as large banks, an approach advocated in broader discussions of fintech oversight [6,7].

Second, transparent algorithmic audits could address the persistent cost gaps observed for minority borrowers at fintech lenders. Requiring regular reporting or third-party validations of automated underwriting models would help regulatory bodies identify and mitigate hidden biases in pricing [10,11].

Third, strengthening oversight and training for credit unions and small banks can help align their community-focused missions with equitable pricing. This might include specialized fair-lending reviews that highlight how add-on fees or discretionary interest rates disproportionately affect minority applicants, as well as improved data reporting on outcomes by race and ethnicity [13].

Although HMDA provides a broad lens on mortgage activity, it lacks direct credit metrics (e.g., FICO scores) that could further illuminate whether risk-based pricing alone explains the observed differentials [3,5]. Future work could merge HMDA with credit-bureau data to measure how much of these disparities remain after accounting for credit scores. Another fruitful line of research would be granular lender-level analyses of underwriting algorithms—especially among fintechs—to identify the specific model inputs or processes that sustain racial/ethnic pricing penalties.

In sum, our study confirms that the U.S. mortgage market remains stratified along racial and ethnic lines, even amid the rise of technology-focused lenders and diverse institutional structures. While certain practices—such as the more inclusive approvals seen at fintechs—show promise, the continuing presence of cost disparities highlights the need for ongoing policy intervention and deeper transparency in credit decisions to ensure equitable mortgage outcomes for all borrowers.

6. Conclusions

This study provides nuanced insights into how different lender types—large banks, fintech lenders, credit unions, small banks, and non-bank lenders—impact mortgage outcomes for minority borrowers. Using HMDA data from 2018 to 2023 and controlling for borrower and loan characteristics, we examine disparities in credit access, rate spreads, and origination charges.

Our findings suggest that large banks impose significant barriers to credit access for minority borrowers, reflected in higher denial rates compared to White borrowers. However, once approved, large banks generally offer better pricing for minority borrowers, with lower rate spreads and fewer pricing penalties. Despite this, minority borrowers often face higher upfront origination charges, increasing their total costs and potentially offsetting the benefits of lower pricing.

Fintech lenders, characterized by their reliance on technology and data-driven decision-making, show greater inclusivity in regard to credit access. Denial disparities for minority borrowers are narrower, and origination charges for minorities—particularly Black and Hispanic borrowers—are notably lower. However, fintech lenders impose higher rate spreads on approved minority borrowers, suggesting that while they improve access, the cost of borrowing remains a challenge for minorities.

Credit unions, despite their consumer-friendly image, exhibit mixed results. They offer the lowest overall rate spreads and origination charges, but their treatment of minority borrowers varies widely. Hispanic borrowers often face significant pricing penalties, with higher rate spreads and origination charges, while Black borrowers benefit from reduced costs and more favorable terms. This duality highlights the variability in credit union practices and raises questions about their equity in lending.

Small banks provide moderate credit access, with denial rates less stringent than those of large banks. However, the pricing outcomes for minority borrowers are inconsistent. Hispanic borrowers face higher rate spreads and origination charges, while Black borrowers receive more favorable terms and reduced costs compared to White borrowers. These mixed patterns suggest that small banks' localized and discretionary lending practices may exacerbate disparities for some groups while benefiting others.

Non-bank lenders offer relatively higher approval rates for minorities, improving credit access. However, their pricing and cost structures remain uneven. Hispanic borrowers frequently encounter higher rate spreads and origination charges, while Black borrowers experience reduced origination costs but still face elevated rate spreads. This variability underscores both the opportunities and risks associated with non-bank lenders in addressing lending disparities.

In sum, this study reveals that while fintech and non-bank lenders improve credit access for minority borrowers, they fail to eliminate disparities in pricing and costs. Large banks demonstrate relatively equitable pricing once minority borrowers are approved, but their stringent credit access standards remain a significant hurdle. Credit unions, despite offering lower baseline costs, impose severe penalties on certain minority groups, particularly Hispanic borrowers. Small banks and non-banks display inconsistent practices that result in varied outcomes for different minority groups. These findings highlight the need for enhanced regulatory oversight, standardized lending practices, and transparent algorithms to address persistent disparities in the mortgage market. Without targeted interventions, systemic inequities will continue to hinder equitable access to homeownership for minority borrowers.

However, the absence of direct credit risk measures, such as FICO scores, presents a limitation in fully isolating the impact of borrower creditworthiness on observed disparities. Nonetheless, this is not a critical concern, as prior research has found that credit scores do not vary significantly across lender types and are unlikely to account for the observed differences [5,6,23].

Author Contributions: Conceptualization, Z.L. and H.L.; methodology, Z.L.; software, Z.L.; validation, Z.L. and H.L.; formal analysis, Z.L.; investigation, Z.L.; resources, Z.L. and H.L.; data curation, Z.L.; writing—original draft preparation, Z.L.; writing—review and editing, Z.L. and H.L.; visualization, Z.L.; supervision, Z.L.; project administration, Z.L. and H.L. All authors have read and agreed to the published version of the manuscript.

Funding: This research received no external funding.

Institutional Review Board Statement: Not applicable.

Informed Consent Statement: Not applicable.

Data Availability Statement: The data used in this study are publicly available through the Home Mortgage Disclosure Act (HMDA) database for the years 2018 to 2023. The dataset can be accessed at https://ffiec.cfpb.gov/data-publication/ (accessed on 1 December 2024).

Conflicts of Interest: The authors report no conflicts of interest. The authors alone are responsible for the content and writing of the paper.

References

1. Bayer, P.; Ferreira, F.; Ross, S.L. What drives racial and ethnic differences in high-cost mortgages? The role of high-risk lenders. *Rev. Financ. Stud.* **2018**, *31*, 175–205. [CrossRef]
2. Charles, K.K.; Hurst, E. The transition to home ownership and the Black-White wealth gap. *Rev. Econ. Stat.* **2002**, *84*, 281–297. [CrossRef]
3. Munnell, A.H.; Tootell GM, B.; Browne, L.E.; McEneaney, J. Mortgage lending in Boston: Interpreting HMDA data. *Am. Econ. Rev.* **1996**, *86*, 25–53. Available online: https://www.jstor.org/stable/2118254 (accessed on 8 November 2024).

4. Avery, R.B.; Brevoort, K.P.; Canner, G.B. Does credit scoring produce a disparate impact? *Real Estate Econ.* **2012**, *40*, 65–114. [CrossRef]
5. Bhutta, N.; Hizmo, A. Do minorities pay more for mortgages? Review of the evidence. *J. Financ. Regul. Compliance* **2021**, *29*, 203–217.
6. Buchak, G.; Matvos, G.; Piskorski, T.; Seru, A. Fintech, regulatory arbitrage, and the rise of shadow banks. *J. Financ. Econ.* **2018**, *130*, 453–483. [CrossRef]
7. Fuster, A.; Plosser, M.; Schnabl, P.; Vickery, J. The role of technology in mortgage lending. *Rev. Financ. Stud.* **2019**, *32*, 1854–1899. [CrossRef]
8. Jagtiani, J.; Lemieux, C. The roles of alternative data and machine learning in fintech lending: Evidence from the LendingClub consumer platform. *Financ. Manag.* **2019**, *48*, 1009–1029. [CrossRef]
9. Demirgüç-Kunt, A.; Klapper, L.; Singer, D. *The Global Findex Database 2021: Financial Inclusion, Digital Payments, and Resilience in the Age of COVID-19*; World Bank: Washington, DC, USA, 2022.
10. Bartlett, R.; Morse, A.; Stanton, R.; Wallace, N. Consumer-lending discrimination in the FinTech era. *J. Financ. Econ.* **2022**, *143*, 30–56. [CrossRef]
11. Klein, A. *Reducing Bias in AI-Based Financial Services*; Brookings Institution Report; Brookings Institution: Washington, DC, USA, 2020.
12. DeFusco, A.A.; Mondragon, J. The rise of the principal-agent problem in the U.S. mortgage industry. *Am. Econ. Rev.* **2020**, *110*, 1137–1165.
13. Ross, S.L.; Yinger, J. *The Color of Credit: Mortgage Discrimination, Research Methodology, and Fair-Lending Enforcement*; MIT Press: Cambridge, MA, USA, 2002.
14. Gerardi, K.; Lambie-Hanson, L.; Willen, P.S. *Racial Differences in Mortgage Refinancing, Distress, and Housing Wealth Accumulation During COVID-19*; Curr. Policy Perspect. No. 92793; Fed. Reserve Bank of Boston: Boston, MA, USA, 2021.
15. Haupert, T. New Technology, Old Patterns: Fintech Lending, Metropolitan Segregation, and Subprime Credit. *Race Soc. Probl.* **2022**, *14*, 293–307. [CrossRef]
16. Fourcade, M.; Healy, K. Seeing Like a Market. *Socio-Econ. Rev.* **2017**, *15*, 9–29. [CrossRef]
17. Haupert, T. The Racial Landscape of Fintech Mortgage Lending. *Hous. Policy Debate* **2020**, *32*, 337–368. [CrossRef]
18. Faber, J.W. Racial Dynamics of Subprime Mortgage Lending at the Peak. *Hous. Policy Debate* **2013**, *23*, 328–349. [CrossRef]
19. Hammel, D.J.; Nilsson, I. Mortgage Foreclosures, Race, and Postrecession Lending. *Prof. Geogr.* **2019**, *71*, 536–550. [CrossRef]
20. Loya, J. Racial Stratification Among Latinos in the Mortgage Market. *Race Soc. Probl.* **2021**, *14*, 39–52. [CrossRef]
21. Sanchez-Moyano, R. Geography and Hispanic homeownership: A review of the literature. *J. Hous. Built Environ.* **2020**, *36*, 215–240. [CrossRef]
22. Haupert, T.; Lee, C.A. Fintech's relationship with subprime lending in immigrant gateway metropolitan areas. *J. Urban Aff.* **2022**, *46*, 281–297. [CrossRef]
23. Liu, Z.; Liang, H.; Zhao, X.S. *Do Non-Banks Bring Lower Prices for Borrowers in the Government-Sponsored Enterprise (GSE) Mortgage Market?* SSRN: Rochester, NY, USA, 2024.

FinTech

Article

Examining the Drivers and Economic and Social Impacts of Cryptocurrency Adoption

Yongsheng Guo *, Ezaddin Yousef and Mirza Muhammad Naseer

International Business School, Teesside University, Middlesbrough TS1 3BX, UK; e.yousef@tees.ac.uk (E.Y.); m.naseer@tees.ac.uk (M.M.N.)
* Correspondence: y.guo@tees.ac.uk; Tel.: +44-1642-342834

Abstract: This study investigates the key drivers and the economic and social impacts of cryptocurrency adoption. Based on panel data across 37 countries from 2020 to 2023, this research examines the interplay between cryptocurrency adoption and technology development, monetary policies, and economic and social development. Employing a mixed-methods approach, the research incorporates panel data analysis across multiple countries to explore correlations and causal relationships between these variables. The study found that technology development, measured by the Network Readiness Index (NRI) enables cryptocurrency adoption. Economic conditions measured by higher national inflation rates and monetary policy indicators, including lower interest and exchange rates are the key drivers for cryptocurrency adoption. The empirical findings reveal that cryptocurrency adoption has negative relationships with economic development measured by the GDP growth rate, unemployment rate, and social development represented by the governance quality corruption index. It implies that cryptocurrency is used as a virtual anchor (digital gold) for national inflation. Findings reveal how network readiness, economic conditions, and monetary policies contribute to fostering cryptocurrency adoption, while resulting in impacts on economic growth, labour markets, and governance. The research contributes to the literature by integrating technological, economic, and governance perspectives to elucidate the role of cryptocurrency in reshaping the global economic and social systems.

Keywords: cryptocurrency; inflation; monetary policies; GDP growth; governance quality

JEL Classification: C12; E4; O4

1. Introduction

The development of cryptocurrencies has undergone significant evolution [1,2], driven by technological advancements [3] and increased adoption across countries. Blockchain technology remains the backbone of cryptocurrencies, enabling features like immutability, decentralisation, and transparency [4]. The integration of blockchain into financial systems highlights its potential to improve transactional efficiency and foster financial inclusion [5,6]. Cryptocurrency adoption has emerged as a transformative element in global financial ecosystems [7], influencing various aspects of economic development [8]. Its potential to enhance financial inclusion, foster innovation, and streamline cross-border transactions highlights its role in shaping modern economies [9–11].

The adoption of cryptocurrencies and their interplay with national inflation has garnered increasing academic interest due to their disruptive potential in financial systems [12–15]. Specifically, cryptocurrencies, often seen as a hedge against inflation, have found popularity in countries with unstable fiat currencies [16,17]. Cryptocurrencies are often criticised for their price volatility [3,18], which can hinder their utility as a reliable store of value or medium of exchange. This volatility poses risks for economies heavily reliant on digital currencies for development [19,20].

Moreover, issues like fraud, cyberattacks, and insufficient consumer protection mechanisms [1,21] can undermine trust in cryptocurrencies, limiting their adoption and economic impact. Last but not least, energy-intensive mining processes associated with cryptocurrencies like Bitcoin raise environmental sustainability questions [22], particularly in developing economies with limited energy resources [7].

The studies investigate the drivers of cryptocurrency adoption, focusing on the interplay between technology development [16,17], economic conditions [14,23], monetary policies [24–26], non-crypto investors [27] and perceived corruption [28]. Technology development is evaluated using the Network Readiness Index (NRI), which captures a nation's capacity to leverage technology for growth and innovation. Economic conditions are represented by the national inflation rate (INF) and Economic Freedom Index (EFI), highlighting the role of macroeconomic stability in fostering or hindering cryptocurrency adoption. Monetary policy indicators, including the interest rate (INT) and exchange rate (EXR), are analysed to understand their influence on the decision to adopt decentralised digital currencies as alternatives or complements to traditional financial systems. Moreover, this study examines the impact of cryptocurrency adoption on economic and social development [12,14], focusing on key indicators such as the economic growth rate (GDP), unemployment rate (UEMP), and governance quality as represented by the corruption index (CORR).

This study aims to provide insights into how technological preparedness, economic pressures, and monetary dynamics shape the adoption trajectory of cryptocurrencies globally, and to offer a better understanding of the role of cryptocurrency in macroeconomic performance and societal governance. It reveals the advantages of cryptocurrencies in fostering economic opportunities while highlighting the challenges of potential economic and governance risks. By bridging the gap between cryptocurrency adoption and broader developmental outcomes, this study contributes to the growing body of knowledge on financial technology and proposes practical implications for policymakers, investors, and technology developers in navigating the evolving cryptocurrency landscape.

The rest of this paper is designed to provide a critical review of existing studies on cryptocurrency adoption, and economic and social development. The Theoretical Framework and Hypotheses are derived based on identified research gaps. The Research Methodology Section explains the data sources, variables, and econometric models used to examine the relationships between cryptocurrency adoption and developmental indicators. The Results and Discussion Section presents the findings, offering detailed interpretations and comparisons with existing literature. Finally, the Conclusion and Policy Implications Section summarises the study's contributions, suggests practical applications, and highlights avenues for future research.

2. Literature Review

2.1. *Drivers of Cryptocurrency Adoption*

Among others, technological development, national economic conditions, and monetary policies are the main drivers of cryptocurrency adoption. The role of technology in cryptocurrency adoption is critical, as digital currencies are inherently technological innovations [16,17]. The study [29] uses a mixed-methods approach to explore factors influencing the adoption of sustainable cryptocurrencies and investment barriers. It provides insights for investors, policymakers, and industry managers, emphasising the importance of regulatory support, customer trust, and sustainability in promoting cryptocurrency adoption [29]. Other studies show that countries with robust internet penetration, advanced mobile networks, and high rates of digital literacy are more likely to see higher cryptocurrency adoption rates [30]. Moreover, the rapid evolution of blockchain applications, including decentralised finance (DeFi) and non-fungible tokens (NFTs), has further driven adoption [31].

Economic conditions often act as a catalyst for cryptocurrency adoption [32], particularly in regions with high inflation or volatile currencies [33,34]. For instance, studies demonstrate that individuals and businesses in countries with unstable fiat currencies turn to cryptocurrencies as a store of value or medium of exchange to hedge against economic uncertainty [35]. Inflation rates have a significant impact, as seen in nations like Venezuela and Zimbabwe, where hyperinflation led to a surge in cryptocurrency use [36].

Additionally, economic growth indicators such as GDP per capita influence adoption, with higher-income countries showing greater investment in cryptocurrencies as speculative assets. The study [37] utilised Fuzzy-set Qualitative Comparative Analysis an inductive approach whereby causal factors are obtained from prior studies to explore their complex interdependency. It first analyses a larger sample of 101 countries (without cultural values) and further investigates the cultural aspects and their roles in 43 countries. The result shows that social factors and financial development are the central factors for cryptocurrency adoption. Monetary policies, including interest rates and exchange rate stability [38], significantly shape cryptocurrency adoption. Low or negative interest rates reduce the opportunity cost of holding cryptocurrencies, thereby encouraging adoption [39,40]. Similarly, exchange rate volatility incentivises individuals and corporations to adopt cryptocurrencies as a means of preserving value and facilitating cross-border transactions without the risks associated with fluctuating fiat currencies [41]. Regulatory clarity in monetary policies also plays a crucial role; permissive environments foster adoption, while restrictive measures, such as outright bans, hinder it [42].

2.2. *Effects of Cryptocurrency Adoption*

Cryptocurrency adoption has sparked significant debate among researchers [19,21] and policymakers regarding its effects on macroeconomic indicators and social structures. Cryptocurrencies contribute to economic growth by facilitating financial inclusion, reducing transaction costs, and promoting cross-border trade [43]. Blockchain technology, which underpins cryptocurrencies, enhances financial efficiency and transparency, thus encouraging economic activity [30]. For example, decentralised finance (DeFi) platforms allow small- and medium-sized enterprises (SMEs) to access funding in regions where traditional banking systems are underdeveloped.

Studies highlight a positive correlation between cryptocurrency adoption and GDP growth, particularly in emerging markets. Ref. [1] emphasises the role of cryptocurrencies in increasing remittance inflows, which are crucial for economic development in low-income countries. However, critics argue that speculative trading and market volatility could overshadow these benefits, leading to financial instability.

Cryptocurrencies have implications for social development, particularly governance quality and corruption. Blockchain's transparency and immutability make it a valuable tool for combating corruption by ensuring accountability in public financial management [42]. Countries with high levels of corruption often experience increased cryptocurrency adoption as citizens seek alternatives to circumvent corrupt financial systems [35].

Despite these benefits, the anonymity provided by some cryptocurrencies can also enable illicit activities, undermining governance and legal systems. Research by [36] highlights a dual impact: while blockchain fosters transparency, unregulated cryptocurrency markets may facilitate tax evasion and money laundering. Addressing these challenges requires robust regulatory frameworks that balance innovation with accountability.

2.3. Research Gaps

Despite extensive studies on the drivers and effects of cryptocurrency adoption, several gaps remain [19,20]. Firstly, although the literature extensively covers individual drivers, integrated models that examine the interplay between technology, economic conditions, and monetary policies are limited. Secondly, while the impact of inflation is well documented in hyperinflationary economies, more research is needed on stable monetary systems. Thirdly, the long-term effects of cryptocurrency on economic growth and the role of cryptocurrencies in enhancing governance quality calls for nuanced studies on international contexts.

The adoption of cryptocurrencies is a multifaceted phenomenon driven by technological advancements, economic conditions, and monetary policies. Understanding these drivers offers valuable insights for policymakers, businesses, and technology developers, aiming to harness the potential of digital currencies. Future research should adopt a multidisciplinary approach to address existing gaps and provide a holistic view of cryptocurrency adoption dynamics.

The adoption of cryptocurrencies has significant implications for inflation management, economic growth, and social development. While they offer innovative solutions for financial inclusion and governance, challenges such as volatility and regulatory concerns persist. A comprehensive understanding of these dynamics is essential for maximising the benefits of cryptocurrency adoption while mitigating associated risks.

2.4. Theoretical Framework and Hypotheses

This study introduces the multiple-currency model for cryptocurrency where cryptocurrencies coexist or compete with traditional fiat currencies catering for different functions [44]. For example, multiple currencies provide diverse financial tools, enabling access for underserved populations without access to traditional banking systems [1]. A diverse currency ecosystem promotes innovation in payment technologies, transaction efficiencies, and financial products [30].

This study argues that cryptocurrencies can be used as a nominal anchor [45], which suggests that the value of a currency should be tied to a stable measure or "anchor" to maintain price stability and control inflation [46,47]. For example, Bitcoin has been proposed as a potential nominal anchor in a decentralised monetary system [36] because of its fixed supply (capped at 21 million coins), and in environments where fiat currencies are unreliable [35].

Based on the multiple-currency model and nominal anchor theory, this study builds a theoretical framework for cryptocurrency adoption. Factors such as technological development, monetary policies and economic conditions influence the adoption of cryptocurrency. Moreover, cryptocurrency adoption affects national economic and social development. Therefore, this study proposes the following hypotheses:

H1. *Cryptocurrency adoption has positive relationships with technology development, monetary policies and economic conditions;*

H2. *Cryptocurrency adoption has positive relationships with economic growth, labour market and social development.*

3. Research Methodology

3.1. Data and Variables

This study employs a quantitative research design using panel data analysis to investigate the drivers and impacts of cryptocurrency adoption. The data spans 37 countries from 2020 to 2023, covering diverse economic, social, and governance contexts. The dependent variable of the study is the cryptocurrency adoption rate (CAR) measured by the Crypto Adoption Index. Chainalysis produces annual reports known as the Crypto Adoption Index, which aims to measure and track cryptocurrency adoption levels in different countries. The index is based on a comprehensive analysis of blockchain transactions. The global Crypto Adoption Index ranks countries on a scale of 0–1. The closer the score is to 1, the higher the rank [48].

The dependent variables are GDP, INF, UNEMP, EXR, NRI, INTR, CORR, and EFI. GDP is calculated as the total market value of all goods and services produced within a country in a specific year, serving as a key indicator of economic health. To adjust for inflation effects, GDP is often expressed in constant U.S. dollars. INF is quantified through the annual percentage change in the Consumer Price Index, which tracks the cost-of-living adjustments. UNEMP is defined as the proportion of the labour force that is unemployed but actively seeking work. EXR denotes the rate at which a country's currency can be exchanged for the U.S. dollar (USD), reflecting the relative stability of the national currency. NRI measures a country's capability to adopt and utilise digital technologies, including cryptocurrencies. It evaluates aspects such as ICT infrastructure, affordability, digital skills, and usage, with higher scores indicating better readiness for digital advancements and cryptocurrency integration (detailed methodology available at https://networkreadinessindex.org/ accessed on 2 September 2024). Figure 1 illustrates the main pillars of the NRI. INTR is represented by the central bank's policy rate or the short-term interest rate, which influences the cost of borrowing and returns on savings, thereby impacting investment choices and financial behaviour including the uptake of cryptocurrencies. CPI, published by Transparency International, gauges the perceived levels of public sector corruption in a country. Higher corruption may encourage the use of cryptocurrencies to circumvent traditional financial systems seen as corrupt. EFI issued by the Heritage Foundation, evaluates economic freedom within a country, considering elements like property rights, government integrity, and regulatory efficiency. Elevated levels of economic freedom typically correlate with more developed financial markets and greater receptiveness to innovations such as cryptocurrencies.

Figure 1. Pillars of Network Readiness Index (NRI)—source [49].

3.2. Empirical Strategy

Panel data methodology is chosen for its ability to capture both cross-sectional and time-series variations, allowing for robust modelling of the relationships among variables [50]. Based on the theoretical framework hypotheses are derived from literature. The research model below illustrates the relationship between cryptocurrency adoption with technology development, monetary policies, and economic conditions.

$$CAR_{i,t} = A\ X\ (NRI)_{i,t}{}^{a1} X\ (INTR)_{i,t}{}^{a2} X\ (EXR)_{i,t}{}^{a3} X(EF1)_{i,t}{}^{a4} \quad (1)$$

Moreover, the dependent variables and relationships might be dynamic and evolve over time. Equation (2) shows dynamic models.

$$\frac{dCARi_t}{dt} = f\left(CAR_{i(t-n)},\ NRI_{it}, INTR_{it}, EXR_{it}, EFI_t\right) \quad (2)$$

where CAR is the cryptocurrency adoption rate; NRI is the Network Readiness Index; INTR is the National Central Bank interest rate; EXR is the exchange rate; and EFI is the Economic Freedom Index.

Moreover, cryptocurrency adoption may have relationships with economic and social development.

$$CAR_{i,t} = A\ X\ (INF)_{i,t}{}^{5a} X\ (GDP)_{i,t}{}^{a6} X\ (UNEMP)_{i,t}{}^{a7} X(CORR)_{i,t}{}^{a8} \quad (3)$$

Moreover, the dependent variables and relationships might be dynamic and evolve over time. Equation (4) shows the dynamic model.

$$\frac{dCARi_t}{dt} = f\left(CAR_{i(t-n)},\ INF_{it}, GDP_{it}, UNEMP_{it}, CORR_{it}\right) \quad (4)$$

where CAR is the cryptocurrency adoption rate; INF is the national annual inflation rate, representing economic development; GDP is the gross domestic product growth rate, representing economic development; UNEMP is the national unemployment rate, representing social development; and CORR is the corruption index of the quality of governance represents social development.

The study uses secondary data obtained from international databases, including those of the World Bank, IMF, and Transparency International, over a period from 2020 to 2023.

Table 1 shows the variables and data sources.

Table 1. Variables and data source.

Variables	Indicator Name	Definition	Data Source
CAR	Cryptocurrency Adoption Rate	Global Crypto Adoption Index	Chain analysis, data are available at https://www.chainalysis.com/blog/2023-global-crypto-adoption-index (accessed on 10 October 2023)
NRI	Network Readiness Index	Network Readiness Index	Data are available at https://networkreadinessindex.org (accessed on 10 October 2024)
INTR	Interest Rate	National Central Bank Interest rate	International Monetary Fund (IMF) Database

Table 1. *Cont.*

Variables	Indicator Name	Definition	Data Source
EXR	Exchange Rate	EXR is the exchange rate (nominal), which represents the value at which the currency of a specific country can be exchanged for the United States Dollar (USD)	International Monetary Fund (IMF) Database
EFI	Economic Freedom	The impact of liberty and free markets around the globe	The Heritage Foundation's Index of Economic Freedom
INF	Inflation Rate	Consumer Prices Index (CPI)	International Monetary Fund (IMF) Database
GDP	Gross Domestic Product	Gross domestic product (current US $)	World Bank national accounts data, and OECD National Accounts data files
UNEMP	Unemployment Rate	The International Labour Organisation's (ILO) unemployment rate	https://stats.oecd.org (accessed on 10 October 2024)
CORR	Corruption Index	CORR perceives levels of public sector corruption, score 0 (highly corrupt) to 100 (very clean)	https://www.transparency.org (accessed on 10 October 2024)

To examine the relationships among key variables, a comprehensive approach includes pairwise correlations, cross-sectional dependence tests, regression tests, and causality tests are used in this study.

The Pearson correlation coefficient [51] is computed to find the pairwise correlations among variables.

$$\varrho(X,Y) = Cov(X,Y)/\sigma X\sigma Y$$

where $\varrho(X,Y)$ is the Pearson correlation coefficient; Cov (X, Y) is the covariance between variables X and Y; σX and σY are the standard deviations of X and Y, respectively.

To find if the observations are interdependent or correlated, a cross-sectional dependence test is conducted. The Breusch–Pagan LM test [52] is conducted to assess heteroscedasticity. To examine cross-sectional dependence, the Pesaran-scaled LM test [53] is employed to ensure the independence of observations. The Bias-Corrected Scaled LM test is applied to mitigate finite-sample bias [54]. The Pesaran CD test is used to explore cross-sectional dependence [55], which ensures the robustness of detecting dependencies among different cross-sectional units.

In the Breusch–Pagan LM test,

$$\mathrm{LM} = \mathrm{nR}^2$$

where

LM: the test statistic;

n: the number of observations;

R^2: the R-squared from the regression.

In the Pesaran-scaled LM test,

$$\mathrm{LM} = \frac{\mathrm{N}}{\mathrm{N}-1}\frac{\mathrm{T}(\mathrm{T}-1)}{4}\frac{\mathrm{R}^2}{1-\mathrm{R}^2}$$

where

LM: the test statistic;

N: the number of cross-sectional units;

T: the number of time periods;

R^2: the R-squared from the auxiliary regression.

In the Bias-Corrected Scaled LM Test,

$$\mathrm{LM_{BC}} = \mathrm{LM} / \left(1 - \frac{2}{\mathrm{T}}\right)$$

where

$\mathrm{LM_{BC}}$: the Bias-Corrected LM test statistic;

LM: The original LM test statistic;

T: the number of time periods.

In the Pesaran CD test,

$$\mathrm{CD} = \mathrm{N(LM/N)}$$

where

CD: the Pesaran CD test statistic;

LM: the test statistic from the Pesaran-scaled LM test;

N is the number of cross-sectional units.

Ordinary Least Squares (OLS) is used in the Baseline Regression, estimating the parameters in linear regression models. The coefficients derived from OLS provide the magnitude and direction of the relationship [56]. R^2 shows the Goodness-of-Fit measuring the proportion of variance in the dependent variable explained by the independent variables [57].

Feasible Generalised Least Squares (FGLS) is an econometric estimation technique used to address issues of heteroskedasticity and autocorrelation in regression models. FGLS provides more efficient and unbiased parameter estimates under heteroskedasticity or autocorrelation [56]. The technique of Panel-Corrected Standard Errors (PCSEs) is an econometric method developed by [58] to address issues of heteroskedasticity and cross-sectional dependence in panel data regression models. PCSEs adjust the standard errors of regression coefficients to ensure valid statistical inference when the error structure exhibits contemporaneous correlation and heteroskedasticity across panel units. The Generalised Method of Moments (GMM) is a widely used econometric estimation technique [59], which is particularly suitable for models that involve endogeneity, heteroskedasticity, or when the researcher has a set of moment conditions derived from economic theory. It has become a standard tool for dynamic panel data models, time-series analysis, and instrumental variable regressions [60].

The pairwise Dumitrescu–Hurlin panel causality test is employed to identify the causal relationships [61]. The Wald Statistic WStat is used to check the existence of causality in panel data:

$$W_{Stat} = \frac{T(N-1)}{N(T-1)} \left(\sum_{i=1}^{N} \sum_{t=1}^{T} \check{\varepsilon}_{it}^{2} \right)$$

where

$\mathrm{W_{Stat}}$: the Wald Statistic;

T: the number of time periods;

N: the number of cross-sectional units;

$\check{\varepsilon}_{it}$: the residuals from the pooled regression.

4. Findings and Discussion

4.1. Summary Statistics

Table 2 provides descriptive statistics for the variables, summarising their central tendencies and variations based on a dataset of 148 observations. The cryptocurrency adoption rate (CAR) has a mean of 0.11 with a standard deviation of 0.137, and the maximum adoption is 0.93, reflecting an uneven distribution of digital currency penetration. The dataset demonstrates diverse economic, social, and technological contexts across observations. There is significant variability in interest and exchange rates, inflation, and governance quality suggesting heterogeneity among the entities studied.

Table 2. Descriptive statistics.

Variable	Obs	Mean	Std. Dev.	Min	Max
CAR	148	0.110	0.137	0.000	0.931
GDP	148	1.914	4.822	−11.20	16.30
INF	148	4.862	4.142	−1.20	19.70
UNEMP	148	6.322	2.983	2.000	17.60
EXR	148	24.129	62.851	0.630	375.0
NRI	148	67.707	8.745	46.26	82.75
INTR	148	2.350	2.783	−0.75	16.00
CORR	148	64.98	15.679	26.00	90.00
EFI	148	71.816	6.193	53.80	84.20

The table provides descriptive statistics for the study variables. CAR is the cryptocurrency adoption rate, GDP is the gross domestic product, INF is inflation, UNEMP is the unemployment rate, EXR is the exchange rate, NRI is the Network Readiness Index, INTR is interest rates, CORR is the corruption index, and EFI is the economic freedom.

Table 3 provides a correlation matrix showing the relationships between variables of interest. Each entry represents the Pearson correlation coefficient ranging from −1 to 1. The weak but notable correlation between cryptocurrency adoption (CAR) and inflation (INF) suggests that inflationary environments may drive individuals toward alternative financial systems like cryptocurrencies. Strong correlations between the Network Readiness Index (NRI) and governance indicators (CORR and EFI) highlight the critical role of technological infrastructure in promoting better governance and economic freedom. The positive relationship between inflation (INF) and interest rates (INTR) underscores the interplay between monetary policy and price stability.

Table 3. Matrix of correlations.

Variables	(1)	(2)	(3)	(4)	(5)	(6)	(7)	(8)	(9)
(1) CAR	1.000								
(2) GDP	−0.142	1.000							
(3) INF	0.147	0.248	1.000						
(4) UNEMP	−0.063	−0.122	−0.091	1.000					
(5) EXR	−0.030	−0.003	0.236	−0.115	1.000				
(6) NRI	0.110	−0.007	−0.356	−0.422	−0.257	1.000			
(7) INTR	0.077	0.082	0.675	−0.174	0.360	−0.377	1.000		
(8) CORR	−0.098	−0.049	−0.279	−0.354	−0.333	0.880	−0.348	1.000	
(9) EFI	−0.096	0.055	−0.170	−0.389	−0.232	0.674	−0.336	0.788	1.000

The table provides a correlation matrix for the study variables. CAR is the cryptocurrency adoption rate, GDP is the gross domestic product, INF is inflation, UNEMP is the unemployment rate, EXR is the exchange rate, NRI is the Network Readiness Index, INTR is interest rates, CORR is the corruption index, and EFI is the economic freedom.

4.2. Cross-Sectional Dependence and Slope Heterogeneity Test

Table 4 reports the results from multiple tests for cross-sectional dependence among variables by using Breusch–Pagan LM, Pesaran Scaled LM, Bias-Corrected Scaled LM, and Pesaran CD tests. These tests determine whether variables exhibit dependence across cross-sectional units (countries) in panel data. The null hypothesis (H0H_0H0) for all tests is that there is no cross-sectional dependence. All tests indicate substantial cross-sectional dependence for most variables, implying that global or regional factors play a significant role in shaping the variables under study. This finding supports the need for econometric techniques, such as cross-sectional dependence-adjusted models or spatial econometrics, to account for these correlations in further analyses. In particular, the Pesaran CD test, suitable for both small time periods and cross-sections, generally confirms the presence of cross-sectional dependence, although some variables, such as CORR (1.307) and EFI (10.086), show weaker dependence compared to others.

Table 4. Cross-sectional dependence tests and slope heterogeneity.

Variables	Breusch–Pagan LM	Pesaran Scaled LM	Bias-Corrected Scaled LM	Pesaran CD
CAR	2223.08 ***	42.66 ***	36.50 ***	46.71 ***
GDP	2125.31 ***	39.98 ***	33.82 ***	45.41 ***
INF	2277.10 ***	44.144 ***	37.978 ***	47.525 ***
UNEMP	1687.028 ***	27.976 ***	21.809 ***	38.767 ***
EXR	1543.961 ***	32.028 ***	25.862 ***	16.086 ***
NRI	1896.972 ***	33.728 ***	27.562 ***	38.964 ***
INTR	1974.971 ***	41.784 ***	30.731 ***	12.448 ***
CORR	1452.287 ***	21.544 ***	15.377 ***	1.307
EFI	1396.961 ***	20.028 ***	13.862 ***	10.086 ***
Testing for slope heterogeneity [62]. H0: slope coefficients are homogenous.				
Delta	−7.795			
*p*_value	0.000			

The table presents cross-sectional dependence using four different tests and slope heterogeneity using Pesaran and Yamagata (2008) tests [62]. The null hypothesis (H0) for cross-sectional dependence is that underlying variables are independent across different sections while for slope heterogeneity it is slope coefficients are homogenous. Asterisks indicate statistical significance at the 10% one-star, 5% two-star, and 1% three-star levels, respectively. *** $p < 0.01$, ** $p < 0.05$, * $p < 0.1$.

4.3. Baseline Regression

Table 5 presents results from multiple Ordinary Least Squares (OLS) regression models, testing the effects of several independent variables. The results show that Inflation (INF), GDP, technological readiness (NRI), exchange rates (EXR), and governance quality (CORR) emerge as significant drivers of cryptocurrency adoption. Unemployment (UNEMP), interest rates (INTR), and economic freedom (EFI) show limited or no significant effects. It highlights the importance of technological infrastructure in facilitating cryptocurrency usage and the impact of inflation, exchange rates, and governance on shaping adoption patterns.

Table 6 presents the result from three econometric models Feasible Generalised Least Squares (FGLS), Panel-Corrected Standard Errors (PCSEs), and Generalised Method of Moments (GMM) to analyse the relationships between the dependent variable (likely cryptocurrency adoption rate (CAR)) and several independent variables. The lagged cryptocurrency adoption rate in the GMM model has a significant negative relationship (coefficient = −0.518; $p < 0.01$), showing that a high past adoption rate is associated with a reduction in current adoption growth, potentially due to market saturation or diminishing marginal adoption effects. Inflation (INF) is positive and significant across all models (coefficients: 0.018 in FGLS test, 0.017 in PCSE test, and 0.008 in GMM test), which means that higher inflation rates drive cryptocurrency adoption, supporting its role as a hedge against fiat currency instability.

Table 5. Baseline regression.

Variables	(1)	(2)	(3)	(4)	(5)	(6)	(7)	(8)	(9)
GDP	−0.004 *								−0.008 ***
	(0.002)								(0.002)
INF		0.005 *							0.013 ***
		(0.003)							(0.003)
UNEMP			−0.003						0.001
			(0.004)						(0.004)
EXR				−0.002					−0.005 **
				(0.001)					(0.001)
NRI					0.002				0.018 ***
					(0.001)				(0.003)
INTR						0.004			−0.002
						(0.004)			(0.005)
CORR							−0.001		−0.010 ***
							(0.001)		(0.002)
EFI								−0.002	0.001
								(0.002)	(0.003)
Constant	0.118 ***	0.087 ***	0.128 ***	0.112 ***	−0.006	0.101 ***	0.166 ***	0.262 **	−0.572 ***
	(0.012)	(0.017)	(0.026)	(0.012)	(0.088)	(0.015)	(0.048)	(0.131)	(0.213)
Observations	148	148	148	148	148	148	148	148	148
R-squared	0.020	0.022	0.004	0.001	0.012	0.006	0.010	0.009	0.327

This table contains estimates of baseline regression models. The dependent variable is CAR (cryptocurrency adoption rate), GDP is the gross domestic product, INF is inflation, UNEMP is the unemployment rate, EXR is the exchange rate, NRI is the Network Readiness Index, INTR is interest rates, CORR is the corruption index, and EFI is economic freedom. All estimations include OLS. Under the coefficients in the parentheses () standard errors are shown. Statistical significance is indicated by asterisks at the * (10%), ** (5%), and *** (1%).

Table 6. Results using FGLS, PCSEs, and GMM.

	(1)	(2)	(3)
Variables	**FGLS**	**PCSEs**	**GMM**
L.CAR			−0.518 ***
			(0.044)
INF	0.018 ***	0.017 ***	0.008 **
	(0.003)	(0.001)	(0.003)
CORR	−0.006 ***	−0.007 ***	−0.022 ***
	(0.001)	(0.002)	(0.004)
NRI	0.015 ***	0.018 ***	0.023 **
	(0.002)	(0.005)	(0.010)
INTR	−0.017 ***	−0.021 ***	−0.018 ***
	(0.006)	(0.006)	(0.005)
EFI	−0.005 **	−0.006 ***	−0.007 **
	(0.002)	(0.002)	(0.003)
UNEMP	−0.002	−0.007 ***	−0.005
	(0.004)	(0.002)	(0.010)
GDP	−0.005 *	−0.006 ***	−0.006 *
	(0.003)	(0.002)	(0.003)
EXR	−0.004	−0.002	−0.001
	(0.003)	(0.003)	(0.001)
Constant	−0.240	−0.144	0.067
	(0.195)	(0.223)	(0.454)
Observations	148	148	148
R-squared		0.766	
Wald chi2	102.45	734.98	275.70
Prob > chi2	0.000	0.000	0.000

Table 6. *Cont.*

	(1)	(2)	(3)
Variables	**FGLS**	**PCSEs**	**GMM**
AR2			0.768
Sargan			0.396

This table contains estimates of long-run co-integration analysis models. The dependent variable is CAR (cryptocurrency adoption rate), GDP is the gross domestic product, INF is inflation, UNEMP is the unemployment rate, EXR is the exchange rate, NRI is the Network Readiness Index, INTR is interest rates, CORR is the corruption index, and EFI is economic freedom. Estimations include FGLS, PCSE, and GMM. Under the coefficients in the parentheses () standard errors are shown. Statistical significance is indicated by asterisks at the * (10%), ** (5%), and *** (1%).

The Network Readiness Index (NRI) is positive and significant across all models, indicating that technological development strongly promotes cryptocurrency adoption. Interest Rate (INTR) shows negative and significant across all models, which means that higher interest rates discourage cryptocurrency adoption, possibly because traditional savings instruments become more attractive. The Economic Freedom Index (EFI) is negative and significant across all models. It means greater economic freedom reduces cryptocurrency adoption, suggesting that cryptocurrencies thrive more in restrictive environments. exchange rate (EXR) is not significant, indicating limited direct effects on cryptocurrency adoption.

The economic growth rate (GDP) is negative and significant in all models, which reveals that higher GDP levels are associated with reduced cryptocurrency adoption. Maybe stable economies rely less on alternative financial tools, and cryptocurrency is widely used in less-developed nations. The unemployment rate (UNEMP) has mixed results as it may have varying impacts on cryptocurrency adoption depending on model specification. The corruption index (CORR) is negative and significant across all models, showing that higher governance quality is associated with reduced cryptocurrency adoption; possibly, cryptocurrency is widely used in corrupt nations.

4.4. Granger Causality Tests

Table 7 illustrates the results of Granger causality tests conducted between various economic, social, and technological variables. The relationship between cryptocurrency adoption rate (CAR) and inflation (INF) is bidirectional, with stronger evidence that CAR influences inflation, possibly by increasing speculative or transactional demand in high-inflation economies. No predictive relationship is observed between corruption levels and cryptocurrency adoption. Technology development predicts cryptocurrency adoption, reflecting the importance of digital infrastructure. Cryptocurrency adoption predicts economic freedom, possibly by influencing financial innovation or liberalisation.

Table 7. Pairwise Granger causality tests.

X → Y Test (F, *p*)	Y → X Test (F, *p*)	Direction
CORR → CAR: (0.074, 0.786)	CAR → CORR: (1.550, 0.216)	Uni-directional
EFI → CAR: (0.235, 0.629)	CAR → EFI: (8.070, 0.005)	Uni-directional
EXR → CAR: (0.127, 0.723)	CAR → EXR: (0.231, 0.632)	Uni-directional
GDP → CAR: (13.149, 0.000)	CAR → GDP: (7.261, 0.008)	Bi-directional
INF → CAR: (3.777, 0.055)	CAR → INF: (10.725, 0.001)	Bi-directional
INTR → CAR: (1.845, 0.177)	CAR → INTR: (0.184, 0.669)	No
NRI → CAR: (3.962, 0.049)	CAR → NRI: (2.289, 0.133)	Uni-directional
UNEMP → CAR: (0.006, 0.939)	CAR → UNEMP: (0.098, 0.754)	No
EFI → CORR: (1.137, 0.289)	CORR → EFI: (9.976, 0.002)	Uni-directional
EXR → CORR: (1.804, 0.182)	CORR → EXR: (0.001, 0.974)	No

Table 7. *Cont.*

X → Y Test (F, p)	Y → X Test (F, p)	Direction
GDP → CORR: (0.050, 0.824)	CORR → GDP: (3.330, 0.071)	Uni-directional
INF → CORR: (10.204, 0.002)	CORR → INF: (0.988, 0.322)	Uni-directional
INTR → CORR: (2.951, 0.089)	CORR → INTR: (2.559, 0.113)	Uni-directional
NRI → CORR: (0.000, 0.988)	CORR → NRI: (5.098, 0.026)	Uni-directional
UNEMP → CORR: (2.256, 0.136)	CORR → UNEMP: (0.598, 0.441)	No
EXR → EFI: (2.098, 0.150)	EFI → EXR: (0.097, 0.756)	No
GDP → EFI: (3.128, 0.080)	EFI → GDP: (1.044, 0.309)	Uni-directional
INF → EFI: (2.220, 0.139)	EFI → INF: (32.592, 0.000)	Uni-directional
INTR → EFI: (0.892, 0.347)	EFI → INTR: (38.784, 0.000)	Uni-directional
NRI → EFI: (3.365, 0.069)	EFI → NRI: (4.524, 0.036)	Bi-directional
UNEMP → EFI: (0.361, 0.549)	EFI → UNEMP: (2.779, 0.098)	No
GDP → EXR: (0.237, 0.627)	EXR → GDP: (0.279, 0.598)	No
INF → EXR: (6.509, 0.012)	EXR → INF: (4.872, 0.029)	Bi-directional
INTR → EXR: (2.817, 0.096)	EXR → INTR: (25.935, 0.000)	Uni-directional
NRI → EXR: (0.015, 0.904)	EXR → NRI: (0.197, 0.658)	No
UNEMP → EXR: (0.362, 0.549)	EXR → UNEMP: (0.179, 0.673)	No
INF → GDP: (38.903, 0.000)	GDP → INF: (47.989, 0.000)	Bi-directional
INTR → GDP: (37.933, 0.000)	GDP → INTR: (25.004, 0.000)	Bi-directional
NRI → GDP: (64.697, 0.000)	GDP → NRI: (1.688, 0.197)	Uni-directional
UNEMP → GDP: (8.406, 0.005)	GDP → UNEMP: (1.313, 0.254)	Uni-directional
INTR → INF: (0.716, 0.399)	INF → INTR: (10.532, 0.002)	Uni-directional
NRI → INF: (7.949, 0.006)	INF → NRI: (57.435, 0.000)	Bi-directional
UNEMP → INF: (1.791, 0.184)	INF → UNEMP: (4.263, 0.041)	Uni-directional
UNEMP → INTR: (0.259, 0.612)	INTR → UNEMP: (3.727, 0.056)	Uni-directional

This table contains estimates of Granger causality tests. CAR is the cryptocurrency adoption rate, GDP is the gross domestic product, INF is inflation, UNEMP is the unemployment rate, EXR is the exchange rate, NRI is the Network Readiness Index, INTR is interest rates, CORR is the corruption index, and EFI is economic freedom. After the variable pair in parentheses (), the first value is f-stat, and the second value following the comma is the *p*-value.

The bidirectional causality suggests that GDP growth fosters cryptocurrency adoption, and adoption might influence economic output, possibly through financial innovation. No significant Granger causality is observed between CAR and unemployment (UNEMP) or exchange rate (EXR) in either direction.

In addition, the results show that corruption drives inflation but not vice versa. Inflation impacts technological readiness, and vice versa, reflecting economic interdependencies. GDP and inflation mutually influence each other, which is consistent with macroeconomic theory. Economic freedom and technological readiness reinforce each other. Interest rates and GDP growth interact closely, consistent with monetary policy theory.

4.5. Discussion

The finding that inflation significantly drives cryptocurrency adoption aligns with prior studies. Studies [27] suggest that sophisticated investors are more inclined to invest in assets that serve as hedges against economic downturns, including scenarios characterised by high future inflation. High inflation erodes the value of fiat currencies, pushing individuals toward cryptocurrencies as a hedge. For example, studies on hyperinflationary economies, such as Venezuela and Zimbabwe, demonstrate how cryptocurrencies like Bitcoin offer an alternative store of value and medium of exchange when traditional currencies collapse [35,36]. It implies that cryptocurrencies act as "digital gold", reinforcing their utility as a store of value in times of economic instability [39]. This supports theories of money that highlight the importance of scarcity and stability for value retention.

The negative relationship between corruption and cryptocurrency adoption contrasts with some studies suggesting that cryptocurrencies are often used in highly corrupt environments to circumvent opaque traditional financial systems. However, lower adoption in less corrupt environments might reflect trust in existing institutions and regulatory clarity [30,42]. It suggests that cryptocurrencies are used in corruptive systems and as a speculative asset and therefore improved governance may reduce the perceived need for decentralised alternatives.

The positive association between technological readiness and cryptocurrency adoption is consistent with studies emphasising the role of digital infrastructure in facilitating blockchain use. Advanced technological ecosystems lower barriers to entry for adopting decentralised systems and integrating them into economic activities [1]. This finding reinforces the innovation diffusion theory, which posits that the adoption of new technologies depends on access to infrastructure and societal readiness.

The negative effect of interest rates on cryptocurrency adoption mirrors findings where low or negative interest rates reduce the opportunity cost of holding cryptocurrencies, making them more attractive relative to fiat savings [39]. This aligns with monetary substitution theories, where individuals shift to alternative currencies when traditional instruments offer lower returns.

Lower economic freedom and higher corruption drive cryptocurrency adoption, underscoring its appeal in restrictive environments. This finding supports studies showing higher adoption rates in developing nations with limited financial access [63]. This supports financial innovation theory, which highlights the disruptive potential of decentralised systems.

The finding that inflation Granger causes cryptocurrency adoption aligns with prior research highlighting the role of economic instability. Cryptocurrencies serve as a hedge in high-inflation environments, particularly in economies with unstable fiat currencies, such as Venezuela and Zimbabwe [36]. This finding supports the view that individuals and businesses increasingly turn to decentralised assets to preserve value during monetary crises [35]. This reinforces monetary substitution theory, where agents opt for alternative currencies when the domestic currency loses purchasing power.

The positive causality from GDP to CAR may reflect the role of economic activity in driving innovation and investment in cryptocurrencies. Wealthier economies tend to have greater resources and infrastructure to support technological adoption [1]. Conversely, the feedback effect (CAR impacts GDP) suggests that cryptocurrencies can spur economic activity by enabling financial inclusion and reducing transaction costs [39]. This relationship underscores financial innovation theory, which posits that digital currencies foster economic activity by creating alternative financial ecosystems.

The finding that technological readiness predicts CAR aligns with literature emphasising the importance of digital infrastructure for cryptocurrency adoption. NRI captures a country's capacity to leverage ICT (Information and Communication Technology), which is critical for enabling blockchain-based systems [30]. This supports the innovation diffusion theory, which highlights that access to technology and digital literacy are prerequisites for adopting disruptive financial technologies.

The mutual relationship between CAR and GDP suggests that cryptocurrency adoption not only depends on economic conditions but also contributes to economic growth. Previous studies indicate that cryptocurrencies facilitate cross-border trade, lower remittance costs, and provide financial tools for unbanked populations, thereby fostering economic expansion [42].

The influence of CAR on EFI reflects cryptocurrencies' potential to liberalise economies. By reducing dependence on traditional financial systems, cryptocurrencies promote individual financial autonomy and stimulate regulatory changes [63]. These findings align with institutional economics theory, which suggests that technological innovations like cryptocurrencies can drive institutional reform and economic liberalisation.

The observed mutual causality among inflation, GDP, and governance quality (CORR) reflects the complex interdependence of economic and institutional factors. Inflation and GDP are tightly linked through monetary policy and economic cycles, while governance quality mediates the effectiveness of these policies [38].

The role of governance (CORR) is particularly nuanced. On the one hand, lower corruption improves financial stability, reducing the need for alternative systems like cryptocurrencies. On the other hand, weak governance in some contexts drives adoption by undermining trust in traditional systems [42]. This supports the theory of economic institutionalism, which posits that institutional quality determines economic outcomes and shapes the adoption of disruptive innovations.

5. Conclusions

5.1. Summary

This study examined cryptocurrency adoption's key drivers and impacts across 37 countries from 2020 to 2023. This study found that inflation emerged as a critical driver of cryptocurrency adoption, particularly in economies with volatile fiat currencies. This supports the view of cryptocurrencies as a hedge against inflation [36]. The Network Readiness Index (NRI) significantly influences adoption, highlighting the necessity of digital infrastructure and technological ecosystems [30]. Lower interest rates (INTRs) encourage adoption, while higher GDP is associated with reduced adoption, reflecting the influence of economic stability and monetary policy on adoption patterns [39].

Moreover, cryptocurrencies not only respond to but also impact GDP and economic freedom (EFI), creating feedback loops that promote financial inclusion and economic liberalisation [42]. Lower corruption levels (CORR) correlate with reduced cryptocurrency adoption, possibly due to increased trust in traditional financial systems [63]. Furthermore, this study found that inflation, GDP, and governance are interconnected, influencing both cryptocurrency adoption and broader economic conditions. This highlights the complex interplay between economic and institutional dynamics in shaping financial innovation.

5.2. Theoretical Implications

Cryptocurrencies act as an alternative monetary system, especially in inflationary environments. This supports the Monetary Substitution Theory that economic instability pushes individuals and institutions toward decentralised currencies [33,35].

Technological readiness (NRI) is critical for the adoption of disruptive innovations like cryptocurrencies, which has implications for innovation diffusion theory. Policymakers must focus on enhancing digital infrastructure to maximise the benefits of these technologies [30].

The feedback effects between cryptocurrency adoption and governance quality reinforce the role of institutional frameworks in facilitating or hindering adoption, which supports the institutional economics theory. Cryptocurrencies can promote financial liberalisation in restrictive environments but require robust governance to prevent misuse [42].

5.3. Policy Recommendations

This study suggests that policymakers should first focus on reducing corruption and increasing transparency to improve trust in traditional financial systems while enabling regulated cryptocurrency adoption. Secondly, investments in technology readiness are essential to leverage the economic benefits of cryptocurrencies. Developing countries should prioritise digital literacy and ICT infrastructure. Thirdly, regulatory frameworks should aim to mitigate the risks of cryptocurrency misuse without stifling innovation. Clear guidelines on taxation, anti-money laundering (AML), and investor protection are critical.

Finally, countries facing high inflation should explore the integration of cryptocurrencies into their monetary systems while addressing underlying economic instability.

5.4. Limitations and Future Research Directions

While this research offers valuable insights into the drivers and impacts of cryptocurrency adoption, several limitations need to be acknowledged to contextualise the findings and guide future studies.

The study uses data spanning 2020–2023, but comprehensive, reliable, and consistent data on cryptocurrency adoption are only available from the late 2010s. This temporal limitation may affect the robustness of the findings, particularly in the early years when adoption rates were negligible. The dataset includes 37 countries, which may not represent the global diversity in economic, technological, and governance conditions. The exclusion of countries with nascent cryptocurrency markets or limited data availability may introduce selection bias.

Despite efforts to address endogeneity using dynamic models (e.g., GMM), the study cannot entirely rule out omitted variable bias, particularly in complex relationships such as CAR and governance quality (CORR) [39]. While Granger causality tests suggest predictive relationships, they do not imply true causality. For example, the bidirectional relationships between CAR and GDP may reflect simultaneous influences rather than clear causal pathways [35].

Although governance quality (CORR) and economic freedom (EFI) were included as proxies for social development, other dimensions such as income inequality, education, or gender equality were not explored. These could provide a broader perspective on the societal implications of cryptocurrency adoption [1].

The cryptocurrency ecosystem is rapidly evolving, with the emergence of stablecoins, decentralised finance (DeFi), and central bank digital currencies (CBDCs). These innovations were not fully accounted for in the analysis, potentially limiting their applicability to current market dynamics [30].

The study does not account for cultural or behavioural drivers of cryptocurrency adoption, such as trust in technology or societal attitudes toward financial innovation. These factors could significantly influence adoption rates and require qualitative or survey-based research to understand fully [63].

This study treats all cryptocurrencies as a homogeneous group, which simplifies the analysis but does not account for the distinct characteristics of different cryptocurrencies. Variations in technology, market acceptance, and regulatory treatment among cryptocurrencies like Bitcoin and Ethereum versus smaller digital currencies could influence adoption rates and economic impacts differently. This approach may limit the generalizability of our findings across the diverse landscape of digital currencies. Future research should consider differentiating cryptocurrencies by their unique attributes and market positions to provide a more nuanced understanding of their adoption and impacts.

Future research may expand the dataset, integrating qualitative methods, and incorporating emerging trends such as DeFi and CBDCs, which provides a more comprehensive understanding of the dynamics and implications of cryptocurrencies in global economies. The long-term effects of cryptocurrency adoption on economic growth, governance, and inequality could be conducted in future studies. Sector-specific analysis might be another future research opportunity, for example, examining how cryptocurrencies impact remittances or cross-border trade.

Author Contributions: Conceptualization: Y.G.; data collection: E.Y.; data analysis: M.M.N. All authors have read and agreed to the published version of the manuscript.

Funding: This research received no external funding.

Institutional Review Board Statement: The study was approved by the Ethics Committee of Teesside University.

Informed Consent Statement: Not applicable.

Data Availability Statement: Research data will be shared if required.

Conflicts of Interest: The authors declare no conflicts of interest.

References

1. Almeida, J.; Gonçalves, T.C. A Decade of Cryptocurrency Investment Literature: A Cluster-Based Systematic Analysis. *Int. J. Financ. Stud.* **2023**, *11*, 71. [CrossRef]
2. García-Corral, F.J.; Cordero-García, J.A.; de Pablo-Valenciano, J.; Uribe-Toril, J. A bibliometric review of cryptocurrencies: How have they grown? *Financ. Innov.* **2022**, *8*, 2. [CrossRef] [PubMed]
3. Aslam, F.; Memon, B.A.; Hunjra, A.I.; Bouri, E. The dynamics of market efficiency of major cryptocurrencies. *Glob. Financ. J.* **2023**, *58*, 100899. [CrossRef]
4. Nakamoto, S. Bitcoin: A Peer-to-Peer Electronic Cash System. (White Paper). 2008. Available online: https://www.klausnordby.com/bitcoin/Bitcoin_Whitepaper_Document_HD.pdf (accessed on 2 September 2024).
5. Viviana, A.C.; Kamin, S.; Zampolli, F. Central bank digital currencies (CBDCs) in Latin America and the Caribbean. *Lat. Am. J. Cent. Bank.* **2024**, 100140. [CrossRef]
6. Viviana, A.C.; Kamin, S.; Zampolli, F. Central bank digital currencies (CBDCs) in Latin America and the Caribbean. 2022. Bank for International Settlements. Available online: https://www.bis.org/publ/work989.htm (accessed on 8 May 2023).
7. Li, Z.; Meng, Q. Time and frequency connectedness and portfolio diversification between cryptocurrencies and renewable energy stock markets during COVID-19. *N. Am. J. Econ. Financ.* **2022**, *59*, 101565. [CrossRef]
8. Au, A. Cryptocurrencies and the promise of individual economic sovereignty in an age of digitalization: A critical appraisal. *Sociol. Rev.* **2022**, *71*, 992–1011. [CrossRef]
9. Bogusz, C.I.; Laurell, C.; Sandström, C. Tracking the Digital Evolution of Entrepreneurial Finance: The Interplay Between Crowdfunding, Blockchain Technologies, Cryptocurrencies, and Initial Coin Offerings. *IEEE Trans. Eng. Manag.* **2020**, *67*, 1099–1108. [CrossRef]
10. Abdelkaoui, F.; Sidaoui, A.; Nasser, F.; Bouzidi, M. Cryptocurrency and Macroeconomic Dynamics: Case of 10 Asian Economies. *South Asian J. Macroecon. Public Financ.* **2024**, *13*, 100–126. [CrossRef]
11. Sadraoui, T.; Nasr, A.; Mgadmi, N. Studding relationship between bitcoin, exchange rate and financial development: A panel data analysis. *Int. J. Manag. Financ. Account.* **2021**, *13*, 232–252. [CrossRef]
12. Conlon, T.; Corbet, S.; McGee, R.J. Inflation and cryptocurrencies revisited: A time-scale analysis. *Econ. Lett.* **2021**, *206*, 109996. [CrossRef]
13. Elsayed, A.H.; Sousa, R.M. International monetary policy and cryptocurrency markets: Dynamic and spillover effects. *Eur. J. Financ.* **2024**, *30*, 1855–1875. [CrossRef]
14. Vo, A.; Chapman, T.A.; Lee, Y.-S. Examining Bitcoin and Economic Determinants: An Evolutionary Perspective. *J. Comput. Inf. Syst.* **2022**, *62*, 572–586. [CrossRef]
15. Bouri, E.; Lucey, B.; Roubaud, D. Cryptocurrencies and the downside risk in equity investments. *Financ. Res. Lett.* **2020**, *33*, 101211. [CrossRef]
16. Bhimani, A.; Hausken, K.; Arif, S. Do national development factors affect cryptocurrency adoption? *Technol. Forecast. Soc. Change* **2022**, *181*, 121739. [CrossRef]
17. Huynh, T.L.D.; Shahbaz, M.; Nasir, M.A.; Ullah, S. Financial modelling, risk management of energy instruments and the role of cryptocurrencies. *Ann. Oper. Res.* **2022**, *313*, 47–75. [CrossRef]
18. Bouri, E.; Gabauer, D.; Gupta, R.; Tiwari, A.K. Volatility connectedness of major cryptocurrencies: The role of investor happiness. *J. Behav. Exp. Financ.* **2021**, *30*, 100463. [CrossRef]
19. Angerer, M.; Hoffmann, C.H.; Neitzert, F.; Kraus, S. Objective and subjective risks of investing into cryptocurrencies. *Financ. Res. Lett.* **2021**, *40*, 101737. [CrossRef]
20. Corbet, S.; Lucey, B.; Urquhart, A.; Yarovaya, L. Cryptocurrencies as a financial asset: A systematic analysis. *Int. Rev. Financ. Anal.* **2019**, *62*, 182–199. [CrossRef]
21. Li, R.; Li, S.; Yuan, D.; Zhu, H. Investor attention and cryptocurrency: Evidence from wavelet-based quantile Granger causality analysis. *Res. Int. Bus. Financ.* **2021**, *56*, 101389. [CrossRef]
22. Alonso, S.L.; Jorge-Vázquez, J.; Echarte Fernández, M.Á.; Reier Forradellas, R.F. Cryptocurrency Mining from an Economic and Environmental Perspective. Analysis of the Most and Least Sustainable Countries. *Energies* **2021**, *14*, 4254. [CrossRef]

23. Hsu, S.-H.; Sheu, C.; Yoon, J. Risk spillovers between cryptocurrencies and traditional currencies and gold under different global economic conditions. *N. Am. J. Econ. Financ.* **2021**, *57*, 101443. [CrossRef]
24. Mnif, E.; Jarboui, A.; Mouakhar, K. How the cryptocurrency market has performed during COVID 19? A multifractal analysis. *Financ. Res. Lett.* **2020**, *36*, 101647. [CrossRef] [PubMed]
25. Papadamou, S.; Kyriazis, N.A.; Tzeremes, P.G. Non-linear causal linkages of EPU and gold with major cryptocurrencies during bull and bear markets. *N. Am. J. Econ. Financ.* **2021**, *56*, 101343. [CrossRef]
26. Kyriazis, N.; Papadamou, S.; Corbet, S. A systematic review of the bubble dynamics of cryptocurrency prices. *Res. Int. Bus. Financ.* **2020**, *54*, 101254. [CrossRef]
27. Colombo, J.A.; Yarovaya, L. Are crypto and non-crypto investors alike? Evidence from a comprehensive survey in Brazil. *Technol. Soc.* **2024**, *76*, 102468. [CrossRef]
28. Alnasaa, M.; Gueorguiev, N.; Honda, J.; Imamoglu, E.; Mauro, P.; Primus, K.; Rozhkov, D. Crypto-assets, corruption, and capital controls: Cross-country correlations. *Econ. Lett.* **2022**, *215*, 110492. [CrossRef]
29. Drăgan, G.B.; Ben Arfi, W.; Tiberius, V.; Ammari, A.; Khvatova, T. Navigating the green wave: Understanding behavioral antecedents of sustainable cryptocurrency investment. *Technol. Forecast. Soc. Change* **2025**, *210*, 123909. [CrossRef]
30. Mikhaylov, A. Understanding the risks associated with wallets, depository services, trading, lending, and borrowing in the crypto space. *J. Infrastruct. Policy Dev.* **2023**, *7*, 2223. [CrossRef]
31. Corbet, S.; Goodell, J.W.; Günay, S. What drives DeFi prices? Investigating the effects of investor attention. *Financ. Res. Lett.* **2022**, *48*, 102883. [CrossRef]
32. Jiang, Y.; Wu, L.; Tian, G.; Nie, H. Do cryptocurrencies hedge against EPU and the equity market volatility during COVID-19?—New evidence from quantile coherency analysis. *J. Int. Financ. Mark. Inst. Money* **2021**, *72*, 101324. [CrossRef]
33. Benigno, P. Monetary Policy in a World of Cryptocurrencies. *J. Eur. Econ. Assoc.* **2023**, *21*, 1363–1396. [CrossRef]
34. Haq, I.U.; Maneengam, A.; Chupradit, S.; Suksatan, W.; Huo, C. Economic Policy Uncertainty and Cryptocurrency Market as a Risk Management Avenue: A Systematic Review. *Risks* **2021**, *9*, 163. [CrossRef]
35. Yermack, D. Chapter 2—Is Bitcoin a Real Currency? An Economic Appraisal. In *Handbook of Digital Currency*, 2nd ed.; Lee Kuo Chuen, D., Ed.; Academic Press: San Diego, CA, USA, 2024; pp. 29–40. [CrossRef]
36. Bouri, E.; Jalkh, N. Spillovers of joint volatility-skewness-kurtosis of major cryptocurrencies and their determinants. *Int. Rev. Financ. Anal.* **2023**, *90*, 102915. [CrossRef]
37. Nguyen, L.T.M.; Nguyen, P.T. Determinants of cryptocurrency and decentralized finance adoption—A configurational exploration. *Technol. Forecast. Soc. Chang.* **2024**, *201*, 123244. [CrossRef]
38. Benigno, P.; Schilling, L.M.; Uhlig, H. Cryptocurrencies, currency competition, and the impossible trinity. *J. Int. Econ.* **2022**, *136*, 103601. [CrossRef]
39. Cheah, E.-T.; Mishra, T.; Parhi, M.; Zhang, Z. Long Memory Interdependency and Inefficiency in Bitcoin Markets. *Econ. Lett.* **2018**, *167*, 18–25. [CrossRef]
40. Zhang, S.; Gregoriou, A. Cryptocurrencies in portfolios: Return–liquidity trade-off around China forbidding initial coin offerings. *Appl. Econ. Lett.* **2021**, *28*, 1036–1040. [CrossRef]
41. Bespalova, O.; Appendino, M.; Bhattacharya, R.; Clevy Aguilar, J.F.; Geng, N.; Komatsuzaki, T.; Lesniak, J.; Lian, W.; Marcelino, S.; Villafuerte, M.; et al. Crypto assets and CBDCs in Latin America and the Caribbean: Opportunities and risks. *Lat. Am. J. Cent. Bank.* **2024**, 100157, *in press*. [CrossRef]
42. OECD. *OECD Economic Outlook, Volume 2023 Issue 2*; OECD: Paris, France, 2023.
43. Yue, Y.; Li, X.; Zhang, D.; Wang, S. How cryptocurrency affects economy? A network analysis using bibliometric methods. *Int. Rev. Financ. Anal.* **2021**, *77*, 101869. [CrossRef]
44. Zhang, Z.J. Cryptopricing: Whence comes the value for cryptocurrencies and NFTs? *Int. J. Res. Mark.* **2023**, *40*, 22–29. [CrossRef]
45. Mishkin, F. *Money, Banking and Financial Markets*; New Horizons: Paris, France, 2007.
46. Wang, P.; Zhang, H.; Yang, C.; Guo, Y. Time and frequency dynamics of connectedness and hedging performance in global stock markets: Bitcoin versus conventional hedges. *Res. Int. Bus. Financ.* **2021**, *58*, 101479. [CrossRef]
47. Shen, D.; Urquhart, A.; Wang, P. A three-factor pricing model for cryptocurrencies. *Financ. Res. Lett.* **2020**, *34*, 101248. [CrossRef]
48. Chainalysis. *The Chainalysis 2023 Geography of Cryptocurrency Report*; Chainalysis: New York, NY, USA, 2023.
49. NRI. *Network Readiness Index 2024*; Portulans Institute: Washington, DC, USA, 2024.
50. Hsiao, C. *Analysis of Panel Data*; Cambridge University Press: Cambridge, UK, 2022.
51. Pearson, K. Notes on regression and inheritance in the case of two parents. *Proc. R. Soc. Lond.* **1895**, *58*, 240–242.
52. Breusch, T.S.; Pagan, A.R. A Simple Test for Heteroscedasticity and Random Coefficient Variation. *Econometrica* **1979**, *47*, 1287–1294. [CrossRef]
53. Pesaran, M.H. General diagnostic tests for cross section dependence in panels. Cambridge Working Papers. *Economics* **2004**, *1240*, 1.

54. Baltagi, B.H.; Feng, Q.; Kao, C. A Lagrange Multiplier test for cross-sectional dependence in a fixed effects panel data model. *J. Econom.* **2012**, *170*, 164–177. [CrossRef]
55. Pesaran, M.H. A simple panel unit root test in the presence of cross-section dependence. *J. Appl. Econom.* **2007**, *22*, 265–312. [CrossRef]
56. Wooldridge, J.M.; Wadud, M.; Lye, J. *Introductory Econometrics: Asia Pacific Edition with Online Study Tools 12 Months*; Cengage AU: Molbourne, Australia, 2016.
57. Gujarati, D.N. *Basic Econometrics*; McGraw-Hill: New York, NY, USA, 2009.
58. Beck, N.; Katz, J.N. What To Do (and Not to Do) with Time-Series Cross-Section Data. *Am. Political Sci. Rev.* **1995**, *89*, 634–647. [CrossRef]
59. Hansen, L.P. Large Sample Properties of Generalized Method of Moments Estimators. *Econometrica* **1982**, *50*, 1029–1054. [CrossRef]
60. Arellano, M.; Bond, S. Some Tests of Specification for Panel Data: Monte Carlo Evidence and an Application to Employment Equations. *Rev. Econ. Stud.* **1991**, *58*, 277–297. [CrossRef]
61. Dumitrescu, E.-I.; Hurlin, C. Testing for Granger non-causality in heterogeneous panels. *Econ. Model.* **2012**, *29*, 1450–1460. [CrossRef]
62. Hashem Pesaran, M.; Yamagata, T. Testing slope homogeneity in large panels. *J. Econom.* **2008**, *142*, 50–93. [CrossRef]
63. Murugappan, M.; Nair, R.; Krishnan, S. Global Market Perceptions of Cryptocurrency and the Use of Cryptocurrency by Consumers: A Pilot Study. *J. Theor. Appl. Electron. Commer. Res.* **2023**, *18*, 1955–1970. [CrossRef]

FinTech

MDPI

Article

The Contribution of Robo-Advisors as a Key Factor in Commercial Banks' Performance After the Global Financial Crisis

Félix Zogning [1,*] and Pascal Turcotte [2]

[1] School of Management, Université de Sherbrooke, Sherbrooke, QC J1K 2R1, Canada
[2] Canadian Imperial Bank of Commerce, Toronto, ON M5J 0E7, Canada; pascal.turcotte@cibc.com
* Correspondence: felix.zogning@usherbrooke.ca

Abstract: In several countries, digital financial advisory services, particularly those supported by robo-advisors, are becoming increasingly popular in retail banking. These tools assist users with financial decisions such as risk assessment, portfolio selection, and rebalancing—all at a reduced cost. Recent studies suggest that, over time, robo-advisors could complement human financial advisors. Building on this research, which evaluates robo-advisors' effectiveness in asset allocation, this study aims to assess the impact of this strategic shift on retail banks' profitability. It compares the Canadian and French banking sectors, where robo-advisors were introduced in the 2010s. Results indicate that implementing robo-advisors enhances profitability in non-interest activities, with this effect being more pronounced in France than in Canada.

Keywords: robo-advisor; retail banking; profitability; portfolio management; non-interest margin

JEL Classification: G21; G01; G17; G32; O33

1. Introduction

Since 2012, financial technologies (fintechs) have experienced significant growth, continuously introducing new services and tools. Among the most notable innovations are 'robo-advisors', which represent the culmination of nearly two decades of technological advancements in the banking sector. These digital financial advisory services, including those powered by robo-advisors, are gaining popularity in retail banking across many countries. They support users in making financial decisions, including risk assessment, portfolio selection, and rebalancing, all at a lower cost. Recent studies indicate that, in the long term, robo-advisors could complement human financial advice.

Over the past decade, the growth of fintech has reshaped banking operations and customer interactions. Robo-advisors have emerged as a flagship innovation in this domain, offering low-cost, algorithm-driven financial advisory services. In Canada and France, major banks have adopted these tools to diversify revenue streams, reduce operating costs, and better serve tech-savvy customers. This dual-country approach allows for a comparative analysis of how different regulatory and market structures influence the adoption and impact of robo-advisors.

In Canada, even the major banks have embarked on the adventure to take advantage of this innovation. The National Bank of Canada created Invest Cube, and the Bank of Montreal developed the Smart Portfolio. On the other side of the Atlantic, in France,

BNP Paribas and Society General, to name but a few, have also taken up the challenge of artificial intelligence. Designing an investment portfolio in the comfort of their own home or between appointments gives clients more latitude in terms of availability. The development of exchange-traded funds (ETFs) has made it possible to advance this type of solution. ETFs make it possible to recreate the effect of stock market indices within an investment portfolio. They are less costly at the base since they involve less human intervention and rely on algorithms that track the effects of the stock market and the components of the indices.

If the implementation of robo-advisors requires large investments, it could be beneficial in the long term because it should significantly reduce the payroll and structural costs of financial institutions. It then becomes interesting to examine the impact of the adoption of this fintech tool on the performance of financial institutions.

In addition to work that evaluates the effectiveness of such a device for allocating financial assets or that examines the benefit of these platforms for investors, the objective of this article is to measure the impact of such a strategic orientation on the profitability of financial institutions. This exploratory study compares the Canadian and French banking sectors, where robo-advisors have been deployed since the 2010 decade. This allows us to compare the effect of these robo-advisors in two types of financial systems, across two countries that have adopted this tool in comparable proportions.

Specifically, the study aims to evaluate how the adoption of robo-advisors affects the profitability of commercial banks, with a specific focus on non-interest activities. By comparing the experiences of the Canadian and French banking systems, this research identifies key operational and strategic levers for improving bank performance. The results provide actionable insights for financial institutions, regulators, and fintech developers regarding the integration of robo-advisors into their business models.

The choice of the Canadian and French banking systems is motivated by the diversity of their financial approaches. Canada represents a market-based financial system, while France illustrates a bank-based system. These differences allow for a relevant comparative analysis of the effect of robo-advisors. Moreover, both systems apply IFRS standards and Basel III agreements, thereby ensuring the comparability of financial performance indicators.

The remainder of this article is structured as follows: Section 2 introduces the concept of robo-advisors and their functioning. Section 3 provides a literature review and an analysis of the current situation regarding the adoption of robo-advisors in Canada and France. Section 4 outlines the research methodology and the data used. The results are presented and analyzed in Section 5, and the article concludes by highlighting the main contributions of this study and suggesting avenues for future research.

2. The Robo-Advisor

The concept of a robo-advisor may seem abstract at first glance. However, it is a concrete and practical innovative tool aimed at automating a process that is sometimes biased by emotions and human error. The robo-advisor is designed to answer a question that is sometimes complex for some advisors: what is the best investment for me?

It is therefore a market analysis tool governed by an algorithm that acts on the markets according to certain signals and modifies the investments made in the client's portfolio. Sometimes it is composed solely of ETFs that attempt to replicate one of the major known stock market indices such as the S&P/TSX. An ETF that tracks this index would allow the investor to obtain a return that is very close to the performance of the New York, Paris, or Toronto stock exchanges. Of course, commission fees are withdrawn by the manufacturer of the product as well as by the distributor.

Initially, the robo-advisor serves as a neutral decision support tool for clients who wish to choose a solution that suits them. The client fills out an online questionnaire to determine his risk tolerance and at the end of the process, the system recommends that he can accept or refuse. Once the administrative formality is in place, the client can integrate the solution, and investments are then executed according to his investment policy. However, a human advisor who will validate the questionnaire completed by the client and validate whether the investment choice made corresponds to his investor profile must analyze his investment choices. In most cases, a diversified portfolio of ETFs is put in place, since this solution is of the passive management type and management fees are then lower for the client. Passive management results from the fact that an investment fund attempts to copy the composition of a stock market index in order to replicate the associated return. The robo-advisor, therefore, uses various algorithms to track these indices and rebalance the portfolio periodically.

In theory, the robo-advisor thus significantly reduces the payroll, which is costly for financial institutions. Few, if any, humans interact with the client since they switch to online investment management mode independently. In Europe, where legislation is different from that in Canada, a human advisor does not have to revalidate client questionnaires and transactions. This considerably reduces the cost of the advisor-boot option and makes it possible to tangibly notice the positive effects of the savings generated for the financial institution.

In addition, this means fewer costly assets for the financial institution. In fact, since it is no longer necessary to go to the office to meet with someone, certain points of business are no longer required. The implementation of a virtual platform, a computerized management system, and excellent servers is only required for this type of operation. The client, therefore, sees himself in the hands of a machine whose emotional biases related to the markets are less than those of a traditional portfolio manager—and all at a lower cost to him.

However, the client does not receive financial advice from an expert in the field. The investor is left to his own devices and in some cases, he may miss out on interesting market opportunities, not know about tax issues that would allow him to save significant amounts of money, or have an expert follow up on a retirement plan through a well-detailed project. Most financial institutions offer this service free of charge for their clients who have a dedicated advisor. However, if the client becomes self-employed, this type of service is not necessarily included, and the client will have to pay significant amounts for a consultation with a private firm. Without having a business relationship with a human, it would also be likely that the client would then be less loyal, and in the case of a better offer, he would be freer to leave for another institution. Knowing that customer retention is already an issue, banks do not want to multiply the chances of losing market share to their competitors. In short, while this type of strategy may have advantages, it also has drawbacks.

The table below presents the particularities of the main robo-advisors used by financial institutions.

Table 1 highlights the variability in fees associated with robo-advisors. Notably, fee structures vary significantly depending on the balance threshold, with lower fees for larger portfolios. This variability may influence the customer segments targeted by financial institutions.

Table 1. Service fees for robo-advisor (in USD).

Robo-Advisors	Balance Minimum	$5000	$10,000	$50,000	$100,000	$1,000,000	$10,000,000
Acorns	$0	0.25%	0.25%	0.25%	0.25%	0.25%	0.25%
Betterment	$0	0.35%	0.25%	0.25%	0.25%	0.15%	0.15%

Table 1. *Cont.*

Robo-Advisors	Balance Minimum	$5000	$10,000	$50,000	$100,000	$1,000,000	$10,000,000
Hedgeable	$0	0.75%	0.75%	0.7%	0.65%	0.3%	0.3%
WiseBanyan	$10	0%	0%	0%	0%	0%	0%
Wealthfront	$500	0%	0%	0.25%	0.25%	0.25%	0.25%
TradeKing Advisors Core	$500	0.25%	0.25%	0.25%	0.25%	0.25%	0.25%
SigFig	$2000	0%	0%	0.25%	0.25%	0.25%	0.25%
Schwab Intelligent Portfolios	$5000	0%	0%	0%	0%	0%	0%
Liftoff	$5000	0.4%	0.4%	0.4%	0.4%	0.4%	0.4%
TradeKing Advisors Momentum	$5000	0.5%	0.5%	0.5%	0.5%	0.5%	0.5%
FutureAdvisor	$10,000	X	0.5%	0.5%	0.5%	0.5%	0.5%
Personal Capital	$25,000	X	X	0.89%	0.89%	0.89%	0.59%
Vanguard VPAS	$50,000	X	X	0.3%	0.3%	0.3%	0.3%
AssetBuilder	$50,000	X	X	0.45%	0.45%	0.3%	0.25%
Rebalance IRA	$100,000	X	X	X	0.5%	0.5%	0.5%

Source: Business Insider Magazine. Website accessed on 13 November 2024. https://www.businessinsider.com/bis-robo-investing-reviews-performance-and-fees-comparison-2017-1?r=DE&IR=T?r=US&IR=T.

3. Implementation of Robo-Advisors: A Review of the Current Situation and Literature

The first robo-advisors were introduced after the global financial crisis of 2008. These tools primarily served as passive and automated asset allocation and portfolio management instruments, designed to automatically rebalance a client's portfolio in response to significant market fluctuations. Their emergence coincided with a period when investors exhibited a preference for low-risk portfolios, reflecting their apprehension after the adverse effects of the global financial crisis.

Thanks to aggressive marketing efforts, robo-advisors rapidly gained popularity in the United States. However, growth in the adoption of these tools was comparatively slower in France and Canada. Notably, Investors Group was among the first financial institutions to introduce this alternative. The implementation of its robo-advisor, Wealthsimple, required a significant investment of approximately CAD 30 million [1]. In response, several major Canadian banks followed suit, introducing exchange-traded fund (ETF) solutions with lower management fees. For instance, the National Bank of Canada and the Bank of Montreal launched portfolio management solutions powered by robo-advisors. The Bank of Montreal developed two distinct offerings: one for investments ranging from CAD 1000 to CAD 49,999 and another for amounts exceeding CAD 50,000. For its part, the National Bank set an investment floor of CAD 10,000 for its robo-advisor platform [2].

As the market for robo-advisors expands, investors have increasingly welcomed these innovations. Growing awareness of the fee structures of mutual funds and turnkey portfolios provided by most financial institutions has driven demand for cost-effective alternatives. Consequently, financial institutions have embraced robo-advisors as a means of demonstrating a competitive advantage and highlighting substantial savings opportunities for investors. For example, Wealthsimple, a prominent robo-advisor in Canada, has transformed the investment landscape by offering accessible, low-fee digital portfolio management. Similarly, BMO's 'SmartFolio' allows Canadian retail investors to create customized ETF portfolios, demonstrating the strategic role of robo-advisors in diversifying bank offerings.

Moreover, the use of financial algorithms, as opposed to the subjective judgement of fund managers, offers a more cost-effective and error-resistant solution. Robo-advisors rely on predefined algorithms that swiftly analyze market fluctuations and execute large-scale transactions to capitalize on emerging opportunities. This approach also supports the implementation of passive ETF solutions, whereby the robo-advisor tracks and adjusts holdings in accordance with predetermined stock market indices, thereby reducing costs and limiting human intervention.

However, regulatory standards vary across regions. In Canada, for instance, regulations mandate that a human advisor must assess the client's risk tolerance and validate the suitability of the transaction to ensure regulatory compliance. This step introduces an additional layer of human involvement, which imposes an operational cost on financial institutions [3]. For comparison, European regulations are less stringent, allowing for a more automated process [4]. This regulatory divergence explains part of the cost differences observed between European and Canadian financial institutions using robo-advisors.

In the United States, where robo-advisors have seen record levels of adoption, the Securities and Exchange Commission (SEC) has raised concerns. The SEC has warned that robo-advisors may sometimes issue investment recommendations based on incorrect assumptions, incomplete information, or irrelevant circumstances for individual investors. This underscores the importance of the oversight and continuous refinement of these algorithms to protect investors and enhance the reliability of the recommendations they receive.

According to Phoon and Koh (2018) [5], the introduction of such retail platforms has not only improved efficiency but also inclusiveness, giving a higher percentage of the US population the opportunity to participate in the economy as shareholders. Active investment strategies are often costly and do not, on average, provide real added value to investors in the context of diversified market exposure. Uhl and Rohner (2018) [6] empirically show that these robo-advisor investors save more than 4% per year in direct and indirect costs compared to traditional solutions, such as advisory fund solutions in banks or asset managers, because robo-advisors offer more efficient solutions on three key levels: passive access to the active market, profitability, and possible investor behavioural biases.

While approximately one-third of the outstanding shares are now held by passive investors, the authors predict that passive investors, through the use of robo-advisors, should control half of the US stock market by 2021. They conclude that robo-advisors will not only become the preferred investment solution for retail clients but will also become an increasingly important device for traditional banks and wealth managers.

Tertilt and Scholz (2018) [7] analyze how robo-advisors determine the risk tolerance of their users and what equity exposure is derived from the individual risk profile. Their results indicate significant differences in the quality of the investment advice offered. Robo-advisors generally ask relatively few questions in assessing the risk profile of their users, and it is particularly surprising that some of the questions asked do not seem to influence risk categorization. In addition, the recommended exposure to equities is relatively conservative.

There is little empirical literature on this relatively new tool, which is often based on its practicality, effectiveness, or benefit to users. Conversely, this study aims to examine the extent to which the adoption of such a tool influences the profitability of a financial institution. We make the general hypothesis that, given the strategic dimension of the decision to switch to automated teller robots and the size of the investment required, financial institutions will only adopt this innovation if it allows them to make substantial savings or gives them access to an additional clientele.

4. Methodology

The purpose of this study is to examine the contribution of robo-advisors to the profitability of financial institutions. This is carried out in a comparative approach between two countries that have adopted the use of robo-advisors in the last decade: Canada and France. As the banking sector is not as important within the financial system in continental Europe as it is in North America (Zogning, 2017) [8], this comparison is essential to ensure that the observed effects of the use of robo-advisors are not solely an American reality. We hypothesize that the adoption of robo-advisors enhances the profitability of banks through improved revenue diversification and operational efficiency. This impact is expected to be more pronounced in bank-based systems (France) than in market-based systems (Canada) due to differences in regulatory structures and business models.

4.1. Sampling and Data

Financial institutions include custodian institutions such as banks and non-depository institutions such as mutual funds, asset management companies, and pension funds, to name but a few. Since regulation in this second category is markedly different on both sides of the Atlantic, we focus here only on banks, whose prudential and accounting standards are international. We, therefore, include two countries that apply IFRS and subscribe to the Basel III agreements, in order to make their performance indicators comparable. We selected banks based on their asset size, market share, and availability of data on robo-advisor adoption from annual reports and public sources.

Although asset management or investment in securities is not a bank's core business, most large commercial banks are highly diversified, with a division or subsidiary dedicated to portfolio management. Therefore, we will further analyze the results of these non-core activities of banks.

In Canada, although there are more than eighty banks, 90% of assets are managed by the seven largest banks, leaving very small market shares for the dozens of banks that follow them, most of which are not publicly traded. We will focus on these seven banks that have national coverage, which we will compare to the seven largest French banks, which also concentrate the bulk of banking assets. In each of the two countries, the sample is split into two sub-groups: banks that have adopted robo-advisors and those that did not use them over the observed period. Data on the adoption of robo-advisors by these banks are available in their annual reports.

Canadian Financial Institutions		French Financial Institutions	
Without robo-advisor	With robo-advisor	Without robo-advisor	With robo-advisor
Royal Bank CIBC Scotiabank Laurentian Bank of Canada TD Bank	Bank of Montreal National Bank	CM-CIC Postal Bank BCPE Group Crédit Agricole	BNP Paribas Society General CM-ARKEA

The financial indicators and ratios of all the banks in our sample were obtained through the Bloomberg database. French financial institutions have been using robo-advisors since 2012 and Canadian institutions since 2014. The data collected therefore cover the period 2012–2019 for French banks and 2014–2019 for Canadian banks. Due to the small sample size, we covered all years from the introduction of robo-advisors to the time of the study.

4.2. Variables and Design

The variables used to represent the banks' profitability include ROE and ROA, which are the main profitability ratios in all business sectors, to which we add the non-interest margin, the proportion of non-interest income to total income, and non-interest expenses, which are more relevant indicators here. This choice to invest in non-interest income and expenses is so as not to contaminate the results by the performance of the banks' financial intermediation activity, which is little or not affected by the use of a robo-advisor.

Our results are based on two series of analyses: an analysis of variance and a multivariate model.

The chosen methodology combines analysis of variance (ANOVA) and multivariate regression to account for the distinct effects of robo-advisors on bank profitability. This dual approach allows for a comprehensive assessment of both direct and indirect relationships, which are essential for capturing the nuanced role of technology adoption in bank performance.

The first series involves an analysis of variance between the performance of robo and non-robo banks. This analysis is first performed at the level of the total sample and then within each country. For fourteen banks and over a period of 8 years, the number of observations fulfils the requirements for a one-factor analysis of variance. Then, a correlation analysis is performed to confirm the effect of the digitalization of financial services and to decipher the country's effect on this relationship.

The second set of analyses consists of developing an explanatory model of the profitability of commercial banks. To the traditional determinants of this performance, we add our variable of interest, which is the use of a robot.

Previous work has shown that commercial bank profitability is affected by both macroeconomic and bank-specific factors. Schepens et al. (2016) [9] test GDP growth, the inflation rate, the US dollar exchange rate, and the presence of a financial crisis as macroeconomic variables. These indicators are of little relevance to this study, as banks in comparison within each country are subject to the same economic reality. They all have national coverage, experience the same rate of inflation, and did not experience any financial crisis in the period considered by the study. However, since the economic reality is different between Canada and France, we include the country in our model as a control variable.

At the level of variables specific to the financial institution, we find size (Singh and Sharma, 2019) [10], level of deposits (Naeem et al., 2017) [11], capital adequacy (Salike and Ao, 2017) [12], asset quality (Anbar and Alper, 2011) [13], liquidity (Francis, 2013) [14], operational efficiency (Rashid and Jabeen, 2016) [15], financial risk (Almaqtari et al., 2019) [16], and asset management (Yahya et al., 2017) [17].

The level of deposits, the capital adequacy ratio (regulatory capital/total risk-weighted assets), the quality of assets (total loans or performing assets/total assets), and the degree of liquidity (liquid assets/total assets) are variables that directly affect the performance of the bank's financial intermediation activity. While they are relevant in explaining ROE and ROA, which are two indicators of overall profitability, they are much less relevant in explaining the profitability associated with the bank's asset management activities. This is why we focus here on operational efficiency (operating expenses/total income), asset management efficiency (total income/total assets), financial risk (total liabilities/total assets), and the size of the bank (logarithm of total assets). To these variables, we add the country control variable and our variable of interest, the use of a robo-advisor. The robo-advisor variable is a binary dummy variable where '1' indicates that the bank has adopted robo-advisor technology, and '0' indicates otherwise.

The model adopted is therefore as follows:

$$Non\ interest\ margin = \alpha + \beta_1 EP + \beta_2 GA + \beta_3 Risk + \beta_4 Size + \beta_5 Country + \beta_6 Robot + \varepsilon$$

$$\frac{Non\ interest\ income}{Total\ income} = \alpha + \beta_1 EP + \beta_2 GA + \beta_3 Risk + \beta_4 Size + \beta_5 \text{Country} + \beta_6 Robot + \varepsilon$$

$$\frac{Non\ interest\ expenses}{Total\ assets} = \alpha + \beta_1 EP + \beta_2 GA + \beta_3 Risk + \beta_4 Size + \beta_5 Country + \beta_6 Robot + \varepsilon$$

where

EP = operational efficiency;

GA = Asset management effectiveness;

Risk = financial risk.

The non-interest margin is calculated as follows $= \frac{(Non\ interest\ income - Non\ interest\ expenses)}{Total\ assets}$

The country variable is a dichotomous variable (1 for Canada or 0 for France).

The assumptions of normality and homogeneity were tested using the Shapiro–Wilk and Levene tests, respectively, to ensure the validity of the ANOVA and multivariate models.

5. Results

5.1. Descriptive Statistics

A comparative analysis of the profitability of Canadian and French banks according to their adoption robots shows the following picture (see Table 2):

Table 2. Description of the sample.

		N	Minimum	Maximum	Average	Standard Deviation
Total Sample						
	ROE	98	−16.3856	19.7843	9.681099	5.532078
	ROA	98	−0.3825	0.9898	0.480578	0.2885229
	Non-int income/total income	98	0.2913	1	0.546341	0.1376793
	Non-interest margin	98	0.0038	0.067	0.01586	0.0122449
	Non-int expenses/total assets	98	0.007	0.066	0.01847	0.0116958
Statistics by Country						
Country		N	Minimum	Maximum	Average	Standard Deviation
Canada	ROE	42	6.8986	19.7843	14.685888	3.22064
	ROA	42	0.2692	0.9898	0.766333	0.179145
	Non-int income/total income	42	0.2913	0.5861	0.467055	0.0757846
	Non-interest margin	42	0.0064	0.0213	0.013566	0.0034173
	Non-int expenses/total assets	42	0.0148	0.0226	0.017886	0.0021295
France	ROE	56	−16.3856	9.524	5.927507	3.5733404
	ROA	56	−0.3825	0.4052	0.266261	0.1173384
	Non-int income/total income	56	0.2921	1	0.605806	0.1440435
	Non-interest margin	56	0.0038	0.067	0.017581	0.0157701
	Non-int expenses/total assets	56	0.007	0.066	0.018908	0.0154082

Table 2. *Cont.*

Robotized Banks vs. Non-robotized Banks						
	Robot	N	Minimum	Maximum	Average	Standard Deviation
NO	ROE	62	−16.3856	19.7843	10.278882	5.7665477
	ROA	62	−0.3825	0.9898	0.511044	0.310762
	Non-int income/total income	62	0.2913	1	0.504052	0.1148178
	Non-interest margin	62	0.0038	0.0213	0.012588	0.0038626
	Non-int expenses/total assets	62	0.007	0.0262	0.015793	0.0047622
YES	ROE	36	−0.1014	18.3569	8.651583	5.0137745
	ROA	36	0.0081	0.844	0.428108	0.2406657
	Non-int income/total income	36	0.4801	0.9295	0.619173	0.1446848
	Non-interest margin	36	0.0112	0.067	0.021495	0.0183825
	Non-int expenses/total assets	36	0.0112	0.066	0.02308	0.017465

It is therefore possible to note at the outset that all Canadian banks stand out with higher ROE and ROA over the period considered. They, therefore, appear to have better returns on equity invested and even more optimal asset management. In both cases, this effect can be explained by the fact that there is less competition in the Canadian market compared to the French market, which is flooded with European competitors, given the mobility of capital in the European Union's economic area. The fact that the Canadian government has put in place stricter rules governing the activities of financial institutions and some protectionism with respect to the activities of foreign banks means that the market is mainly dominated by the seven large banks that we have selected for this study (Banking Act, https://laws-lois.justice.gc.ca/fra/lois/b-1.01/, accessed on 14 November 2024) [18].

French banks have a higher net margin excluding interest and higher non-interest expenses, both in absolute and relative terms. There is therefore every reason to believe that other non-banking financial activities have a more important place within French banks.

In light of the last segment of this table, we realize that banks operating a robo-advisor have a lower average ROE and ROA than non-robotized banks. Conversely, non-interest margin and non-interest expenses are higher for financial institutions that have chosen to integrate robo-advisors. This finding suggests that banks with low overall profitability or limited profitability with their intermediation activity are more likely to turn to digital solutions in order to obtain additional revenues or reduce their costs and improve profitability for shareholders.

5.2. Analysis of Variance

The analysis of variances allows us to determine whether there is a significant difference in profitability indicators between banks that invest in the robo-advisor and those that do not.

For the entire sample selected, the above Tables 3 and 4 show a significant difference in the non-interest margin, the share of non-interest income in total income, and non-interest expenses in relation to the level of assets. It is therefore presumed at this stage that robo banks have different profitability than non-robot banks.

Table 3. Analysis of Variance (Robotized Banks vs. Non-Robotized Banks).

1 Factor ANOVA						
		Sum of Squares	**ddl**	**Average of Squares**	**F**	**Sig.**
ROE	Inter-groups	60.312	1	60.312	1.991	0.161
	Intra-groups	2908.265	96	30.294		
	Total	2968.577	97			
ROA	Inter-groups	0.157	1	0.157	1.899	0.171
	Intra-groups	7.918	96	0.082		
	Total	8.075	97			
Non-int income/total income	Inter-groups	0.302	1	0.302	18.855	0.000
	Intra-groups	1.537	96	0.016		
	Total	1.839	97			
Non-interest margin	Inter-groups	0.002	1	0.002	13.618	0.000
	Intra-groups	0.013	96	0		
	Total	0.015	97			
Non-int expenses/total assets	Inter-groups	0.001	1	0.001	9.627	0.003
	Intra-groups	0.012	96	0		
	Total	0.013	97			

Table 4. Analysis of Variance by Country (Robo Banks vs. Non-Robo Banks).

1 Factor ANOVA							
Country			**Sum of Squares**	**ddl**	**Average of Squares**	**F**	**Sig.**
Canada	ROE	Inter-groups	0.475	1	0.475	0.045	0.834
		Intra-groups	424.799	40	10.62		
		Total	425.273	41			
	ROA	Inter-groups	0.013	1	0.013	0.385	0.539
		Intra-groups	1.303	40	0.033		
		Total	1.316	41			
	Non-int income/total income	Inter-groups	0.047	1	0.047	10.021	0.003
		Intra-groups	0.188	40	0.005		
		Total	0.235	41			
	Non-interest margin	Inter-groups	0	1	0	2.367	0.132
		Intra-groups	0	40	0		
		Total	0	41			
	Non-int expenses/total assets	Inter-groups	0	1	0	0.846	0.363
		Intra-groups	0	40	0		
		Total	0	41			

Table 4. *Cont.*

1 Factor ANOVA							
Country			Sum of Squares	ddl	Average of Squares	F	Sig.
France	ROE	Inter-groups	5.973	1	5.973	0.463	0.499
		Intra-groups	696.309	54	12.895		
		Total	702.282	55			
	ROA	Inter-groups	0.002	1	0.002	0.123	0.727
		Intra-groups	0.756	54	0.014		
		Total	0.757	55			
	Non-int income/total income	Inter-groups	0.166	1	0.166	9.214	0.004
		Intra-groups	0.975	54	0.018		
		Total	1.141	55			
	Non-interest margin	Inter-groups	0.002	1	0.002	10.386	0.002
		Intra-groups	0.011	54	0		
		Total	0.014	55			
	Non-int expenses/total assets	Inter-groups	0.002	1	0.002	8.583	0.005
		Intra-groups	0.011	54	0		
		Total	0.013	55			

However, when analyzing the two sub-samples separately by country, it should be noted that of all the profitability indicators tested, only the proportion of non-interest income to total income shows a significant difference on the Canadian side. In France, on the other hand, all profitability indicators related to activities other than financial intermediation (non-interest margin, non-interest income/total income, and non-interest expenses/total assets) show a significant difference between robotized and non-robotized banks. ROE and ROA show no significant difference. This can be explained by the fact that these are general profitability indicators, which largely include net interest income from financial intermediation, an activity for which robo-advisors are not used. The latter is more required in the context of the bank's market activities. In addition, the maintenance expenses of such devices are included in the non-interest expense category, while the income from these activities contributes to the non-interest margin.

5.3. Correlation Analysis

Elements other than the arrival of robo-advisors in these banks can influence the profitability indicators we have selected. The correlation analysis here sheds more light on the preliminary results.

This Table 5 reveals a strong and very significant association between the presence of a robo-advisor and the level of non-interest income, non-interest expenses, and non-interest margin. The use of robo-advisors also appears to be related to greater financial risk and low operational efficiency. These results highlight that Canadian banks are significantly more likely to have higher overall profitability than French banks (with higher ROE and ROA) and that non-robotized banks also have higher overall profitability than robotized banks. In addition, the most profitable banks invest less in non-interest activities and consequently have the lowest non-interest margins. Naturally, banks that invest more in robo-advisors have more comfortable non-interest margins, which is also the objective.

Table 5. Correlations.

		1	2	3	4	5	6	7	8	9	10	11
1	ROE	1										
2	ROA	0.947 **	1									
3	Non-int. mg	−0.245 *	−0.258 *	1								
4	Non-int inc/tot inc	−0.075	−0.051	0.775 **	1							
5	Non-int exp/tot ass	−0.016	0.001	0.619 **	0.963 **	1						
6	Assets Manag.	0.147	0.187	0.580 **	0.949 **	0.976 **	1					
7	Fin risk	−0.471 **	−0.534 **	0.567 **	0.647 **	0.621 **	0.493 **	1				
8	Oper eff.	−0.230 *	−0.218 *	0.744 **	0.964 **	0.929 **	0.877 **	0.754 **	1			
9	Size	−0.054	0.049	−0.133	−0.363 **	−0.474 **	−0.396 **	−0.462 **	−0.401 **	1		
10	Robot	−0.143	−0.139	0.405 **	0.352 **	0.302 **	0.274 **	0.309 **	0.362 **	−0.008	1	
11	Country	−0.788 **	−0.862 **	0.501 **	0.163	0.043	−0.098	0.514 **	0.274 **	0.163	0.147	1

* Significant at 0.05 level. ** Significant at 0.01 level.

5.4. Multivariate Analysis

In order to determine the substantial contribution of the use of robo-advisors to bank profitability, we analyze regressions of profitability indicators by adding the robot variable to the traditional determinants of profitability in banks, namely optimal asset management, operational efficiency, and financial risk. All this is controlled for size and country factors (See Table 6).

Table 6. Model results.

	1			2			3		
	Coef.	**T**	***p*-Value**	**Coef.**	**T**	***p*-Value**	**Coef.**	**T**	***p*-Value**
Constant	0.0106302	0.40	0.693	2.398058	1.34	0.184	−0.0207603	−0.87	0.384
Asset management	0.6329441	10.10	0.000	3.016701	1.46	0.148	0.8666632	24.08	0.000
Financial risk	−0.0240928	−2.46	0.363	−2.284565	−1.25	0.213	0.0270216	1.12	0.267
Operational efficiency	0.0022416	2.31	0.000	0.0304644	2.54	0.013	0.0003789	1.77	0.080
Size	0.0022416	−1.74	0.525	−0.0092544	−0.33	0.745	−0.002574	−5.97	0.000
Country	0.0028096	1.77	0.000	0.1399631	4.32	0.000	0.0023876	4.09	0.000
Robot	0.0006856	8.92	0.018	0.0448961	2.97	0.004	0.0003089	1.06	0.294
N		98			98			98	
Significance		0.0000			0.0000			0.0000	
R2 adjusted		0.6833			0.6999			0.7864	

1: Non-interest margin = α + β1EP + β2GA + β3Risk + β1Size + β5Country + β6Robot + ε. 2: Proportion of non-interest income = α + β1EP + β2GA + β3Risk + β1Size + β5Country + β6Robot + ε. 3: Non-interest expenses/total assets = α + β1EP + β2GA + β3Risk + β1Size + β5Country + β6Robot + ε.

The regression carried out on the whole sample shows significance for the robot variable in terms of explaining the non-interest margin and the share of non-interest income in the total income of the banks. However, this variable is not significant for the variable relating to non-interest expenses in relation to the volume of assets. In almost all cases, operational efficiency and effective asset management are important determinants of profitability.

In light of these findings, it is clear that there is a relationship between the use of a robo-advisor and the level of non-interest income. This link seems stronger in France than in Canada. It is likely that the fact that these robots have been installed for a slightly longer period of time in France explains why their effect is a little more marked there. In addition to the novelty effect in Canada compared to France, another more important factor could affect these results, namely the distinct environment of the two countries.

The three equations conducted on the total sample clearly show that both Canadian and French banks operate in almost impervious environments. This makes it difficult to compare Canadian banking activity with that of France. This is mainly because of the legislative differentiation in place and the opening of doors to the European Union for

France. Still, on an institutional level, Zogning (2017) [8] shows that France has a financial system strongly influenced by the banking sector, whereas Canada embodies a financial system more focused on financial markets. This state of affairs largely explains why banks in France are major players, even in securities investments where they act as brokers and intermediaries. Whereas in Canada, investment in securities is primarily the preserve of pension funds, mutual funds, and income trusts. Banks access this market because of their financial expertise and the potential it offers in terms of liquidity.

For example, at the end of 2018, there were 632 portfolio management companies in France and 75% of the top 20 players in this market are subsidiaries of commercial banks. These account for 66.2% of assets under management (Report of the Autorité des Marchés Financiers on assets under management by management companies—November 2019). In contrast, Canada had 3535 asset management and investment advisory firms as of the same date. Moreover, in the ranking, only 2 of the top 7 banks included in this study are among the top 40 players in the market. Herein lies an attempt to explain the fact that Canada does not show a significant difference in the comparison of certain profitability indicators between robotized and non-robotized banks. This is because they use the robo-advisor in a segment of activity where they are highly competitive. Although this robot improves their profitability in market activities, the difference with banks without robots, although perceptible, is not yet significant.

Pellerin (2008) [19], who analyzed the effect of off-balance-sheet activities on the volatility of Canadian banks' revenues, highlights the role of the Bank Act, which came into effect in the early 1990s, as an important factor in the diversification of financial institutions' revenues in Canada. Revenues derived from the use of credit cards, group or personal insurance, real estate, and securities commissions are good examples of sectors in which financial institutions have invested in order to increase their revenues. Now that technology and digital technology are becoming ubiquitous in the daily lives of many countries, these institutions are integrating them into their business models.

Robo-advisors are still a recent concept. The first appearances outside the United States took place in 2012. It is therefore likely that more conclusive results as to their influence on financial results, especially on banks' non-interest income, will come after the current investment phase and the running-in of this phase with clients. Indeed, with the process in the start-up phase, the additional market shares that the implementation of the robo-advisors should confer have probably not yet reached the proportions necessary to make a noticeable difference in results.

Moreover, a reading of the financial statements of these banks indicates a rationalization of expenditures and the addition of new activities between 2012 and 2019. Indeed, even the French banks in this study that stood out in terms of non-interest expenses and revenues were clearly engaged in a strategy to develop different avenues for the benefits of financial intermediation. As an example, in 2011, CM-ARKEA set up a venture capital subsidiary that invests in equity in unlisted companies and another subsidiary that operates in securitization (CM-ARKEA, 2012 Registration Document, website: https://www.arkea.com/banque/assurance/credit/upload/docs/application/pdf/2014-01/document-de-reference-credit-mutuel-arkea-31122012.pdf consulted on 3 May 2020). These two areas clearly influence a bank's non-interest activities. Moreover, the fact that financial institutions with lower ROE and ROA performance are diversifying shows that financial intermediation revenues tend to peak and that banks are constantly looking for new activities to improve their profitability. As a result, they are developing a technological watch by investing in fintech. The increase in the performance of robotized banks between 2012 and 2019 may therefore not be due solely to robot-advisors but also to a broader diversification strategy, which relies, among other things, on the use of robo-advisors to rationalize costs.

6. Conclusions

With regard to the previous lines, the arrival of the robo-advisors is a response to the desire of financial institutions to diversify the type of income they have beyond simple intermediation. Long before the 2008 crisis, banks were already seeking to differentiate their activities, by seeking income where they had never done so before.

The integration of digital technologies, in the age of banking automation and artificial intelligence, offers new ways to reach customers and take advantage of growing technology. The robot-advisor fulfils an important task in meeting the needs of bank customers who no longer want to travel but still want advice about their investments and asset management. It manages a series of exchange-traded funds in exchange for a commission for the bank, which is, however, lower than that of a conventional mutual fund. However, in theory, the lack of human interaction means that the costs incurred to manage these funds are lower for the bank.

In order to properly analyze the effect of advisors coming to the banks, fourteen banks were selected from among the largest. Seven were selected in Canada and seven in France.

The results bring out two important observations. Financial institutions with low overall profitability (lower ROE and ROA) are turning to the use of robo-advisors. These banks have higher net non-interest margins and non-interest income per asset than their counterparts that do not invest in robo-advisors. These results show that banks using robo-advisors experienced a 5% increase in non-interest income compared to non-adopters. Two traits appear to be more pronounced in France than in Canada.

This study contributes to the academic literature on digital banking transformation by providing empirical evidence on the role of robo-advisors in bank profitability. It offers insights into the influence of regulatory and operational differences across financial systems. For practitioners, the findings underscore the potential of robo-advisors to optimize operational efficiency and diversify revenue streams, offering a pathway for strategic decision-making.

Can we believe that it is only the introduction of robo-advisors that is influencing these changes to the financial statements of these banks? Probably not. In fact, other sectors of activity such as insurance and real estate management, among others, are diversifying banks' revenues. However, the role of robo-advisors seems to be becoming clearer and would be an avenue to watch out for in the longer term.

It is likely that this study was conducted a little early in the process of implementing robo-advisors and that the system has not yet reached cruising speed, particularly among Canadian banks that compete fiercely in this segment of activity against many non-depositary financial institutions, which adopted robo-advisors long before the banks.

This study presents certain limitations, particularly regarding the availability of data on the performance of banks that have adopted robo-advisors. The recent implementation period of robo-advisors does not yet allow for the observation of long-term effects. Therefore, the results should be interpreted with caution, and future studies could extend this research by relying on more recent data and longer observation periods. Future research could extend the observation period and incorporate a larger sample of banking systems from other countries that comply with IFRS and Basel III agreements.

Another investigation will be required once the robo-advisors have taken a greater share of the banks' activities. All in all, there is every reason to believe that the virtualization of banking services will continue at a rapid pace and that these changes will have an impact on the financial statements of financial institutions. In any case, interest in robo-advisors continues to grow. As evidence of this, Canada's two largest banks, the Royal Bank of Canada (RBC) and Toronto Dominion Bank (TD) in turn adopted a robo-advisor in the very last months of the reference period of this study.

Author Contributions: Conceptualization, F.Z. and P.T.; methodology, F.Z.; software, F.Z.; validation, F.Z. and P.T.; formal analysis, F.Z. and P.T.; writing—original draft preparation, F.Z. and P.T.; writing—review and editing, F.Z.; visualization, F.Z.; supervision, F.Z. All authors have read and agreed to the published version of the manuscript.

Funding: This research received no external funding.

Institutional Review Board Statement: Not applicable.

Informed Consent Statement: Not applicable.

Data Availability Statement: The data can be shared up on request.

Conflicts of Interest: Author Pascal Turcotte was employed by the Canadian Imperial Bank of Commerce. The authors declare no conflicts of interest.

References

1. Les Affaires. Les Robots-Conseillers: Est-ce Pour Vous? 2020. Available online: https://www.lesaffaires.com/dossier/maximiser-ma-retraite-et-mon-patrimoine/les-robots-conseillers-est-ce-pour-vous/595111 (accessed on 14 November 2024).
2. Hard Bacon. Comparez les Robots-Conseillers au Canada. 2020. Available online: https://hardbacon.ca/fr/comparez-les-robots-conseillers-au-canada/ (accessed on 14 November 2024).
3. Mondaq. CSA provides guidance on Canadian robo-advisers. *Mondaq*. 2015. Available online: https://www.mondaq.com/canada/fund-management-reits/434698/csa-provides-guidance-on-canadian-robo-advisers (accessed on 14 November 2024).
4. European Parliament. Robo-advisors in the EU: Market developments and regulatory framework. Policy Department for Economic, Scientific and Quality of Life Policies. 2021. Available online: https://www.europarl.europa.eu/RegData/etudes/STUD/2021/662928/IPOL_STU(2021)662928_EN.pdf (accessed on 14 November 2024).
5. Phoon, K.; Koh, F. Robo-advisors and wealth management. *J. Altern. Invest.* **2018**, *20*, 79–94. [CrossRef]
6. Uhl, M.W.; Rohner, P. Robo-advisors versus traditional investment advisors: An unequal game. *J. Wealth Manag.* **2018**, *21*, 44–50. [CrossRef]
7. Tertilt, M.; Scholz, P. To advise, or not to advise—How robo-advisors evaluate the risk preferences of private investors. *J. Wealth Manag.* **2018**, *21*, 70–84. [CrossRef]
8. Zogning, F. Comparing Financial Systems around the World: Capital Markets, Legal Systems, and Governance Regimes. *Econ. Manag. Financ. Mark.* **2017**, *12*, 43–58.
9. Schepens, G. Taxes and Bank capital structure. *J. Financ. Econ.* **2016**, *120*, 585–600. [CrossRef]
10. Singh, A.; Sharma, A.K. An empirical analysis of macroeconomic and bank-specific factors affecting liquidity of Indian banks. *Future Bus. J.* **2016**, *2*, 40–53. [CrossRef]
11. Naeem, M.; Baloch, Q.B.; Khan, A.W. Factors affecting banks' profitability in Pakistan. *Int. J. Bus. Stud. Rev.* **2017**, *2*, 33–49.
12. Salike, N.; Ao, B. Determinants of bank's profitability: Role of poor asset quality in Asia. *China Financ. Rev. Int.* **2017**, *8*, 216–231. [CrossRef]
13. Anbar, A.; Alper, D. Bank specific and macroeconomic determinants of commercial bank profitability: Empirical evidence from Turkey. *Bus. Econ. Res. J.* **2011**, *2*, 139.
14. Francis, M.E. Determinants of commercial bank profitability in sub-Saharan Africa. *Int. J. Econ. Financ.* **2013**, *5*, 134–147.
15. Rashid, A.; Jabeen, S. Borsa_Istanbul review analyzing performance determinants: Conventional versus Islamic banks in Pakistan. *Borsa Istanb. Rev.* **2016**, *16*, 92–107. [CrossRef]
16. Almaqtari, F.A.; Al-Homaidi, E.A.; Tabash, M.I.; Farhan, N.H. The determinants of profitability of Indian commercial banks: A panel data approach. *Int. J. Financ. Econ.* **2019**, *24*, 168–185. [CrossRef]
17. Yahya, A.T.; Akhtar, A.; Tabash, M.I. The impact of political instability, macroeconomic and bank-specific factors on the profitability of Islamic banks: An empirical evidence. *Invest. Manag. Financ. Innov.* **2017**, *14*, 30–39.
18. Canada, J. Government of Canada. Bank Act. Available online: https://laws-lois.justice.gc.ca/fra/lois/b-1.01/ (accessed on 14 November 2024).
19. Pellerin, N. *The Effect of Off-Balance Sheet Activities on the Profitability and Revenue Volatility of Canadian Banks*; Working paper; Université du Québec en Outaouais: Gatineau, QC, Canada, 2008.

FinTech

Article

Using Precious Metals to Reduce the Downside Risk of FinTech Stocks

Perry Sadorsky

Schulich School of Business, York University, Toronto, ON M3J 1P3, Canada; psadorsky@schulich.yorku.ca

Abstract: FinTech stocks are an important new asset class that reflects the rapidly growing FinTech sector. This paper studies the practical implications of using gold, silver, and basket-of-precious-metals (gold, silver, platinum, palladium) ETFs to diversify risk in FinTech stocks. Downside risk reduction is estimated using relative risk ratios based on CVaR. The analysis shows that gold provides the most downside risk protection. For a 5% CVaR, a 30% portfolio weight for gold reduces the downside risk by about 25%. The minimum variance and minimum correlation three-asset (FinTech, gold, and silver) portfolios (with portfolio weights estimated using a TVP-VAR model) have the highest risk-adjusted returns (Sharpe ratio, Omega ratio) followed by the fixed-weight FinTech and gold portfolio. These results show the benefits of diversifying an investment in FinTech stocks with precious metals. These results are robust to weekly or monthly portfolio rebalancing and reasonable transaction costs.

Keywords: FinTech stocks; downside risk; minimum variance portfolio; gold; portfolio analysis

JEL Classification: G1; G11; G15

1. Introduction

In the past ten years, financial technology (FinTech) has evolved to create some amazing new financial products and services. Examples of FinTech include mobile payments via smartphones, securing transactions through blockchain, peer-to-peer lending, robo-investment advising, cybersecurity, cloud computing, and crowdfunding [1]. FinTech can increase efficiency in the financial sector [2,3] and promote financial inclusion [4–7]. The growth of FinTech has been accompanied by a rapid growth in investing in FinTech stocks. For example, in July 2023, publicly traded FinTech companies had a market capitalization of USD 550 billion, which is a two-time increase versus 2019 [8].

The growing interest in FinTech stocks has inspired a literature looking at the dynamic connectedness between FinTech stocks and other assets. To date, there is research looking at the relationship between FinTech stocks and other financial assets like Bitcoin, green bonds, and AI [9], robotics and AI stocks [10], conventional finance [11–15], renewable energy [16], green bonds [17], and related FinTech assets [18–20].

While the abovementioned studies provide important perspective on the relationship between FinTech stocks and other financial markets, the risk management of FinTech stocks is understudied. The risk management of FinTech stocks is important because investors need to identify and measure downside risk and either accept the impact these downsides have on risk-adjusted returns or mitigate downside risk in order to achieve higher risk-adjusted returns. One way to mitigate the downside risk associated with FinTech stocks is to combine FinTech stocks with another unrelated (uncorrelated) asset class—a tactic referred to as portfolio diversification. According to modern portfolio theory, an investment portfolio experiences two types of risk: systematic risk and unsystematic risk or specific risk [21]. Systematic risk is the risk associated with the volatility in the entire capital market and cannot be diversified away. Specific risk is the volatility associated with a specific security and can be diversified away by investing in other securities. In the context of FinTech stocks, Henriques and Sadorsky [22] find that combining FinTech stocks with clean energy stocks produces higher risk-adjusted returns than an investment only in FinTech stocks. They do not, however, investigate the role of precious metals in reducing FinTech downside risk.

The purpose of this research is to examine the ability of precious metals to reduce the downside risk for an investment in FinTech stocks. In this paper, risk reduction is measured using risk ratios [23,24]. A risk ratio is constructed where the numerator is the risk of a portfolio that mixes FinTech with precious metals and the denominator is the risk of an investment in FinTech. The value of this ratio shows the share of portfolio risk remaining after diversifying with precious metals. Lower values of this ratio indicate greater risk reduction. Risk ratios are often used by practitioners because they are easy to calculate and easy to interpret. The analysis in this paper uses conditional value at risk (CVaR) as the risk measure. CVaR, also referred to as expected shortfall (ES), is a risk measure that quantifies tail risk in the return distribution. More explicitly, CVaR is computed by taking a weighted average of the loses below the value at risk (VaR) value. VaR measures how much an investment will lose (with given probability α) over a specific time period [25]. CVaR is often preferred in practice over VaR because CVaR is a coherent measure of risk, while VaR is not [26]. A comparison is made between fixed-weight two-asset portfolios and three-asset (FinTech, gold, silver) changing-weight minimum-variance, minimum-correlation, and minimum-connectedness portfolios where the portfolio weights are estimated using a TVP-VAR model.

Precious metals are chosen as the financial assets to reduce FinTech downside risk because of the long history of using these assets as diversifiers. Gold is often used by investors as a hedge against inflation or adverse economic times [27–44]. For example, gold prices increased during the 2008–2009 global financial crisis (GFC) and during the COVID-19 pandemic as investors sought safe-haven investments. In addition to gold, there is research showing that other precious metals like silver, platinum, and palladium also have diversification and hedging properties [40,45–49].

For the purposes of this research, a FinTech company is defined to be a small, technology-enabled, new entrant to financial services that disrupts the incumbents [50]. FinTech stock prices and the prices of gold, silver, and a basket of precious metals are measured using exchange-traded funds (ETFs). ETFs are collections of traded securities used by individual and institutional investors to build portfolios. ETFs have low management fees and are widely traded. The daily data set covers the time period 16 September 2016 to 28 June 2024. In addition to estimating and comparing downside risk ratios for different weights of precious metals, risk and return analysis is provided by comparing an investment in FinTech stocks with portfolios that combine FinTech and precious metals.

Risk ratios computed using CVaR show that gold provides the most downside risk reduction. For a 5% CVaR, a 30% portfolio weight for gold reduces the downside risk by about 25%. Silver has the least downside risk reduction. Portfolio analysis shows that combining FinTech stocks with either gold, silver, or a precious metals basket in a fixed-weight two-asset portfolio produces higher risk-adjusted returns and lower maximum drawdowns than an investment solely in FinTech stocks. Overall, the three-asset (FinTech, gold, silver) minimum-variance portfolio (MVP) and minimum-correlation portfolio (MCP) have the highest risk-adjusted returns and lowest drawdown. The MVP and MCP portfolio weights are estimated using a TVP-VAR model. These results are robust to weekly or monthly rebalancing of portfolios and transaction costs.

This study proceeds as follows. Section 2 describes the methodology, while Section 3 details the data. The results are presented in Section 4. Section 5 presents a discussion and conclusion.

2. Methods

This section describes the empirical methods used in the analysis. There are two main empirical methods of analysis used in this paper—relative risk ratios and investment portfolio performance.

2.1. Relative Risk Ratios

Relative risk ratios are computed as the ratio $CVaR_{mix}/CVaR_{ft}$, where "*mix*" is a portfolio that mixes FinTech stocks with precious metals and "*ft*" is the investment in FinTech stocks. The $CVaR_p$ is the average expected portfolio loss larger than a VaR_p for a confidence interval of $(1 - \alpha)$:

$$CVaR_p(1-\alpha) = E(R_p | R_p < VaR_p(1-\alpha) \tag{1}$$

Rp is the portfolio return and VaR_p is the portfolio VaR_p calculated at the α level. *VaR* quantifies an investment loss for a specific time period and probability (α). Typical values for α are 0.01 (1%) and 0.05 (5%). The expression for VaR_p is:

$$Prob(R_p \leq VaR_p(1-\alpha)) = \alpha \tag{2}$$

VaR can be calculated parametrically or non-parametrically [26]. The analysis in this paper uses a historical *VaR* (non-parametric) and a modified VaR (parametric) [51]. The historical *VaR* is the α percentile value of the return distribution. The modified *VaR* uses a Cornish–Fisher expansion to modify the Gaussian *VaR* to account for skewness and kurtosis [51].

2.2. Portfolio Construction

Portfolios were constructed for two-asset portfolios and three-asset portfolios. The two-asset portfolios (FinTech and one precious metal) are estimated using fixed weights and do not require econometric techniques.

The three-asset portfolios (FinTech, gold, and silver) are estimated with changing portfolio weights and require econometric techniques. Three portfolios are estimated, (1) minimum-variance portfolio (*MVP*) [52], (2),minimum-correlation portfolio (*MCP*) [53], and (3) minimum-connectedness portfolio (*MPC*) [54].

The *MVP* minimizes total variance where $\sum_t$ is the 3×3 variance–covariance matrix of the asset returns at time period t. The portfolio weights for the *MVP* are:

$$w_{MVPt} = \frac{\sum_t^{-1} I}{I \sum_t^{-1} I} \tag{3}$$

The matrix I is the 3×3 identity matrix.

The objective of *MCP* is to determine portfolio weights by minimizing the portfolio correlation. The portfolio weights for the *MCP* are:

$$w_{MCPt} = \frac{CC_t^{-1} I}{CC_t^{-1} I} \tag{4}$$

where $CC_t = \text{diag}(\sum_t)^{-0.5} \sum \text{diag}(\sum_t)^{-0.5}$ is the conditional correlations of asset returns.

The portfolio weights for the *MPC* are:

$$w_{MPCt} = \frac{PCI_t^{-1} I}{IPCI_t^{-1} I} \tag{5}$$

Here, PCIs are pairwise correlations estimated from a TVP-VAR(1) connectedness model. The Antonakakis et al. [55] TVP-VAR approach to estimating connectedness has several advantages over the VAR approach first proposed by Diebold and Yilmaz [56,57].

The TVP-VAR captures the time-varying nature in the data, taking into account changing dynamics over different periods and assessing the extent and direction of market spillovers [58]. This approach also avoids the problem of arbitrarily selecting a rolling window size. The SIC selected one as the order of the TVP-VAR lag length. The TVP-VAR connectedness was estimated using 20-step-ahead generalized forecast error variance decompositions.

2.3. Portfolio Comparison

The risk-adjusted returns of portfolios are compared using the Sharpe ratio and the Omega ratio. The Sharpe ratio divides the average portfolio return (net of a risk-free rate) by the portfolio standard deviation. Higher Sharpe ratios indicate higher risk-adjusted returns. The Omega ratio is the probability weighted ratio of gains versus loses relative to a threshold target. While the Sharpe ratio takes mean and standard deviation into account, the Omega ratio also accounts for skewness and kurtosis. A higher Omega ratio indicates higher risk-adjusted returns.

In addition to the Sharpe ratio and Omega ratio, maximum drawdown, value-at-risk (VaR), and expected shortfall (ES) are calculated. A discussion of these measures can be found in Cogneau and Huber [59].

All computations were performed using R [60] with the help of the following packages—ConnectednessApproach [61], quantmod [62], and PerformanceAnalytics [63].

3. Data

FinTech stock prices are measured using the adjusted closing prices of the Global X FinTech ETF (FINX). FINX is one of the largest (in terms of assets under management) ETFs specializing in FinTech stocks and has the longest trading history. Gold prices are measured by the GLD ETF and silver prices are measured by the SLV ETF. The ETF GLTR is a basket of precious metals (gold, silver, platinum, and palladium). The daily data set covers the period 13 September 2016 to 28 June 2024. GLD, SLV, and GLTR are the three largest precious metal ETFs in terms of assets under management. As of 1 August 2024 GLD, SLV, and GLTR had USD 55 billion, USD 10 billion, and USD 930 million, respectively, in assets under management (data sourced from Yahoo Finance). The starting date of the analysis is determined by the inception of FINX. The data are in USD and were downloaded from Yahoo Finance.

The time series pattern of FINX displays considerable variability (Figure 1). Between March 2018 and March 2020, FINX increased from USD 20 to USD 50. Most of this increase occurred during the onset of the COVID-19 lockdowns as consumers shifted more of their economic activity online [64]. The price appreciation was short lived and by September 2022, FINX was trading around USD 20.

The time series plots of the precious metals display a similar pattern of price appreciation from January 2019 to June 2020, although gold appreciated the most. Afterwards, gold and GLTR show the strongest performance. Over the sample period studied, gold has the strongest upwards trend followed by GLTR.

FINX, measured in continuously compounded daily percent returns, had a small positive average daily value of 0.03% over the sample period (Table 1). For the precious metals, GLD had the largest average daily return (0.027%) and SLV had the smallest (0.020%). Notice that while the variables have similar mean values, they display considerable variability. According to the coefficient of variation, SLV is the most variable while GLD is the least. The distribution of each variable is lightly skewed to the left and has heavier tails than a normal distribution. Each variable is stationary because the KPSS unit root test statistics are below the 5% critical value. Each variable is non-normally distributed.

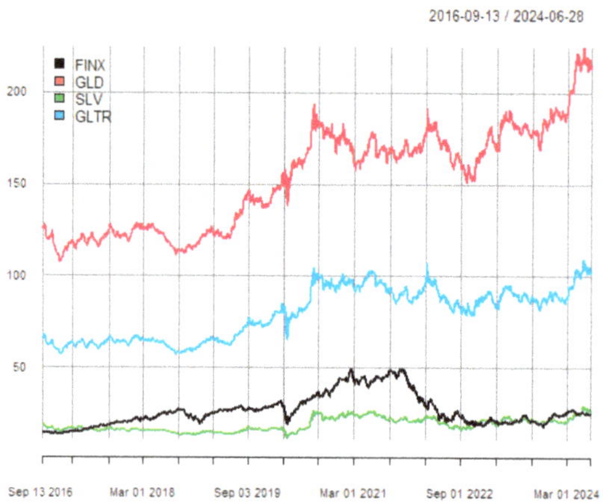

Figure 1. Time series plot of FINX, GLD, SLV, and GLTR adjusted closing prices.

Table 1. Summary statistics.

	Median	Mean	Std.dev	Coef.var	Skewness	Kurtosis	KPSS	W	W(p)
FINX	0.145	0.030	1.804	60.532	−0.490	5.600	0.287	0.938	0.000
GLD	0.055	0.027	0.865	31.595	−0.314	3.275	0.098	0.966	0.000
SLV	0.040	0.020	1.708	85.116	−0.418	7.627	0.080	0.924	0.000
GLTR	0.066	0.023	1.098	48.471	−0.486	5.513	0.053	0.949	0.000

Notes. All variables measured in continuously compounded daily percent returns. W is the Shapiro–Wilk test for normality and W(p) is the associated probability value. KPSS is the Kwiatkowski–Phillips–Schmidt–Shin test for unit roots (5% critical value is 0.463).

The Pearson correlation coefficients indicate that FINX is positively correlated with each precious metal (Table 2). The lowest correlation is between FINX and GLD while the highest correlation is between GLTR and SLV. Pearson correlation analysis indicates that GLD may be the best diversifier for FINX.

Table 2. Pearson correlation coefficients.

	FINX	GLD	SLV	GLTR
FINX	1.000	0.105	0.239	0.223
GLD	0.105	1.000	0.783	0.902
SLV	0.239	0.783	1.000	0.909
GLTR	0.223	0.902	0.909	1.000

Notes: See Table 1.

4. Results

The relative risk ratio plots show how relative risk varies by the precious metal portfolio weight (Figure 2). The top panel of Figure 2 shows relative risk ratios computed for 5% CVaR coverage (α value), while the lower panel shows ratios for 1% coverage. CVaR ratios are computed using either the historical or modified approach. Looking first at the top panel of Figure 2, gold has the greatest risk reduction. A 30% portfolio weight for gold reduces the downside risk by about 25% (relative risk ratio value is 0.75). Notice also that both GLD and GLTR show a smooth decline in relative risk as their portfolio weights increase until a weighting of 80%—after which higher weights add little to reducing downside risk. Silver is different in that relative risk is never reduced below 0.75. It is also important to point out that for each precious metal, the risk ratio computed using the historical method is similar to that using the modified method.

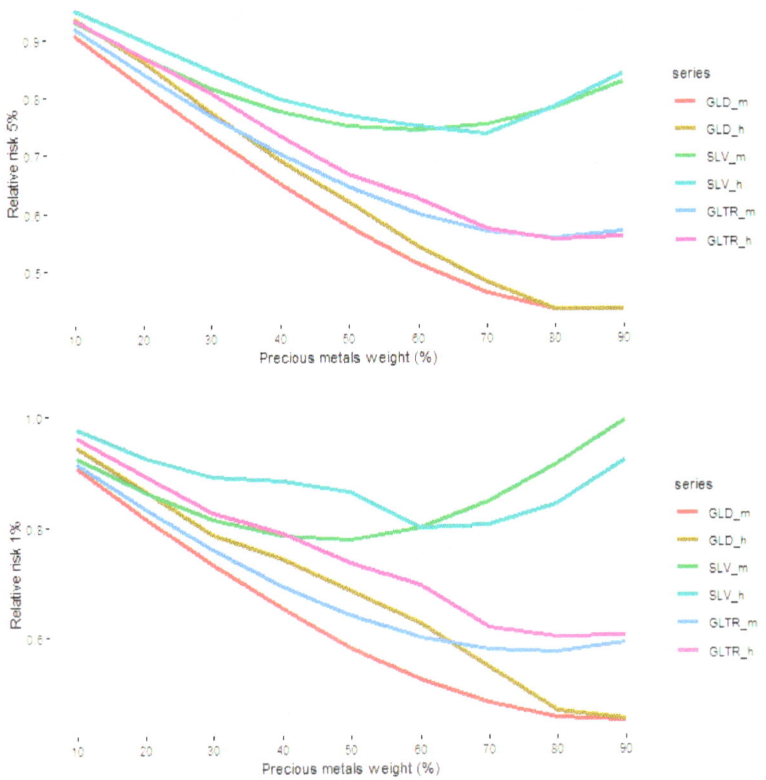

Figure 2. Relative risk ratio plots. The suffixes _m and _h denote modified and historical CVaR.

The lower panel of Figure 2 shows relative risk ratios computed using coverage at 1%. It is still the case that GLD and GLTR show the greatest risk reduction as the precious metal portfolio weight increases. Notice, however, that for each precious metal the choice of CVaR method (historical, modified) affects the pattern of the plots. This is expected because there are not many observations in the 1% tail of the return distribution, and this affects the precision of the CVaR calculation.

Since risk reduction may vary across time, it is also of interest to see how relative risk varies across time. For this analysis, the relative risk ratios are computed using a fixed rolling window of length 500 observations (two years of daily data) and a precious metals portfolio weighting of 25%. CVaR is calculated using the modified method. At a portfolio weighting of 25%, gold and precious metals show relative risk ratios of around 80%, which is enough of a risk reduction to accommodate trading costs in the portfolio analysis presented below. Regulators require that at least 250 daily observations be used for calculating VaR [65,66] and in practice 500 days is often used. The impact of the COVID-19 lockdowns on the relative risk (at 5% loss) is clear (Figure 3). All risk ratios experienced large increases during March 2020 when the COVID-19 lockdowns began. Thus, risk reduction is reduced during times of economic stress. Risk ratios remained elevated until January 2023. GLD provides the greatest amount of risk reduction across the sample period with a risk ratio that never exceeds 80%. GLTR has the next best risk reduction, while SLV provides the least amount of risk reduction.

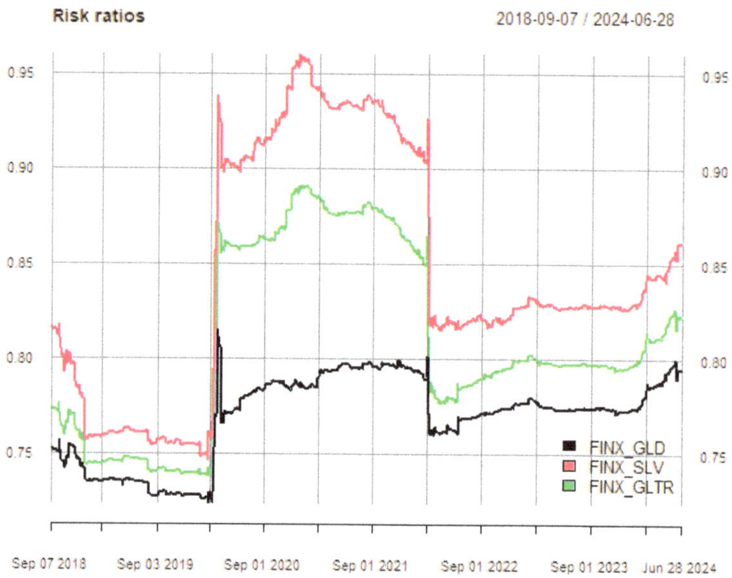

Figure 3. Risk ratios (at 5% loss) across time.

Risk ratios calculated for a 1% loss (Figure 4) show a similar pattern to those calculated for a 5% loss. GLD provides the greatest risk reduction, while SLV provides the least. Notice that gold's risk reduction during the COVID-19 period is higher than silver's risk reduction in the pre-COVID-19 period.

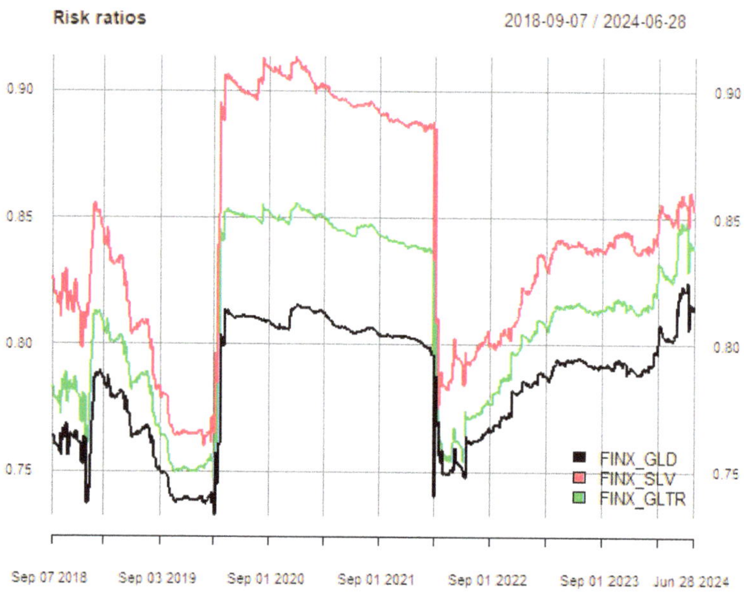

Figure 4. Risk ratios (at 1% loss) across time.

4.1. Two-Asset Portfolios

Turning now to portfolio performance comparisons, it is interesting to see how portfolios that combine FinTech stocks with precious metals compare to an investment only in FinTech stocks. For each two-asset portfolio, the precious metals weighting is 25%. Portfolio rebalancing occurs weekly and the transaction costs are 50 basis points per trade (50 cents per USD 100 transacted). A transaction cost of 50 basis points is generous as many discount brokers allow ETF trading for less than 10 basis points.

Equity curves (Figure 5) show how USD 1 in each portfolio evolves across time. The investment in FinTech stocks shows the greatest amount of variability while the portfolios that combine FinTech stocks with precious metals show less variability. At the endpoint of the time period, the FINX_GLD portfolio has a slightly higher return than the other portfolios.

Figure 5. Equity curves—weekly rebalancing.

This figure shows how USD 1 invested in each portfolio evolves across time. For each two-asset portfolio, the precious metals weighting is 25%. Portfolio rebalancing occurs weekly and the transaction costs are 50 basis points per trade.

Portfolio summary statistics show that each of the portfolios that combine FinTech stocks with precious metals has a higher Sharpe ratio and Omega ratio and a lower standard deviation than an investment in FinTech stocks (Table 3. Portfolios that mix FinTech stocks with precious metals also have lower maximum drawdown, VaR, and ES. For example, an investment in FINX has an annualized return, Sharpe ratio, and maximum drawdown of 0.075, 0.153, and 0.635, respectively. In comparison a portfolio that combines FINX with GLD has an annualized return, Sharpe ratio, and maximum drawdown of 0.080, 0.218, and 0.521, respectively. While the annualized returns of the portfolios are similar, the risk-adjusted returns are higher for portfolios that combine FinTech stocks with precious metals. The FINX_GLD portfolio has the highest risk-adjusted returns (Sharpe ratio and Omega ratio).

Table 3. Portfolio summary statistics (two-asset portfolios).

	FINX	FINX_GLD	FINX_SLV	FINX_GLTR
Annualized Return	0.075	0.080	0.076	0.076
Annualized Std Dev	0.286	0.220	0.239	0.227
Annualized Sharpe	0.153	0.218	0.187	0.196
Maximum Drawdown	0.635	0.521	0.543	0.531
Historical VaR (95%)	−0.030	−0.023	−0.024	−0.024
Historical ES (95%)	−0.043	−0.033	−0.036	−0.034
Modified VaR (95%)	−0.029	−0.022	−0.024	−0.023
Modified ES (95%)	−0.051	−0.039	−0.047	−0.043
Omega (L = 0%)	1.074	1.086	1.080	1.082

Notes: The risk-free rate is set at 3% per year. For each two-asset portfolio, the precious metals weighting is 25%. Decimal returns reported. Portfolios rebalanced weekly. Transaction costs are 50 basis points per transaction.

4.2. Three-Asset Portfolios

The variation across time in the downside risk ratios shows that portfolio weights may need to be rebalanced and estimated frequently. This section reports results for three-asset (FINX, GLD, SLV) MVP, MCP, and MPC portfolios where the portfolio weights are estimated using a TVP-VAR model.

The total connectedness index (TCI) plot, estimated using a TVP-VAR(1) model, shows how total connectedness varies across time (Figure 6). The mean value of the TCI is 45%, indicating that on average 45% of the forecast error variance comes from spillovers. September of 2016, March of 2020, and November of 2022 exhibited periods of higher than average spillovers. Spillovers increased in 2016 as the strong performance of gold in the first half of the year (concerns over rising interest rates, Brexit, and the US presidential election) was offset by weakness in the second half of the year as concerns over these issues mitigated. Spillovers increased in March 2020 as COVID-19 was declared by the World Health Organization as a global heath pandemic. In 2022, central banks in North America and Europe began hiking interest rates to slow inflation and this led to higher spillovers and TCI.

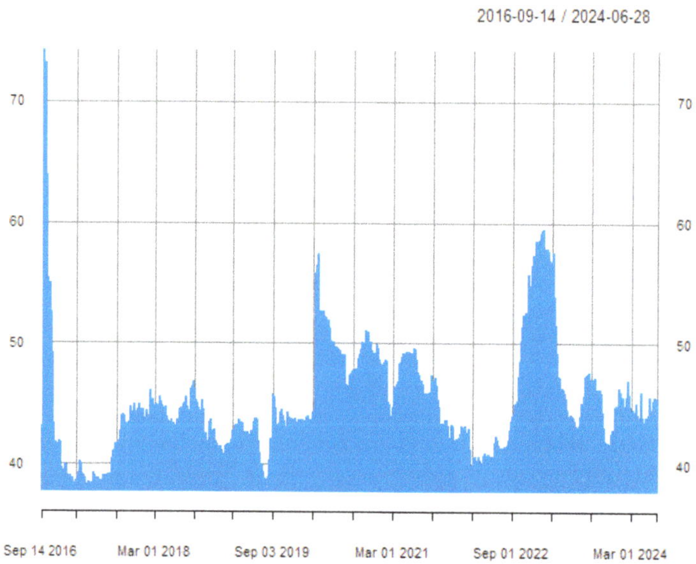

Figure 6. Total connectedness index estimated from a TVP-VAR(1) model.

The network connectedness plot shows average pairwise connectedness (Figure 7). Silver is the net contributor to spillovers, while gold and FINX are net receivers. This plot shows that gold is a better diversifier for FinTech than silver.

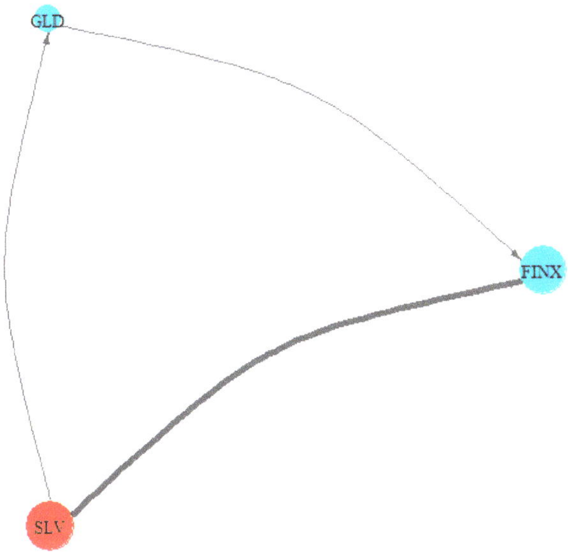

Figure 7. Network connectedness.

Equity curves for the three-asset portfolios show that the MVP has the highest end period returns, followed by the MCP and MPC (Figure 8). Notice that during the COVID-19 period, the MCP had the best performance. The MVP, which minimizes risk, underperforms during periods of high risk.

Figure 8. Equity curves for three-asset portfolios (FINX, GLD, SLV)—weekly rebalancing.

This figure shows how USD 1 invested in each portfolio evolves across time. Portfolio weights are constructed using a TVP-VAR(1) model. Portfolio rebalancing occurs weekly and the transaction costs are 50 basis points per transaction.

Portfolio summary statistics show that the MVP had the highest return, Sharpe ratio, and Omega ratio (Table 4). The MVP also had the lowest standard deviation, drawdown, value at risk, and expected shortfall. In comparing the Sharpe ratios in Table 4 with those in Table 3, notice that the MVP has the highest value overall and the MCP has the second highest value overall. The FINX-GLD portfolio has the third highest overall Sharpe ratio. All of the portfolios in Tables 3 and 4 have higher Sharpe ratios than an investment solely in FINX—illustrating the benefits of diversification.

Table 4. Portfolio summary statistics (three-asset (FinTech, gold, silver) portfolios).

	MVP	MCP	MPC
Annualized Return	0.085	0.072	0.062
Annualized Std Dev	0.127	0.171	0.177
Annualized Sharpe	0.458	0.269	0.199
Maximum Drawdown	0.235	0.412	0.425
Historical VaR (95%)	−0.013	−0.017	−0.018
Historical ES (95%)	−0.018	−0.025	−0.026
Modified VaR (95%)	−0.013	−0.017	−0.018
Modified ES (95%)	−0.021	−0.031	−0.035
Omega (L = 0%)	1.131	1.091	1.078

Notes: The risk-free rate is set at 3% per year. Decimal returns reported. Portfolios rebalanced weekly. Portfolio weights are constructed using a TVP-VAR(1) model. Transaction costs are 50 basis points per trade.

Although not reported in detail, the results in Tables 3 and 4 are robust to portfolios rebalanced monthly.

5. Discussion and Conclusions

FinTech stocks are an important new asset class that reflects the rapidly growing FinTech sector. Investors invest in FinTech stocks in the hopes of realizing large future gains. Many FinTech companies are young and emerging and FinTech stocks display considerable risk. In accordance with modern portfolio theory, investors are advised to combine FinTech stocks with uncorrelated assets to diversify the risk of an investing in only in FinTech stocks.

This paper studies the practical implications of using gold, silver, and basket-of-precious-metals (gold, silver, platinum, palladium) ETFs to diversify risk in Fintech stocks. Downside risk reduction is estimated using relative risk ratios based on CVaR. Relative risk ratios are computed using the ratio $CVaR_{mix}/CVaR_{ft}$, where mix is a portfolio that mixes FinTech stocks with precious metals and ft is the investment in FinTech stocks. The analysis shows that gold provides the most downside risk protection. For a 5% CVaR, a 30% portfolio weight for gold reduces the downside risk by about 25%. These findings add to the existing literature demonstrating the diversification benefits of gold [27–43]. Silver has the least protection for downside risk. Downside risk ratios vary across time. In the case of gold, for example, the downside risk ratio was below 75% in late 2019 and then increased rapidly to over 80% in early 2020 as the COVID-19 pandemic spread. The risk ratio for silver during this time period spiked to over 90%, offering little in downside protection.

The variation across time in the downside risk ratios indicates that portfolio weights may need to be updated and rebalanced frequently. To investigate this further, three-asset (FinTech, gold, silver) MVP, MCP, and MPC portfolios were estimated where the portfolio weights are estimated using a TVP-VAR model. The MVP and MCP portfolios with time varying weights have the highest risk-adjusted returns (Sharpe ratio, Omega ratio), followed by the fixed-weight FinTech and gold portfolio. The MVP, MCP, and MPC portfolios have lower drawdown than any of the fixed-weight two-asset portfolios—

illustrating the benefits of diversification with time varying portfolio weights. This analysis is robust to portfolios rebalanced weekly or monthly and reasonable transaction costs. These results are important in adding to the literature on using gold to diversify portfolio risk.

Future research could look at comparing different measures of risk for computing downside risk ratios. For example, one could use maximum drawdown or risk measures from extreme value theory as the basis to form risk ratios. Future research could also look into how useful platinum or palladium are for reducing downside risks.

Funding: This research received no external funding.

Informed Consent Statement: Not applicable.

Data Availability Statement: The data are publicly available.

Acknowledgments: This research is part of York University's Catalyzing Interdisciplinary Research Cluster on Digital Currencies. I thank the three reviewers for their helpful comments.

Conflicts of Interest: The author declares no conflicts of interest.

References

1. Goldstein, I.; Jiang, W.; Karolyi, G.A. To FinTech and Beyond. *Rev. Financ. Stud.* **2019**, *32*, 1647–1661. [CrossRef]
2. Abbasi, K.; Alam, A.; Du, M.; Huynh, T.L.D. FinTech, SME Efficiency and National Culture: Evidence from OECD Countries. *Technol. Forecast. Soc. Chang.* **2021**, *163*, 120454. [CrossRef]
3. Wang, Y.; Xiuping, S.; Zhang, Q. Can Fintech Improve the Efficiency of Commercial Banks? —An Analysis Based on Big Data. *Res. Int. Bus. Financ.* **2021**, *55*, 101338. [CrossRef]
4. Senyo, P.; Osabutey, E.L.C. Unearthing Antecedents to Financial Inclusion through FinTech Innovations. *Technovation* **2020**, *98*, 102155. [CrossRef]
5. Girma, A.G.; Huseynov, F. The Causal Relationship between FinTech, Financial Inclusion, and Income Inequality in African Economies. *J. Risk Financ. Manag.* **2024**, *17*, 2. [CrossRef]
6. Amnas, M.B.; Selvam, M.; Parayitam, S. FinTech and Financial Inclusion: Exploring the Mediating Role of Digital Financial Literacy and the Moderating Influence of Perceived Regulatory Support. *J. Risk Financ. Manag.* **2024**, *17*, 108. [CrossRef]
7. Ashenafi, B.B.; Dong, Y. Financial Inclusion, Fintech, and Income Inequality in Africa. *FinTech* **2022**, *1*, 376–387. [CrossRef]
8. Mckinsey The Future of Fintech Growth. McKinsey. Available online: https://www.mckinsey.com/industries/financial-services/our-insights/fintechs-a-new-paradigm-of-growth (accessed on 29 June 2024).
9. Abakah, E.J.A.; Tiwari, A.K.; Ghosh, S.; Doğan, B. Dynamic Effect of Bitcoin, Fintech and Artificial Intelligence Stocks on Eco-Friendly Assets, Islamic Stocks and Conventional Financial Markets: Another Look Using Quantile-Based Approaches. *Technol. Forecast. Soc. Chang.* **2023**, *192*, 122566. [CrossRef]
10. Adekoya, O.B.; Oliyide, J.A.; Saleem, O.; Adeoye, H.A. Asymmetric Connectedness between Google-Based Investor Attention and the Fourth Industrial Revolution Assets: The Case of FinTech and Robotics & Artificial Intelligence Stocks. *Technol. Soc.* **2022**, *68*, 101925. [CrossRef]
11. Li, J.; Li, J.; Zhu, X.; Yao, Y.; Casu, B. Risk Spillovers between FinTech and Traditional Financial Institutions: Evidence from the U.S. *Int. Rev. Financ. Anal.* **2020**, *71*, 101544. [CrossRef]
12. Chaudhry, S.M.; Ahmed, R.; Huynh, T.L.D.; Benjasak, C. Tail Risk and Systemic Risk of Finance and Technology (FinTech) Firms. *Technol. Forecast. Soc. Chang.* **2022**, *174*, 121191. [CrossRef]
13. Chen, Y.; Chiu, J.; Chung, H. Givers or Receivers? Return and Volatility Spillovers between Fintech and the Traditional Financial Industry. *Financ. Res. Lett.* **2022**, *46*, 102458. [CrossRef]
14. Chen, Y.; Wang, G.-J.; Zhu, Y.; Xie, C.; Uddin, G.S. Quantile Connectedness and the Determinants between FinTech and Traditional Financial Institutions: Evidence from China. *Glob. Financ. J.* **2023**, *58*, 100906. [CrossRef]
15. Wang, Z.; Xia, Y.; Fu, Y.; Liu, Y. Volatility Spillover Dynamics and Determinants between FinTech and Traditional Financial Industry: Evidence from China. *Mathematics* **2023**, *11*, 4058. [CrossRef]
16. Croutzet, A.; Dabbous, A. Do FinTech Trigger Renewable Energy Use? Evidence from OECD Countries. *Renew. Energy* **2021**, *179*, 1608–1617. [CrossRef]
17. Le, T.-L.; Abakah, E.J.A.; Tiwari, A.K. Time and Frequency Domain Connectedness and Spill-over among Fintech, Green Bonds and Cryptocurrencies in the Age of the Fourth Industrial Revolution. *Technol. Forecast. Soc. Chang.* **2021**, *162*, 120382. [CrossRef]
18. Alshater, M.M.; Polat, O.; El Khoury, R.; Yoon, S.-M. Dynamic Connectedness among Regional FinTech Indices in Times of Turbulences. *Appl. Econ. Lett.* **2022**, *31*, 670–675. [CrossRef]
19. Bhatnagar, M.; Özen, E.; Taneja, S.; Grima, S.; Rupeika-Apoga, R. The Dynamic Connectedness between Risk and Return in the Fintech Market of India: Evidence Using the GARCH-M Approach. *Risks* **2022**, *10*, 209. [CrossRef]
20. Rafiuddin, A.; Gaytan, J.C.T.; Mohnot, R.; Sisodia, G.S.; Ahmed, G. Growth Evaluation of Fintech Connectedness with Innovative Thematic Indices—An Evidence through Wavelet Analysis. *J. Open Innov. Technol. Mark. Complex.* **2023**, *9*, 100023. [CrossRef]

21. Bodie, Z.; Kane, A.; Marcus, A.J. *Investments*, 13th ed.; McGraw-Hill Education: New York, NY, USA, 2023; ISBN 978-1-264-41266-2.
22. Henriques, I.; Sadorsky, P. Do Clean Energy Stocks Diversify the Risk of FinTech Stocks? Connectedness and Portfolio Implications. *Glob. Financ. J.* **2024**, *62*, 101019. [CrossRef]
23. Kuang, W. Are Clean Energy Assets a Safe Haven for International Equity Markets? *J. Clean. Prod.* **2021**, *302*, 127006. [CrossRef]
24. Bredin, D.; Conlon, T.; Potì, V. The Price of Shelter—Downside Risk Reduction with Precious Metals. *Int. Rev. Financ. Anal.* **2017**, *49*, 48–58. [CrossRef]
25. Jorion, P. *Value at Risk: The New Benchmark for Managing Financial Risk*, 2nd ed.; McGraw-Hill: New York, NY, USA, 2000; ISBN 978-0-07-135502-5.
26. Poncet, P.; Portait, R. Value at Risk, Expected Shorfall, and Other Risk Measures. In *Capital Market Finance: An Introduction to Primitive Assets, Derivatives, Portfolio Management and Risk*; Poncet, P., Portait, R., Eds.; Springer International Publishing: Cham, Switzerland, 2022; pp. 1103–1169; ISBN 978-3-030-84600-8.
27. Baur, D.G.; Lucey, B.M. Is Gold a Hedge or a Safe Haven? An Analysis of Stocks, Bonds and Gold. *Financ. Rev.* **2010**, *45*, 217–229. [CrossRef]
28. Baur, D.G.; McDermott, T.K. Is Gold a Safe Haven? International Evidence. *J. Bank. Financ.* **2010**, *34*, 1886–1898. [CrossRef]
29. Bekiros, S.; Boubaker, S.; Nguyen, D.K.; Uddin, G.S. Black Swan Events and Safe Havens: The Role of Gold in Globally Integrated Emerging Markets. *J. Int. Money Financ.* **2017**, *73*, 317–334. [CrossRef]
30. Ciner, C.; Gurdgiev, C.; Lucey, B.M. Hedges and Safe Havens: An Examination of Stocks, Bonds, Gold, Oil and Exchange Rates. *Int. Rev. Financ. Anal.* **2013**, *29*, 202–211. [CrossRef]
31. Hood, M.; Malik, F. Is Gold the Best Hedge and a Safe Haven under Changing Stock Market Volatility? *Rev. Financ. Econ.* **2013**, *22*, 47–52. [CrossRef]
32. Junttila, J.; Pesonen, J.; Raatikainen, J. Commodity Market Based Hedging against Stock Market Risk in Times of Financial Crisis: The Case of Crude Oil and Gold. *J. Int. Financ. Mark. Inst. Money* **2018**, *56*, 255–280. [CrossRef]
33. Baur, D.G.; McDermott, T.K.J. Why Is Gold a Safe Haven? *J. Behav. Exp. Financ.* **2016**, *10*, 63–71. [CrossRef]
34. Beckmann, J.; Berger, T.; Czudaj, R. Does Gold Act as a Hedge or a Safe Haven for Stocks? A Smooth Transition Approach. *Econ. Model.* **2015**, *48*, 16–24. [CrossRef]
35. Blose, L.E. Gold Prices, Cost of Carry, and Expected Inflation. *J. Econ. Bus.* **2010**, *62*, 35–47. [CrossRef]
36. Hoang, T.H.V.; Lahiani, A.; Heller, D. Is Gold a Hedge against Inflation? New Evidence from a Nonlinear ARDL Approach. *Econ. Model.* **2016**, *54*, 54–66. [CrossRef]
37. Reboredo, J.C. Is Gold a Safe Haven or a Hedge for the US Dollar? Implications for Risk Management. *J. Bank. Financ.* **2013**, *37*, 2665–2676. [CrossRef]
38. Iqbal, J. Does Gold Hedge Stock Market, Inflation and Exchange Rate Risks? An Econometric Investigation. *Int. Rev. Econ. Financ.* **2017**, *48*, 1–17. [CrossRef]
39. O'Connor, F.A.; Lucey, B.M.; Batten, J.A.; Baur, D.G. The Financial Economics of Gold—A Survey. *Int. Rev. Financ. Anal.* **2015**, *41*, 186–205. [CrossRef]
40. Hillier, D.; Draper, P.; Faff, R. Do Precious Metals Shine? An Investment Perspective. *Financ. Anal. J.* **2006**, *62*, 98–106. [CrossRef]
41. Tronzano, M. Financial Crises, Macroeconomic Variables, and Long-Run Risk: An Econometric Analysis of Stock Returns Correlations (2000 to 2019). *J. Risk Financ. Manag.* **2021**, *14*, 127. [CrossRef]
42. Areal, N.; Oliveira, B.; Sampaio, R. When Times Get Tough, Gold Is Golden. *Eur. J. Financ.* **2015**, *21*, 507–526. [CrossRef]
43. Valadkhani, A.; Nguyen, J.; Chiah, M. When Is Gold an Effective Hedge against Inflation? *Resour. Policy* **2022**, *79*, 103009. [CrossRef]
44. Bredin, D.; Conlon, T.; Potì, V. Does Gold Glitter in the Long-Run? Gold as a Hedge and Safe Haven across Time and Investment Horizon. *Int. Rev. Financ. Anal.* **2015**, *41*, 320–328. [CrossRef]
45. Mensi, W.; Hammoudeh, S.; Kang, S.H. Precious Metals, Cereal, Oil and Stock Market Linkages and Portfolio Risk Management: Evidence from Saudi Arabia. *Econ. Model.* **2015**, *51*, 340–358. [CrossRef]
46. Mensi, W.; Aslan, A.; Vo, X.V.; Kang, S.H. Time-Frequency Spillovers and Connectedness between Precious Metals, Oil Futures and Financial Markets: Hedge and Safe Haven Implications. *Int. Rev. Econ. Financ.* **2023**, *83*, 219–232. [CrossRef]
47. Lahiani, A.; Mefteh-Wali, S.; Vasbieva, D.G. The Safe-Haven Property of Precious Metal Commodities in the COVID-19 Era. *Resour. Policy* **2021**, *74*, 102340. [CrossRef]
48. Kangalli Uyar, S.G.; Uyar, U.; Balkan, E. The Role of Precious Metals in Extreme Market Conditions: Evidence from Stock Markets. *Stud. Econ. Financ.* **2021**, *39*, 63–78. [CrossRef]
49. Low, R.K.Y.; Yao, Y.; Faff, R. Diamonds vs. Precious Metals: What Shines Brightest in Your Investment Portfolio? *Int. Rev. Financ. Anal.* **2016**, *43*, 1–14. [CrossRef]
50. McWaters, R.J.; Galaski, R. *Beyond Fintech: A Pragmatic Assessment of Disruptive Potential in Financial Services*; World Economic Forum: Geneva, Switzerland, 2017.
51. Favre, L.; Galeano, J.-A. Mean-Modified Value-at-Risk Optimization with Hedge Funds. *J. Altern. Invest.* **2002**, *5*, 21–25. [CrossRef]
52. Markowitz, H. Portfolio Selection. *J. Financ.* **1952**, *7*, 77–91.
53. Christoffersen, P.; Errunza, V.; Jacobs, K.; Jin, X. Correlation Dynamics and International Diversification Benefits. *Int. J. Forecast.* **2014**, *30*, 807–824. [CrossRef]

54. Broadstock, D.C.; Chatziantoniou, I.; Gabauer, D. Minimum Connectedness Portfolios and the Market for Green Bonds: Advocating Socially Responsible Investment (SRI) Activity. In *Applications in Energy Finance: The Energy Sector, Economic Activity, Financial Markets and the Environment*; Floros, C., Chatziantoniou, I., Eds.; Springer International Publishing: Cham, Switzerland, 2022; pp. 217–253, ISBN 978-3-030-92957-2.
55. Antonakakis, N.; Chatziantoniou, I.; Gabauer, D. Refined Measures of Dynamic Connectedness Based on Time-Varying Parameter Vector Autoregressions. *J. Risk Financ. Manag.* **2020**, *13*, 84. [CrossRef]
56. Diebold, F.X.; Yilmaz, K. Better to Give than to Receive: Predictive Directional Measurement of Volatility Spillovers. *Int. J. Forecast.* **2012**, *28*, 57–66. [CrossRef]
57. Diebold, F.X.; Yilmaz, K. Measuring Financial Asset Return and Volatility Spillovers, with Application to Global Equity Markets. *Econ. J.* **2009**, *119*, 158–171. [CrossRef]
58. Abakah, E.J.A.; Abdullah, M.; Dankwah, B.; Lee, C.-C. Asymmetric Dynamics between the Baltic Dry Index and Financial Markets during Major Global Economic Events. *North Am. J. Econ. Financ.* **2024**, *72*, 102126. [CrossRef]
59. Cogneau, P.; Hübner, G. The 101 Ways to Measure Portfolio Performance. *SSRN Electron. J.* **2009**. [CrossRef]
60. R Core Team. *R: A Language and Environment for Statistical Computing*; R Core Team: Vienna, Austria, 2022.
61. Gabauer, D. *Connectedness Approach: Connectedness Approach*; R Core Team: Vienna, Austria, 2022.
62. Ryan, J.A.; Ulrich, J.M.; Smith, E.B.; Thielen, W.; Teetor, P.; Bronder, S. Quantmod: Quantitative Financial Modelling Framework 2023.
63. Peterson, B.G.; Carl, P.; Boudt, K.; Bennett, R.; Ulrich, J.; Zivot, E.; Cornilly, D.; Hung, E.; Lestel, M.; Balkissoon, K.; et al. PerformanceAnalytics: Econometric Tools for Performance and Risk Analysis 2020.
64. Fu, J.; Mishra, M. Fintech in the Time of COVID−19: Technological Adoption during Crises. *J. Financ. Intermediation* **2022**, *50*, 100945. [CrossRef]
65. Committee of European Securities Regulators. *CESR's Guidelines on Risk Measurement and the Calculation of Global Exposure and Counterparty Risk for UCITS CESR/10-788*; Committee of European Securities Regulators: Paris, France, 2010.
66. Basel Committee on Banking Supervision. *An Internal Model-Based Approach to Market Risk Capital Requirements*; Basel Committee on Banking Supervision: Basel, Switzerland, 1995.

FinTech

Review

Exploring Financial Literacy in Higher Education with the Help of FinTech: A Bibliometric Analysis of Linkages to Access, Behavior, and Well-Being Through Digital Innovation

Ionut Marius Croitoru [1,*], Paula-Paraschiva Dragan (SPIRIDON) [2], Nicoleta Daniela Ignat [1] and Romanita Jumanca [3]

[1] Faculty of Entrepreneurship, Business Engineering and Management, National University of Science and Technology Politehnica, 060042 Bucharest, Romania; nicoleta.ignat@upb.ro
[2] Doctoral School of Economics and Business Administration, West University of Timisoara, 300223 Timisoara, Romania; paula.dragan84@e-uvt.ro
[3] Romanian and Foreign Languages Department, University of Medicine and Pharmacy Timisoara, 300041 Timisoara, Romania; romanita.jumanca@umft.ro
* Correspondence: ionut.croitoru0208@upb.ro

Abstract: This study explores the dynamic interaction between financial literacy and higher education, focusing on the critical role of financial education in improving individual financial well-being. Using bibliometric analysis and the VOSviewer software, this research examines thematic clusters in financial literacy, categorized into access, behavior, health, and education. By analyzing 469 articles from the Web of Science database (2020–2024), this study identifies trends and key linkages between financial literacy and societal well-being, highlighting the role of digital innovation. While FinTech is discussed as a facilitator of financial inclusion and education, the primary focus lies in understanding how financial literacy drives behavioral change, capacity building, and economic resilience. This paper provides information for policymakers and educators to design inclusive, behaviorally focused educational programs that address specific demographic needs, ultimately contributing to societal and economic resilience.

Keywords: FinTech; higher education; bibliometric research; VOSviewer

JEL Classification: B26; D53; G32; I25; P34

1. Introduction

FinTech represents a set of technologies that innovate and improve current financial services. These include solutions such as blockchain technology, online platforms, mobile applications, artificial intelligence (AI), and more.

The impact of FinTech technologies on financial inclusion has been widely studied, highlighting the way they reduce costs and expand access to financial services. FinTech offers users the opportunity to manage their financial activities through automated platforms that use specific algorithms, thus facilitating the financial decision-making process. Technologies such as blockchain and digital payments contribute significantly to the modernization and efficiency of financial services, offering users more accessible and flexible solutions. Financial technology (FinTech) contributes significantly to increasing operational efficiency, improving the quality of services, and increasing managerial transparency and security while providing increased comfort for users, which justifies the rapid expansion of this field in recent years [1].

In addition, big data analysis plays an essential role in gaining in-depth insights into consumer behaviors and needs, supporting the development of personalized solutions [2,3].

The impact of FinTech on higher education institutions can be noted in the context of the COVID-19 pandemic, which has generated movement and interaction restrictions. This context has accelerated the level of innovation and the digitization of universities by offering online payment services, digitizing the registration process, managing and archiving documents electronically, carrying out collection and payment operations via electronic means, as well as implementing online teaching services [4].

Recent global events and changes in financial practices have underscored the need for a financially educated population capable of making informed decisions amid economic uncertainty. The implementation of digital technologies in higher education institutions, along with the involvement of the business environment and the banking sector, has created a favorable environment for increasing the level of digital and financial education globally. In this context, digital innovations, including financial technologies, provide new opportunities for enhancing financial literacy by enabling more inclusive and accessible education tools [5]. However, educational challenges associated with FinTech persist, highlighting the need for an appropriate regulatory framework and the integration of these technologies to ensure the long-term success of financial education [5,6].

While financial education is a broad field, key themes are emerging that influence its effectiveness. This study aims to investigate the role of financial education and digitization in higher education institutions, emphasizing on their contributions to the development of the public sector, private sector, and civil society. It will also aim to identify and contextualize the main topic areas in financial literacy through the analysis of related keyword clusters.

This study examines financial literacy in higher education, with a focus on its linkages to access, behavior, and well-being. While financial technologies (FinTechs) serve as a supportive mechanism, the analysis emphasizes the foundational role of financial literacy in societal and economic resilience.

This paper brings into discussion a bibliometric analysis to approach the subject of FinTech as an element of change. Bibliometric analysis is a relatively new research method that has gained popularity in several academic fields, including finance. It is part of a broader scientometric discipline, defined as the study of the quantitative characteristics of science and scientific research [7].

Recent bibliometric analyses have shown that the number of publications on FinTech has doubled in the last five years, with a focus on emerging topics such as data security and digital inclusion [2,8].

By examining 469 articles from the Web of Science database (2020–2024), this paper aims to identify trends and perspectives on financial education and information technology innovation impacting higher education.

The objectives include understanding the way financial education, information technology innovation, and the implementation of digitization can contribute to reducing economic discrepancies between various sectors, optimize organizational processes, and support digital transformation and accessibility within higher education institutions.

In the context of the diversification and increasing complexity of financial education, the perspective on the intercorrelation between the FinTech field and higher education can be expanded, leading to the adaptation, development, and progression of economic entities through FinTech mechanisms [9–11].

FinTech has opened up new career opportunities for students in areas such as AI-based financial services, cyber security, and RegTech (regulatory technology). Universities collaborate with FinTech companies to provide students with hands-on experience in these sectors. Through FinTech internships and incubation programs, students gain direct access to the cutting-edge technologies that are transforming the financial industry.

The intersection of FinTech and higher education is a dynamic and constantly evolving space. The Markets in Crypto-Assets Regulation (MiCA) legislation is specific to the European Union and was adopted by the European Parliament and the Council of 31 May 2023 on markets in crypto assets in the "Regulation (EU) 2023/1114", Revised Payment Services Directive (PSD2); this legislation is specific to the European Union and was adopted by the European Parliament through the "Directive (EU) 2015/2366 of the European Parliament and of the Council of 25 November 2015 on payment services in the internal market, amending Directives 2002/65/EC, 2009/110/EC and 2013/36/EU and Regulation (EU) No 1093/2010, and repealing Directive 2007/64/EC (Text with EEA relevance)" for updates, and it enhances the EU rules put in place by the initial PSD, which was adopted in 2007. The PSD2 entered into force on 12 January 2016, and EU Member States were given until 13 January 2018 to transpose it into national law and Digital Operational Resilience Act (DORA); this legislation is specific to the European Union and was adopted by the European Parliament and the Council of 14 December 2022 in the "Regulation (EU) 2022/2554 on digital operational resilience for the financial sector and amending Regulations (EC) No 1060/2009, (EU) No 648/2012, (EU) No 600/2014, (EU) No 909/2014 and (EU) 2016/1011"; this regulation entered into force on 16 January 2023 and will apply as of 17 January 2025. Although this legislation is mainly aimed at financial institutions, it has significant implications for universities as well. As institutions adopt new financial technologies and incorporate FinTech into their curricula, they simultaneously navigate the challenges of regulatory compliance and cybersecurity.

2. Literature Review

FinTech represents a new paradigm in finance, aiming for an equally innovative approach to regulation such as 'smart regulation' and the use of regulatory technologies (RegTechs) to monitor and enforce compliance. Key regulatory strategies, including sandbox environments, innovation hubs, and new frameworks, are essential to ensure that FinTech innovations are well regulated while promoting financial stability, inclusion, and sustainability [12].

Starting from the 19th century to the present, looking at the historical evolution of FinTech, we can discuss the increasing role of technology in finance, focusing in particular on the rise in artificial intelligence (AI), blockchain-distributed ledger technology (DLT), cryptocurrencies, and central bank digital currencies (CBDCs). These technological advances are transforming traditional financial services and institutions by creating efficiencies, improving financial inclusion, and providing innovative solutions in both society and higher education institutions.

The integration of artificial intelligence (AI) and chatbots into the financial technology (FinTech) industry and the education system is transforming the way companies interact with customers and teachers with their students while also leading to advances in predictive analytics. AI and machine learning (ML) enable FinTech companies and higher education institutions to automate repetitive tasks, improve security, and provide personalized experiences for customers and students. These technologies are particularly useful in areas such as fraud detection, customer service, financial advice, and financial education, providing solutions that were previously unimaginable for human brain processing.

The emergence of FinTech offers tools that enhance financial education, such as AI-based learning platforms and digital finance management applications. These tools complement broader efforts to promote financial literacy by improving accessibility and user engagement.

Higher education institutions play a key role in researching FinTech developments, including distributed ledger technologies, decentralized finance (DeFi), and central bank digital currencies (CBDCs). EU regulations such as MiCA and DORA shape the framework in which universities conduct research on these technologies, ensuring that innovations align with legal and ethical standards [13].

As FinTech becomes a dominant force in global finance, universities are increasingly incorporating FinTech-related subjects into their curricula. Courses in blockchain, artificial intelligence in finance, and digital payments have become an integral part of business and finance curricula across Europe, reflecting a growing trend to adapt curricula to new emerging technologies in the financial sector. Renowned universities such as the University of Hong Kong and Harvard University are leaders in integrating FinTech education at the academic level. These institutions have adopted innovative strategies to support the development of student's skills in emerging fields such as blockchain, artificial intelligence, and digital payments. Their collaborations with the FinTech industry contribute to the development of study programs that meet the needs of a constantly changing financial sector [10,12,13].

One of the most significant applications of AI in FinTech is its ability to handle large amounts of data, performing complex analyses to identify patterns and risks. As noted in the literature, AI can streamline processes such as payment processing, credit scoring, and fraud detection, allowing financial institutions to mitigate risk more effectively. AI can also support researchers and teachers by analyzing large data sets of information to obtain results in the shortest possible time and in the most efficient way with the aim of sharing them with students and the civil society to increase the well-being and the education level of the population [14].

AI is also used in predictive analytics to forecast customer behavior and financial trends. By analyzing historical data, AI can help FinTech companies predict future outcomes, such as changes in stock prices, interest rates, or market trends. This information enables companies to make more informed decisions by optimizing their cross-selling strategies, risk management, and portfolio management [14].

Developments in AI are proceeding at a rapid pace. While AI has already played a role in our daily lives for several years, AI and robotics are driving innovation, leading to new business models and playing a key role in transforming our societies and digitizing the economy in many sectors, including industry, education, health, construction, and transport [15].

Despite the many benefits of AI and chatbots in FinTech, there are challenges associated with their implementation. A major problem is the shortage of skilled AI professionals, which has slowed the adoption of AI technologies in some financial institutions as well as in some sectors such as higher education institutions. Furthermore, although AI can provide accurate predictions and improve security, it is not immune to errors, and the consequences of such mistakes can be significant in the financial industry, in various sectors of the economy, and in the research area [14].

FinTech, in addition to the undeniable benefits that it has brought and continues to bring to society, also presents potential risks that can be associated in particular with those related to cyber security, data privacy, and market dominance by large technology companies (BigTechs). The literature also addresses the critical role of regulation in mitigating systemic risks, ensuring that the benefits of digital finance are realized in both developed and developing economies.

AI and chatbots have revolutionized and are revolutionizing the FinTech industry by improving customer experience, improving operational efficiency, and providing valuable predictive insights. As FinTech companies continue to adopt these technologies, they are reshaping the way financial services are delivered, making them more personalized, secure, and accessible. However, overcoming the challenges of talent shortages and customer trust will be crucial to the successful integration of AI into financial, research, and education ecosystems. As AI and chatbots continue to evolve, their roles in FinTech will expand, providing new opportunities for innovation both in customer and student services, as well as in the financial management of companies and higher education institutions.

3. Research Methodology

By means of bibliometric analysis, frequently used keywords and evolving ideas can be identified, offering perspectives on future trends [15,16]. This analysis is based on quantitative measurements and investigative techniques applied to written documents [17].

In order to accomplish the bibliometric analysis, the Web of Science database was used, whereas for their processing, the VOSviewer application was used. Taking into consideration the fact that the FinTech field and the academic environment of higher education have visible connections only in the economic sphere, we intended to make a correlation between the two categories and find an area of intercorrelation in the valuable scientific literature contained in the Web of Science. By applying tagging techniques and using specific filters from the Web of Science database, 469 relevant scientific articles were identified. By processing their specific data (article title, keywords, abstract country of origin of authors, and connections between articles) new points of view can be generated in terms of FinTech higher education intercorrelation. The research was based on a systematic analysis of the scientific literature by applying several comparative bibliometric analyzes on 469 scientific research articles that offer some perspectives on the manifestation of the FinTech higher education correlation.

Bibliometrics, although a useful method for analyzing the scientific literature, can encounter significant difficulties in capturing all relevant aspects of a research field, due to the large and ever-expanding volume of information. Thus, carrying out a comprehensive and high-quality bibliometric analysis requires a considerable effort in the organization and interpretation of data, and their diversity requires substantial resources [18–20].

The Web of Science database query began with the primary tag "higher education FinTech", resulting in 345 articles. To maximize the breadth of identified connections be-tween FinTech and the educational environment, additional labels such as "personal fi-nance management", "modern financial technologies", and "financial education" were included. The following Boolean operators facilitated this process:

- AND Operator: This was used to combine the primary tag with related subtopics to ensure relevance to the core topic. For example, the query

TS = ("FinTech in Higher Education") AND TS = ("personal finance management") AND TS = ("financial education") AND TS = ("modern financial management"), ensures results that address FinTech while simultaneously incorporating key subtopics. In this query, the TS (topic) field searches for specified terms within article titles, abstracts, or keywords.

- OR Operator: This operator broadened the search to include synonyms or closely related terms, enriching the findings. For instance,

TS = ("FinTech in Higher Education") AND (TS = ("personal finance manage-ment") OR TS = ("digital finance management")) AND (TS = ("financial education") OR TS = ("financial literacy")) expanded the scope of the search by considering alternative terminologies, such as "financial literacy" alongside "financial education".

The authors wanted the conclusions drawn from this bibliometric analysis to be based on accessible and up-to-date scientific research. This was achieved by using the following filters that exist in the Web of Science database:

- Articles, because the published papers are filtered through the reviews specific to each journal;
- Open Access, because articles published in this form can be studied for free;
- Publication years 2020–2024, because we wanted to study the content of articles published in the last 5 years.

By applying these three filters, our selection provided 469 articles, which was then subjected to bibliometric analysis.

The first approach within the bibliometric analysis was the analysis according to the years of publication and according to the country of origin of the authors of the scientific articles.

To capture new aspects and correlations between FinTech and the educational environment resulting from clustering analysis, we used the VOSviewer software by applying the following filters: *co-occurrence filters*, *author keywords*, and *minimum 9 co-occurrences*. Clusters within the VOSviewer program are generated as item pairs.

Through this process, keywords were grouped, where each keyword's occurrence and link strength were calculated to determine its association with others. The strength of the link between the terms, based on co-occurrence, enabled the identification of clusters within the broader field of financial literacy. The data set generated four primary clusters whose composition is presented in the following Table in Results and Discussion. Each cluster comprises terms related to specific thematic areas in financial literacy, highlighting aspects such as access, attitudes, behavior, and well-being.

The objective of this bibliometric analysis is to examine key themes in financial literacy research, including access, behavior, and well-being, while considering the role of digital innovations such as FinTech in facilitating these outcomes.

4. Results and Discussion

The evolution of the number of articles in the sample is presented in Table 1, with information on the number of articles included when applying Keywords and Keywords added.

Table 1. Tags and additional tags used to base the database.

Filter Applied	Item Number in the Selection
Keywords "higher education FinTech"	345
Keywords added "personal finance management"	395
Keywords added "modern financial technologies"	404
Keywords added "financial education"	1984

Source: Web of Science database (accessed on 4 November 2024).

The authors wanted this selection of scientific works to capture current theoretically grounded aspects to which we have access. That is why we used consecutive filters to select articles, specifically with open access and published in the last 5 years. The evolution of the number of articles in the selection following the successful application of the filters is presented in Table 2.

The number of 469 articles is the number in which the bibliometric analysis was performed using the specific filters of Web of Science and the VOSviewer application [21].

From the analysis of the annual distribution over the 5 years, an increase in the number of articles can be observed every year, excluding the year 2024 which has not been completed, which leads us to a conclusion that in the course of the development of the FinTech field, more and more bridges to higher education academia are found. The evolution of the number of scientific articles is presented in Table 3 [21].

Table 2. Order of Web of Science filters used to query the database.

Filter Applied	Number of Items After Applying Filter
Articles	1612
Open Access	716
Publication years 2020–2024	469

Source: Web of Science database (accessed on 4 November 2024).

Table 3. Distribution of the 469 articles by year.

Year	2020	2021	2022	2023	2024
Number of articles	57	88	117	127	80

Source: Web of Science database (accessed on 4 November 2024).

In Figure 1, the first 12 countries according to the number of existing articles in the database subject to our research are analyzed with the help of the analysis of the bibliometric results from the Web of Science database and the density analysis of the countries of origin of the authors [21]. From the analysis of the distribution of the articles by country, we see that there are countries from all continents, which leads us to the conclusion that the analysis undertaken by us is of worldwide interest.

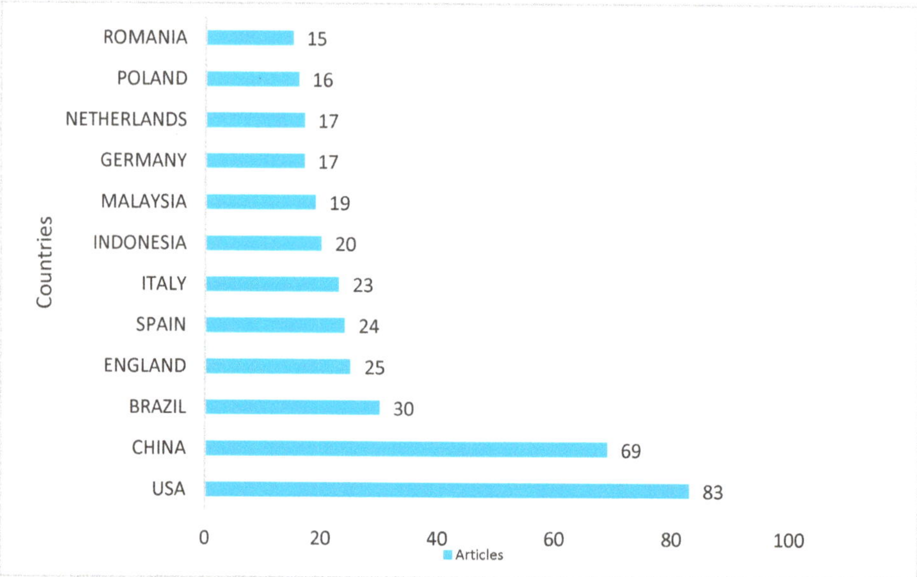

Figure 1. Authors' countries of origin according to the number of published articles. Source: own conceptualization; data processing from WOS (accessed on 4 November 2024).

Another analysis carried out was on the research area presented in Figure 2 [21]. We see that the predominant fields are related to the economic field and the information technology field.

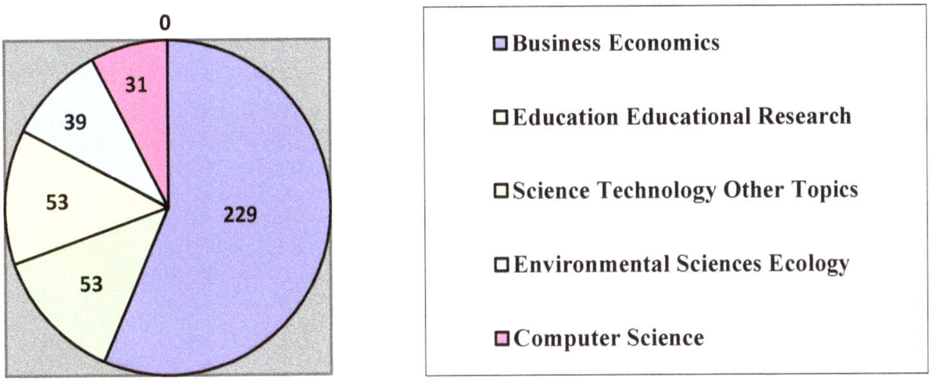

Figure 2. Research areas. Source: own conceptualization; data processing from WOS (accessed on 4 November 2024).

A new analysis regarding the density of phrases or words used in the 469 selected articles was carried out with the help of the VOSviewer program by applying the co-occurrence filter for all keywords with an appearance of at least 9 times. Only 44 words/phrases out of the 2148 analyzed met this criterion, and Figure 3 shows the distribution and links between words/phrases resulting from the application of the filters.

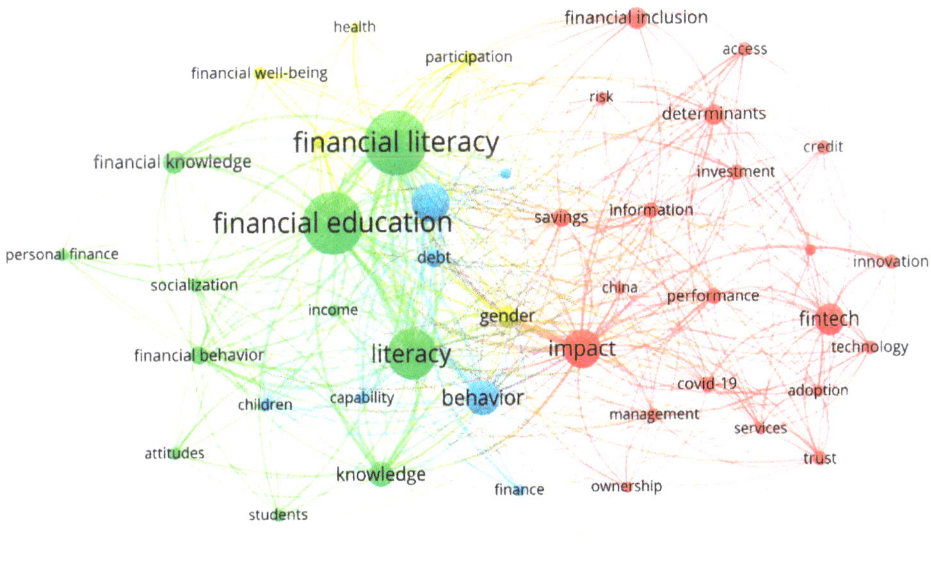

Figure 3. Density of phrases and words that have at least 9 *co-occurrences*. Source: WOS database (accessed on 4 November 2024) and made with the VOSviewer software version 1.6.20.

After processing the data with the help of the VOSviewer program, the words and phrases that have the highest density included financial literacy, financial education, literacy, impact, education, behavior, knowledge, financial behavior, and financial knowledge. Also, through the VOSviewer program, we obtained the classification of words according to total link strength, which is presented in Table 4.

From the analysis of the VOSviewer program on the 44 keywords/phrases that appear at least 9 times within the 469 articles, four clusters emerged; their composition is presented in Table 5. The cluster represents a set of elements included in a bibliometric map; articles belong to only one cluster, and we can have articles that do not belong to any cluster. Based on the information contained in each cluster, we will deepen the analysis for each cluster separately, taking into account the strength of the links of the keywords with the highest density and the links in these and other clusters. Thus, these bibliometric maps give us a new picture of the subject matter and existing orientations within the scientific articles.

Table 4. Link strength between articles analyzed according to Keyword.

Keyword	Occurrences	Total Link Strength
financial literacy	135	340
financial education	131	286
literacy	93	280
impact	62	200
education	63	190
behavior	53	182
knowledge	33	125
financial behavior	20	82
financial knowledge	28	82

Source: own conceptualization; data processing from WOS with the VOSviewer software.

Table 5. VOSviewer clusters and related colors.

Cluster 1 (21 items)	Cluster 2 (11 items)
access adoption China COVID-19 credit determinants financial inclusion FinTech impact information innovation investment management ownership performances personal finance management risk savings technology trust	attitudes financial behavior financial education financial knowledge financial literacy income knowledge literacy personal finance socialization students
Cluster 3 (7 items)	**Cluster 4 (5 items)**
capability children debt education finances exemplary	financial well-being gender health participation women

Source: own conceptualization; data processing with VOSviewer (accessed 4 November 2024).

Next, we will comment on the content of the four clusters and try to present some aspects of the FinTech higher education relationship.

Within cluster 1, we can see that articles included in it have channeled the fundamental aspects of financial literacy, such as "access", "adoption-of strategies", "impact", and "credit". High-frequency terms such as "financial literacy" (135 occurrences) and "education" (63 occurrences) emphasize the importance of making financial knowledge accessible. Additionally, terms such as "COVID-19" suggest that recent global events have impacted financial access, shaping the educational needs and challenges people face in the financial realm [22].

Within cluster 2, the behavioral components of financial literacy are addressed, including "attitudes", "financial behaviour", and "financial knowledge". With 'financial behaviour' and 'capability' as central themes, this cluster captures the intersection between knowledge and actionable behavior. The emphasis on behavioral terms reflects the growing need for financial education programs that not only impart knowledge but also promote positive financial habits.

Cluster 3 is focused on ability and demographics; this group includes keywords such as "children", "debt", and "education". Here, the focus on young people ("kids") suggests an awareness of the critical role that early financial education plays in building long-term financial literacy. Terms like "ability" and "debt" indicate that financial literacy is critical to managing financial challenges from an early age, ultimately contributing to better financial decision-making in adulthood.

Culture 4, the smallest but a significant group, focuses on financial health and well-being, with keywords such as "gender", "health", and "participation". This cluster reflects the growing awareness of the impact of financial education on quality of life and overall well-being. The inclusion of "gender" highlights the need for inclusive financial education efforts that address the specific financial challenges faced by various demographic groups, including women.

The results of these groups reveal how financial literacy encompasses more than just acquiring knowledge. Instead, it is a multi-faceted field that addresses accessibility, behavioral development, capacity building, and well-being. Cluster 1's focus on access and education reflects fundamental needs such as creating opportunities for financial learning, while cluster 2 demonstrates that financial literacy must go beyond knowledge to drive behavior change. Cluster 3, focused on youth and capability, and this indicates a proactive approach to financial education, focusing on early education. Finally, cluster 4 aligns with recent trends that view financial well-being as part of overall health, suggesting that financial literacy contributes to a holistic sense of quality of life.

The group also emphasizes the need for targeted approaches in financial education. For example, financial education programs could tailor content to specific demographic needs, such as youth or underrepresented groups, to maximize their impact.

To analyze the links between and within the clusters, we chose one word from each, with the strongest links within each, according to the data in Table 5:

- For cluster 1: "keyword *impact* with link strength 200", (Figure 4);
- For cluster 2: "keyword *financial literacy* with link strength 340", (Figure 5);
- For cluster 3: "keyword *behavior* with link strength 182", (Figure 6);
- For cluster 4: "keyword *gender* with link strength 74", (Figure 7);

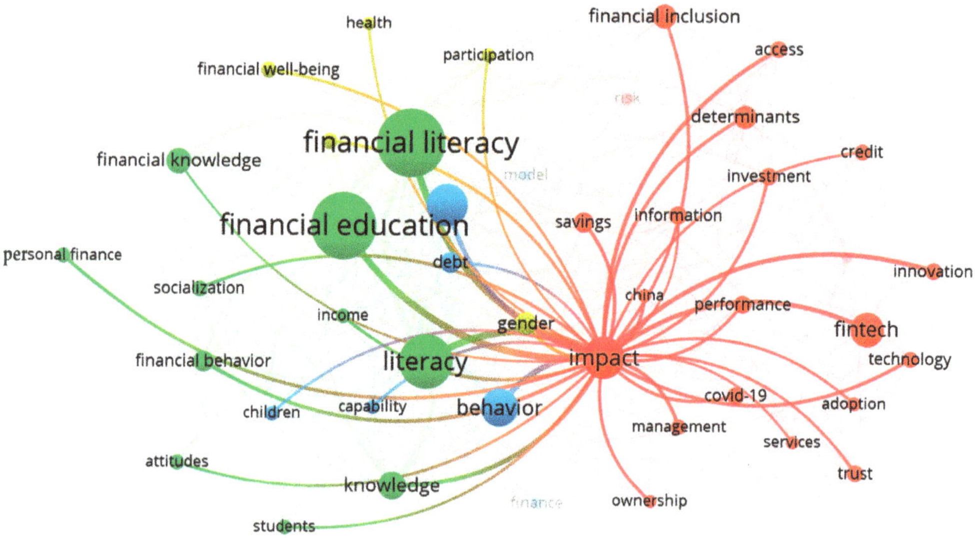

Figure 4. Cluster 1 keyword *impact* with link strength 200. Source: WOS database (accessed on 4 November 2024) and made with the VOSviewer software.

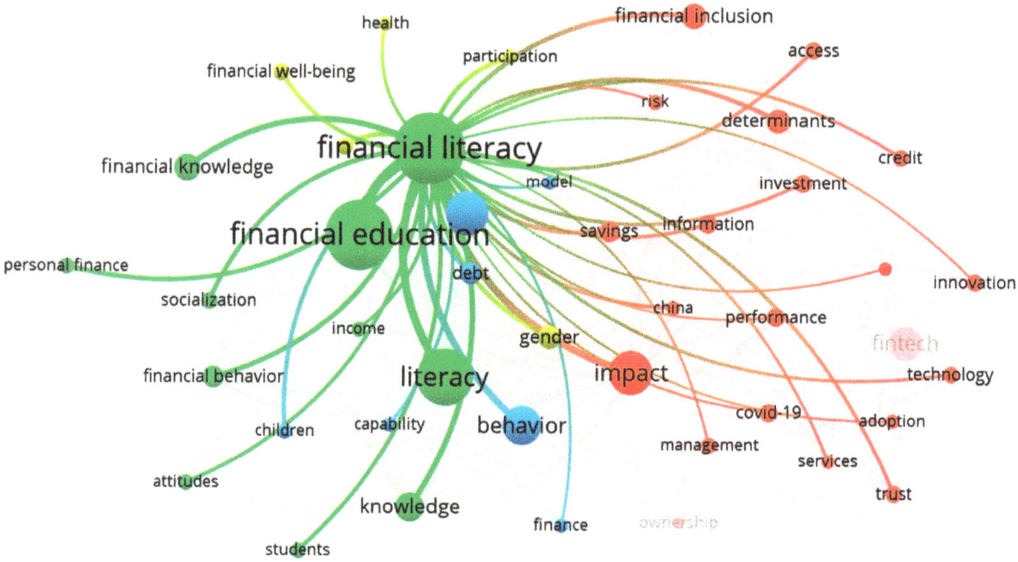

Figure 5. Cluster 2 keyword *financial literacy* with link strength 340. Source: WOS database (accessed on 4 November 2024) and made with the VOSviewer software.

Starting from the dominant keyword within this cluster, impact, we can group together several economic notions to formulate a perspective on the correlations within the cluster:

- **access, adoption, financial inclusion, FinTech, and technology:** articles containing these keywords suggest that "impact" could be related to how technology influences access to and the use of financial services;

- **investment, credit, and savings:** articles containing these keywords suggest that "impact" could be related to financial results or effects on these areas;
- **risk and trust:** articles dealing with this research area can address the impact of financial technology on risk perception and trust in financial systems;
- **innovation, management, and performance:** articles specific to this area can refer to the operational and strategic impact in the FinTech landscape.
- **COVID-19 and China:** we may have articles that present external or geographic impacts on FinTech development or access, given the effects of the pandemic globally.

Cluster analysis highlights the significance of access and education as foundational aspects of financial literacy. Digital innovations, including FinTech, contribute to these outcomes by facilitating easier access to financial information and tools, though their role is secondary to broader educational initiatives. By facilitating more inclusive, efficient, and transparent financial systems, FinTech continues to play a vital role in modern economic development [23].

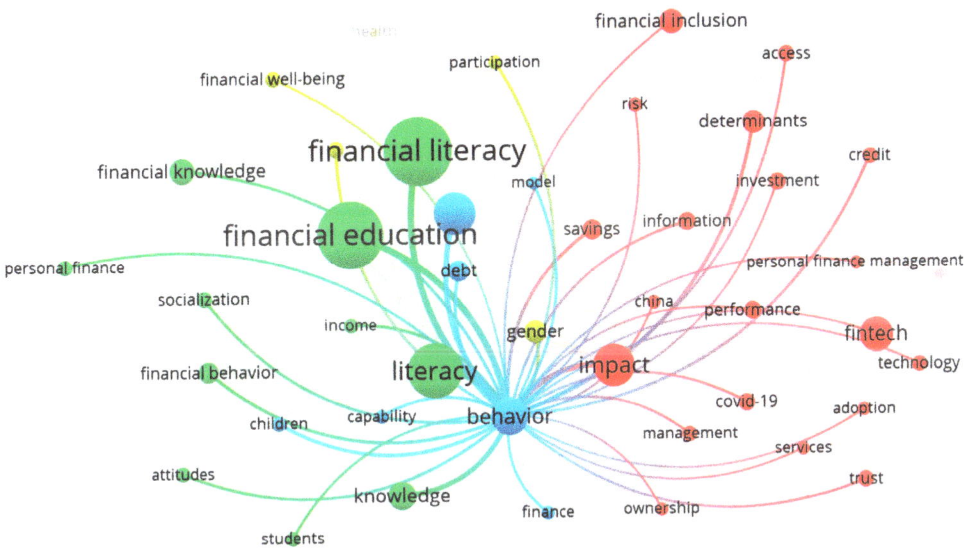

Figure 6. Cluster 3 keyword *behavior* with link strength 182. Source: WOS database (accessed on 4 November 2024) and made with the VOSviewer software.

To analyze the relationship between "financial literacy" and other words in this cluster, we will evaluate potential connections based on context, thematic similarities, or typical associations found in financial research. Thus, we analyze the terms present in the cluster in relation to "financial literacy".

The term "financial literacy" is associated with the following words in cluster 2:

- attitudes: often reflect how beliefs and perceptions influence financial decisions, closely related to financial literacy;
- financial behavior: refers to actions such as budgeting and saving, which are influenced by the level of financial literacy;
- financial education: a direct source for improving financial literacy;
- financial literacy: fundamental to financial literacy as it involves the understanding needed to make informed financial decisions;

- income: although not directly literacy itself, it is often related to how well people manage their finances;
- knowledge: general cognitive skills essential for literacy in any field, including finance;
- literacy: generally, it refers to financial skills and understanding;
- personal finance: practical application of financial literacy to money management;
- socialization: influences how individuals learn financial habits and attitudes, shaping financial literacy;
- students: a key group often studied in relation to the development of financial literacy.

These connections indicate that "financial literacy" serves as a central node interconnected with education, behavior, knowledge, and attitudes, all of which contribute to or are influenced by an individual's financial competence.

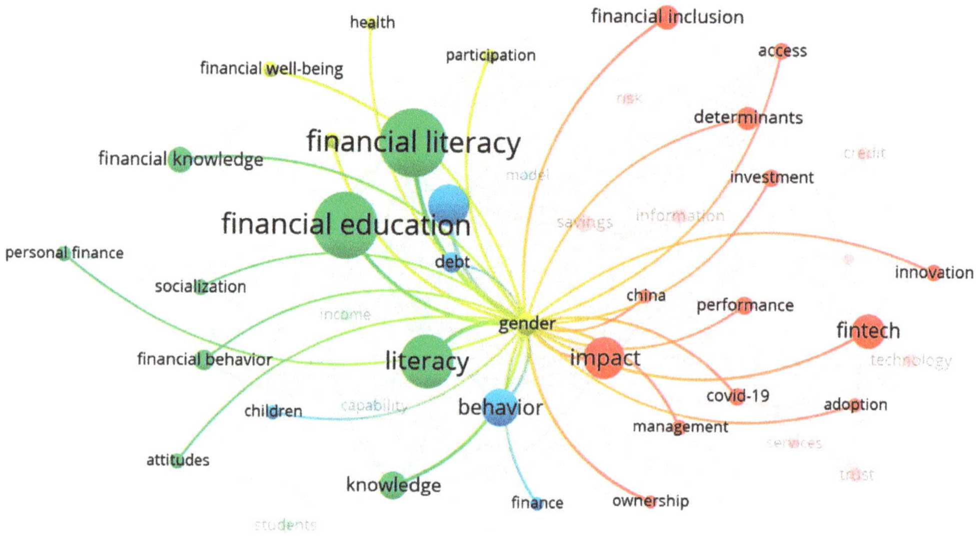

Figure 7. Cluster 4 keyword *gender* with link strength 74. Source: WOS database (accessed on 4 November 2024) and made with the VOSviewer software.

Measuring the impact of financial literacy involves evaluating how financial education or literacy programs influence individuals' financial knowledge, behavior, and outcomes.

By using a combination of these measurement methods, researchers and policymakers can assess not only the short-term knowledge gains but also the long-term behavioral and economic benefits of financial education initiatives.

Leveraging technological advances in the financial literacy process leads to the acquisition of knowledge and the development of tools necessary to make the better financial decisions needed to build long-term financial security. By incorporating these factors, financial literacy programs can go beyond simply imparting knowledge and foster lasting behavior changes that lead to improved long-term financial well-being.

The results obtained within this cluster confirm that financial education remains a major challenge, thereby having a significant impact on citizens' financial decisions. These findings are also supported by previous research, such as that carried out by Șimandan, Leuștean, and Dobrescu (2022), who emphasize that, despite economic progress and expanded access to financial services, financial education directly influences the financial behaviors of individuals and contributes to the perpetuation of existing economic inequalities [24].

Articles within this cluster may highlight thematic relationships that may involve behavioral aspects in various contexts, such as financial capability, education, interactions with children, financial modeling, and debt management [25].

Financial capability refers to the ability of individuals to effectively manage their financial resources. Behavioral patterns such as spending habits, saving tendencies, and risk aversion play a crucial role in determining financial capability. Responsible financial behavior can enhance capacity, while poor financial habits can impair it.

In the broader context of finance, behavior is a critical factor that drives market trends and investment decisions. Behavioral finance is an entire field that examines how psychological factors and biases affect the behavior of investors and financial analysts. Understanding behavior can reveal why markets might react irrationally to news or why individuals make poor financial choices despite having access to information.

In financial modeling, assumptions about human behavior are often integrated to predict financial trends and outcomes. Models can take into account behavioral patterns such as herd mentality in trading, consumer spending behavior, or the psychological impact of market volatility on investment strategies [26]. These behavioral insights can make financial models more realistic and applicable in predicting real-world scenarios.

In conclusion, behavior intertwines with financial terms to shape both individual and financial health. By leveraging these technological resources, parents, teachers, and educators can make financial literacy more accessible, interactive, and engaging for children, preparing them for a future of informed and responsible money management.

Insights into behavioral trends enable better financial planning, policy making, and the development of tools that support healthier financial practices [27].

To analyze the relationship between "gender" and the other words in this group, we will look at potential associations, themes, or contexts where the keywords might interconnect:

- gender and financial well-being: These examine how gender influences financial stability or access to economic resources. These could include studies on gender pay gaps, disparities in financial literacy, or access to financial services;
- gender and health: These explore how gender influences health outcomes and access to healthcare. This relationship often covers differences in life expectancy, health risks, and how medical research and healthcare policies might respond differently to different genders;
- gender and participation: These investigate gender differences in participation in different sectors such as the workforce, education, or political representation. This analysis may reveal gender-specific barriers or opportunities;
- gender and women-directly related: The examination of gender often involves a focus on the rights, roles, and challenges of women in society. This includes issues such as gender equality, empowerment, and specific policies aimed at improving conditions for women.

Cluster 4 reflects the critical connection between financial literacy and well-being. Gender and participation themes underscore the need for inclusive educational efforts, addressing disparities and promoting equitable access to financial resources.

5. Conclusions

The analyses carried out in this article emphasize the importance of grouping in understanding the various components of financial education. The content of the four clusters—access and literacy, behavior, capability, and well-being—captures key areas of focus in the field, reflecting a spectrum of educational needs. Financial literacy extends beyond knowledge to include behavior, health, and inclusion. Policymakers and educators can leverage these insights to design programs that address the full spectrum of financial literacy, contributing to a financially secure and capable society. Thus, some suggestions are required for future financial education strategies:

- Educational programs should focus on fundamental topics such as budgeting, savings, and credit management, ensuring that these resources reach people who do not have and understand the concepts specific to this area or are less financially literate. Post-crisis resilience training could also be valuable [28];
- FinTech and educational actors should develop educational initiatives that emphasize behavioral change, including strategies for positive financial habits, impulse control, and long-term financial planning. Programs could also integrate insights from behavioral psychology to address the emotional aspects of financial decision-making;
- Educational programs should target a younger audience, perhaps by integrating basic financial education into school curricula. These programs could cover topics such as budgeting, savings, and understanding debt to better prepare young adults for financial independence;
- Supporting the development of inclusive, tailored financial education programs that address the specific needs of different demographics (e.g., women and marginalized communities). These programs can focus on financial independence, reducing financial stress and promoting financial security as part of overall wellness.

This study underscores the multifaceted nature of financial literacy, linking it to access, behavior, and well-being. While FinTech provides innovative tools that support these outcomes, the core emphasis remains on financial education as a driver of behavioral change and societal resilience. Policymakers and educators should prioritize inclusive financial literacy programs that address demographic-specific needs, leveraging digital innovations to enhance accessibility and impact.

By analyzing 469 scientific articles using bibliometric methods and the VOSviewer software, this study identified key thematic clusters that highlight the various aspects of financial education and its integration into digital innovation. Universities are increasingly including FinTech subjects in their curricula, giving students the opportunity to develop skills in areas such as AI-based financial services, cyber security and regulatory technologies.

Collaborative initiatives between academia and the FinTech industry, such as internships and incubators, provide hands-on exposure and align education with market demands.

In conclusion, financial education is often overlooked due to a combination of systemic, cultural, and policy factors. Addressing these barriers requires coordinated efforts by educational institutions, governments, and communities to prioritize financial literacy and recognize its critical role in fostering economic stability and personal well-being.

Overcoming these challenges requires coordinated efforts among educators, policymakers, and industry leaders to ensure equitable access and the adoption of financial technologies.

The intersection of FinTech and higher education is a dynamic and evolving field with the potential to drive both technological innovation and societal progress. By using FinTech to address gaps in financial literacy, institutions and governments can foster a financially capable population, enhance economic stability, and build resilience in the face of global uncertainties. Future research should explore deeper interconnections and develop innovative and inclusive strategies for promoting financial literacy in the digital age.

Limitations of the Study

To properly understand the results, discussions, and conclusions resulting from a bibliometric analysis, the limitations must be contextualized by the authors. In this article, data were collected exclusively from the **Web of Science platform**, and querying other databases may reveal additional aspects. The authors chose this database because they believed it to be representative and relevant to the research being conducted.

Author Contributions: Conceptualization, I.M.C., P.-P.D., N.D.I. and R.J.; Data curation, I.M.C., P.-P.D. and N.D.I.; Formal analysis, I.M.C., P.-P.D. and N.D.I.; Investigation, I.M.C., P.-P.D., N.D.I. and R.J.; Methodology, I.M.C., P.-P.D., N.D.I. and R.J.; Supervision, I.M.C., P.-P.D., N.D.I. and R.J.; Validation, I.M.C., P.-P.D., N.D.I. and R.J.; Visualization, I.M.C., P.-P.D., N.D.I. and R.J.; Writing—Original draft, I.M.C., P.-P.D., N.D.I. and R.J.; Writing—Review and editing, N.D.I. and R.J. All authors have read and agreed to the published version of the manuscript.All authors have read and agreed to the published version of the manuscript.

Funding: This research received no external funding.

Institutional Review Board Statement: Not applicable.

Informed Consent Statement: Not applicable.

Data Availability Statement: No new data were created or analyzed in this study. Data sharing is not applicable to this article.

Conflicts of Interest: The authors declare that they have no conflict of interest.

References

1. Brika, S.K.M. A Bibliometric Analysis of Fintech Trends and Digital Finance. *Front. Environment. Sci.* **2022**, *9*, 696. [CrossRef]
2. Dissanayake, H.; Popescu, C.; Iddagoda, A. A Bibliometric Analysis of Financial Technology: Unveiling the Research Landscape. *FinTech* **2023**, *2*, 527–542. [CrossRef]
3. Gabor, D.; Brooks, S. The digital revolution in financial inclusion: International development in the fintech era. *New Political Econ.* **2017**, *22*, 423–436. [CrossRef]
4. Manta, O. Financial Technology and Innovation for Sustainable Development. *FinTech* **2024**, *3*, 424–426. [CrossRef]
5. Lusardi, A. Financial literacy and the need for financial education: Evidence and implications. *Swiss J. Econ. Stat.* **2019**, *155*, 1. [CrossRef]
6. Morgan, P. Fintech, financial literacy, and financial education. In *The Routledge Handbook of Financial Literacy*, 1st ed.; Nicolini, G., Cude, B.J., Eds.; Routledge International Handbooks: London, UK, 2021; p. 20.
7. Aysan, A.F.; Nanaeva, Z. Fintech as a Financial Disruptor: A Bibliometric Analysis. *FinTech* **2022**, *1*, 412–433. [CrossRef]
8. Sahabuddin, M.; Sakib, M.N.; Rahman, M.M.; Jibir, A.; Fahlevi, M.; Aljuaid, M.; Grabowska, S. The Evolution of FinTech in Scientific Research: A Bibliometric Analysis. *Sustainability* **2023**, *15*, 7176. [CrossRef]
9. Siddiqui, Z.; Rivera, C.A. Embedding FinTech-Specific content in higher education. *Risk Gov. Control. Financ. Mark. Inst.* **2023**, *13*, 18–29. [CrossRef]
10. The Intersection of Academia and Fintech: Unpacking Harvard's Integration Strategies. TechBullion, 30 November 2023. Available online: https://techbullion.com/the-intersection-of-academia-and-fintech-unpacking-harvards-integration-strategies/ (accessed on 19 November 2024).
11. Militaru, A.M.; Fleacă, B.; Dumitrescu, C.I.; Fleacă, E. Romanian Youth Enhancing Innovation Mindset and Organizational Change in the Business Environment. In Proceedings of the European Conference on Innovation and Entrepreneurship, Porto, Portugal, 21–22 September 2023; Volume 18, pp. 626–635.
12. Buckley, R.; Arner, D.; Zetzsche, D. *FinTech: Finance, Technology and Regulation*; Cambridge University Press: Cambridge, MA, USA, 2023; pp. 27–57.
13. Building Better Financial Systems, HKU FinTech. Available online: https://www.hkufintech.com/research (accessed on 5 November 2024).
14. Arnone, G. *AI and Chatbots in FinTech Revolutionizing Digital Experiences and Predictive Analytics*; Springer Nature: Cham, Switzerland, 2024; pp. 4–20, 55–68, 71–77.
15. Kosmas, I.; Papadopoulos, T.; Dede, G.; Michalakelis, C. The Use of Artificial Neural Networks in the Public Sector. *FinTech* **2023**, *2*, 138–152. [CrossRef]
16. Donthu, N.; Kumar, S.; Mukherjee, D.; Pandey, N.; Lim, W.M. How to conduct a bibliometric analysis: An overview and guidelines. *J. Bus. Res.* **2021**, *133*, 285–296. [CrossRef]
17. Ellegaard, O.; Wallin, J.A. The bibliometric analysis of scholarly production: How great is the impact? *Scientometrics* **2015**, *105*, 1809–1831. [CrossRef] [PubMed]

18. Rialti, R.; Mardi, G.; Ciappei, C.; Busso, D.J. Big data and dynamic capabilities: A bibliometric analysis and systematic literature review. *Manag. Decis.* **2019**, *57*, 2052–2068. [CrossRef]
19. Maria, M.R.; Ballini, R.; Souza, R.F. Evolution of Green Finance: A Bibliometric Analysis through Complex Networks and Machine Learning. *Sustainability* **2023**, *15*, 967. [CrossRef]
20. Passas, I. Bibliometric Analysis: The Main Steps. *Encyclopedia* **2024**, *4*, 1014–1025. [CrossRef]
21. Web of Science Results Analysis for 469 Records from Web of Science Core Collection. Available online: https://www.webofscience.com/wos/woscc/summary/12602235-4895-41ab-8ddc-703d2a9fd1d3-011f0ef258/relevance/1 (accessed on 4 November 2024).
22. Manea, N.; Dumitrescu, C.I.; Niculescu, N.; Dobrescu, R.M.; Puiu, R.A.; Sirbu, S.A. An Analysis of the Impact of the COVID-19 Pandemic on Air Transport Services in Romania. *J. East. Eur. Res. Bus. Econ.* **2022**, *2022*, 232829. [CrossRef]
23. Song, N.; Appiah-Otoo, I. The impact of fintech on economic growth: Evidence from China. *Sustainability* **2022**, *14*, 6211. [CrossRef]
24. Šimandan, R.; Leustean, B.; Dobrescu, R.M. An Uphill Battle: Financial Education in Romania in the Midst of Societal Transformation. *J. Risk Financ. Manag.* **2022**, *15*, 494. [CrossRef]
25. Khan, M.T.I.; Tze, W.L.; Xue, Y.L. Fintech literacy among millennials: The roles of financial literacy and education. *Cogent Soc. Sci.* **2023**, *9*, 2281046. [CrossRef]
26. Chen, F.; Lu, J.; Li, J.; Wang, W.; Bissielou, H. Sustainable financial education and consumer life satisfaction. *Sustainability* **2020**, *12*, 1150. [CrossRef]
27. Pham, K.D.; Le, V.L.T. Nexus between Financial Education, Literacy, and Financial Behavior: Insights from Vietnamese Young Generations. *Sustainability* **2023**, *15*, 14854. [CrossRef]
28. Paunică, M.; Manole, A.; Motofei, C.; Tănase, G.L. Resilience of the European Union Economies. An Analysis of the Granger Causality at the Level of the Gross Domestic Product. *Amfiteatru Econ.* **2021**, *23*, 914–933. [CrossRef]

FinTech

Review

A Comprehensive Review of Generative AI in Finance

David Kuo Chuen Lee [1], Chong Guan [2], Yinghui Yu [1] and Qinxu Ding [1,*]

[1] School of Business, Singapore University of Social Sciences, 463 Clementi Road, Singapore 599494, Singapore
[2] SUSS Academy, Singapore University of Social Sciences, Singapore 408601, Singapore
* Correspondence: qinxuding@suss.edu.sg

Abstract: The integration of generative AI (GAI) into the financial sector has brought about significant advancements, offering new solutions for various financial tasks. This review paper provides a comprehensive examination of recent trends and developments at the intersection of GAI and finance. By utilizing an advanced topic modeling method, BERTopic, we systematically categorize and analyze existing research to uncover predominant themes and emerging areas of interest. Our findings reveal the transformative impact of finance-specific large language models (LLMs), the innovative use of generative adversarial networks (GANs) in synthetic financial data generation, and the pressing necessity of a new regulatory framework to govern the use of GAI in the finance sector. This paper aims to provide researchers and practitioners with a structured overview of the current landscape of GAI in finance, offering insights into both the opportunities and challenges presented by these advanced technologies.

Keywords: generative AI; large language models; finance; topic modeling; BERTopic

JEL Classification: G20; O33; C63

1. Introduction

The intersection of generative AI (GAI) and finance has emerged as a rapidly developing area of research and application, revolutionizing various facets of the financial industry. GAI encompasses a broad range of models, such as variational autoencoders (VAEs), generative adversarial networks (GANs), large language models (LLMs), and diffusion models. It has demonstrated significant potential in enhancing financial analytics, improving decision-making processes, and generating synthetic financial data for various applications. This review paper aims to provide a comprehensive overview of recent trends and advancements in GAI's application within the financial sector.

Before the advent of GAI models, traditional methods for financial text mining were primarily used to analyze financial reports and forecast stock prices. However, these methods often relied on the bag-of-words approach to generate word embeddings, which failed to capture the contextual information within sentences. In contrast, pre-trained LLMs, which leverage transformer architecture, are able to capture the complex dependency relationships between words, resulting in more nuanced and contextually aware embeddings. Consequently, GAI models, such as LLMs, have shown significant potential to enhance various financial tasks [1]. Over the past few years, there has been a growing body of research investigating how GAI can address these tasks, evaluating both the results and the associated risks.

In this paper, we aim to evaluate the current state of research on GAI in finance and provide guidance for newcomers in this field. Notably, Ding et al. [2] conducted an extensive analysis of LLMs, while Li et al. [3] provided a broader perspective by examining the current advancements in LLM techniques and their applications. However, neither study explores the intricate relationship between GAI and finance in detail. Lee et al. [4] offered surveys that focus specifically on the impact of LLMs in finance, though they do not address other GAI models, and their topics were predefined manually. Additionally, Barde and Kulkarni [5], Krause [6], and Mbanyele [7] concentrated on general-purpose LLMs, such as ChatGPT, Bard, and Bing AI.

However, our paper expands the scope by exploring the intersection of GAI and finance, going beyond the focus on LLMs. Additionally, we utilize the advanced topic modeling technique, BERTopic [8], to systematically cluster and analyze the existing research. By leveraging the BERTopic model, we introduce a novel framework for categorizing the current body of work on GAI in finance. In light of the identified gaps and the evolving application of GAI models in finance, this paper aims to address the following research questions:

- RQ1. What are the current trends and advancements in the application of GAI within the financial sector?
- RQ2. How does GAI, beyond LLMs, contribute to solving financial tasks and challenges?
- RQ3. How can BERTopic be used to systematically classify and analyze research on GAI in finance?
- RQ4. What are the risks and challenges associated with the use of GAI in finance, and how have these been addressed in the literature?

The structure of our paper is as follows. In Section 2, we examine the papers relevant to this topic. In Section 3, we introduce the dataset and the topic modeling method used in this study. Section 4 presents the results of our analysis. In Section 5, we provide an in-depth discussion based on the new framework obtained through the topic modeling method. In Section 6, we discuss our contribution, future directions, and potential areas for further research. Finally, we give a conclusion in Section 7.

2. Literature Review

The field of GAI has experienced rapid advancement in recent years. One of the famous GAI methods is the VAE algorithm, developed by Kingma and Welling in 2013 [9]. VAEs applied probabilistic frameworks to generate new data points based on latent representations learned during training. Therefore, it enhances the ability to model complex distributions in data. Subsequently, in 2014, Goodfellow et al. [10] introduced the GAN model, which represented a paradigm shift in generative modeling. It is an adversarial process involving two neural networks: a generative model to capture the data distribution and a discriminative model to distinguish between real data and generated samples. This adversarial framework enabled GANs to produce remarkably realistic outputs across various domains, such as images and texts.

In 2017, Transformers was introduced by Vaswani et al. [11]. It leverages self-attention mechanisms to capture long-range dependencies in sequential data, making them highly effective for various natural language tasks. This innovation inspired the development of LLMs, particularly transformer-based architectures like OpenAI's GPT series [12–15] and Google's BERT [16], which marked a significant advancement in natural language processing. The deployment of LLMs has expanded generative AI into sophisticated applications requiring the comprehension and generation of human-like text. Additionally, Diffusion models have emerged as a novel approach in GAI, focusing on modeling temporal dependencies and irregular patterns in sequential data [17]. These models have shown promise in applications where traditional generative models fall short, particularly in capturing the nuances of dynamic and time-series data.

From the financial researchers' perspective, the impact of LLMs' applications is most significant and far-reaching. In the past two decades, financial text mining has been a popular research area, especially with advancements in computational methods that have made processing large-scale data possible. Beyond conventional financial data sources such as public companies' annual reports and earning announcements, financial researchers have turned to financial news press, regulatory filings, and social media to uncover hidden information and sentimental cues. These insights can be used to predict investment behaviors and trends in stock returns. For instance, Bollen et al. [18] investigated whether measurements of collective mood states derived from large-scale Twitter feeds are correlated to the value of the Dow Jones Industrial Average (DJIA) over time. Wisniewski and Yekini [19] analyzed the qualitative part of annual reports of UK-listed companies and used the frequency of words associated with different language indicators to forecast future stock returns. McGurk et al. [20] examined the relationship between investor sentiment and stock returns by employing textual analysis on Twitter posts and found that their investor sentiment measure has a positive and significant effect on abnormal stock returns.

Most of these earlier studies are still exploratory, often reducing text information to "a bag of words" or representing it through dictionary-based sentiment scores. This is primarily because financial texts frequently lack a regular structure, and verbal/textual communication can be subtle and complex. Additionally, financial jargon can vary in meaning depending on the context. To extract more meaningful insights from financial texts, more advanced models are required. LLMs trained on extensive datasets from diverse sources and themes can provide more sophisticated text representations that capture the nuances of financial language. In the literature we surveyed, Gupta [21] simplified the process of assessing annual reports of all the firms by leveraging the capabilities of LLMs, where the insights generated by the LLM are compiled in a Quant-styled dataset and augmented by historical stock price data. Fatemi et al. [1] showcased the remarkable capabilities of LLMs, even smaller models, in both fine-tuning and in-context learning for financial sentiment analysis. Li et al. [22] reported evidence that general-purpose LLMs, especially GPT-4, could outperform domain-specific models in terms of sentiment analysis. Pavlyshenko [23] demonstrated that Llama 2 can be fine-tuned and multitask; when analyzing financial texts, it can return both a structured response and sentiment data in specified JSON format, which can further be loaded directly into predictive models as features. On the other hand, Xing [24] reported that a design framework with heterogeneous LLM agents can be effective in financial sentiment analysis without fine-tuning.

In general, the financial sector, characterized by its vast and complex data, stands to benefit immensely from these advancements in GAI. Traditional data analysis methods often fall short in handling the scale, variability, and intricate patterns inherent in financial data. GAI offers a promising solution by not only managing large datasets effectively but also generating synthetic data close to real-world financial data. This capability is particularly important for applications such as risk management, fraud detection, algorithmic trading, and financial forecasting. Recent years have seen the emergence of specialized GAI models tailored for financial applications. Finance-specific LLMs, such as FinGPT [25,26] and FinPT [27], have been developed to address domain-specific challenges and have shown superior performance compared to general-purpose models in various financial tasks. Despite the promising advancements, the integration of GAI in finance is not without challenges. Issues such as data privacy, model interpretability, regulatory compliance, and the potential for generating biased or misleading data necessitate careful consideration. The ethical and social implications of deploying generative AI in financial decision making further underscore the need for robust frameworks and guidelines to ensure responsible use [28].

Most importantly, there is a limited body of research that surveys the intersection of GAI and finance [3–7], and none of these studies employ advanced topic modeling techniques to mine potential topics from paper abstracts. Using a topic model like BERTopic [8] for paper reviews offers significant advantages over manual review, especially when dealing with large datasets. They usually provide an objective, unbiased grouping of papers, uncovering hidden patterns and emerging trends that may be missed by human reviewers. Additionally, they ensure consistency across the entire dataset and allow researchers to focus on the most relevant areas, making it easier to manage large-scale literature reviews. From the above review, it is evident that while significant progress has been made in applying GAI to finance, many challenges remain underexplored, particularly in terms of integrating various GAI models and uncovering new insights through more sophisticated topic modeling methods.

3. Materials and Methods

This study leverages the Google Scholar database for its extensive coverage, interdisciplinary reach, and up-to-date research indexing. Given that research on GAI, particularly LLMs, is relatively new and rapidly evolving, Google Scholar's comprehensive indexing of reputable authors and institutions is particularly valuable. Many significant papers are submitted to repositories such as arXiv and SSRN, both of which are well indexed by Google Scholar.

We conducted searches using two key combinations: (1) "generative AI and finance" and (2) "large language models and finance." From these searches, we retrieved a total of 90 papers published between 2018 and 2024. These papers were sourced from a diverse range of publishers, including ACM, ACL, arXiv, Curran Associates, Darcy & RoyPress, Elsevier, IEEE, MDPI, Routledge, SSRN, Taylor & Francis Online, and MIT Press. The dataset consists of academic papers from multiple disciplines, with a primary focus on Finance and Computer Science. It also includes papers from related fields such as Economics, Business, Management, and Accounting, ensuring a comprehensive scope. The authors in the dataset are affiliated with a broad spectrum of institutions, ranging from elite universities like Harvard, MIT, and Stanford to tier 1 institutions such as the University of Oxford and the National University of Singapore. Additionally, the dataset includes contributions from leading technology companies like Amazon, Microsoft, and Alibaba, as well as financial institutions such as JP Morgan and Bloomberg. The dataset reflects a geographically diverse set of authors, with substantial representation from the US, Asia, and Europe. This global distribution was intentional to capture a wide range of perspectives on the trends and insights being discussed. As shown in Figure 1, about half of the papers come from Asia, while roughly one-third are from the US. This distribution is consistent with the fact that the US and China are leading countries in research on generative AI models and their applications.

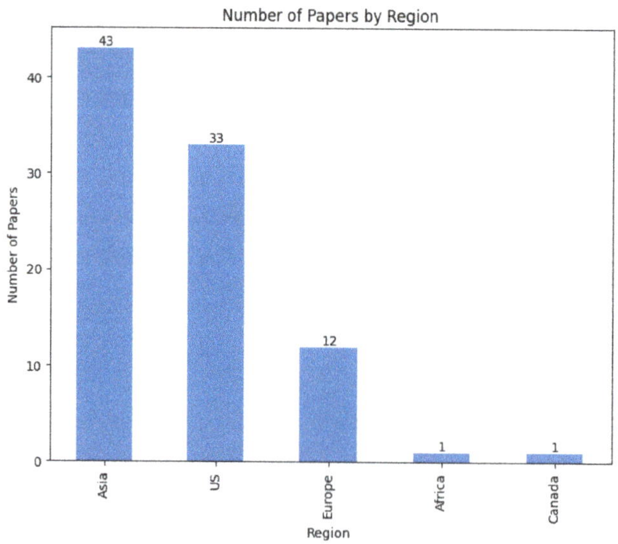

Figure 1. This figure describes data's geographical information. Source: personal processing according to the data.

To effectively cluster and analyze these papers, we applied a robust topic modeling technique known as BERTopic [8]. Topic models are powerful unsupervised tools for uncovering themes and underlying narratives in textual data.

BERTopic Model Specification: To generate coherent topic representations, the BERTopic model will employ three steps. The first step is to generate document embeddings. In this step, the Sentence-BERT (SBERT) framework [29] was employed to convert each paper's abstract into a vector representation. The SBERT uses pre-trained large language models and achieves state-of-the-art performance on various embedding tasks, generating high-quality document vector representations. The second step is to cluster these document embeddings. To achieve a robust cluster result, a dimension reduction technique named UMAP [30] was used, preserving more of the local and global features of high-dimension document embeddings in a lower-dimension space. After that, the HDBSCAN model [31] is used to cluster the reduced embeddings. The benefit of using HDBSCAN is that we can model the outliers as noise, preventing any unrelated documents from being assigned to any cluster. The third step is to model the topic representation with documents in each cluster. The class-based TF-IDF (c-TF-IDF) method [8] is employed to model the importance of a word to a cluster. BERTopic has shown effectiveness in various applications, including systematic reviews [2,21].

BERTopic vs. LDA: While traditional topic modeling methods such as Latent Dirichlet Allocation (LDA) [32] and Non-Negative Matrix Factorization (NMF) [33] represent documents as mixtures of latent topics using a bag-of-words approach, BERTopic enhances this process with advanced techniques. The use of bag-of-words would disregard the semantic relationship among words or lose the context information in a paragraph, resulting in a failure of document representation. In contrast, the BERTopic model takes advantage of pre-trained large language models to encode the meaning of texts into the document embedding. Moreover, the BERTopic model performs better than the LDA and NMF methods with the topic coherence and topic diversity metrics [8].

Our application of BERTopic in this study can be broken down into the following steps:

- Data Preprocessing: First, we convert all text to lowercase to ensure uniformity and reduce redundancy; second, we use nltk.word_tokenize() to split the text into individual tokens and WordNetLemmatizer() to reduce words to their base or root form; finally, we use stopwords.words('english') to eliminate the common stopwords, as they usually do not contribute significantly to the meaning of the text.
- Fit the Model and Transform Documents: We use BERTopic and ClassIFidTransformer to fit the model to our data and transform to discover topics.
- Topics Exploration: After fitting the model, we explore the topics generated by various tools of BERTopic.

4. Results

In this section, we discuss the results obtained from the BERTopic model. After fitting the model, we identified the most frequent topics in our dataset, as shown in Figure 2. Figure 2 reveals four distinct clusters:

- "-1_chatbots_credit_reliable_chatgpt";
- "0_llm_financial_model_task";
- "1_ai_generative_risk_challenge";
- and "2_data_stock_synthetic_market".

Cluster -1 represents all outliers and should be disregarded. Consequently, our focus will be directed towards the examination of the remaining three clusters. Cluster 0 pertains to discussions surrounding the application of LLMs in financial tasks. This cluster highlights the innovative use of LLMs to address various financial modeling and task automation challenges. Cluster 1 delves into the challenges and risks associated with the implementation of GAI within the realm of finance. This cluster underscores the potential risks and regulatory considerations that accompany the deployment of GAI technologies in finance. Cluster 2 centers on the generation of synthetic financial data facilitated by GAI. This cluster emphasizes the role of GAI in creating synthetic datasets, which are essential for tasks such as market simulation and risk assessment.

Additionally, our analysis reveals a significant discrepancy in the distribution of research focus. Specifically, there are approximately 47 papers discussing LLMs in finance, a considerably higher count compared to those addressing the risks and data generation aspects of GAI. This observation underscores that LLMs currently represent the foremost research focus of GAI within the financial domain.

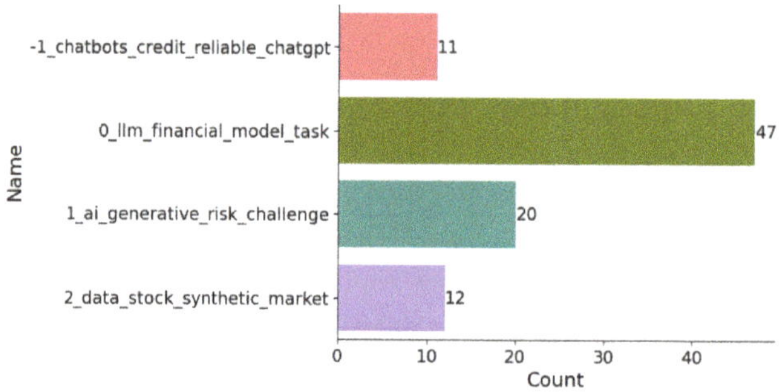

Figure 2. This figure describes the frequent topics obtained from the BERTopic model. Source: personal processing according to the cluster results from BERTopic model.

Observing Table 1, we identify the representative words for each topic generated by the BERTopic model. These words help elucidate the main themes and concepts of each topic, as they are extracted based on their relevance and frequency within the topic. Topic -1 is ignored, as it is an outlier, so our analysis begins with Topic 0: "LLMs for Financial Tasks."

Topic 0: "LLMs for Financial Tasks": In addition to the key terms, such as 'LLM', 'financial', and 'task', that define this topic, other prominent words, like 'model', 'language', and 'large', emphasize the core characteristics of LLMs. These terms highlight the foundational role LLMs play in processing human text and understanding financial language. Financial papers referencing LLMs often focus on the ability of these models to interpret complex financial documents, automate tasks, and assist in decision-making processes. Words like 'benchmark' and 'performance' are frequently used to evaluate how effectively LLMs accomplish financial tasks, whether they are used for explaining phenomena such as market trends, generating reports, or forecasting financial outcomes. The focus on 'benchmark' results indicates the importance of validating LLMs against industry standards, while 'performance' suggests the critical evaluation of their accuracy, speed, and reliability in financial contexts. Thus, these terms collectively indicate that financial research using LLMs aims not only to describe or analyze financial data but also to enhance forecasting and predictive capabilities.

Topic 1: "The Risk and Challenge of Generative AI": Key terms such as 'AI', 'artificial', 'intelligence', 'generative', 'risk', and 'challenge' are central to this topic. These terms reflect the growing discourse around the potential risks and challenges associated with implementing GAI in the financial sector. Additionally, the term 'ethical' frequently appears, highlighting significant concerns about the ethical implications of GAI, particularly in terms of transparency, fairness, and accountability. These ethical considerations are especially critical in the financial industry, where GAI is used to automate decision-making processes, and any misuse or bias in these systems can lead to substantial consequences. Discussions in financial papers often focus on the risks associated with deploying GAI, such as the potential for generating biased or inaccurate financial predictions, or the challenge of ensuring regulatory compliance. Ethical debates are often tied to how GAI is transforming the financial 'industry', affecting everything from risk management to customer service. The common appearance of the word 'paper' in our dataset is largely due to the review-based nature of this article and does not carry significant meaning in this specific context. However, the focus on risks and challenges suggests that researchers are keen on evaluating not only the technical capabilities of GAI but also the broader implications for ethical and responsible use in financial applications.

Topic 2: "Synthetic Financial Data Generation": The words 'synthetic' and 'data' are central to this topic, indicating the focus on the creation of artificial financial datasets. Terms such as 'network', 'GANs', 'learning', and 'adversarial' suggest that many existing studies utilize GANs for generating synthetic financial data, particularly for stock market simulations. In practice, GANs are widely used to produce synthetic 'stock' and 'market' data, such as 'price' 'series', which are essential for financial modeling and analysis. These synthetic datasets play a critical role in financial research, as they allow researchers and practitioners to simulate various market scenarios, test trading strategies, and analyze risk without relying on real-world data, which may be limited or sensitive. In financial papers, the use of synthetic data is typically aimed at overcoming challenges related to data availability, privacy concerns, and the need for large, high-quality datasets for machine learning models. By generating realistic price series and market behaviors, researchers can conduct more robust financial simulations, improving the accuracy and reliability of predictive models. The prominence of terms like 'network' and 'adversarial' reflects the technical focus on GAN architectures, which are key to producing high-fidelity synthetic data that closely mirror actual financial markets. Thus, this topic underscores the practical importance of synthetic data generation for enhancing financial forecasting, risk assessment, and model training.

Table 1. This table includes the representation words of each topic generated by BERTopic model. Source: personal processing according to the cluster results from BERTopic model.

Count	Name	Representation
11	-1_chatbots_credit_reliable_chatgpt	['chatbots', 'credit', 'reliable', 'chatgpt', 'lgp', 'payment', 'user', 'transaction', 'individual', 'process']
47	0_llm_financial_model_task	['llm', 'financial', 'model', 'task', 'language', 'large', 'benchmark', 'performance', 'text', 'instruction']
20	1_ai_generative_risk_challenge	['ai', 'generative', 'risk', 'challenge', 'ethical', 'industry', 'paper', 'intelligence', 'artificial', 'potential']
12	2_data_stock_synthetic_market	['data', 'stock', 'synthetic', 'market', 'network', 'gans', 'learning', 'adversarial', 'series', 'price']

As discussed by Grootendorst [8] in the BERTopic model, the c-TF-IDF method is used to calculate the word score for each cluster or topic. The definition of c-TF-IDF is as follows:

$$W_{x,c} = \|tf_{x,c}\| \times \log(1 + \frac{A}{f_x}), \tag{1}$$

where x is the word, c is the cluster, $tf_{x,c}$ is the frequency of word x in cluster c, f_x refers to word x's frequency across all clusters, and A represents the word's average number per cluster. Figure 3 tells us the 10 most important words for each cluster and their importance. These word scores represent how strongly a word is associated with a particular topic within the model. The higher the score, the more central the word is for defining the topic's theme. Practically speaking, these scores help us identify the most influential terms within each topic, giving us insights into the key concepts driving the discussion in the data. For example, in the context of financial papers, a high score for a word like 'performance' in Topic 0 means that researchers are likely to focus on improving or evaluating financial LLMs' performance in those papers. By identifying the most relevant words, we can better understand the central themes of each topic and how they relate to real-world financial issues like forecasting, strategy optimization, or the evaluation of financial instruments.

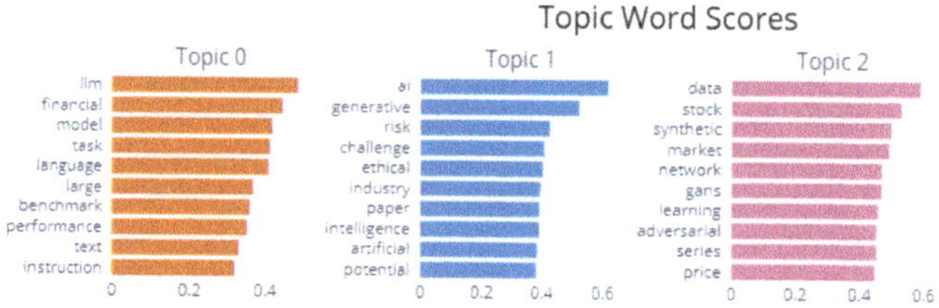

Figure 3. This figure shows the word scores for each topic. Source: personal processing according to the cluster results from BERTopic model.

Figure 4 presents the dendrogram of the hierarchical clustering of the three clusters. The x-axis represents the distance or dissimilarity between clusters, while the vertical lines indicate the points at which clusters are merged. For instance, clusters 0 and 1 merge at a dissimilarity level of approximately 0.6, indicating their relative similarity compared to cluster 2. This visualization helps us understand the relationships and similarities among the identified topics.

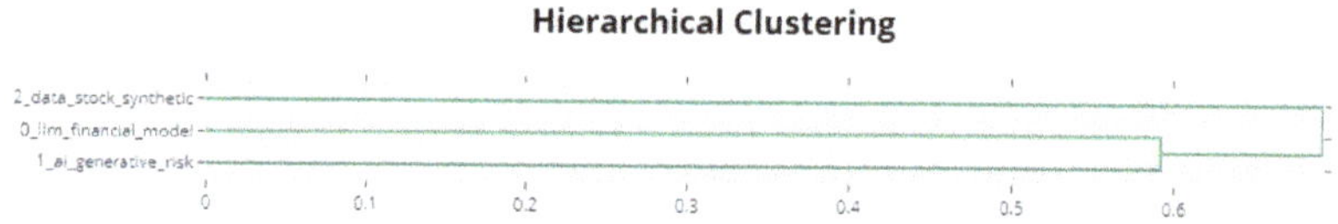

Figure 4. This figure describes the hierarchical clustering result obtained from the BERTopic model. Source: personal processing according to the cluster results from BERTopic model.

5. Discussion

In this section, we delve into three key topics derived from the BERTopic analysis. The first topic explores the application of LLMs in finance across various tasks. This includes discussions on the capability of general-purpose LLMs (e.g., GPTs, Gemini) to address financial problems, the effectiveness of finance-specific LLMs (e.g., FinGPT, FinPT) compared to general-purpose LLMs, and the identification of benchmarks and financial datasets that can be used to fairly evaluate the performance of LLMs in finance. The second topic addresses the potential risks and challenges associated with GAI models for financial applications. This includes an examination of issues such as hallucinations, ethical and social impacts, and financial regulation. Finally, the third topic focuses on the use of GAI for synthetic financial data generation. We will discuss the challenges and areas of focus in this domain, as well as existing work utilizing VAEs, GANs, and diffusion models.

5.1. LLMs for Financial Tasks

5.1.1. General-Purpose LLMs

The rapid advancements in LLMs have ushered in a new era of innovation across various sectors, with finance being a significant beneficiary. Over the past few years, general-purpose LLMs such as GPT-4 have been extensively studied by researchers. Teixeira et al. [34] and Krause [35] presented comprehensive guides to prompt usage in LLMs for financial analysis. Rane et al. [36] explored a comparative analysis of Gemini and ChatGPT, focusing on the discussion of these models' effectiveness and performance in finance and accounting tasks. LLMs have also been tested on a wide range of financial text analytics tasks, demonstrating their versatility and effectiveness [1,21–24,37,38].

General-purpose LLMs can also be used as investment advisors. The potential of LLMs as financial robo-advisors has been rigorously assessed, generally showing good performance [39–42]. Furthermore, Lu et al. [43] demonstrated that ChatGPT could potentially generate portfolios that outperform the markets in out-of-sample tests. Additionally, an innovative LLM multi-agent framework endowed with layered memories has been proposed for stock and fund trading [44]. Their capabilities extend to financial decision making [45,46], financial auditing [47], financial regulatory interpretation [48], financial budgeting [49], financial risk management [50,51], and analyzing climate change issues related to finance [52].

The reasoning capabilities of LLMs have also been studied extensively. Yu et al. [53,54] examined LLMs' ability for explainable financial time series forecasting, demonstrating that these models can generate well-reasoned decisions. Srivastava et al. [55] explored the mathematical reasoning abilities of LLMs on tabular question-answering datasets. Additionally, a comparative study of LLMs for personal financial decision making in a low-resource language, the Yoruba language, was conducted by Sikiru et al. [56]. The results indicate that the performance of LLMs is poor compared to their performance with English financial data, highlighting the need for improvements in low-resource languages. To address the high GPU memory consumption associated with LLMs, Liu et al. [57] presented high-performance GPU-based methods for pretraining and fine-tuning LLMs for financial applications.

5.1.2. Finance-Specific LLMs

General-purpose LLMs offer versatility and adaptability for a wide range of financial tasks but may lack the specialized domain knowledge required for complex financial analyses. In contrast, finance-specific LLMs are exclusively trained on financial data. For instance, BloombergGPT, trained on a diverse range of financial data, showcased superior performance in financial tasks compared to existing general-purpose LLMs [58]. Similarly, FinMA was introduced by fine-tuning LLaMA with a tailored dataset, enabling it to executive various financial tasks [59]. Furthermore, FinGPT emerged as an open-source LLM tailored for the finance sector, providing accessible and transparent resources for researchers and practitioners to develop their FinLLMs [25,26]. Additionally, Li et al. [60] proposed a financial LLM (CFLLM) specially designed to adeptly manage financial texts.

On the other hand, LLMs fine-tuned by financial datasets leverage general-purpose models and enhance their performance in finance-rated tasks through specialized training. For example, Zhang et al. [61] proposed a simple instruction tuning approach to fine-tune general-purpose LLMs, achieving remarkable achievements in financial sentiment analysis. Similarly, Yin et al. [27] introduced FinPT, fine-tuned on LLMs with natural language customer profile text for predictive purposes and pre-trained on a dataset containing Chinese financial data, and a general-purpose dataset. Additionally, Yang et al. [62] presented InvestLM, a financial LLM for investment, tuned on LLaMA with a financial investment instruction dataset. Chen et al. [63] proposed a multiple-expert fine-tuning framework for DISC-FinLLM, a large Chinese financial LLM. Finally, Chu et al. [64] created FLLM, a financial LLM employing multitask prompt-based fine-tuning for data pre-processing and pre-understanding, employing abductive augmentation reasoning (AAR) to overcome manual annotation costs.

Multimodal financial LLMs combine the power of language understanding with the rich information contained in financial data across multiple modalities. By integrating textual, numerical, and visual data, multimodal financial LLMs offer a holistic understanding of financial information, enabling more accurate analyses, predictions, and decision making in the financial domain. For instance, Wang et al. [65] introduced FinVis-GPT, a pioneering multimodal LLM designed to interpret financial charts, marking a significant advancement in the application of multimodal LLMs in finance. Similarly, Bhatia et al. [66] proposed a multimodal financial LLM that integrates textual, numerical, tabular, and image financial data, surpassing the performance of ChatGPT-3.5 in financial tasks.

By leveraging advanced language understanding capabilities and domain-specific knowledge, non-English financial LLMs enable more accurate and nuanced analyses of financial information in languages such as Japanese, Spanish, and beyond. For instance, Hirano [67] developed a Japanese financial-specific LLM through continual pre-training, while Zhang et al. [68] introduced FinMA-ES, an LLM tailored for bilingual financial applications aimed at bridging the gap between Spanish and English financial natural language processing (NLP) capabilities.

5.1.3. Benchmarks of LLMs in Finance

Benchmarks are crucial in evaluating the performance of LLMs in the financial domain. These benchmarks serve as standardized tests or datasets against which various LLMs are assessed, allowing researchers, practitioners, and developers to compare and contrast the effectiveness of different models in handling financial tasks. For instance, Xie et al. [59] proposed a standardized benchmark covering a range of financial tasks, while Zhang et al. [69] introduced FinEval, a benchmark specially tailored for the financial domain knowledge in LLMs, including multiple-choice questions covering various topics in business. Guo et al. [70] presented FinLMEval, offering a comprehensive evaluation of LLMs in financial NLP, and Xie et al. [71] proposed an open-source evaluation benchmark encompassing 35 datasets across 23 financial tasks.

Additionally, Yin et al. [27] provided high-quality datasets on financial risks, Lei et al. [72] introduced CFBenchmark for evaluating LLMs for financial assistance, and Islam et al. [73] proposed FinanceBench for assessing LLMs' performance on open book financial question answering (QA). Zhang et al. [74] curated a practical Text-to-SQL benchmark dataset, beneficial for financial professionals less-skilled in SQL programming. Li et al. [75] introduced the AlphaFin dataset for pretraining or fine-tuning financial analysis LLMs, combining traditional research datasets, real-time financial datasets, and handwritten chain-of-thought (COT) data. Furthermore, Hirano [76] constructed a benchmark specific to the Japanese financial domain, while Xu et al. [77] proposed a benchmark for evaluating Chinese-native financial LLMs.

5.2. *The Risk and Challenge of Generative AI*

5.2.1. Hallucination

In the realm of GAI, the phenomenon of hallucination manifests when a model generates data or information that deviates from accurately representing the underlying patterns or realities. This occurrence can engender misleading predictions, instill false impressions, or prompt erroneous conclusions based on the generated data. The ramifications of such hallucination are particularly acute within the financial domain, where precision in data and prognostications holds paramount importance for informed decision-making processes. An illustrative case in point is the investigation into GPT-3's efficacy in analyzing climate change related to its financial implications, as undertaken by Leippold [52]. Nevertheless, the inquiry unveiled an issue of hallucination during an interview with the GPT-3 model. Further empirical examination of the financial tasks' hallucination behaviors was conducted by Kang and Liu [78], who evaluated the efficacy of various methods, such as few-shot learning and the retrieval augmentation generation method, in mitigating hallucination in LLMs. Their findings underscored the substantial presence of hallucination behaviors in off-the-shelf LLMs when applied to financial tasks.

Consequently, it is imperative that forthcoming research endeavors prioritize strategies aimed at circumventing hallucination by GAI models. Roychowdhury [79] delineated three major stages to design hallucination-minimized LLM-based solutions tailored for the financial domain's decision-makers: prototyping, scaling, and LLM evolution using feedback. These measures ensure that GAI chatbots, autonomous reports, and alerts are reliable and high-quality, thereby facilitating key decision-making processes.

5.2.2. Ethical and Social Impact

GAI represents a remarkable tool for discerning users, yet it necessitates critical reflection on the ethical implications and societal ramifications of its integration into the financial industry. Rane [28] extensively explored the multifaceted role and challenges encountered by GAI tools within the intricate realms of finance and accounting, elucidating both their transformative potential and the hurdles that must be overcome to genuinely revolutionize the financial landscape. Similarly, Kalia [80] scrutinized the impact of GAI on the financial sector, advocating for the establishment of robust privacy frameworks, stringent enforcement of data protection regulations, and the promotion of responsible and ethical deployment of these technologies by organizations and policymakers. Sarker [81] delved into the myriad perspectives on LLMs, highlighting both their potentiality and associated risk factors, underscored by heightened awareness. Additionally, Krause [82] deliberated on the potential risks posed by GAI tools in finance and proposed comprehensive mitigation strategies for businesses, emphasizing the importance of employing GAI tools within closed networks, utilizing secure training data, the implementation of robust security measures, providing employee training, and monitoring outputs.

Moreover, Remolina [83] emphasized the necessity of context- and sector-specific debates to effectively address the risks and challenges inherent in GAI deployment. For instance, generating financial advice content entails different societal implications than generating imagery of a turtle. Lo and Ross [84] focused on three primary challenges confronting most LLM applications: domain-specific expertise tailored to users' unique circumstances, adherence to moral and ethical standards, and compliance with regulatory guidelines and oversight. Lastly, Yusof and Roslan [85] underscored the imperative of continuous evaluation and adaptation of AI technologies within banking to simultaneously maximize benefits and mitigate associated risks. Collectively, these perspectives underscore the intricate interplay between technological advancement, ethical considerations, and regulatory imperatives within the financial domain, urging stakeholders to navigate these complexities with foresight and diligence.

5.2.3. Financial Regulation

The emergence of robo-advisors and advanced GAI models such as GPT-4 and ChatGPT heralds efficiency gains but also presents distinctive regulatory hurdles. Caspi et al. [86] delved into the regulatory landscape surrounding financial advice in an era increasingly shaped by GAI. Their study scrutinized the extant legal framework governing investment advisors and broker-dealers in the United States, while also examining the ascendancy and impact of robo-advisors and GAI. The pivotal role assumed by AI in the provision of financial advice has necessitated a judicious approach to regulatory strategies. Each regulatory strategy, whether predicated on disclosure mandates or outright prohibitions, carries its own array of benefits and potential challenges. A robust regulatory framework demands more than a cursory understanding; it mandates a comprehensive grasp of these AI technologies and their ramifications.

5.3. *Synthetic Financial Data Generation*

5.3.1. Challenges of Generating Synthetic Data

The financial services sector produces an enormous amount of highly intricate and diverse data. These data are frequently compartmentalized within organizations for several reasons, such as regulatory compliance and operational requirements. Consequently, the sharing of data both across various business units and with external entities like the research community is greatly restricted. Therefore, exploring techniques for creating synthetic financial datasets that maintain the characteristics of real data while ensuring the privacy of the involved parties is crucial. Assefa et al. [87] emphasized the growing need for the financial domain's effective synthetic data generation and highlighted the following three areas of focus for the academic community:

- Realistic synthetic dataset generation;
- Similarity calculation between real and generated datasets;
- Ensuring privacy constraints with the generative process.

While these challenges are also present in other domains, the financial sector's additional regulatory and privacy requirements add a layer of complexity. This presents a unique opportunity to study synthetic data generation within the context of financial services.

5.3.2. Existing Works by VAE, GAN, and Diffusion Models

From the literature, it is evident that most existing works on financial synthetic data generation employ GANs. For instance, Zhang et al. [88] introduced a novel GAN architecture to forecast stock closing prices, utilizing a Long Short-Term Memory (LSTM) network as the generator. The LSTM generator captures the data distributions of stocks from the given market data, generating data with similar distributions. Takahashi et al. [89] developed the FIN-GAN model for financial time-series modeling, which learns the properties of data and generates realistic time-series data.

Koshiyama et al. [90] proposed using conditional GANs (cGANs) for trading strategy calibration and aggregation, utilizing the generated samples for ensemble modeling. Bezzina [91] examined the correlation characteristics of synthetic financial time series data generated by TimeGAN, demonstrating that TimeGAN preserves the correlation structure in multi-stock datasets. Ramzan et al. [92] explored GANs for generating synthetic data, emphasizing the generation of datasets that mimic the statistical properties of input data without revealing sensitive information. Vuletić et al. [93] investigated GANs for probability forecasting of financial time series, using a novel economics-driven loss function in the generator. Ljung [94] assessed CTGAN's ability to generate synthetic data, while He and Kita [95] employed a hybrid sequential GAN model with three training strategies using S&P500 data.

In addition to GANs, VAEs and diffusion models have also been employed for financial synthetic data generation. Dalmasso et al. [96] introduced PayVAE, a generative model designed to learn the temporal and relational structure of financial transactions directly from data. Applied to a real peer-to-peer payment dataset, PayVAE demonstrated its capability to generate realistic transactions. Huang et al. [97] developed a novel generative framework called FTS-Diffusion, which consists of three modules designed to model irregular and scale-invariant patterns in financial time series.

6. Contribution and Future Research Agenda

This research unveils significant theoretical and managerial implications, crucial for comprehending and harnessing the potential of advanced GAI technologies within the financial domain. By summarizing key past research themes, the paper elucidates the evolving landscape of AI technologies and their applications in finance, providing a comprehensive synthesis that advances understanding and informs future research directions.

6.1. Theoretical Contribution

Theoretically, this review highlights the transformative potential of LLMs within the financial domain. Building upon previous research that summarizes LLMs in finance [3], it emphasizes the need to differentiate between general-purpose and finance-specific LLMs by categorizing research based on training data and application areas. The review then synthesizes findings on the performance and capabilities of prominent LLMs, such as GPT-4 and BloombergGPT, in diverse financial tasks encompassing text analysis, investment advisory, and decision support. This synthesis establishes a foundational framework for future research endeavors to explore critical aspects like performance benchmarks, evaluation criteria, and optimization strategies tailored for LLMs operating in financial contexts. Additionally, the discussion on LLMs' reasoning abilities and their application in financial forecasting and decision making underscores crucial areas for theoretical exploration. These areas include the development of models capable of generating well-reasoned financial decisions and the enhancement of LLMs to operate effectively within low-resource language environments.

Furthermore, the review delves into the significant ethical and risk considerations surrounding GAI models within the financial sector. Previous research has highlighted the need to address ethical, risk, and synthetic data considerations of GAI [28]. By critically examining the phenomenon of hallucination [79], the paper contributes to the theoretical comprehension of the risks associated with GAI. Additionally, the exploration of ethical concerns, encompassing data privacy and responsible AI utilization, lays the groundwork for the development of robust ethical guidelines and frameworks [2,98]. These frameworks can serve as a foundation for guiding the deployment of GAI technologies in a manner that adheres to ethical principles and aligns with societal expectations. This theoretical foundation is paramount in ensuring that future research and applications of AI in finance are demonstrably ethical and in accordance with societal norms.

The review further underscores the critical role of synthetic financial data generation through the utilization of advanced models like GANs, VAEs, and diffusion models. By synthesizing past research on methodologies for constructing realistic synthetic datasets while adhering to privacy concerns and regulatory compliance, the paper contributes to the theoretical underpinnings of synthetic data generation in a financial context. This synthesis serves as a roadmap for future research endeavors to refine the accuracy, utility, and ethical considerations associated with synthetic financial data.

6.2. Managerial Implications

This review offers valuable managerial insights into the practical applications of GAI technologies within the financial sector. By comprehensively summarizing the capabilities of LLMs across various financial tasks, the paper serves as a practical guide for managers seeking to leverage these models to optimize operational efficiency and enhance decision-making processes. The analysis of performance metrics and evaluation criteria for LLMs equips managers with the tools necessary to develop effective implementation strategies for integrating these technologies into financial operations [3].

Furthermore, the review emphasizes the critical need to address ethical considerations and potential risks associated with the deployment of GAI technologies. Financial managers can benefit from the comprehensive frameworks and risk management strategies outlined within the review, which provide guidance for the responsible use of AI and the mitigation of potential legal and reputational risks. This proactive approach ensures the ethical and responsible implementation of AI technologies, fostering trust and confidence amongst stakeholders [48].

Finally, the review highlights the practical applications of synthetic financial data generation, offering managers valuable insights into how these technologies can be leveraged to enhance decision making and bolster the resilience of financial institutions. By investing in the generation and utilization of synthetic financial data, managers gain access to robust datasets that can be employed for financial modeling, stress testing, and scenario analysis, ultimately leading to improved strategic planning and risk management capabilities [87].

6.3. Future Research Agenda

Our research advocates for a future research agenda that prioritizes the exploration of a synergistic relationship between three key areas: differentiation and performance, ethical and risk considerations, and synthetic financial data generation. As depicted in Figure 5, these domains interact dynamically, where advancements in one area can amplify progress in the others.

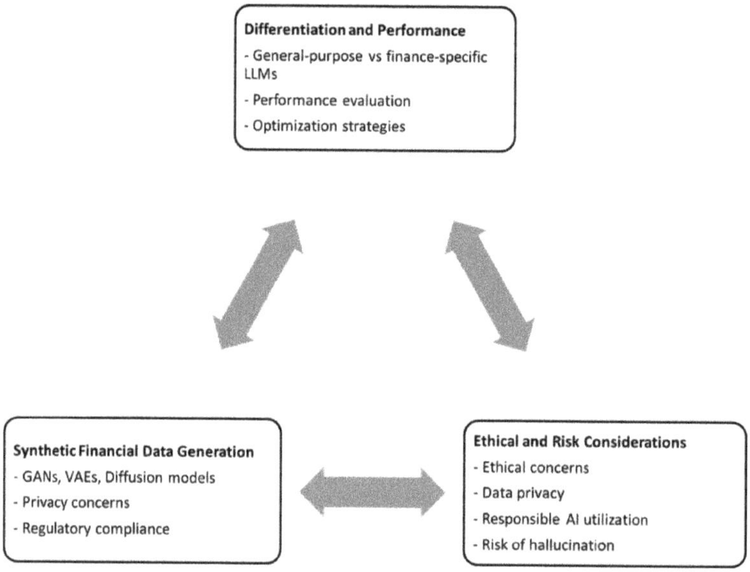

Figure 5. Future research agenda. Source: own processing.

6.3.1. Intertwined Ethics and Performance Optimization

Central to this approach is the integration of ethical considerations within the performance optimization framework for LLMs employed in finance. This entails ensuring that while LLMs are optimized for financial tasks, the resultant outcomes remain fair, transparent, and accountable. Ethical considerations encompassing data privacy, responsible utilization of AI, and the potential for model hallucination (generating irrelevant or misleading outputs) must be embedded within performance evaluation and optimization strategies. This ensures that advancements in model performance do not come at the expense of ethical standards, fostering the development of trustworthy and socially responsible AI applications in the financial domain.

6.3.2. Synthetic Data: A Boon for Performance Benchmarking

Synthetic financial data have the potential to serve as a valuable tool for evaluating and benchmarking the performance of LLMs specifically designed for finance, while simultaneously safeguarding privacy concerns. By leveraging advanced techniques like GANs, VAEs, and diffusion models, researchers can create realistic yet privacy-preserving datasets. These datasets can facilitate extensive testing and validation of models, guaranteeing that performance metrics are reliable and reflect real-world scenarios. It is imperative, however, to address privacy concerns and uphold regulatory compliance during synthetic data generation to maintain public trust and adhere to legal requirements.

6.3.3. Ethical Considerations in Synthetic Data Generation

A crucial aspect of this research agenda involves addressing the ethical risks associated with synthetic data generation. Researchers must meticulously consider the ethical implications and potential risks to ensure responsible use of this data. This entails guaranteeing that the synthetic data are generated in a manner that does not inadvertently introduce biases or other ethical concerns. Specific considerations include potential biases in data generation, the possibility of data misuse, and the need for robust regulatory frameworks to guide ethical practices. By adhering to these principles, researchers can uphold the integrity and reliability of the models trained on such data.

By pursuing research that investigates these interconnected areas, significant contributions can be made towards the development of robust, ethical, and high-performing LLMs within the financial sector. This holistic approach fosters a collaborative environment where advancements in one area bolster developments in the others, ultimately leading to a more integrated and responsible application of LLMs in the realm of finance. Figure 5 serves as a visual representation of the proposed future research agenda, highlighting the critical areas of focus and their interconnections, thereby providing a roadmap for researchers to create comprehensive and ethically sound financial AI systems.

The future research agenda outlined in Figure 5 emphasizes three pivotal areas of exploration to advance the relationship between GAI and finance. First, it calls for a deeper differentiation and performance assessment between general-purpose LLMs and finance-specific models, stressing the need for rigorous performance evaluation and optimization strategies to better align with financial domain requirements. Second, this paper underscores the significance of synthetic financial data generation through sophisticated generative models such as GANs, VAEs, and diffusion models. This approach is paramount for mitigating privacy risks and ensuring adherence to regulatory frameworks, thereby bolstering the trustworthiness and practical utility of GAI in finance. For instance, a worthy avenue of exploration is the potential impact of generative art Non-Fungible Tokens (NFTs) on NFT price volatility [99]. Third, it underscores the necessity of ethical and risk considerations in deploying GAI, particularly regarding data privacy, responsible AI utilization, and minimizing risks such as hallucination. Together, these focal points provide a comprehensive roadmap for future research, advocating for a balanced approach that integrates technical advancement, ethical governance, and domain-specific customization at the intersection of GAI and finance [98].

7. Conclusions

The integration of GAI into the financial sector is revolutionizing various facets of financial technology, particularly in areas such as data analysis, predictive modeling, and synthetic data generation [100]. By harnessing advanced AI techniques, financial institutions can process voluminous datasets with unprecedented efficiency, uncover patterns and trends that were previously hidden, and generate synthetic datasets that are crucial for developing robust models without compromising sensitive information. This review highlights the significant advancements achieved with key generative AI models like VAEs, GANs, LLMs, and diffusion models [101]. These models have opened new avenues for predictive analytics, risk assessment, fraud detection, and personalized financial services. However, while these cutting-edge technologies offer substantial benefits, there are still considerable challenges that need to be addressed, such as ensuring data privacy, improving model interpretability, and maintaining regulatory compliance in an evolving legal landscape. Future research should prioritize enhancing model robustness to better withstand adversarial attacks and market volatility, increasing transparency to build trust among stakeholders, and establishing ethical standards to guide the responsible use of generative AI in finance. This includes developing frameworks for responsible AI governance, ensuring accountability, and minimizing biases that could lead to unfair outcomes [102]. By tackling these challenges comprehensively, the financial industry can fully realize the transformative potential of generative AI, driving innovation while safeguarding the integrity and fairness of financial systems.

Author Contributions: The conceptualization, methodology, validation, formal analysis, investigation, and writing of the paper were completed by all authors equally. All authors have read and agreed to the published version of the manuscript.

Funding: This research is funded by MOE Start-up Research Funding (RFE23003).

Conflicts of Interest: The authors declare no conflicts of interest.

References

1. Fatemi, S.; Hu, Y. A Comparative Analysis of Fine-Tuned LLMs and Few-Shot Learning of LLMs for Financial Sentiment Analysis. *arXiv* **2023**, arXiv:2312.08725.
2. Ding, Q.; Ding, D.; Wang, Y.; Guan, C.; Ding, B. Unraveling the landscape of large language models: A systematic review and future perspectives. *J. Electron. Bus. Digit. Econ.* **2023**, *3, 3–19* . [CrossRef]
3. Li, Y.; Wang, S.; Ding, H.; Chen, H. Large language models in finance: A survey. In Proceedings of the Fourth ACM International Conference on AI in Finance, Brooklyn, NY, USA, 27–29 November 2023; pp. 374–382.
4. Lee, J.; Stevens, N.; Han, S.C.; Song, M. A Survey of Large Language Models in Finance (FinLLMs). *arXiv* **2024**, arXiv:2402.02315.
5. Barde, K.; Kulkarni, P.A. Applications of Generative AI in Fintech. In Proceedings of the Third International Conference on AI-ML Systems, Bangalore, India, 25–28 October 2023; pp. 1–5.
6. Krause, D. Large Language Models and Generative AI in Finance: An Analysis of ChatGPT, Bard, and Bing AI. 2023. Available online: https://papers.ssrn.com/sol3/papers.cfm?abstract_id=4511540 (accessed on 7 June 2024).
7. Mbanyele, W. Generative AI and ChatGPT in Financial Markets and Corporate Policy: A Comprehensive Review. 2024. Available online: https://papers.ssrn.com/sol3/papers.cfm?abstract_id=4745990 (accessed on 7 June 2024).
8. Grootendorst, M. BERTopic: Neural topic modeling with a class-based TF-IDF procedure. *arXiv* **2022**, arXiv:2203.05794.
9. Kingma, D.P.; Welling, M. Auto-encoding variational bayes. *arXiv* **2013**, arXiv:1312.6114.
10. Goodfellow, I.; Pouget-Abadie, J.; Mirza, M.; Xu, B.; Warde-Farley, D.; Ozair, S.; Courville, A.; Bengio, Y. Generative adversarial nets. In *Advances in Neural Information Processing Systems 27*; The MIT Press: Montreal, QC, Canada, 2014.
11. Vaswani, A.; Shazeer, N.; Parmar, N.; Uszkoreit, J.; Jones, L.; Gomez, A.N.; Kaiser, Ł.; Polosukhin, I. Attention is all you need. In *Advances in Neural Information Processing Systems 30*; NeurIPS Foundation: Long Beach, CA, USA, 2017.
12. Radford, A.; Narasimhan, K.; Salimans, T.; Sutskever, I. Improving Language Understanding by Generative Pre-Training. 2018. Available online: https://hayate-lab.com/wp-content/uploads/2023/05/43372bfa750340059ad87ac8e538c53b.pdf (accessed on 7 June 2024).
13. Radford, A.; Wu, J.; Child, R.; Luan, D.; Amodei, D.; Sutskever, I. Language models are unsupervised multitask learners. *OpenAI Blog* **2019**, *1*, 9.
14. Brown, T.; Mann, B.; Ryder, N.; Subbiah, M.; Kaplan, J.D.; Dhariwal, P.; Neelakantan, A.; Shyam, P.; Sastry, G.; Askell, A.; et al. Language models are few-shot learners. *Adv. Neural Inf. Process. Syst.* **2020**, *33*, 1877–1901.
15. Ouyang, L.; Wu, J.; Jiang, X.; Almeida, D.; Wainwright, C.; Mishkin, P.; Zhang, C.; Agarwal, S.; Slama, K.; Ray, A.; et al. Training language models to follow instructions with human feedback. *Adv. Neural Inf. Process. Syst.* **2022**, *35*, 27730–27744.
16. Devlin, J.; Chang, M.W.; Lee, K.; Toutanova, K. Bert: Pre-training of deep bidirectional transformers for language understanding. *arXiv* **2018**, arXiv:1810.04805.
17. Ho, J.; Jain, A.; Abbeel, P. Denoising diffusion probabilistic models. *Adv. Neural Inf. Process. Syst.* **2020**, *33*, 6840–6851.
18. Bollen, J.; Mao, H.; Zeng, X. Twitter mood predicts the stock market. *J. Comput. Sci.* **2011**, *2*, 1–8. [CrossRef]
19. Wisniewski, T.P.; Yekini, L.S. Stock market returns and the content of annual report narratives. In *Proceedings of the Accounting Forum*; Elsevier: Amsterdam, The Netherlands, 2015; Volume 39, pp. 281–294.
20. McGurk, Z.; Nowak, A.; Hall, J.C. Stock returns and investor sentiment: Textual analysis and social media. *J. Econ. Financ.* **2020**, *44*, 458–485. [CrossRef]
21. Gupta, U. Gpt-investar: Enhancing stock investment strategies through annual report analysis with large language models. *arXiv* **2023**, arXiv:2309.03079. [CrossRef]
22. Li, X.; Chan, S.; Zhu, X.; Pei, Y.; Ma, Z.; Liu, X.; Shah, S. Are ChatGPT and GPT-4 General-Purpose Solvers for Financial Text Analytics? A Study on Several Typical Tasks. In Proceedings of the 2023 Conference on Empirical Methods in Natural Language Processing: Industry Track, Singapore, 6–10 December 2023; pp. 408–422.
23. Pavlyshenko, B.M. Financial News Analytics Using Fine-Tuned Llama 2 GPT Model. *arXiv* **2023**, arXiv:2308.13032.
24. Xing, F. Designing Heterogeneous LLM Agents for Financial Sentiment Analysis. *arXiv* **2024**, arXiv:2401.05799. [CrossRef]
25. Liu, X.Y.; Wang, G.; Zha, D. Fingpt: Democratizing internet-scale data for financial large language models. *arXiv* **2023**, arXiv:2307.10485.
26. Yang, H.; Liu, X.Y.; Wang, C.D. Fingpt: Open-source financial large language models. *arXiv* **2023**, arXiv:2306.06031. [CrossRef]
27. Yin, Y.; Yang, Y.; Yang, J.; Liu, Q. FinPT: Financial Risk Prediction with Profile Tuning on Pretrained Foundation Models. *arXiv* **2023**, arXiv:2308.00065.
28. Rane, N. Role and Challenges of ChatGPT and Similar Generative Artificial Intelligence in Finance and Accounting. 2023. Available online: https://papers.ssrn.com/sol3/papers.cfm?abstract_id=4603206 (accessed on 7 June 2024).
29. Reimers, N. Sentence-BERT: Sentence Embeddings using Siamese BERT-Networks. *arXiv* **2019**, arXiv:1908.10084.
30. McInnes, L.; Healy, J.; Melville, J. Umap: Uniform manifold approximation and projection for dimension reduction. *arXiv* **2018**, arXiv:1802.03426.
31. McInnes, L.; Healy, J.; Astels, S. hdbscan: Hierarchical density based clustering. *J. Open Source Softw.* **2017**, *2*, 205. [CrossRef]
32. Blei, D.M.; Ng, A.Y.; Jordan, M.I. Latent dirichlet allocation. *J. Mach. Learn. Res.* **2003**, *3*, 993–1022.
33. Févotte, C.; Idier, J. Algorithms for nonnegative matrix factorization with the β-divergence. *Neural Comput.* **2011**, *23*, 2421–2456. [CrossRef]

34. Teixeira, A.C.; Marar, V.; Yazdanpanah, H.; Pezente, A.; Ghassemi, M. Enhancing Credit Risk Reports Generation using LLMs: An Integration of Bayesian Networks and Labeled Guide Prompting. In Proceedings of the Fourth ACM International Conference on AI in Finance, Brooklyn, NY, USA, 27–29 November 2023; pp. 340–348.
35. Krause, D. Proper Generative AI Prompting for Financial Analysis. 2023. Available online: https://papers.ssrn.com/sol3/papers.cfm?abstract_id=4453664 (accessed on 7 June 2024).
36. Rane, N.; Choudhary, S.; Rane, J. Gemini or ChatGPT? Efficiency, Performance, and Adaptability of Cutting-Edge Generative Artificial Intelligence (AI) in Finance and Accounting. 2024. Available online: https://papers.ssrn.com/sol3/papers.cfm?abstract_id=4731283 (accessed on 7 June 2024).
37. Callanan, E.; Mbakwe, A.; Papadimitriou, A.; Pei, Y.; Sibue, M.; Zhu, X.; Ma, Z.; Liu, X.; Shah, S. Can gpt models be financial analysts? an evaluation of chatgpt and gpt-4 on mock cfa exams. *arXiv* **2023**, arXiv:2310.08678.
38. Zhao, H.; Liu, Z.; Wu, Z.; Li, Y.; Yang, T.; Shu, P.; Xu, S.; Dai, H.; Zhao, L.; Mai, G.; et al. Revolutionizing finance with llms: An overview of applications and insights. *arXiv* **2024**, arXiv:2401.11641.
39. Niszczota, P.; Abbas, S. GPT has become financially literate: Insights from financial literacy tests of GPT and a preliminary test of how people use it as a source of advice. *Financ. Res. Lett.* **2023**, *58*, 104333. [CrossRef]
40. Lakkaraju, K.; Vuruma, S.K.R.; Pallagani, V.; Muppasani, B.; Srivastava, B. Can llms be good financial advisors?: An initial study in personal decision making for optimized outcomes. *arXiv* **2023**, arXiv:2307.07422.
41. Huang, Z.; Che, C.; Zheng, H.; Li, C. Research on Generative Artificial Intelligence for Virtual Financial Robo-Advisor. *Acad. J. Sci. Technol.* **2024**, *10*, 74–80. [CrossRef]
42. Liu, Y.; Wang, J. Analysis of Financial Market using Generative Artificial Intelligence. *Acad. J. Sci. Technol.* **2024**, *11*, 21–25. [CrossRef]
43. Lu, F.; Huang, L.; Li, S. ChatGPT, Generative AI, and Investment Advisory. 2023. Available online: https://papers.ssrn.com/sol3/Papers.cfm?abstract_id=4519182 (accessed on 7 June 2024).
44. Li, Y.; Yu, Y.; Li, H.; Chen, Z.; Khashanah, K. Tradinggpt: Multi-agent system with layered memory and distinct characters for enhanced financial trading performance. *arXiv* **2023**, arXiv:2309.03736.
45. Yu, Y.; Li, H.; Chen, Z.; Jiang, Y.; Li, Y.; Zhang, D.; Liu, R.; Suchow, J.W.; Khashanah, K. FinMem: A performance-enhanced LLM trading agent with layered memory and character design. *Proc. AAAI Symp. Ser.* **2024**, *3*, 595–597. [CrossRef]
46. Lakkaraju, K.; Jones, S.E.; Vuruma, S.K.R.; Pallagani, V.; Muppasani, B.C.; Srivastava, B. LLMs for Financial Advisement: A Fairness and Efficacy Study in Personal Decision Making. In Proceedings of the Fourth ACM International Conference on AI in Finance, Brooklyn, NY, USA, 27–29 November 2023; pp. 100–107.
47. Hillebrand, L.; Berger, A.; Deußer, T.; Dilmaghani, T.; Khaled, M.; Kliem, B.; Loitz, R.; Pielka, M.; Leonhard, D.; Bauckhage, C.; et al. Improving zero-shot text matching for financial auditing with large language models. In Proceedings of the ACM Symposium on Document Engineering 2023, Limerick, Ireland, 22–25 August 2023; pp. 1–4.
48. Cao, Z.; Feinstein, Z. Large Language Model in Financial Regulatory Interpretation. *arXiv* **2024**, arXiv:2405.06808.
49. de Zarzà, I.; de Curtò, J.; Roig, G.; Calafate, C.T. Optimized financial planning: Integrating individual and cooperative budgeting models with llm recommendations. *AI* **2023**, *5*, 91–114. [CrossRef]
50. Chen, B.; Wu, Z.; Zhao, R. From fiction to fact: The growing role of generative AI in business and finance. *J. Chin. Econ. Bus. Stud.* **2023**, *21*, 471–496. [CrossRef]
51. Wang, Y. Generative AI in Operational Risk Management: Harnessing the Future of Finance. 2023. Available online: https://papers.ssrn.com/sol3/papers.cfm?abstract_id=4452504 (accessed on 7 June 2024).
52. Leippold, M. Thus spoke GPT-3: Interviewing a large-language model on climate finance. *Financ. Res. Lett.* **2023**, *53*, 103617. [CrossRef]
53. Yu, X.; Chen, Z.; Lu, Y. Harnessing LLMs for temporal data-a study on explainable financial time series forecasting. In Proceedings of the 2023 Conference on Empirical Methods in Natural Language Processing: Industry Track, Singapore, 6–10 December 2023; pp. 739–753.
54. Yu, X.; Chen, Z.; Ling, Y.; Dong, S.; Liu, Z.; Lu, Y. Temporal Data Meets LLM–Explainable Financial Time Series Forecasting. *arXiv* **2023**, arXiv:2306.11025.
55. Srivastava, P.; Malik, M.; Ganu, T. Assessing LLMs' Mathematical Reasoning in Financial Document Question Answering. *arXiv* **2024**, arXiv:2402.11194.
56. Sikiru, R.D.; Adekanmbi, O.; Soronnadi, A. Comparative Study of LLMs for Personal Financial Decision in Low Resource Language. In Proceedings of the 5th Workshop on African Natural Language Processing, Vienna, Austria, 11 May 2024.
57. Liu, X.Y.; Zhang, J.; Wang, G.; Tong, W.; Walid, A. FinGPT-HPC: Efficient Pretraining and Finetuning Large Language Models for Financial Applications with High-Performance Computing. *arXiv* **2024**, arXiv:2402.13533.
58. Wu, S.; Irsoy, O.; Lu, S.; Dabravolski, V.; Dredze, M.; Gehrmann, S.; Kambadur, P.; Rosenberg, D.; Mann, G. BloombergGPT: A Large Language Model for Finance. *arXiv* **2024**. Available online: https://arxiv.org/pdf/2303.17564.pdf (accessed on 7 June 2024).
59. Xie, Q.; Han, W.; Zhang, X.; Lai, Y.; Peng, M.; Lopez-Lira, A.; Huang, J. Pixiu: A large language model, instruction data and evaluation benchmark for finance. *arXiv* **2023**, arXiv:2306.05443.
60. Li, J.; Bian, Y.; Wang, G.; Lei, Y.; Cheng, D.; Ding, Z.; Jiang, C. Cfgpt: Chinese financial assistant with large language model. *arXiv* **2023**, arXiv:2309.10654.

61. Zhang, B.; Yang, H.; Liu, X.Y. Instruct-fingpt: Financial sentiment analysis by instruction tuning of general-purpose large language models. *arXiv* **2023**, arXiv:2306.12659. [CrossRef]
62. Yang, Y.; Tang, Y.; Tam, K.Y. Investlm: A large language model for investment using financial domain instruction tuning. *arXiv* **2023**, arXiv:2309.13064.
63. Chen, W.; Wang, Q.; Long, Z.; Zhang, X.; Lu, Z.; Li, B.; Wang, S.; Xu, J.; Bai, X.; Huang, X.; et al. Disc-finllm: A chinese financial large language model based on multiple experts fine-tuning. *arXiv* **2023**, arXiv:2310.15205.
64. Chu, Z.; Guo, H.; Zhou, X.; Wang, Y.; Yu, F.; Chen, H.; Xu, W.; Lu, X.; Cui, Q.; Li, L.; et al. Data-centric financial large language models. *arXiv* **2023**, arXiv:2310.17784.
65. Wang, Z.; Li, Y.; Wu, J.; Soon, J.; Zhang, X. Finvis-gpt: A multimodal large language model for financial chart analysis. *arXiv* **2023**, arXiv:2308.01430.
66. Bhatia, G.; Nagoudi, E.M.B.; Cavusoglu, H.; Abdul-Mageed, M. FinTral: A Family of GPT-4 Level Multimodal Financial Large Language Models. *arXiv* **2024**, arXiv:2402.10986.
67. Hirano, M.; Imajo, K. Construction of Domain-specified Japanese Large Language Model for Finance through Continual Pre-training. *arXiv* **2024**, arXiv:2404.10555. [CrossRef]
68. Zhang, X.; Xiang, R.; Yuan, C.; Feng, D.; Han, W.; Lopez-Lira, A.; Liu, X.Y.; Ananiadou, S.; Peng, M.; Huang, J.; et al. Dólares or Dollars? Unraveling the Bilingual Prowess of Financial LLMs Between Spanish and English. *arXiv* **2024**, arXiv:2402.07405.
69. Zhang, L.; Cai, W.; Liu, Z.; Yang, Z.; Dai, W.; Liao, Y.; Qin, Q.; Li, Y.; Liu, X.; Liu, Z.; et al. Fineval: A chinese financial domain knowledge evaluation benchmark for large language models. *arXiv* **2023**, arXiv:2308.09975.
70. Guo, Y.; Xu, Z.; Yang, Y. Is chatgpt a financial expert? evaluating language models on financial natural language processing. *arXiv* **2023**, arXiv:2310.12664.
71. Xie, Q.; Han, W.; Chen, Z.; Xiang, R.; Zhang, X.; He, Y.; Xiao, M.; Li, D.; Dai, Y.; Feng, D.; et al. The FinBen: An Holistic Financial Benchmark for Large Language Models. *arXiv* **2024**, arXiv:2402.12659.
72. Lei, Y.; Li, J.; Jiang, M.; Hu, J.; Cheng, D.; Ding, Z.; Jiang, C. Cfbenchmark: Chinese financial assistant benchmark for large language model. *arXiv* **2023**, arXiv:2311.05812.
73. Islam, P.; Kannappan, A.; Kiela, D.; Qian, R.; Scherrer, N.; Vidgen, B. Financebench: A new benchmark for financial question answering. *arXiv* **2023**, arXiv:2311.11944.
74. Zhang, C.; Mao, Y.; Fan, Y.; Mi, Y.; Gao, Y.; Chen, L.; Lou, D.; Lin, J. FinSQL: Model-Agnostic LLMs-based Text-to-SQL Framework for Financial Analysis. *arXiv* **2024**, arXiv:2401.10506.
75. Li, X.; Li, Z.; Shi, C.; Xu, Y.; Du, Q.; Tan, M.; Huang, J.; Lin, W. AlphaFin: Benchmarking Financial Analysis with Retrieval-Augmented Stock-Chain Framework. *arXiv* **2024**, arXiv:2403.12582.
76. Hirano, M. Construction of a japanese financial benchmark for large language models. *arXiv* **2024**, arXiv:2403.15062. [CrossRef]
77. Xu, L.; Zhu, L.; Wu, Y.; Xue, H. SuperCLUE-Fin: Graded Fine-Grained Analysis of Chinese LLMs on Diverse Financial Tasks and Applications. *arXiv* **2024**, arXiv:2404.19063.
78. Kang, H.; Liu, X.Y. Deficiency of Large Language Models in Finance: An Empirical Examination of Hallucination. *arXiv* **2023**, arXiv:2311.15548.
79. Roychowdhury, S. Journey of hallucination-minimized generative ai solutions for financial decision makers. In Proceedings of the 17th ACM International Conference on Web Search and Data Mining, Mérida, Mexico, 4–8 March 2024; pp. 1180–1181.
80. Kalia, S. Potential Impact of Generative Artificial Intelligence (AI) on the Financial Industry. *Int. J. Cybern. Inform.* **2023**, *12*, 37. [CrossRef]
81. Sarker, I.H. LLM potentiality and awareness: A position paper from the perspective of trustworthy and responsible AI modeling. *Discov. Artif. Intell.* **2024**, *4*, 40. [CrossRef]
82. Krause, D. Mitigating Risks for Financial Firms Using Generative AI Tools. 2023. Available online: https://papers.ssrn.com/sol3/papers.cfm?abstract_id=4452600 (accessed on 7 June 2024).
83. Remolina, N. *Generative AI in Finance: Risks and Potential Solutions*; Singapore Management University School of Law Research Paper Forthcoming, SMU Centre for AI & Data Governance Research Paper Forthcoming: Singapore, 2023.
84. Lo, A.W.; Ross, J. Can ChatGPT Plan Your Retirement?: Generative AI and Financial Advice. 2024. Available online: https://papers.ssrn.com/sol3/papers.cfm?abstract_id=4722780 (accessed on 7 June 2024).
85. Yusof, S.A.B.M.; Roslan, F.A.B.M. The Impact of Generative AI in Enhancing Credit Risk Modeling and Decision-Making in Banking Institutions. *Emerg. Trends Mach. Intell. Big Data* **2023**, *15*, 40–49.
86. Caspi, I.; Felber, S.S.; Gillis, T.B. Generative AI and the Future of Financial Advice Regulation. In Proceedings of the Generative AI and Law Workshop at ICML 2023, Hawaii Convention Center, Honolulu, HI, USA, 28–29 July 2023.
87. Assefa, S.A.; Dervovic, D.; Mahfouz, M.; Tillman, R.E.; Reddy, P.; Veloso, M. Generating synthetic data in finance: Opportunities, challenges and pitfalls. In Proceedings of the First ACM International Conference on AI in Finance, New York, NY, USA, 15–16 October 2020; pp. 1–8.
88. Zhang, K.; Zhong, G.; Dong, J.; Wang, S.; Wang, Y. Stock market prediction based on generative adversarial network. *Procedia Comput. Sci.* **2019**, *147*, 400–406. [CrossRef]
89. Takahashi, S.; Chen, Y.; Tanaka-Ishii, K. Modeling financial time-series with generative adversarial networks. *Phys. A Stat. Mech. Appl.* **2019**, *527*, 121261. [CrossRef]

90. Koshiyama, A.; Firoozye, N.; Treleaven, P. Generative adversarial networks for financial trading strategies fine-tuning and combination. *Quant. Financ.* **2021**, *21*, 797–813. [CrossRef]
91. Bezzina, P. Improving Portfolio Construction Using Deep Generative Machine Learning Models Applying Generative Models on Financial Market Data. Master's Thesis, University of Malta, Msida, Malta, 2023.
92. Ramzan, F.; Sartori, C.; Consoli, S.; Reforgiato Recupero, D. Generative Adversarial Networks for Synthetic Data Generation in Finance: Evaluating Statistical Similarities and Quality Assessment. *AI* **2024**, *5*, 667–685. [CrossRef]
93. Vuletić, M.; Prenzel, F.; Cucuringu, M. Fin-GAN: Forecasting and classifying financial time series via generative adversarial networks. *Quant. Financ.* **2024**, *24*, 175–199. [CrossRef]
94. Ljung, M. Synthetic Data Generation for the Financial Industry Using Generative Adversarial Networks. 2021. Available online: https://www.diva-portal.org/smash/get/diva2:1591892/FULLTEXT01.pdf (accessed on 7 June 2024).
95. He, B.; Kita, E. Stock price prediction by using hybrid sequential generative adversarial networks. In Proceedings of the 2020 International Conference on Data Mining Workshops (ICDMW), Sorrento, Italy, 17–20 November 2020; pp. 341–347.
96. Dalmasso, N.; Tillman, R.E.; Reddy, P.; Veloso, M. Payvae: A generative model for financial transactions. In Proceedings of the AAAI 2021 Workshop on Knowledge Discovery from Unstructured Data in Financial Services Workshop, Virtual, 9 February 2021.
97. Huang, H.; Chen, M.; Qiao, X. Generative Learning for Financial Time Series with Irregular and Scale-Invariant Patterns. In Proceedings of the Twelfth International Conference on Learning Representations, Vienna, Austria, 7 May 2024.
98. Guan, C.; Ding, D.; Gupta, P.; Hung, Y.C.; Jiang, Z. A Systematic Review of Research on ChatGPT: The User Perspective. In *Exploring Cyber Criminals and Data Privacy Measures*; IGI Global: Hershey, PA, USA, 2023; pp. 124–150.
99. Guan, C.; Ding, D.; Ren, J.; Guo, J. Unveiling the aesthetic "wow factor": The role of aesthetic incongruity and image quality in NFT art valuation with computer vision. *Electron. Mark.* **2024**, *34*, 38. [CrossRef]
100. Rajath, K. Fintech's Generative AI Revolution How AI is shaping the Future of Banking and Financial Services. *Int. Res. J. Mod. Eng. Technol. Sci.* **2023**, *5*, 1812–1814.
101. Cao, X.; Li, S.; Katsikis, V.; Khan, A.T.; He, H.; Liu, Z.; Zhang, L.; Peng, C. Empowering financial futures: Large language models in the modern financial landscape. *EAI Endorsed Trans. AI Robot.* **2024**, *3*. [CrossRef]
102. Ranković, M.; Gurgu, E.; Martins, O.; Vukasović, M. Artificial intelligence and the evolution of finance: Opportunities, challenges and ethical considerations. *EdTech J.* **2023**, *3*, 20–23. [CrossRef]

MDPI AG
Grosspeteranlage 5
4052 Basel
Switzerland
Tel.: +41 61 683 77 34

FinTech Editorial Office
E-mail: fintech@mdpi.com
www.mdpi.com/journal/fintech

www.ingramcontent.com/pod-product-compliance
Lightning Source LLC
Chambersburg PA
CBHW061449210926
51850CB00008B/1663